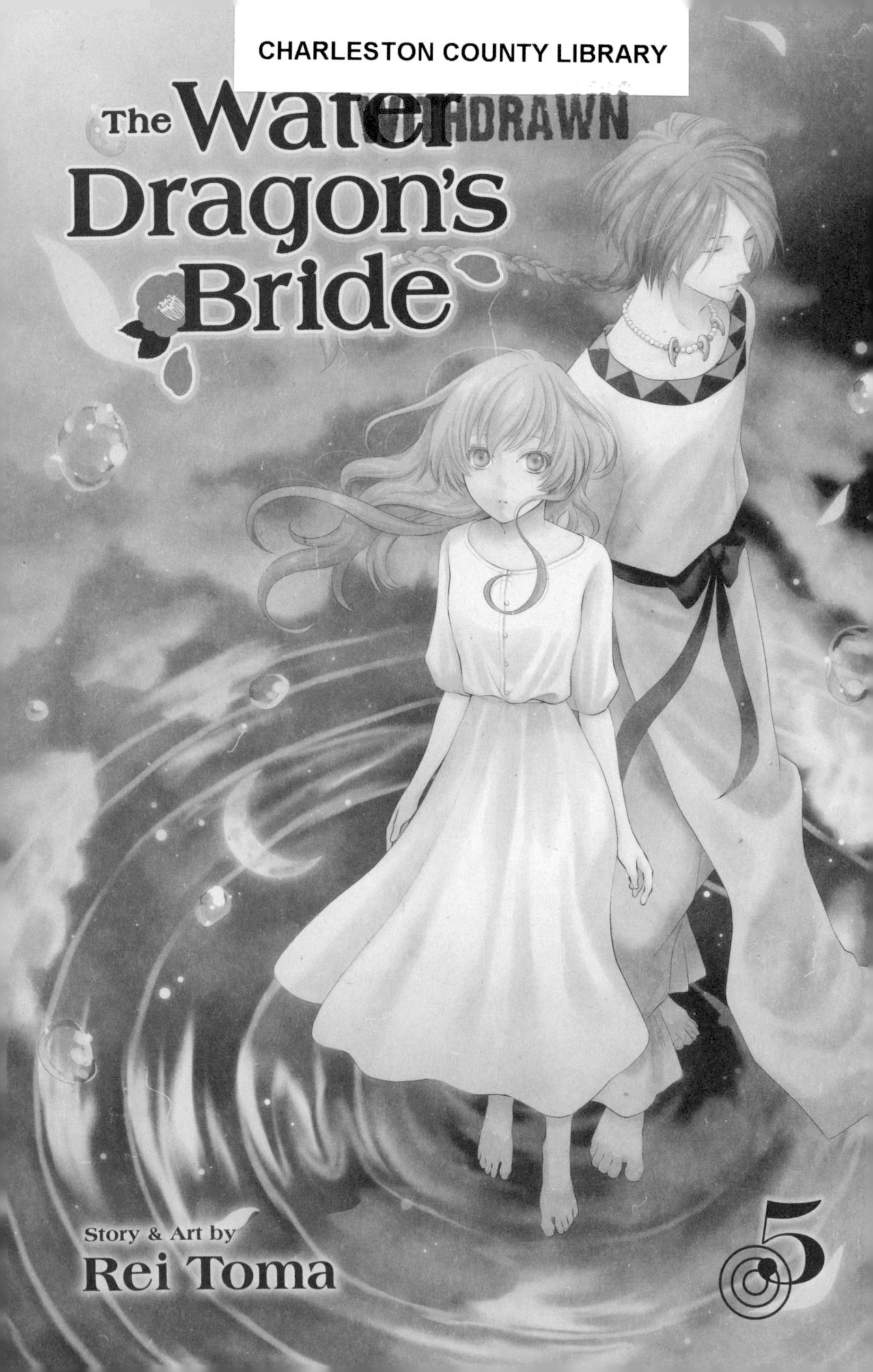
The Water Dragon's Bride
Story & Art by
Rei Toma
5

The Water Dragon's Bride

CHARACTER INTRODUCTIONS

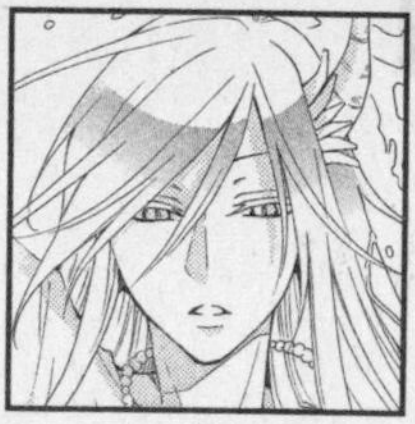

The Water Dragon God

The god who rules over the waters. Though he hates humans, he seems to be intrigued by Asahi and feels compassion for her.

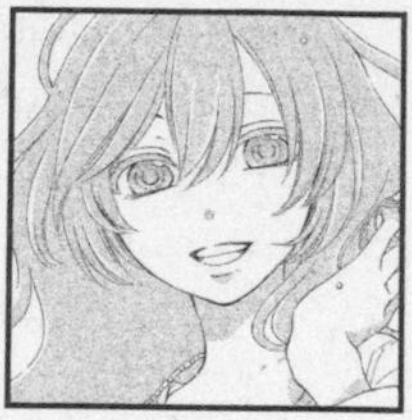

Asahi

She was transported to another world when she was young. Subaru's mother sacrificed her to the water dragon god.

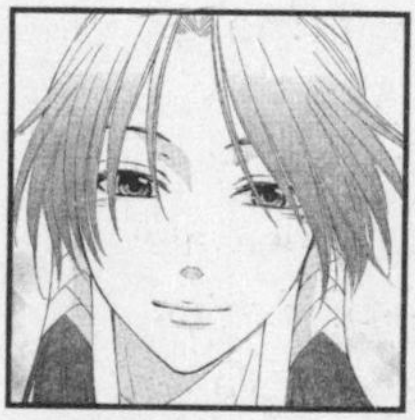

Subaru

He is drawn to Asahi and has resolved to protect her.

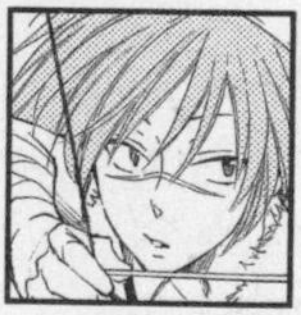

Kogahiko

He's seeking the water dragon god's power by targeting Asahi.

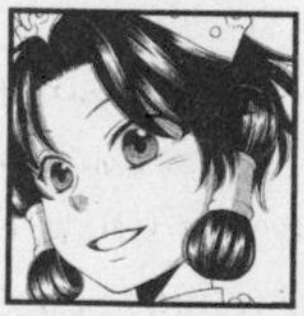

The Emperor

A young boy, the emperor of the country of Naga.

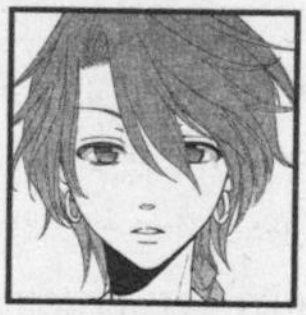

Tsukihiko

Asahi's caretaker. He has the ability to sense people's thoughts and emotions.

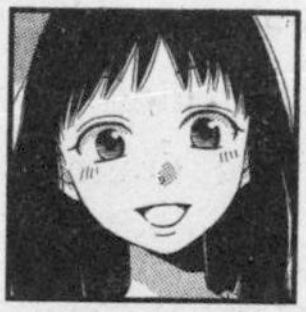

Shiina

Subaru's younger sister. She thinks Asahi is strange and frightening.

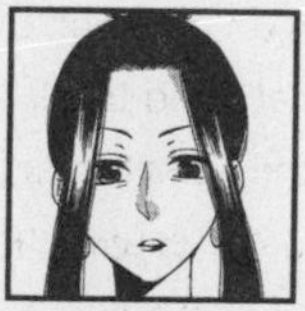

Subaru's Mother

She despises Asahi.

STORY THUS FAR

◎ Asahi is living a normal, sheltered life when she suddenly gets pulled into a pond and is transported to a strange new world. She meets Subaru, the son of the most prominent family in his village, and he helps her and brings her to his home. Subaru's mother dislikes Asahi, however, and plots to sacrifice her as a bride to the water dragon god in the Great Lake.

◎ The water dragon god decrees that Asahi will become his wife and takes her voice from her. He also gifts her with strange powers, which results in the villagers revering her as the water priestess. Since she is unable to return home, Asahi lives her life in the village. Each year, she spends time with the water dragon god as part of a ritual, and their relationship begins to subtly change. Then, a man named Kogahiko starts a war against the village because he wants to obtain Asahi's power.

◎ The water dragon god sees that Asahi is miserable that a war has been started over her, so he returns her voice and stops the war. He asks Asahi to marry him, but she says the two of them don't have special feelings for one another. In response, the water dragon god appears in human guise and tells her he will live with her in the human world.

◎ Asahi, the water dragon and Subaru decide to use the interim of the ritual to travel around the land. But the priestess of a village they are visiting sees through the water dragon god's disguise. She notifies the emperor of Naga, and he orders Asahi to lend him her power. Asahi's persuasive ability allows her to escape without issue, at least for now...

The Water Dragon's Bride

5

CONTENTS

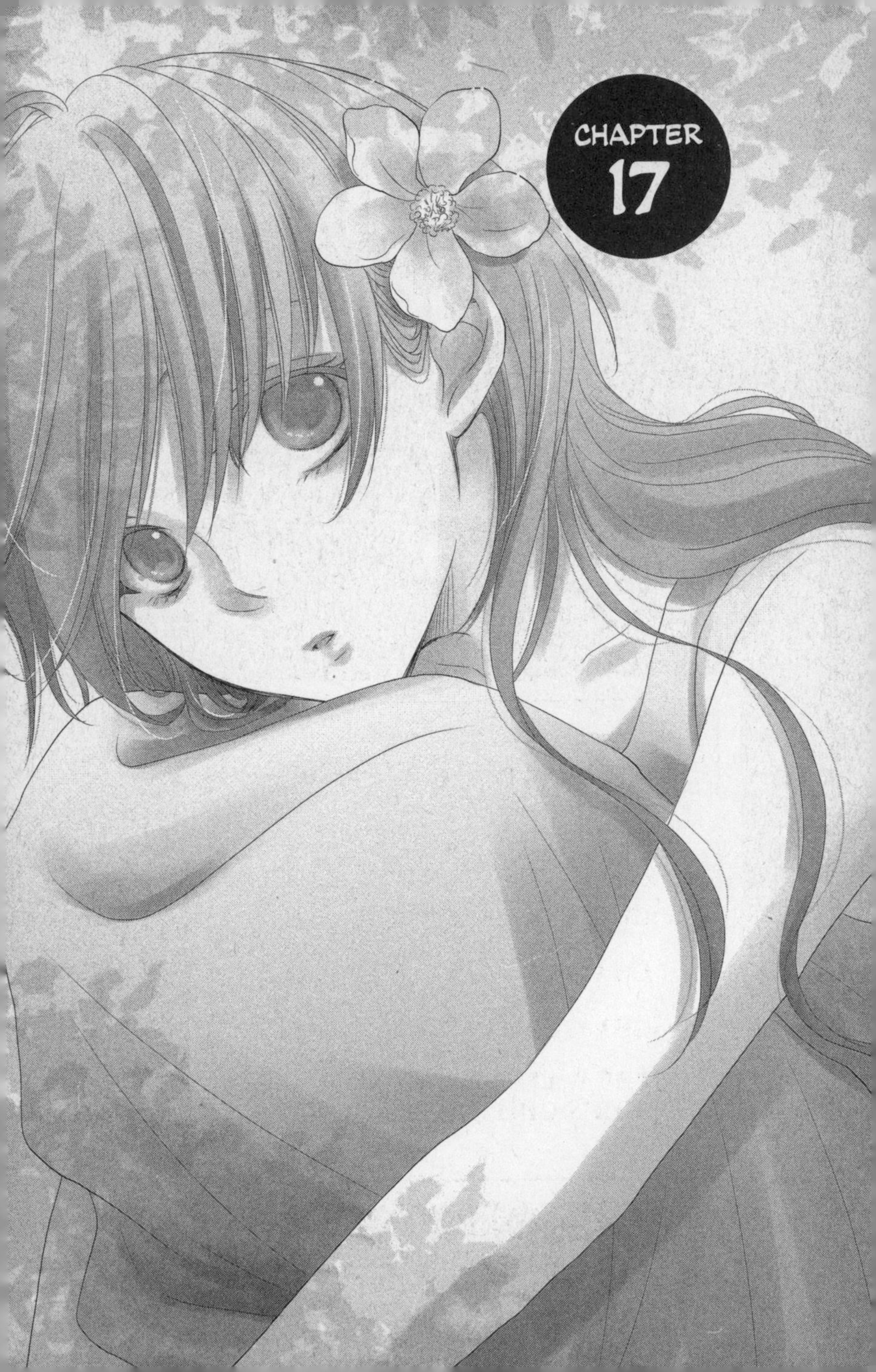
CHAPTER
17

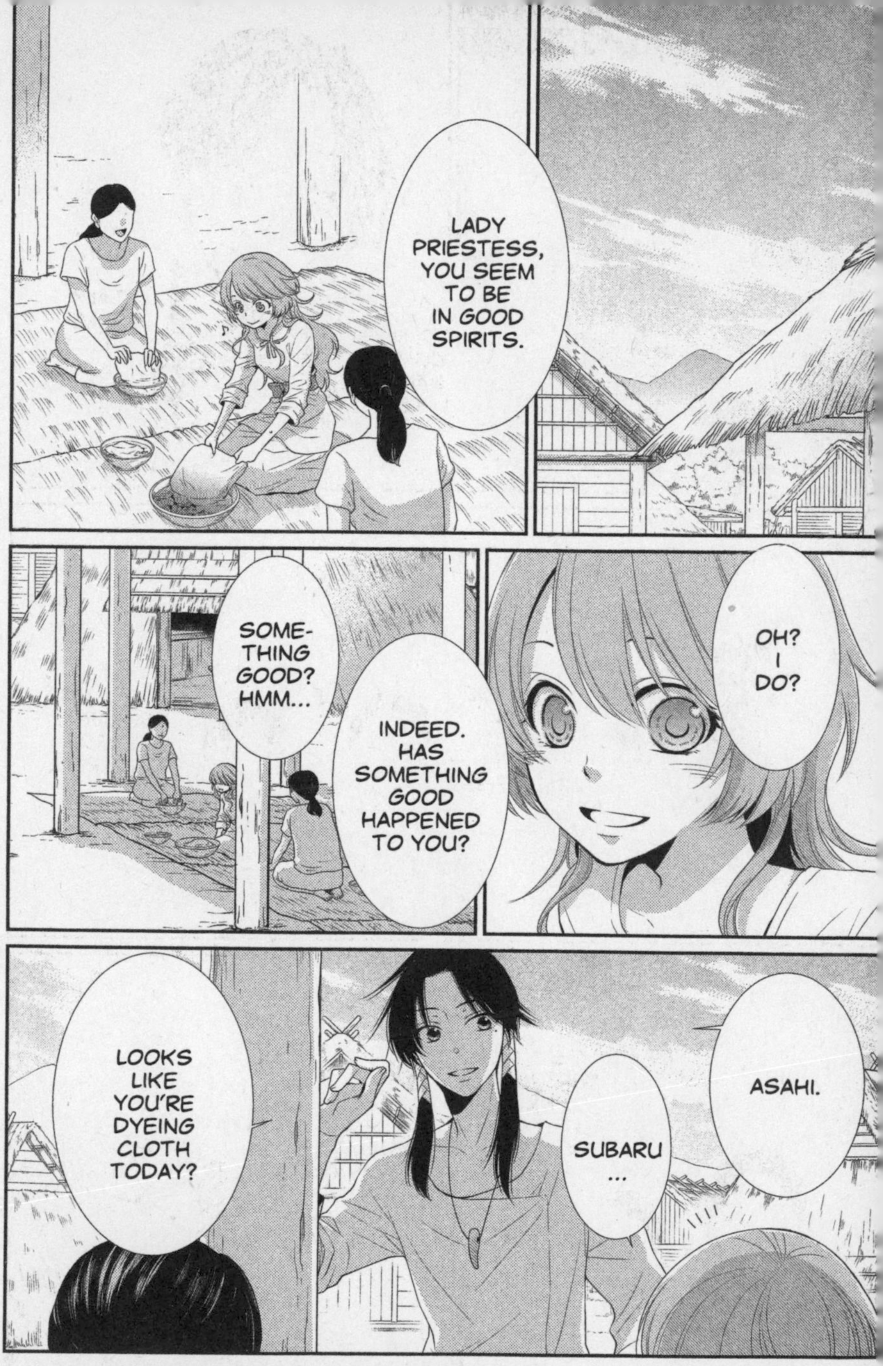
LADY PRIESTESS, YOU SEEM TO BE IN GOOD SPIRITS.
OH? I DO?
INDEED. HAS SOMETHING GOOD HAPPENED TO YOU?
SOME-THING GOOD? HMM...
ASAHI.
SUBARU...
LOOKS LIKE YOU'RE DYEING CLOTH TODAY?

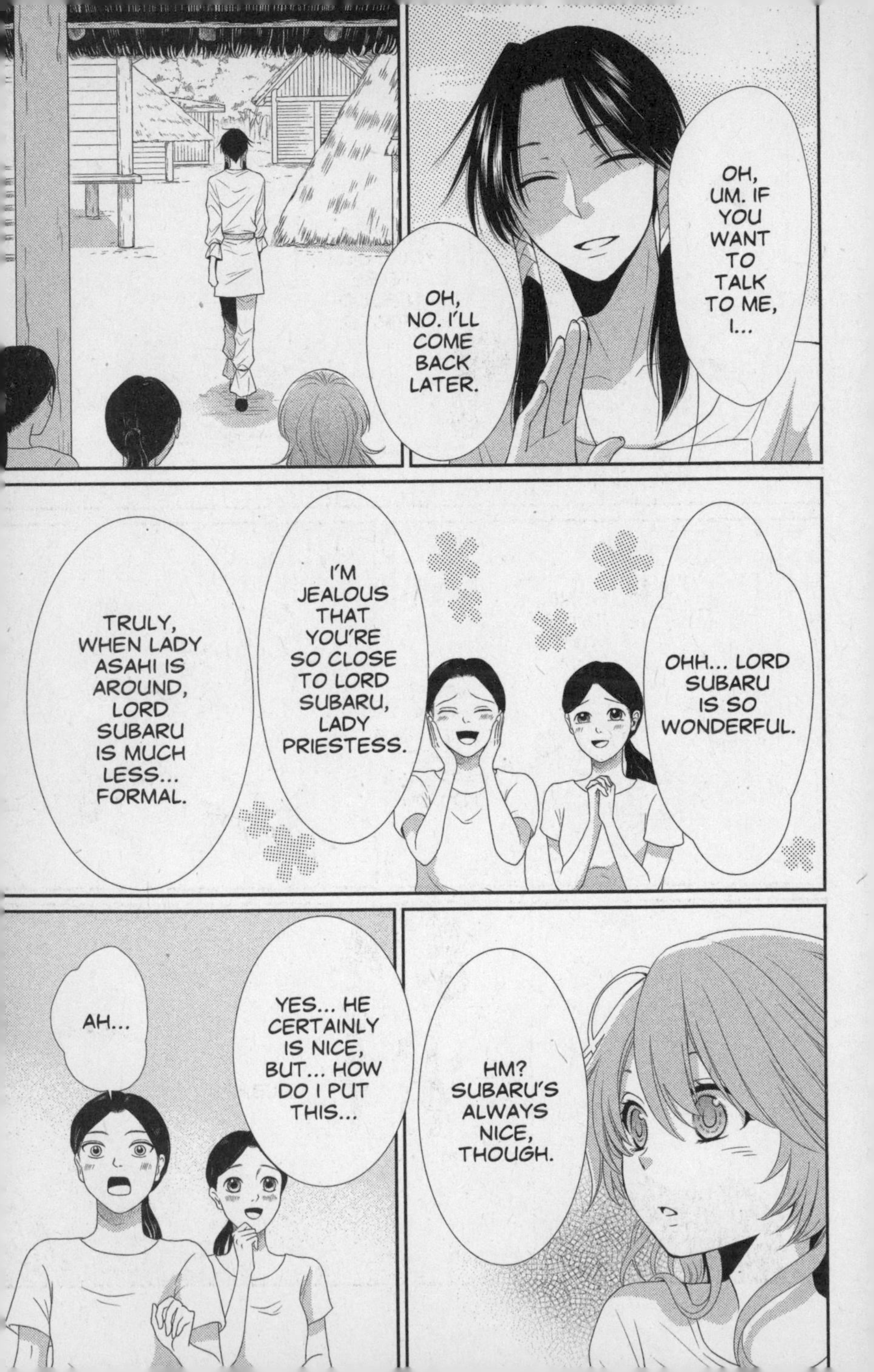
OH, UM. IF YOU WANT TO TALK TO ME, I...
OH, NO. I'LL COME BACK LATER.
OHH... LORD SUBARU IS SO WONDERFUL.
I'M JEALOUS THAT YOU'RE SO CLOSE TO LORD SUBARU, LADY PRIESTESS.
TRULY, WHEN LADY ASAHI IS AROUND, LORD SUBARU IS MUCH LESS... FORMAL.
HM? SUBARU'S ALWAYS NICE, THOUGH.
YES... HE CERTAINLY IS NICE, BUT... HOW DO I PUT THIS...
AH...

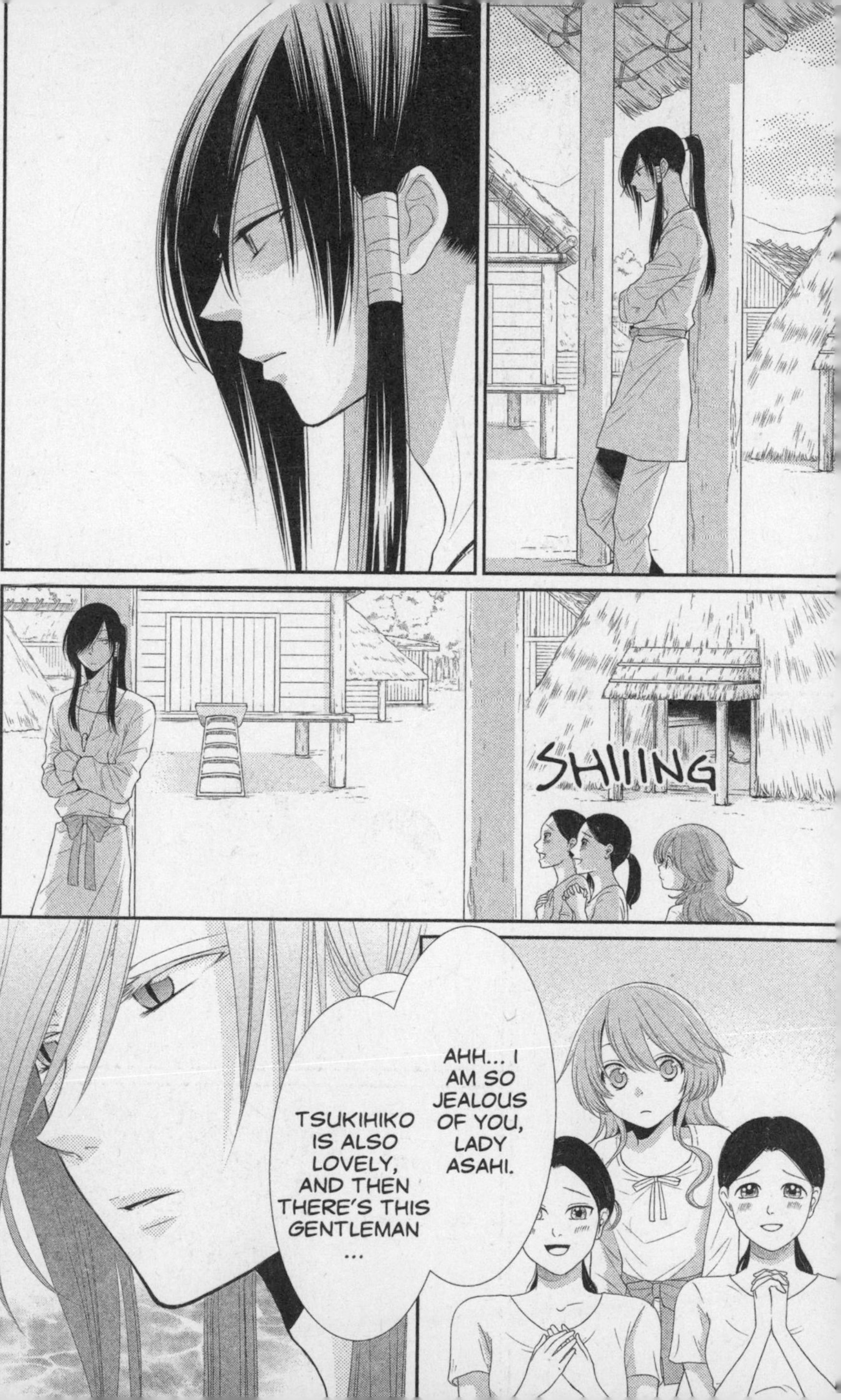
SHIIING
AHH... I AM SO JEALOUS OF YOU, LADY ASAHI.
TSUKIHIKO IS ALSO LOVELY, AND THEN THERE'S THIS GENTLEMAN ...

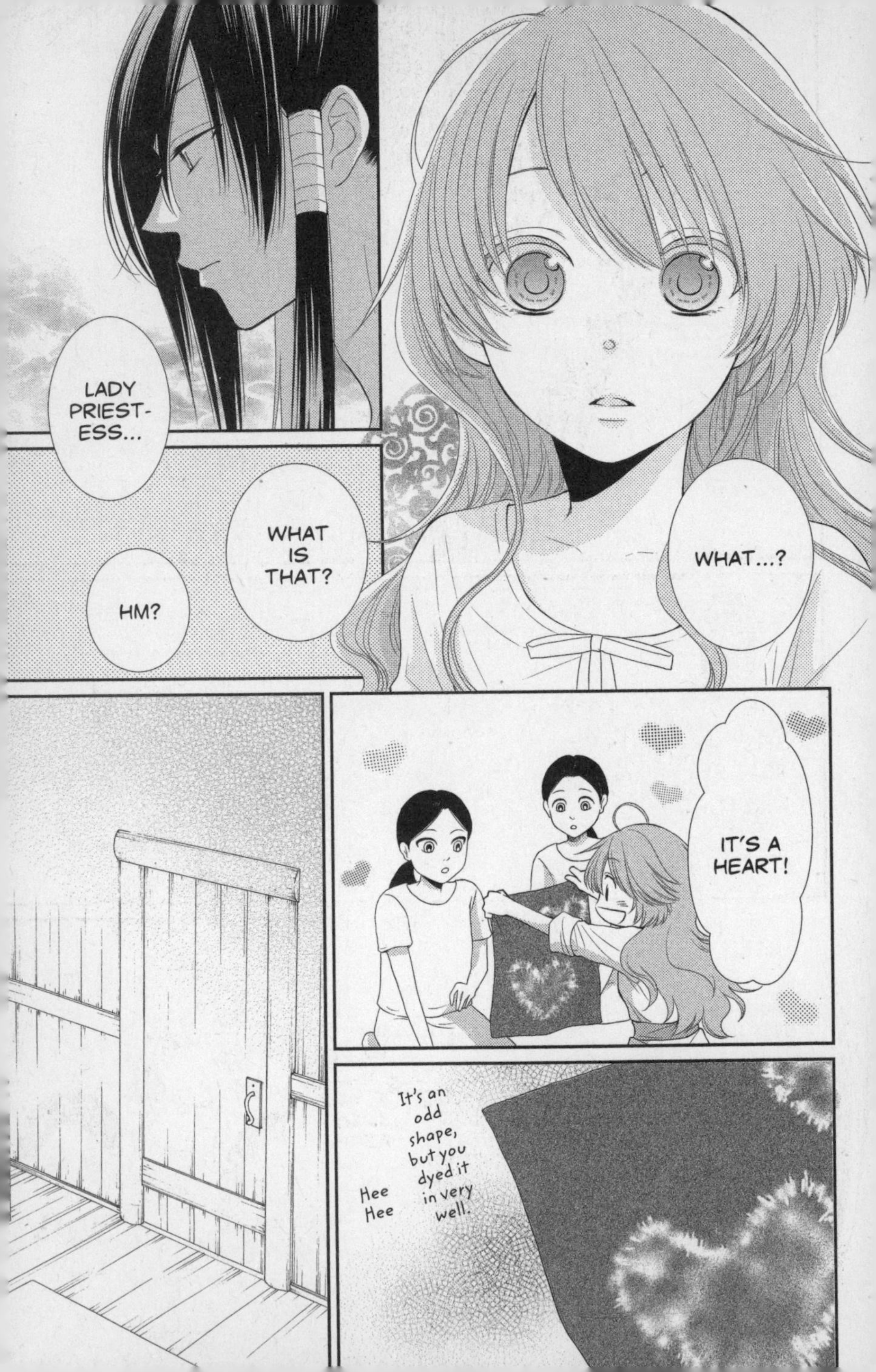
WHAT...?
LADY PRIEST-ESS...
WHAT IS THAT?
HM?
IT'S A HEART!
It's an odd shape, but you dyed it in very well.
Hee Hee

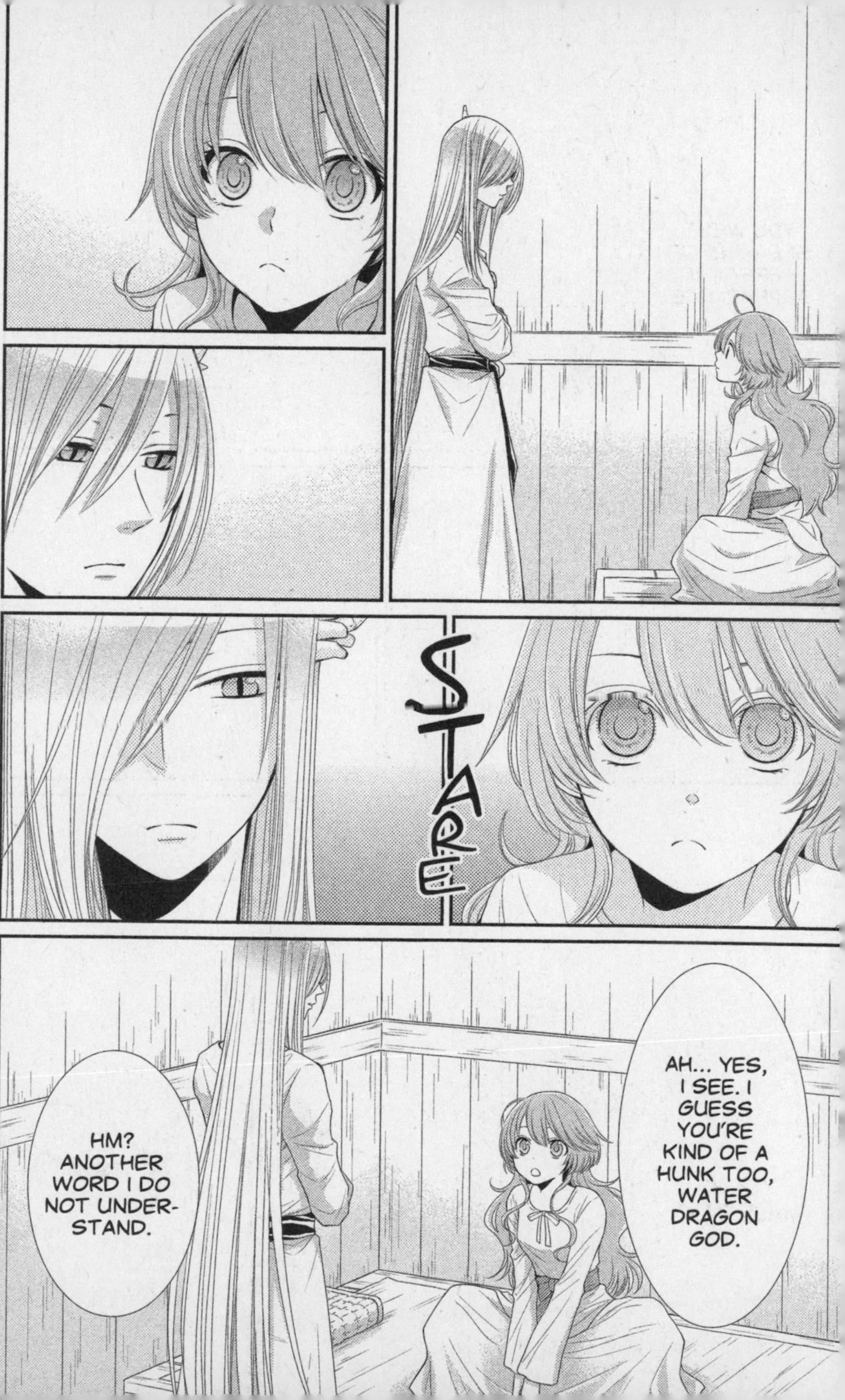
STARE
AH... YES, I SEE. I GUESS YOU'RE KIND OF A HUNK TOO, WATER DRAGON GOD.
HM? ANOTHER WORD I DO NOT UNDER-STAND.

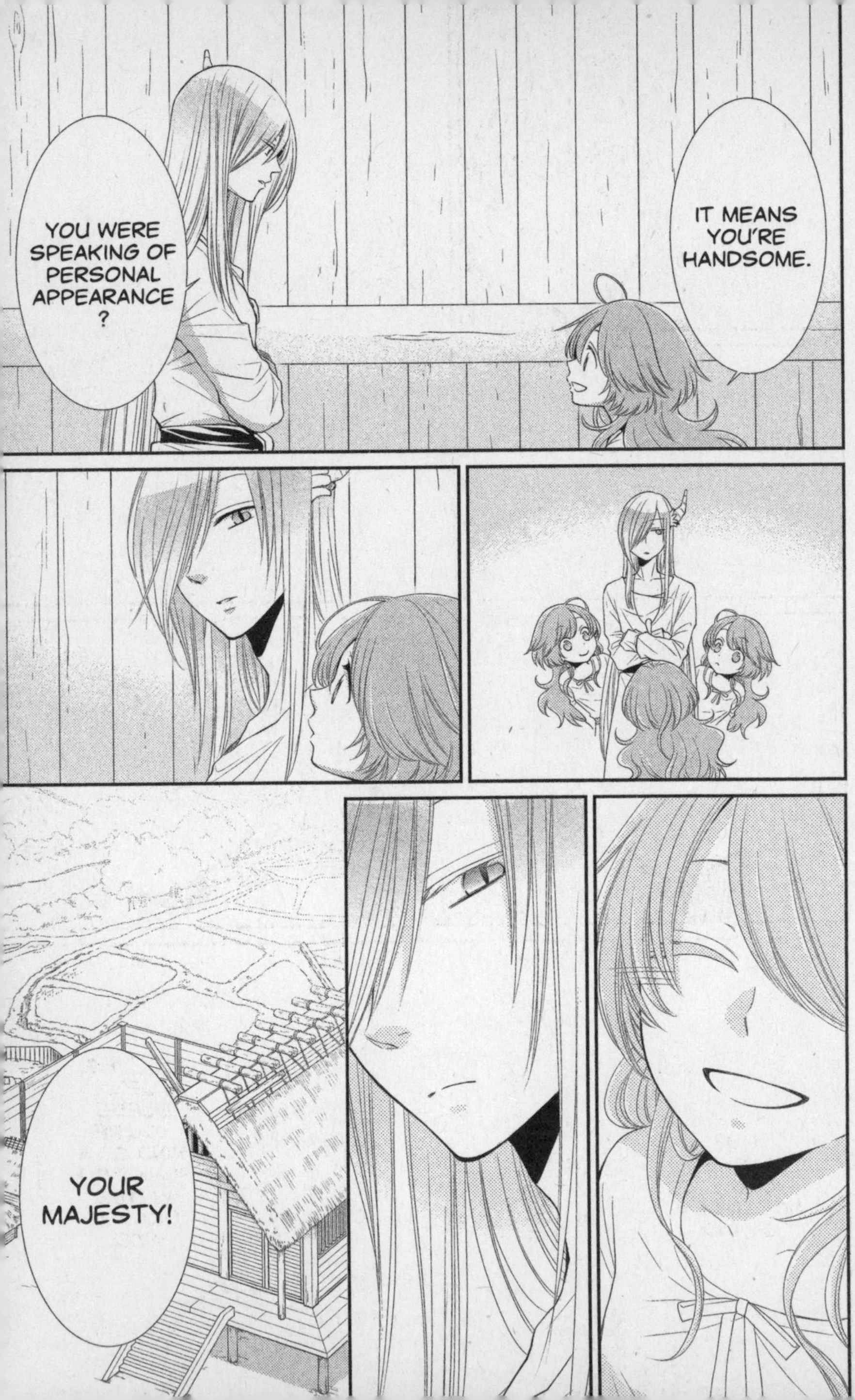
IT MEANS YOU'RE HANDSOME.
YOU WERE SPEAKING OF PERSONAL APPEARANCE?
YOUR MAJESTY!

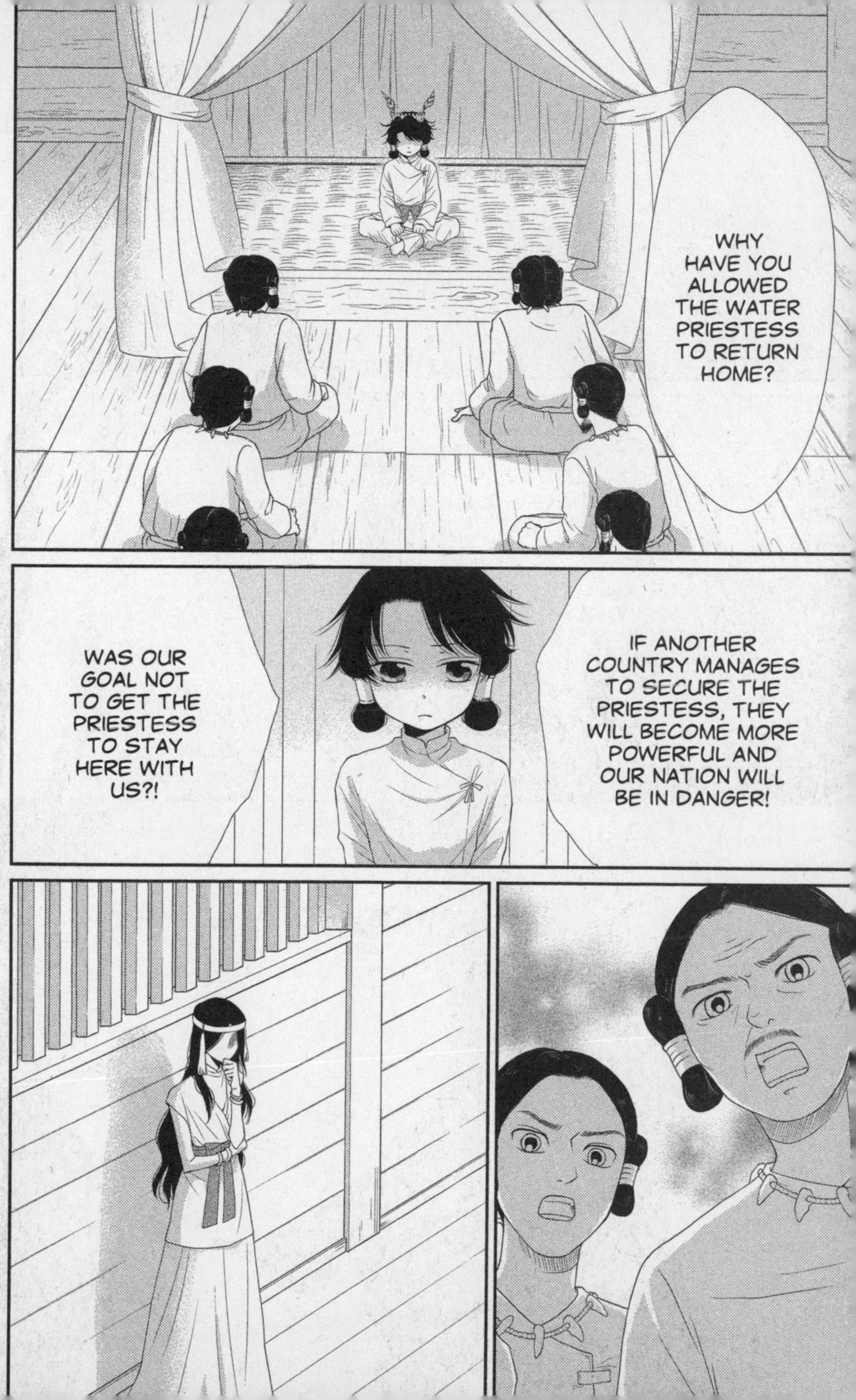
WHY HAVE YOU ALLOWED THE WATER PRIESTESS TO RETURN HOME?
IF ANOTHER COUNTRY MANAGES TO SECURE THE PRIESTESS, THEY WILL BECOME MORE POWERFUL AND OUR NATION WILL BE IN DANGER!
WAS OUR GOAL NOT TO GET THE PRIESTESS TO STAY HERE WITH US?!

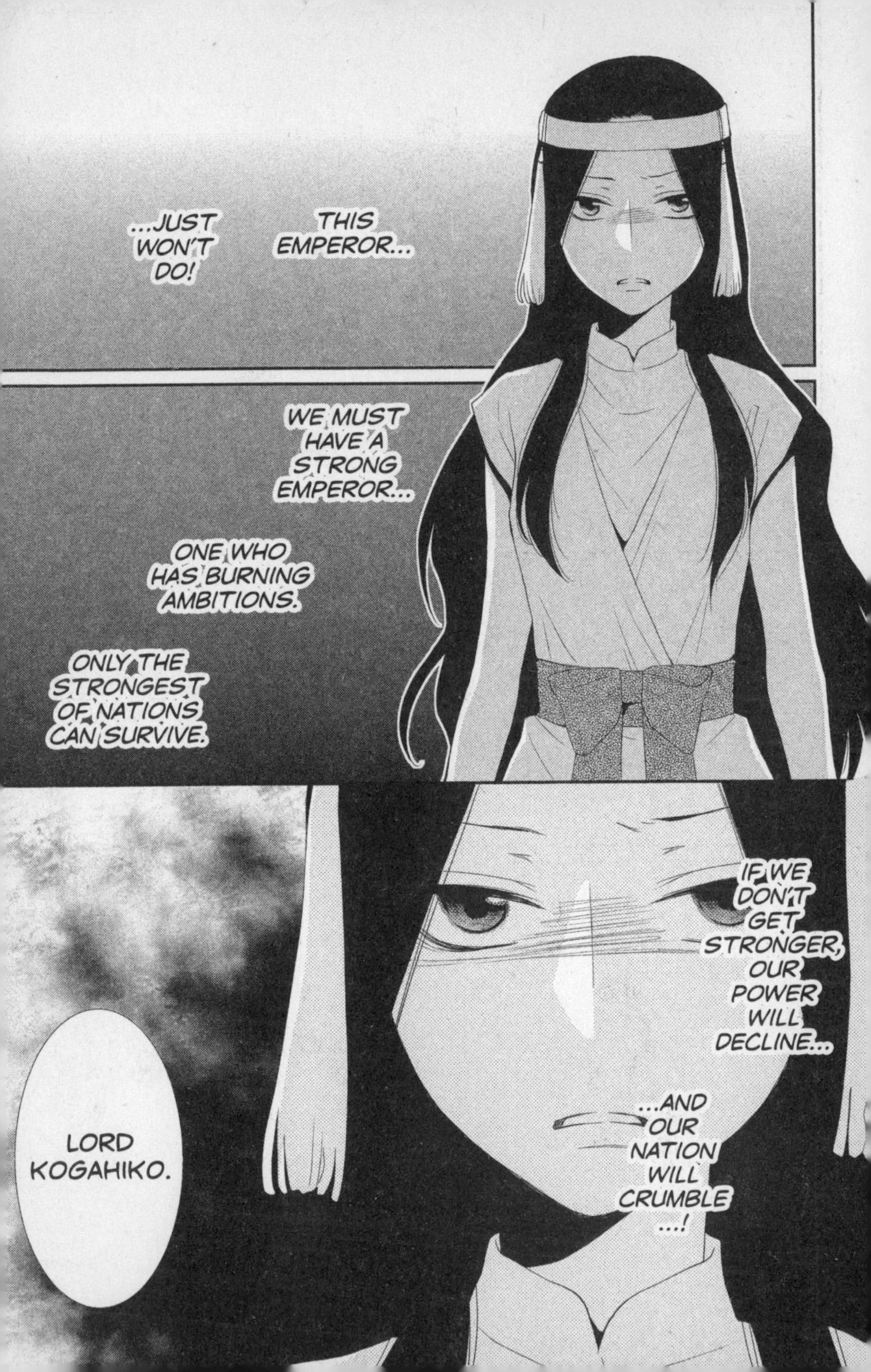
THIS EMPEROR...
...JUST WON'T DO!
WE MUST HAVE A STRONG EMPEROR...
ONE WHO HAS BURNING AMBITIONS.
ONLY THE STRONGEST OF NATIONS CAN SURVIVE.
IF WE DON'T GET STRONGER, OUR POWER WILL DECLINE...
...AND OUR NATION WILL CRUMBLE...!
LORD KOGAHIKO.

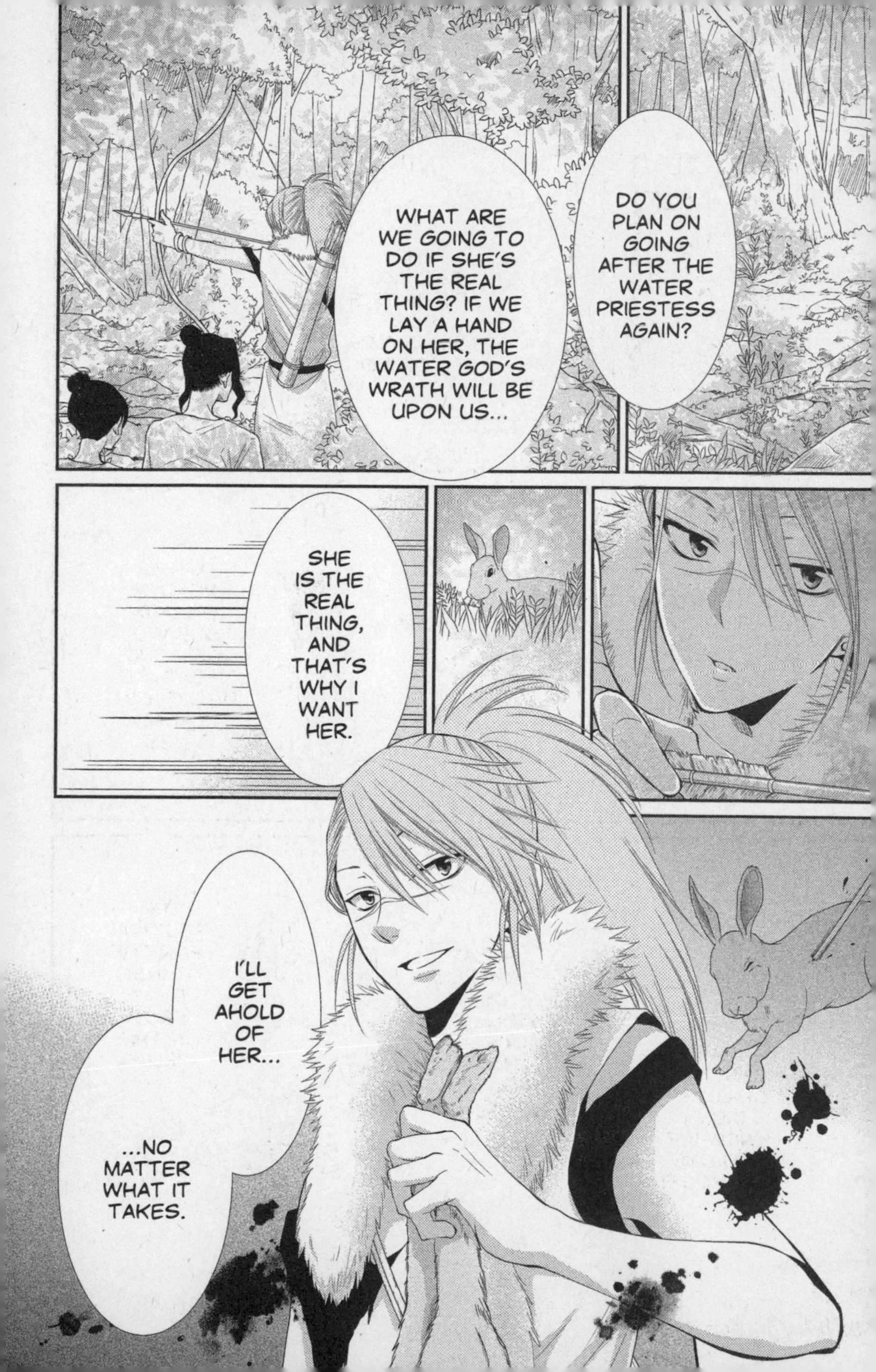
DO YOU PLAN ON GOING AFTER THE WATER PRIESTESS AGAIN?
WHAT ARE WE GOING TO DO IF SHE'S THE REAL THING? IF WE LAY A HAND ON HER, THE WATER GOD'S WRATH WILL BE UPON US...
SHE IS THE REAL THING, AND THAT'S WHY I WANT HER.
I'LL GET AHOLD OF HER...
...NO MATTER WHAT IT TAKES.

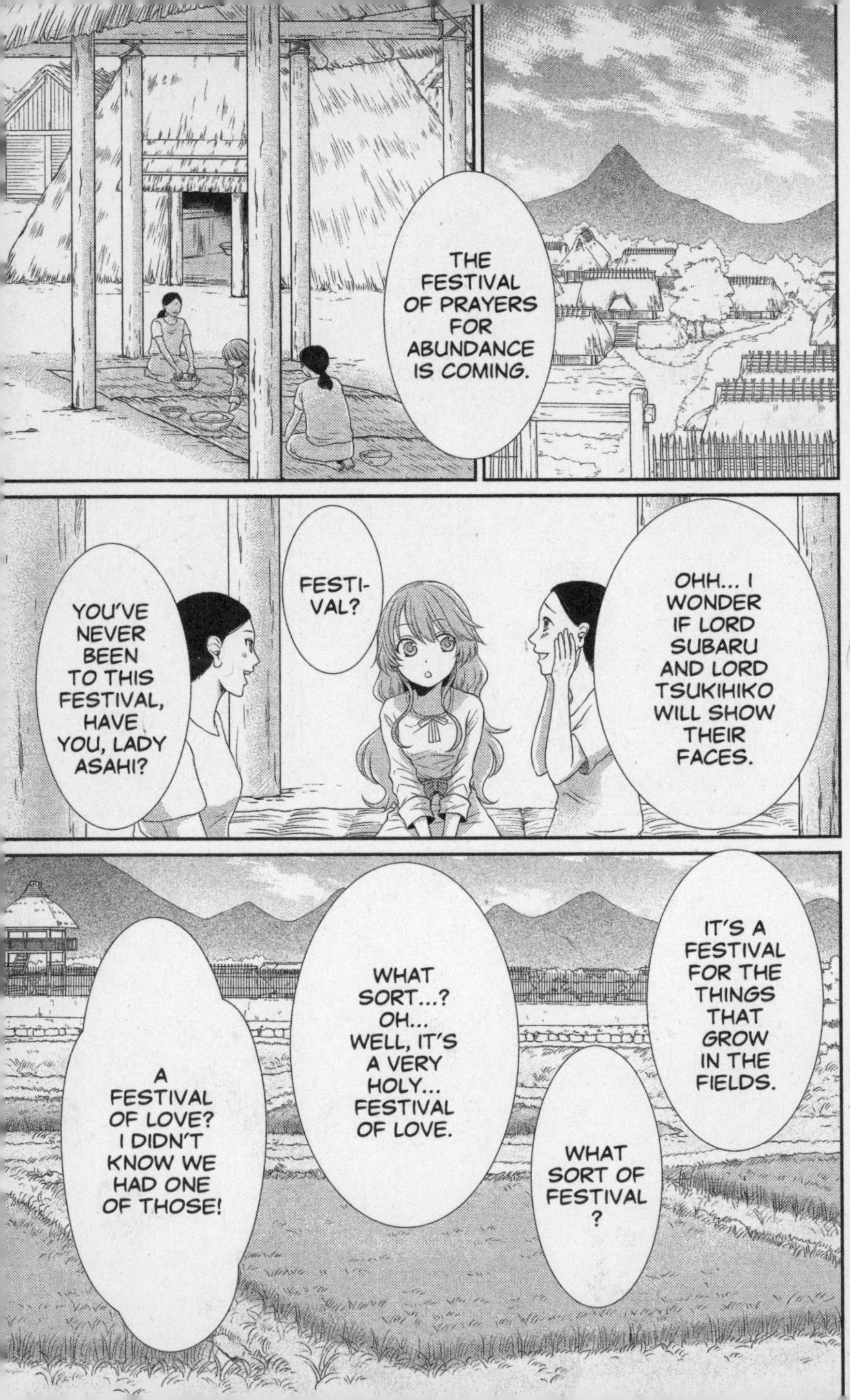
THE FESTIVAL OF PRAYERS FOR ABUNDANCE IS COMING.
OHH... I WONDER IF LORD SUBARU AND LORD TSUKIHIKO WILL SHOW THEIR FACES.
FESTI-VAL?
YOU'VE NEVER BEEN TO THIS FESTIVAL, HAVE YOU, LADY ASAHI?
IT'S A FESTIVAL FOR THE THINGS THAT GROW IN THE FIELDS.
WHAT SORT OF FESTIVAL?
WHAT SORT...? OH... WELL, IT'S A VERY HOLY... FESTIVAL OF LOVE.
A FESTIVAL OF LOVE? I DIDN'T KNOW WE HAD ONE OF THOSE!

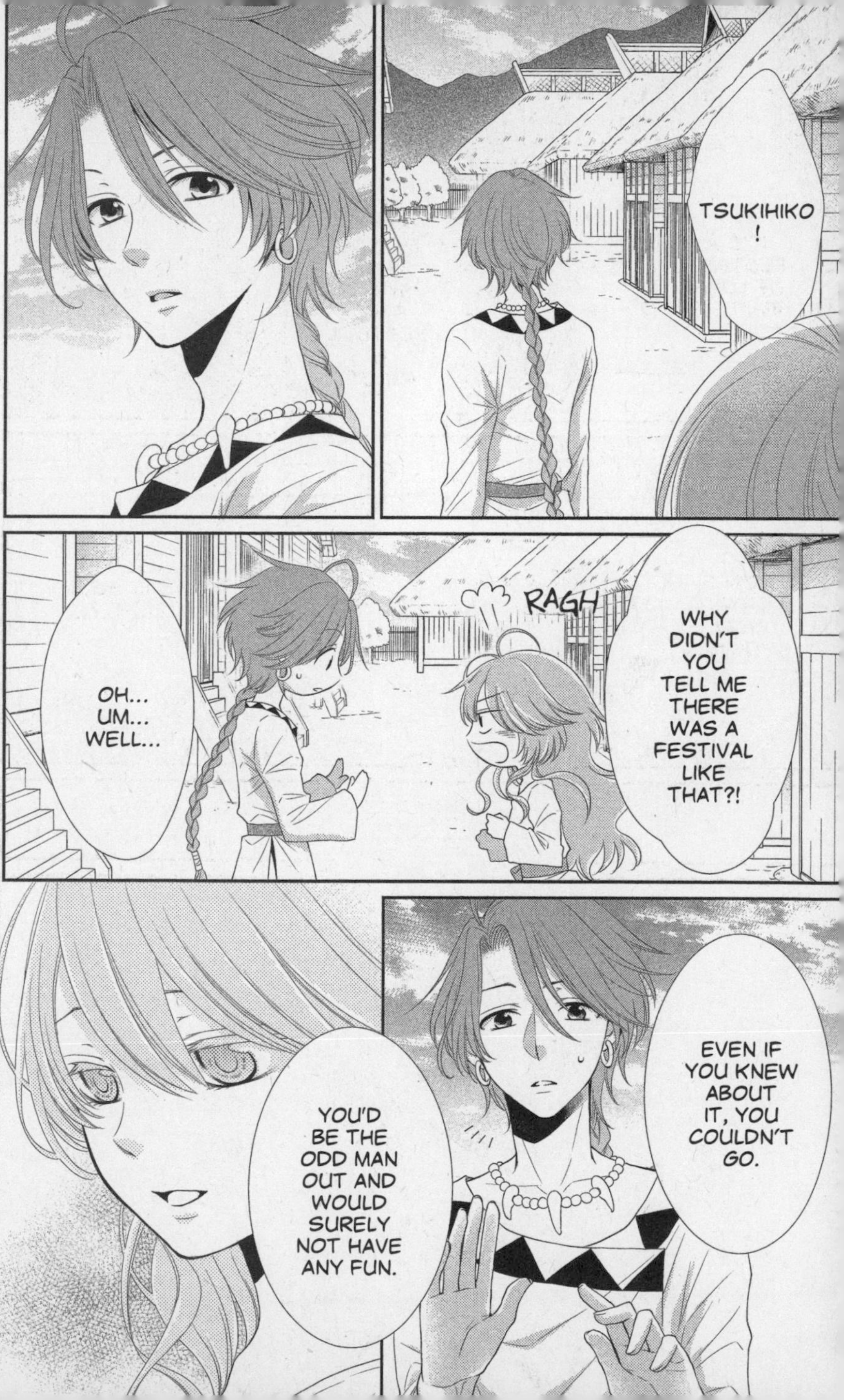
TSUKIHIKO!
WHY DIDN'T YOU TELL ME THERE WAS A FESTIVAL LIKE THAT?!
RAGH
OH... UM... WELL...
EVEN IF YOU KNEW ABOUT IT, YOU COULDN'T GO.
YOU'D BE THE ODD MAN OUT AND WOULD SURELY NOT HAVE ANY FUN.

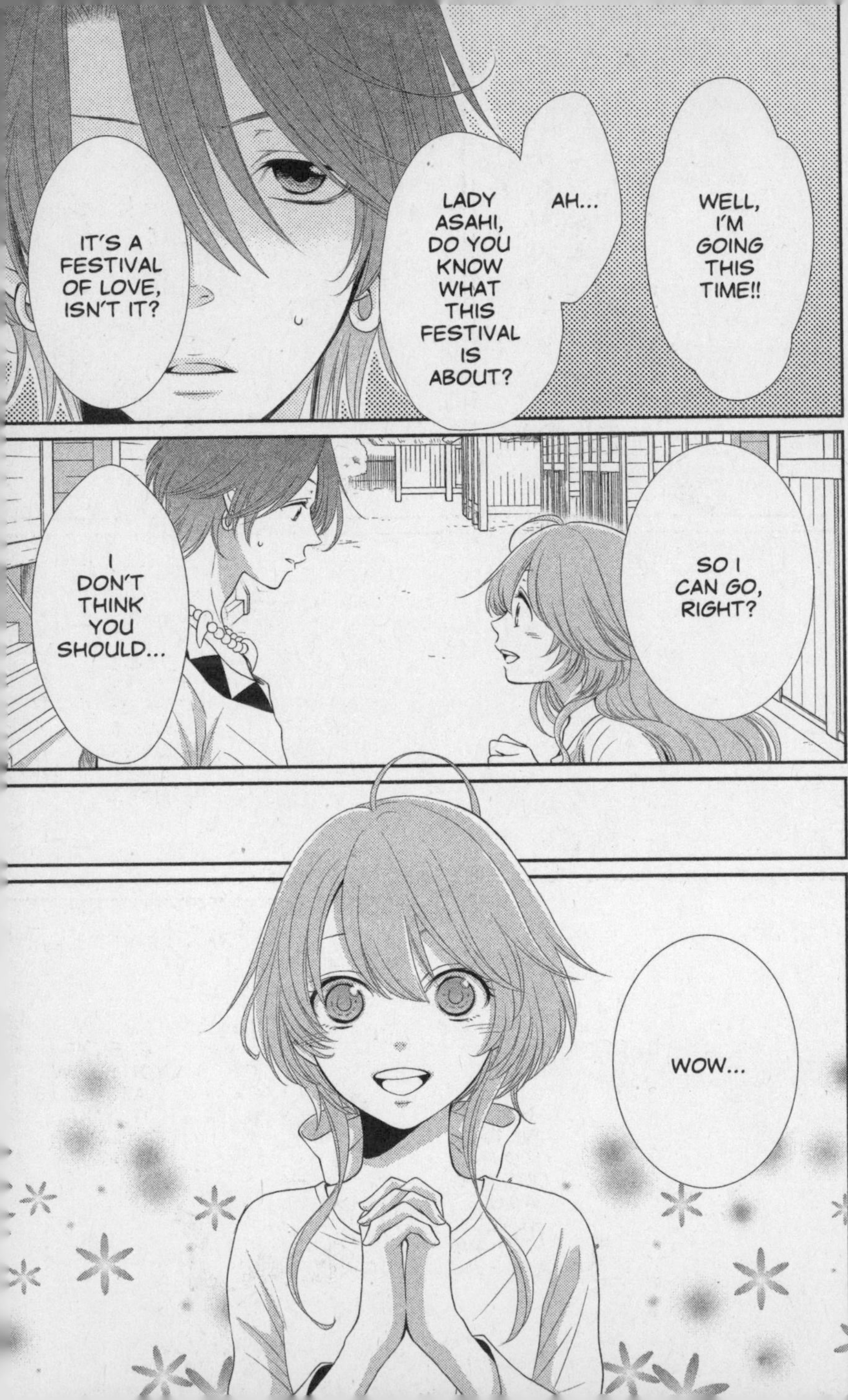
WELL, I'M GOING THIS TIME!!
AH...
LADY ASAHI, DO YOU KNOW WHAT THIS FESTIVAL IS ABOUT?
IT'S A FESTIVAL OF LOVE, ISN'T IT?
SO I CAN GO, RIGHT?
I DON'T THINK YOU SHOULD...
WOW...

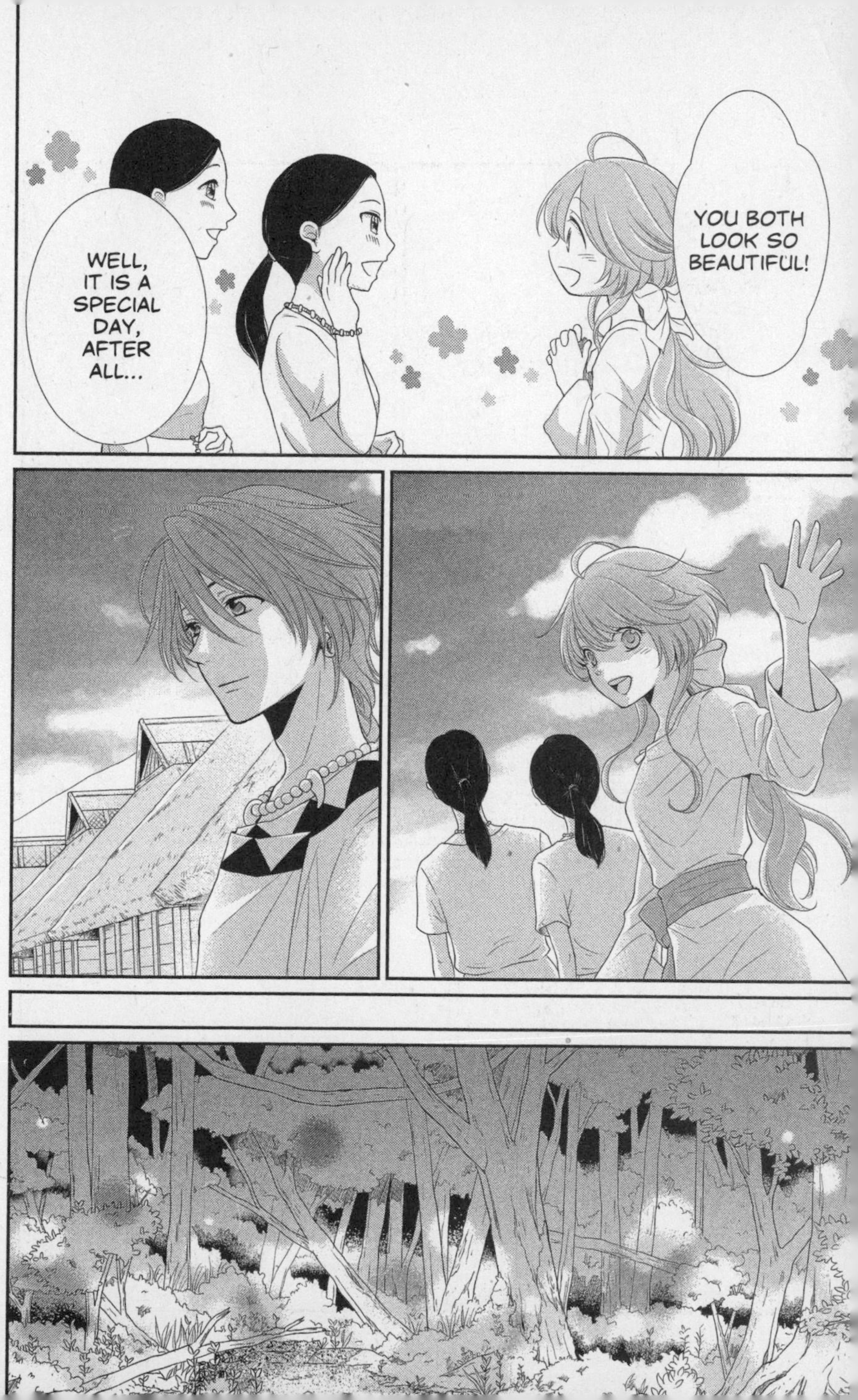
YOU BOTH LOOK SO BEAUTIFUL!
WELL, IT IS A SPECIAL DAY, AFTER ALL...

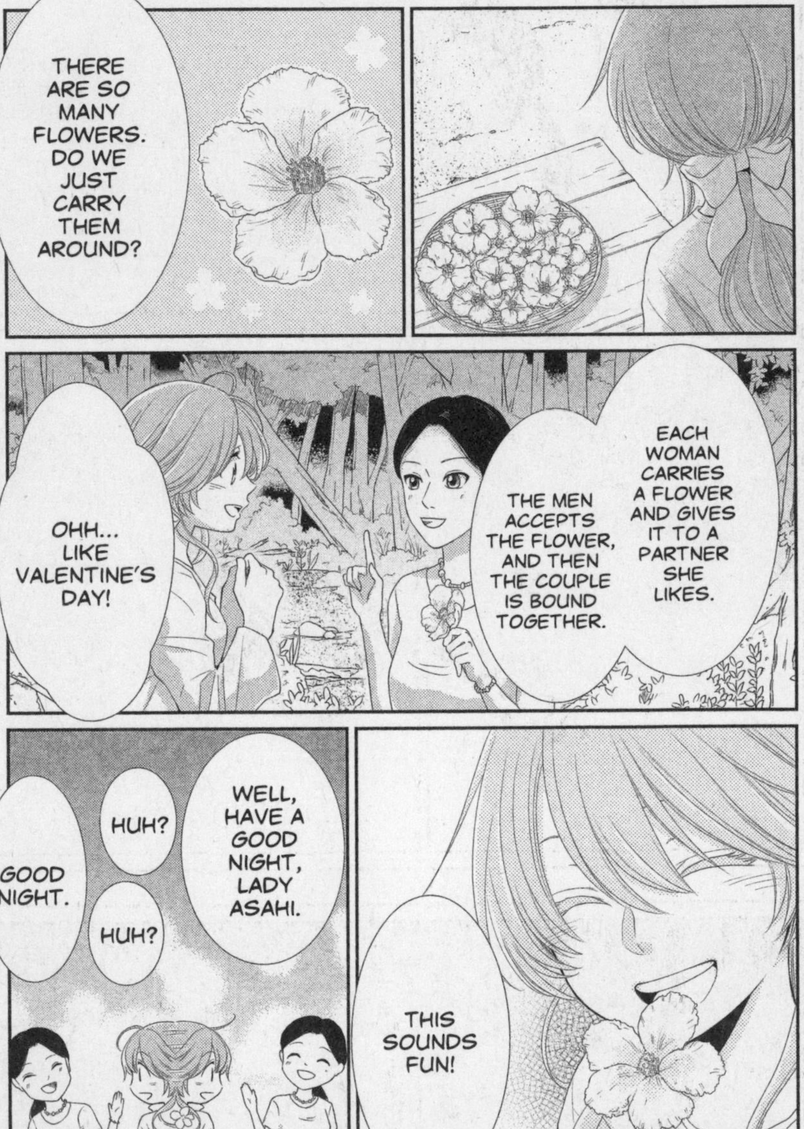
THERE ARE SO MANY FLOWERS. DO WE JUST CARRY THEM AROUND?
EACH WOMAN CARRIES A FLOWER AND GIVES IT TO A PARTNER SHE LIKES.
THE MEN ACCEPTS THE FLOWER, AND THEN THE COUPLE IS BOUND TOGETHER.
OHH... LIKE VALENTINE'S DAY!
THIS SOUNDS FUN!
WELL, HAVE A GOOD NIGHT, LADY ASAHI.
HUH?
HUH?
GOOD NIGHT.

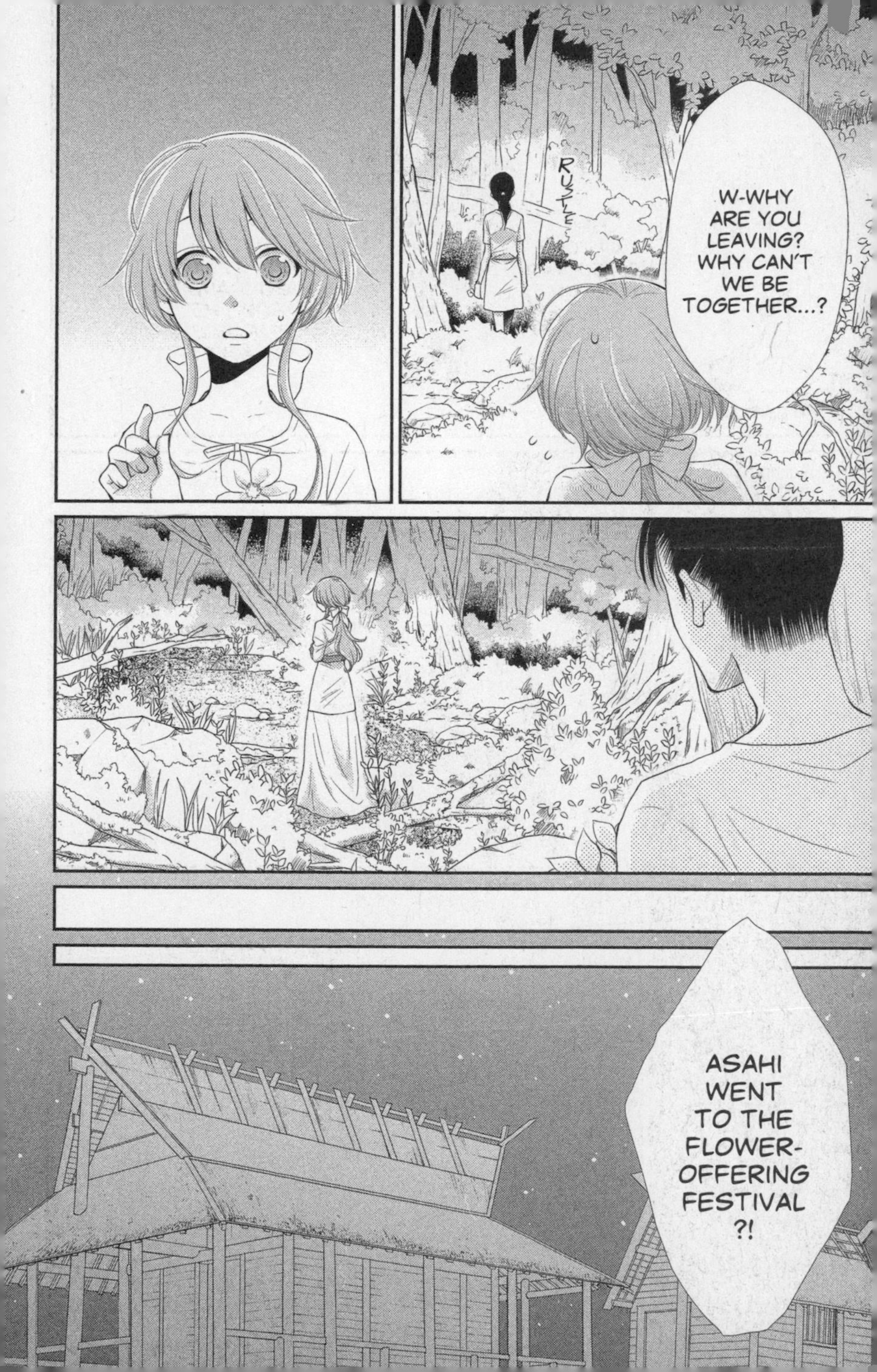
W-WHY ARE YOU LEAVING? WHY CAN'T WE BE TOGETHER...?
RUSTLE
ASAHI WENT TO THE FLOWER-OFFERING FESTIVAL?!

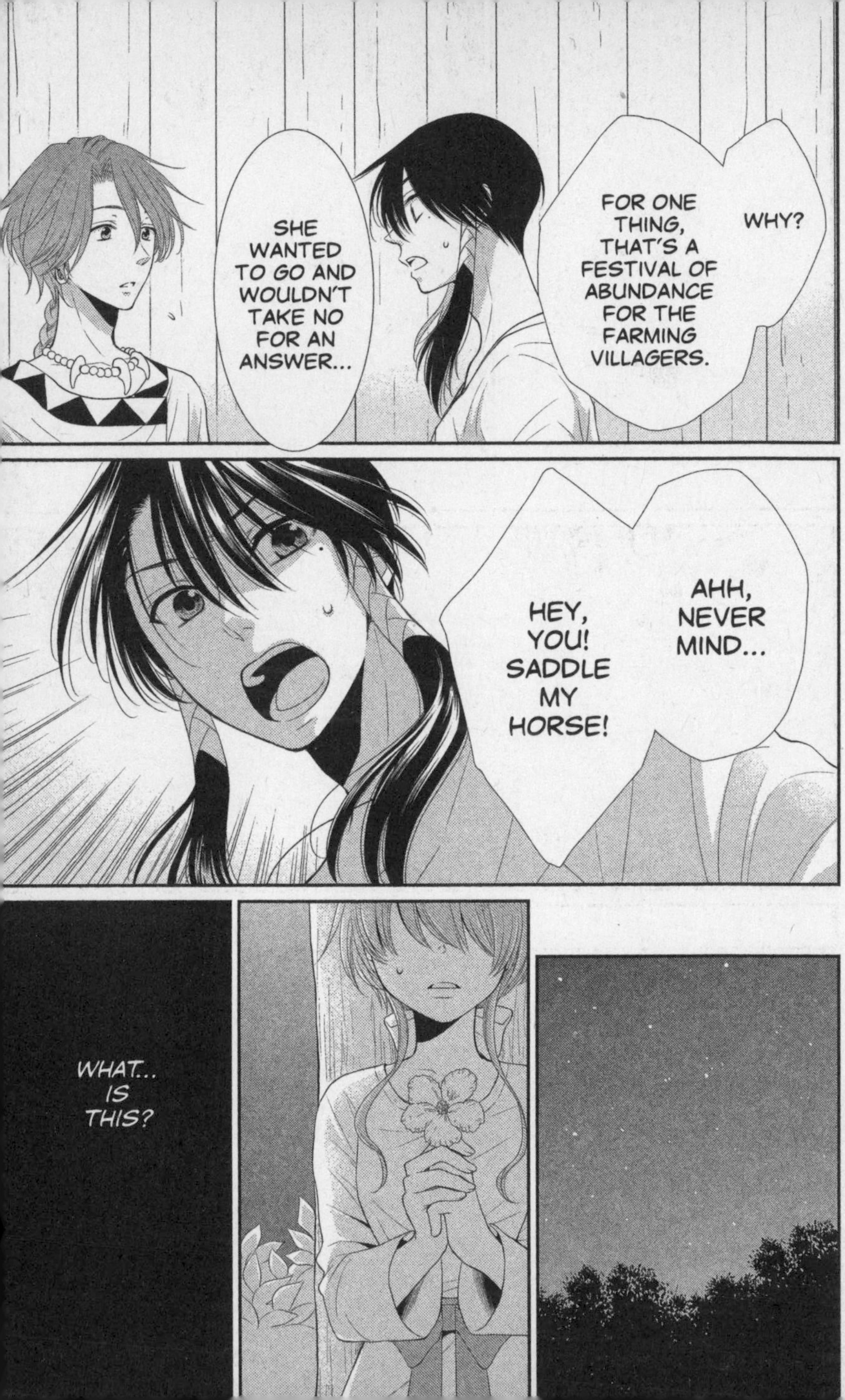
WHY?
FOR ONE THING, THAT'S A FESTIVAL OF ABUNDANCE FOR THE FARMING VILLAGERS.
SHE WANTED TO GO AND WOULDN'T TAKE NO FOR AN ANSWER...
AHH, NEVER MIND...
HEY, YOU! SADDLE MY HORSE!
WHAT... IS THIS?

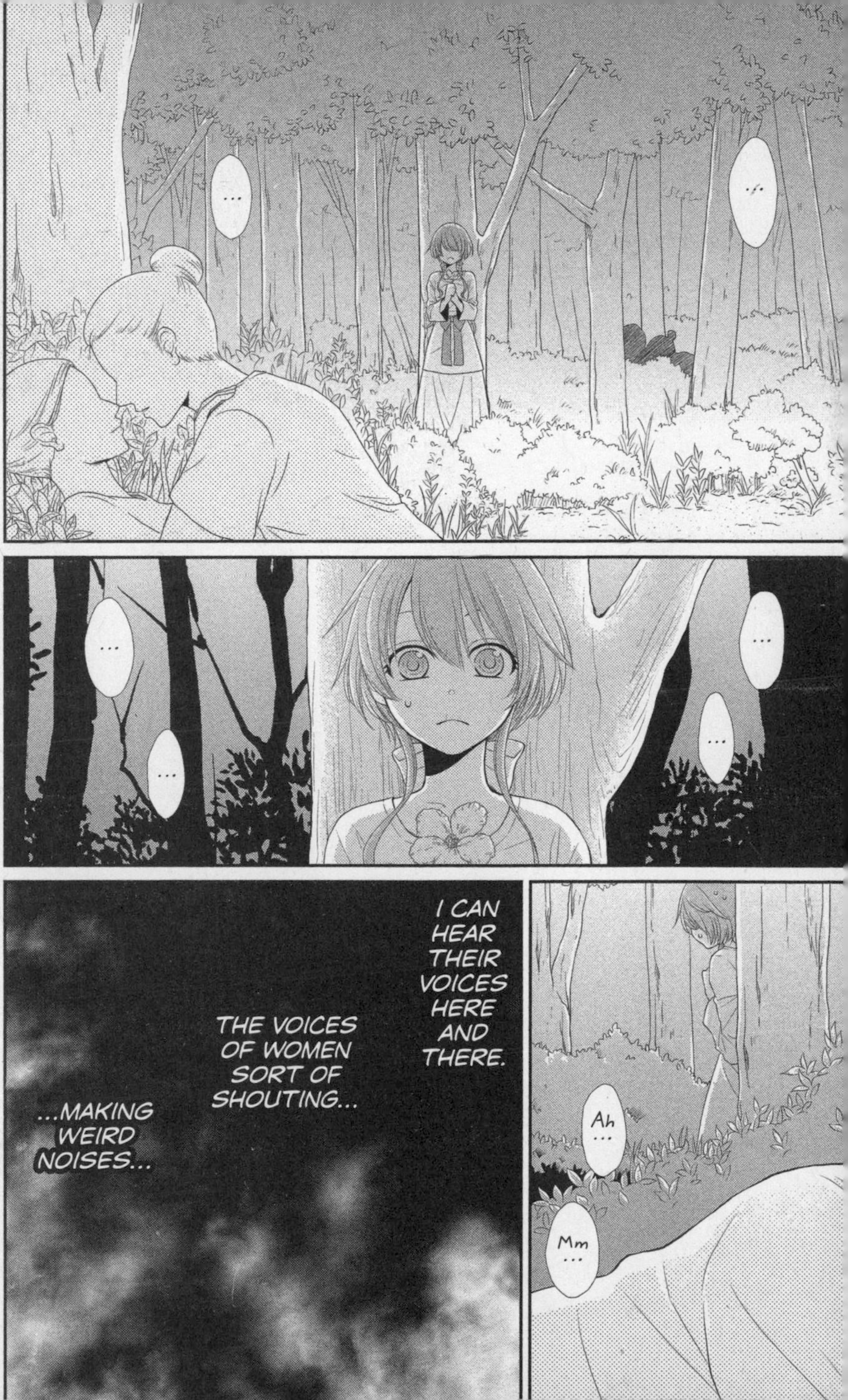
...
...
...
...
...
...
Ah...
Mm...
I CAN HEAR THEIR VOICES HERE AND THERE.
THE VOICES OF WOMEN SORT OF SHOUTING...
...MAKING WEIRD NOISES...

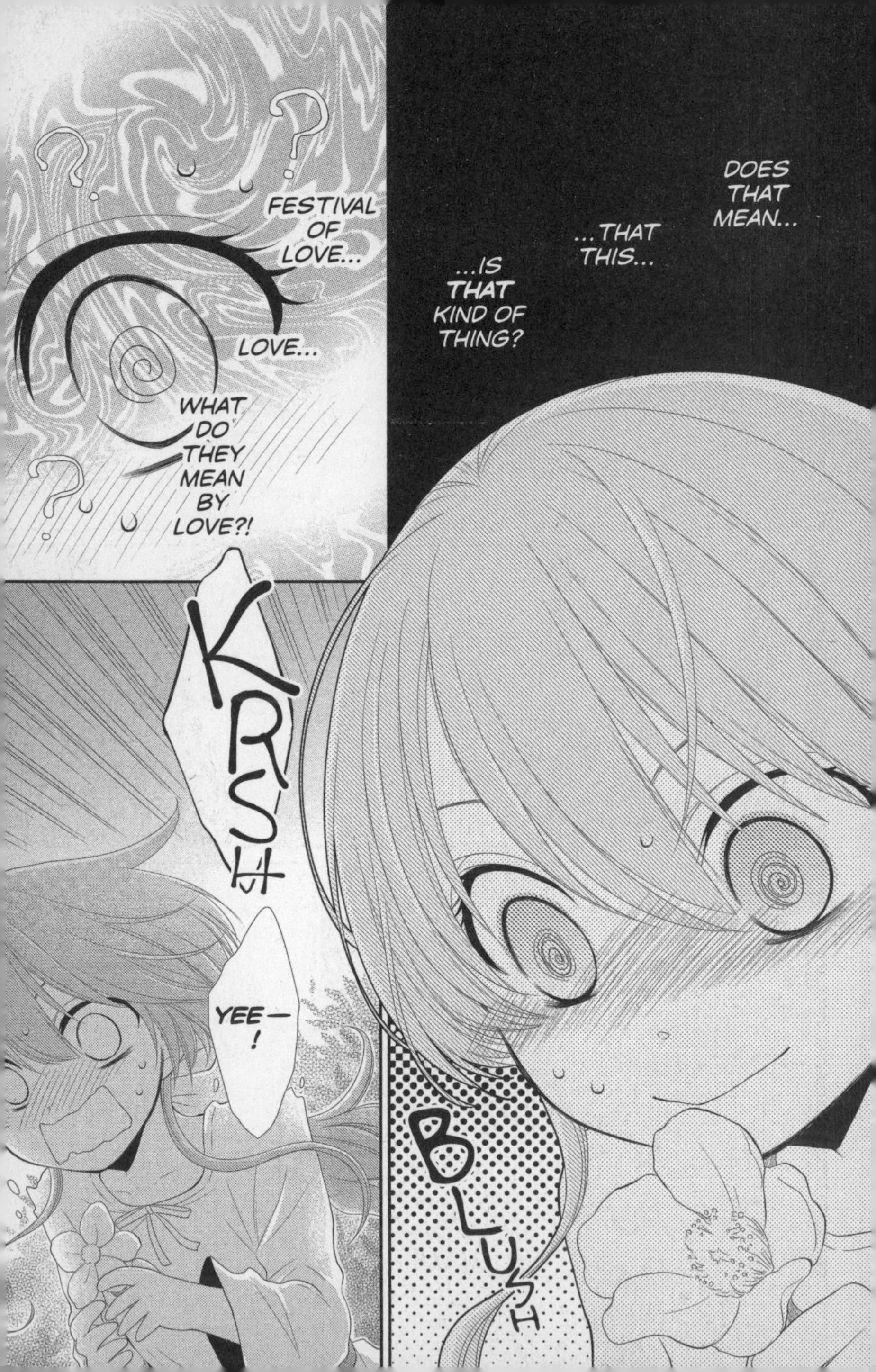
DOES THAT MEAN...
...THAT THIS...
...IS **THAT** KIND OF THING?
FESTIVAL OF LOVE...
LOVE...
WHAT DO THEY MEAN BY LOVE?!
BLUSH
KRSH
YEE—!

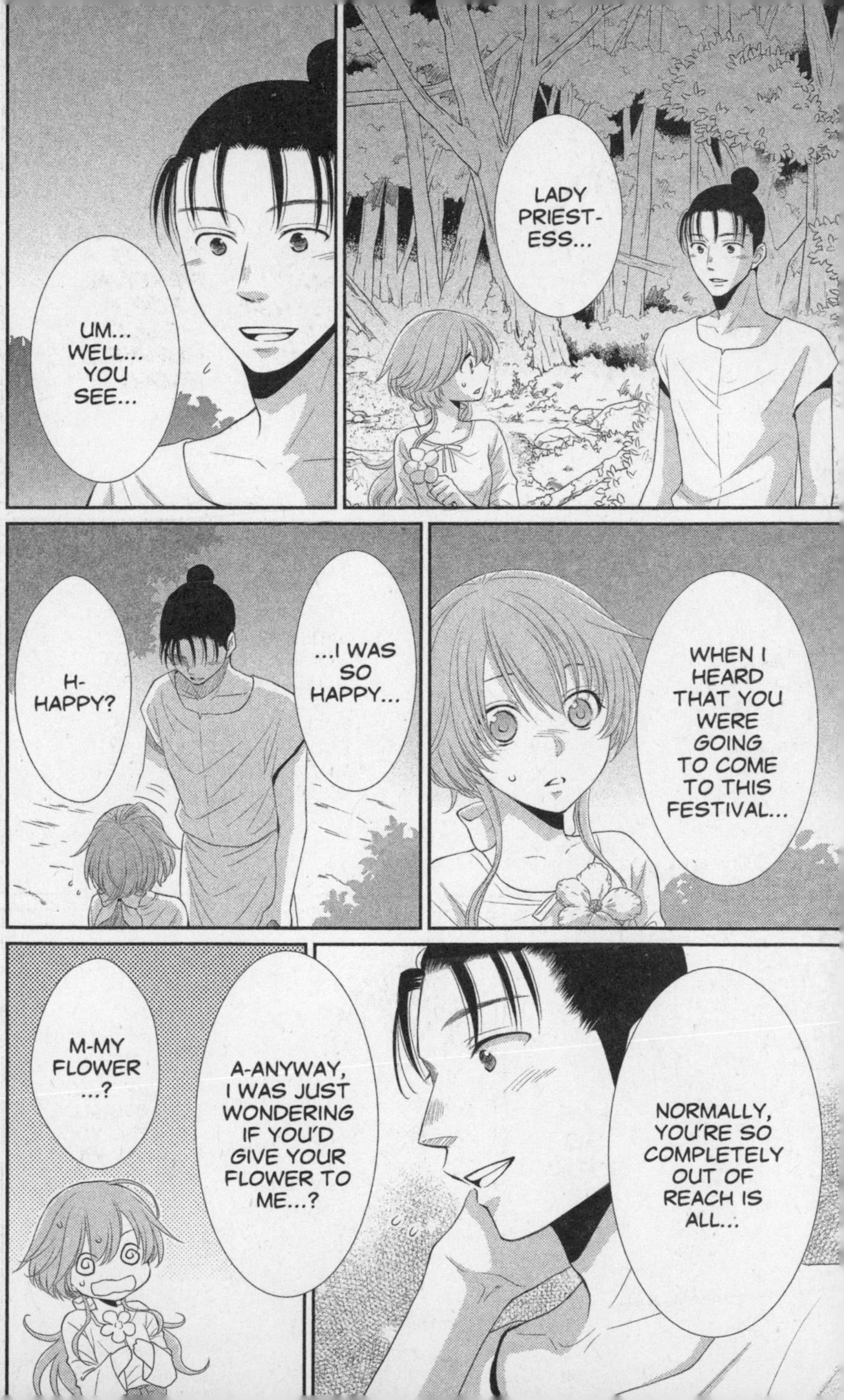
LADY PRIEST-ESS...
UM... WELL... YOU SEE...
WHEN I HEARD THAT YOU WERE GOING TO COME TO THIS FESTIVAL...
...I WAS SO HAPPY...
H-HAPPY?
NORMALLY, YOU'RE SO COMPLETELY OUT OF REACH IS ALL...
A-ANYWAY, I WAS JUST WONDERING IF YOU'D GIVE YOUR FLOWER TO ME...?
M-MY FLOWER ...?

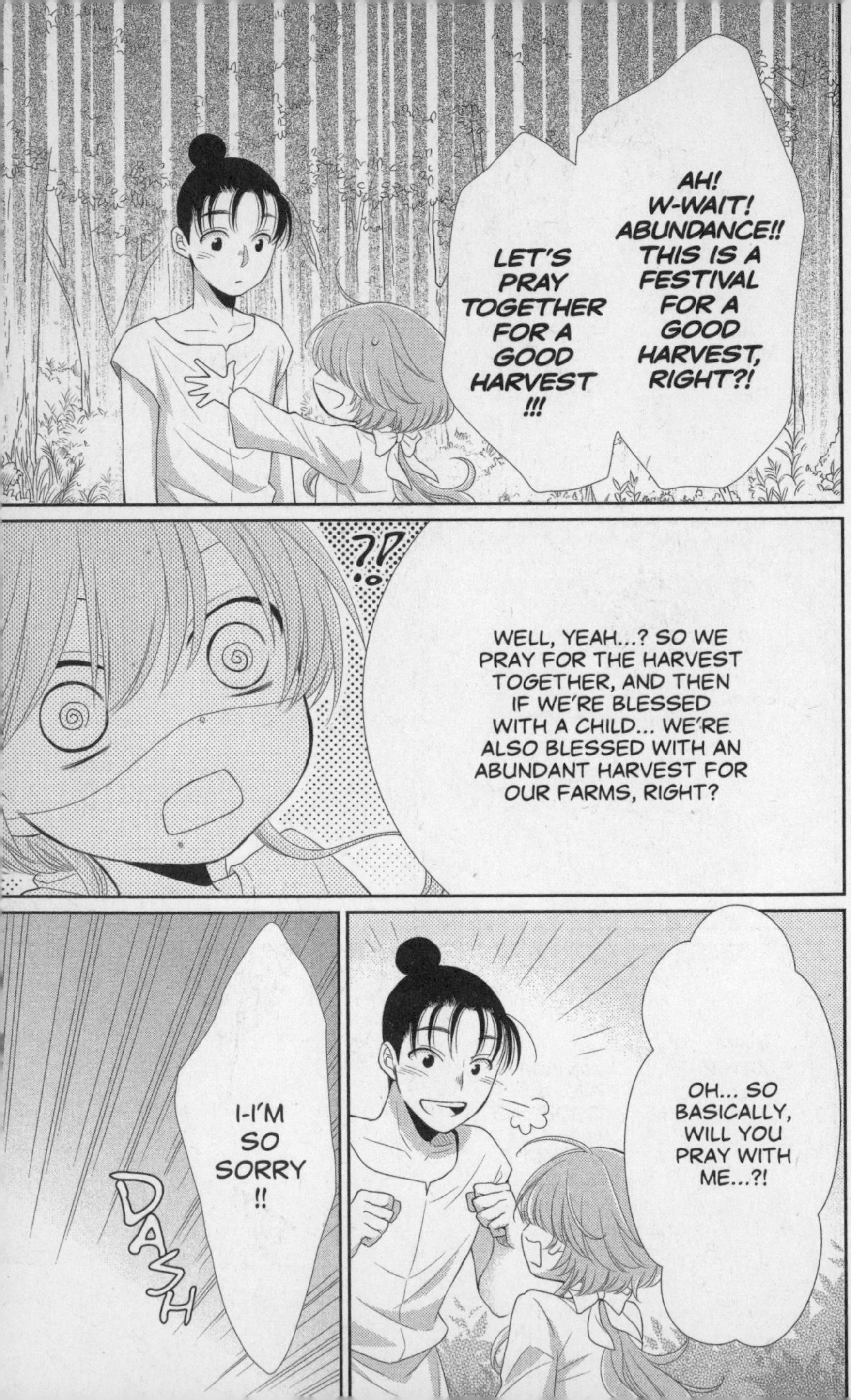
AH! W-WAIT! ABUNDANCE!! THIS IS A FESTIVAL FOR A GOOD HARVEST, RIGHT?!
LET'S PRAY TOGETHER FOR A GOOD HARVEST !!!
?!
WELL, YEAH...? SO WE PRAY FOR THE HARVEST TOGETHER, AND THEN IF WE'RE BLESSED WITH A CHILD... WE'RE ALSO BLESSED WITH AN ABUNDANT HARVEST FOR OUR FARMS, RIGHT?
OH... SO BASICALLY, WILL YOU PRAY WITH ME...?!
I-I'M SO SORRY !!
DASH

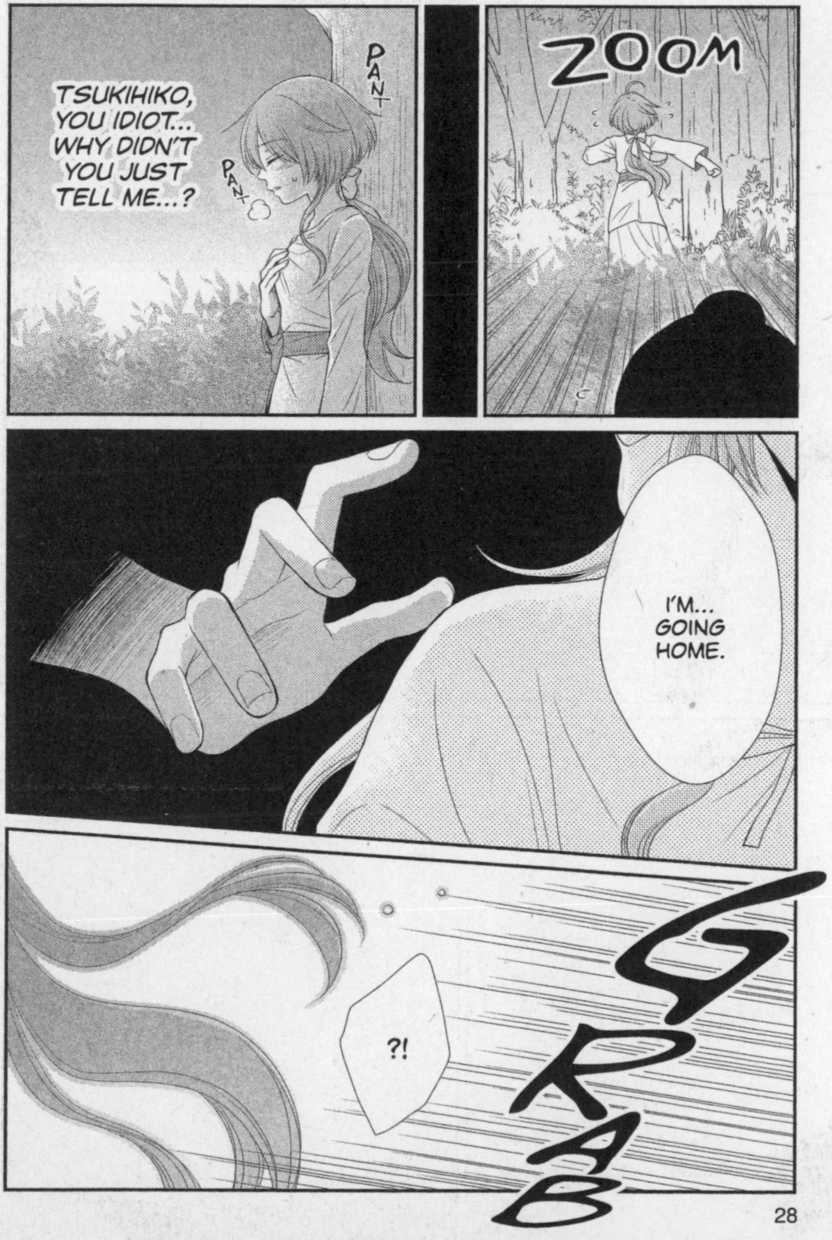

ZOOM
PANT
PANT
TSUKIHIKO, YOU IDIOT... WHY DIDN'T YOU JUST TELL ME...?
I'M... GOING HOME.
GRAB
?!

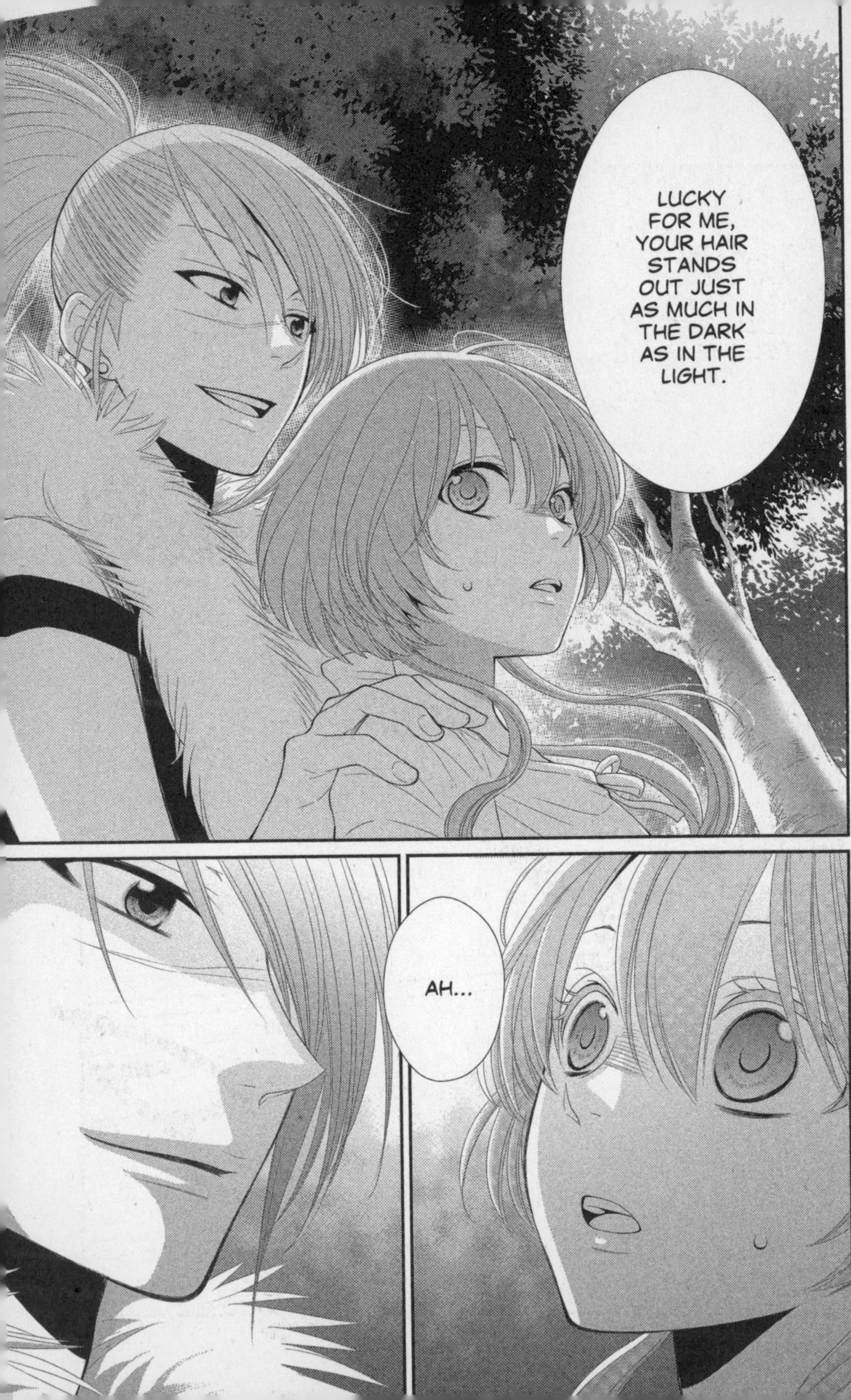
LUCKY FOR ME, YOUR HAIR STANDS OUT JUST AS MUCH IN THE DARK AS IN THE LIGHT.
AH...

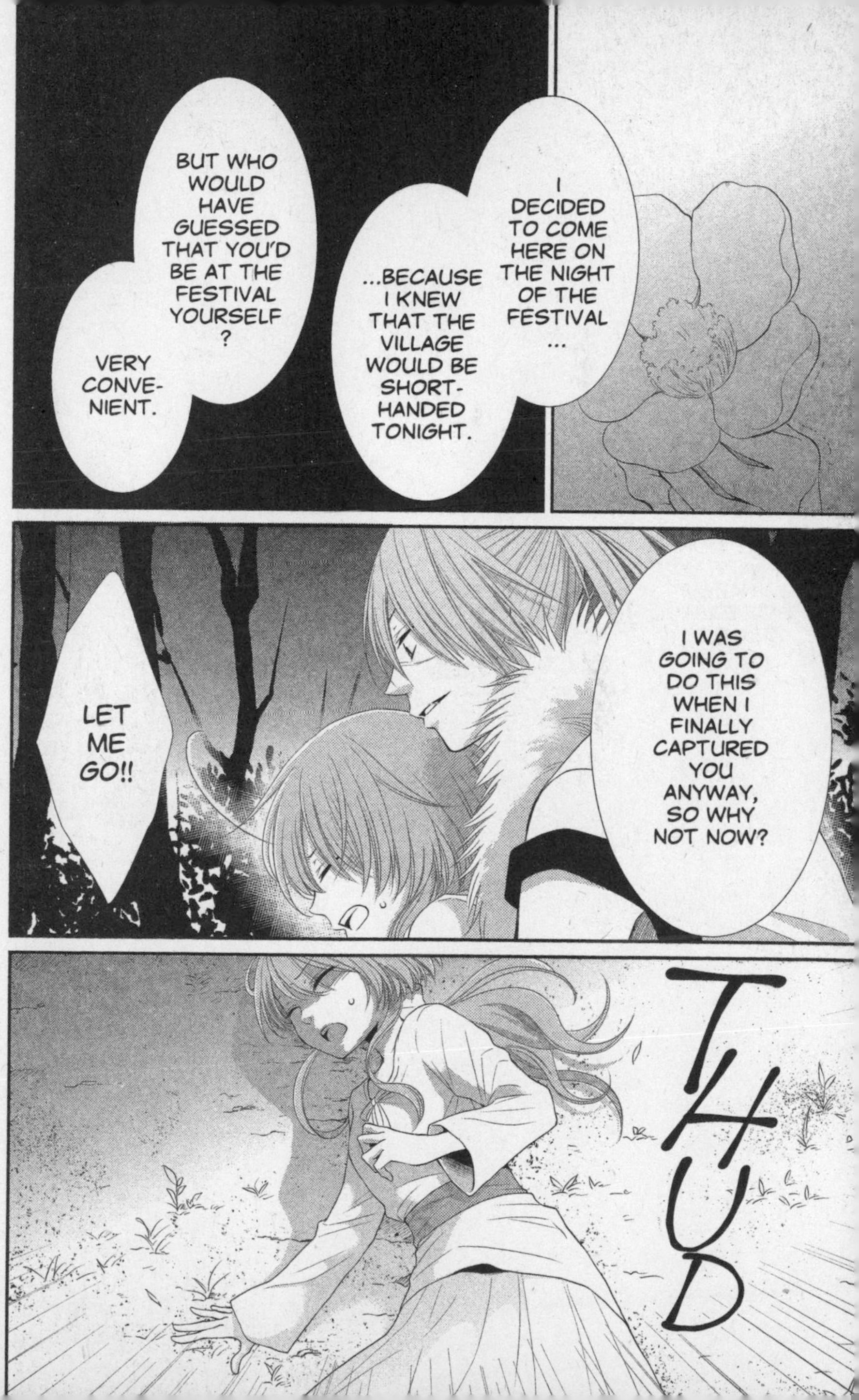
I DECIDED TO COME HERE ON THE NIGHT OF THE FESTIVAL...
...BECAUSE I KNEW THAT THE VILLAGE WOULD BE SHORT-HANDED TONIGHT.
BUT WHO WOULD HAVE GUESSED THAT YOU'D BE AT THE FESTIVAL YOURSELF?
VERY CONVE-NIENT.
I WAS GOING TO DO THIS WHEN I FINALLY CAPTURED YOU ANYWAY, SO WHY NOT NOW?
LET ME GO!!
THUD

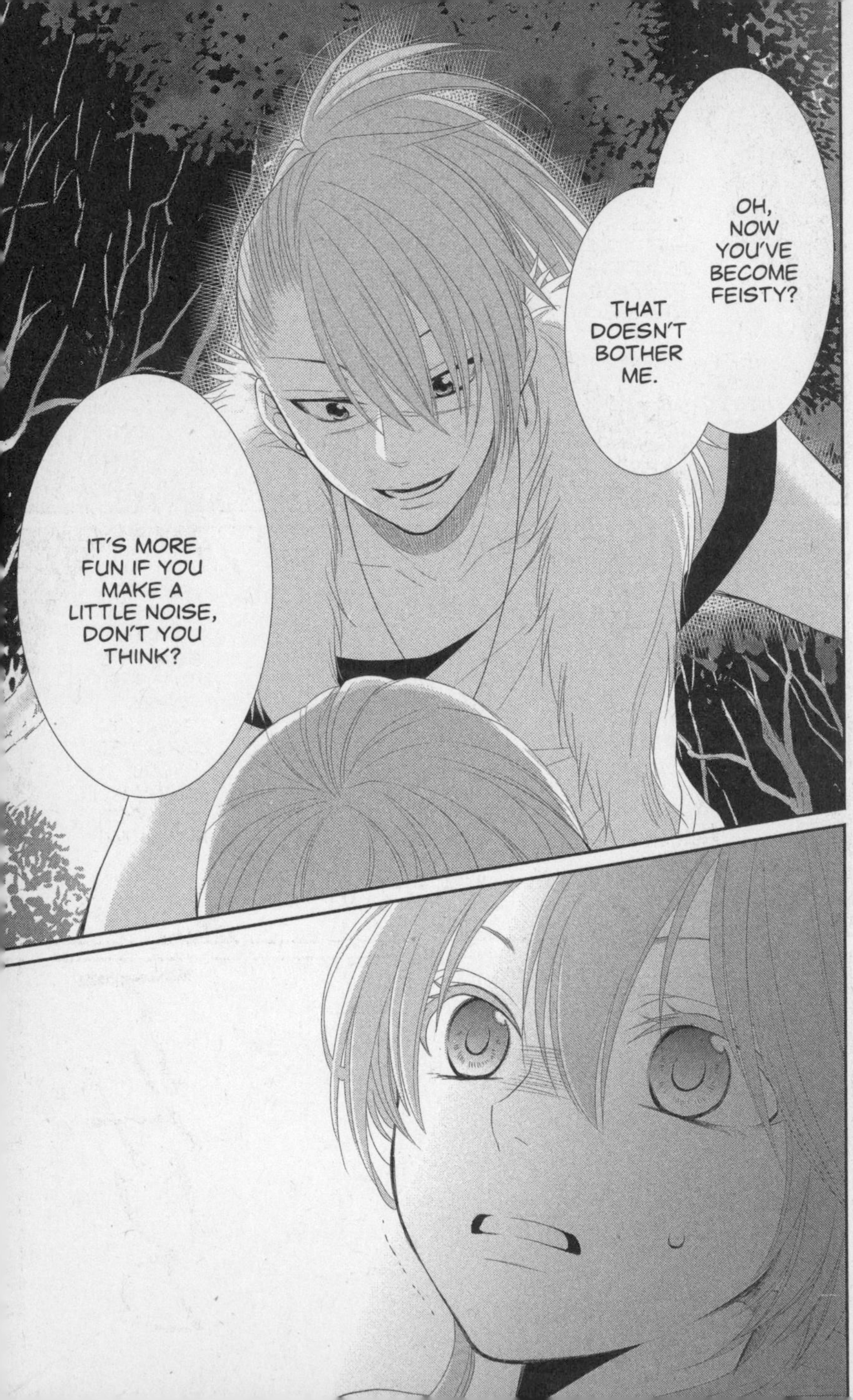
OH, NOW YOU'VE BECOME FEISTY?
THAT DOESN'T BOTHER ME.
IT'S MORE FUN IF YOU MAKE A LITTLE NOISE, DON'T YOU THINK?

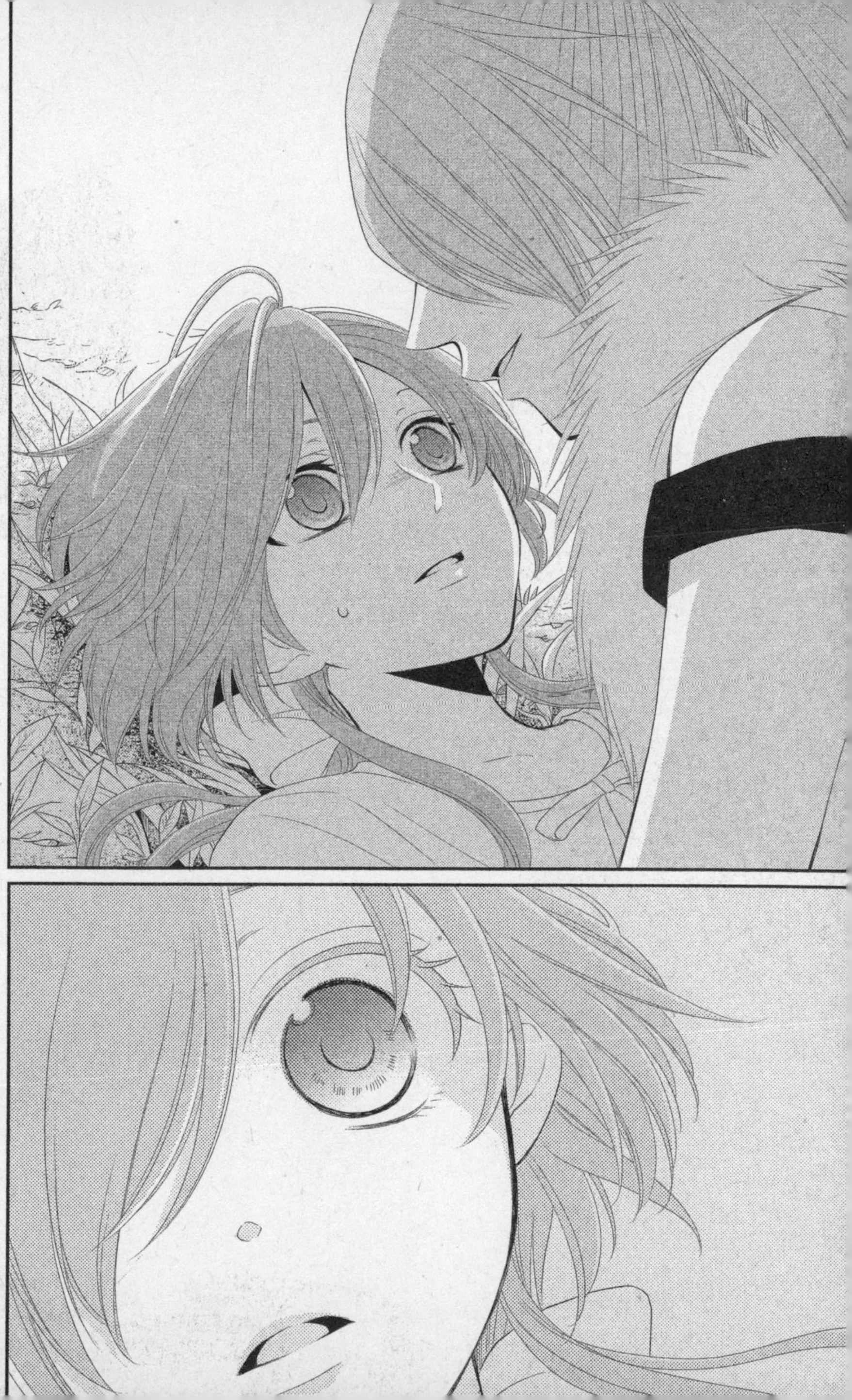

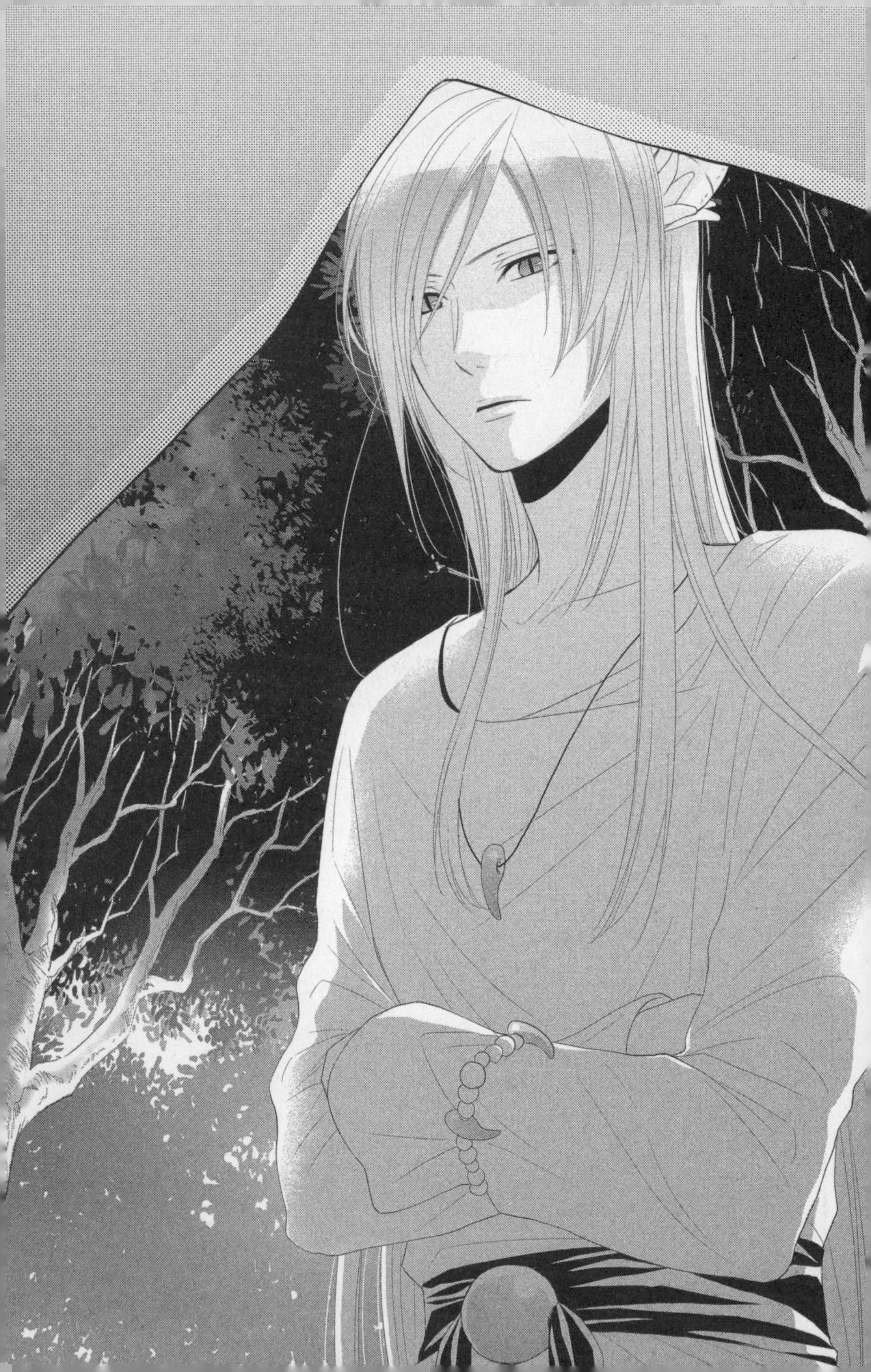

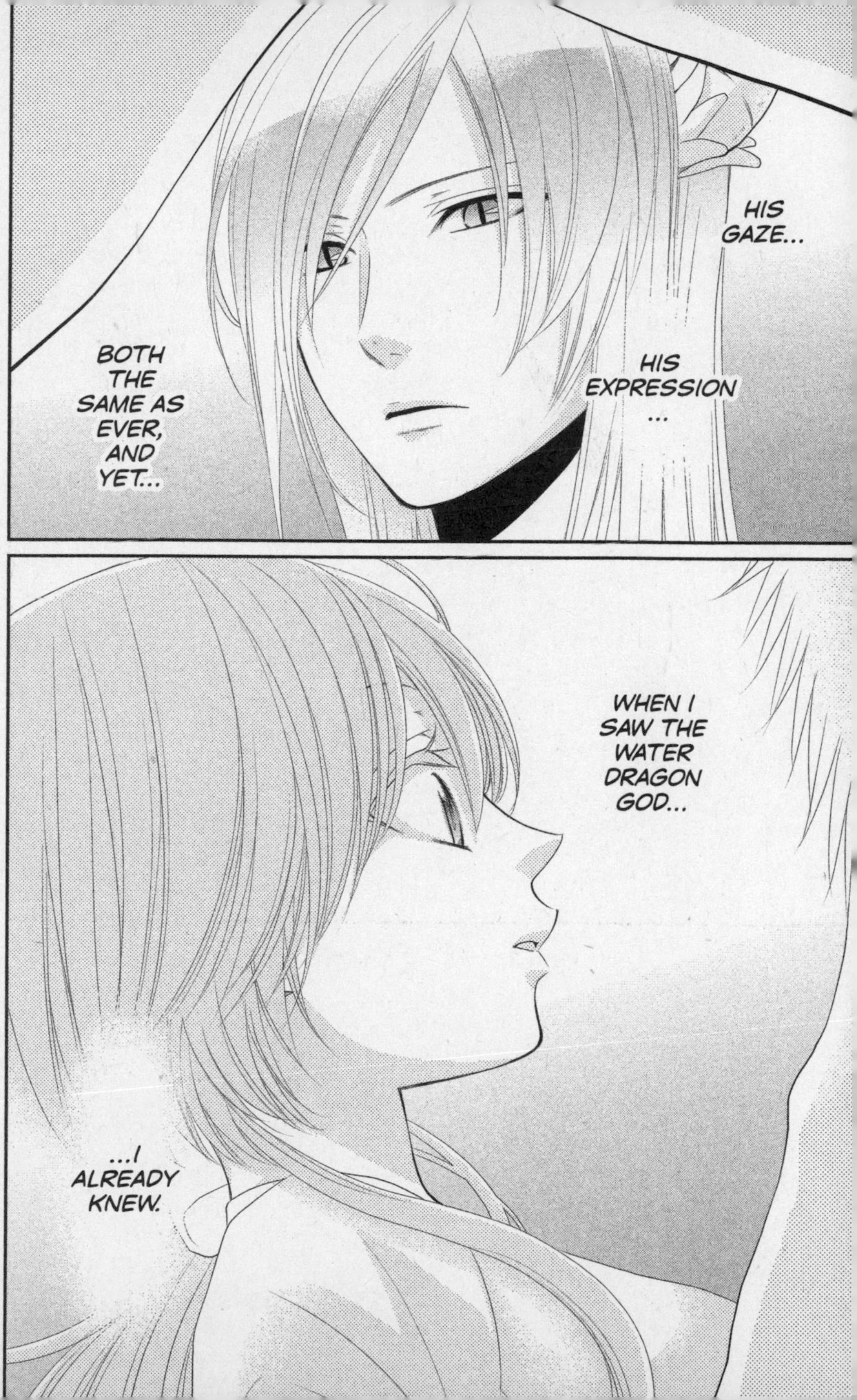
HIS GAZE...
HIS EXPRESSION ...
BOTH THE SAME AS EVER, AND YET...
WHEN I SAW THE WATER DRAGON GOD...
...I ALREADY KNEW.

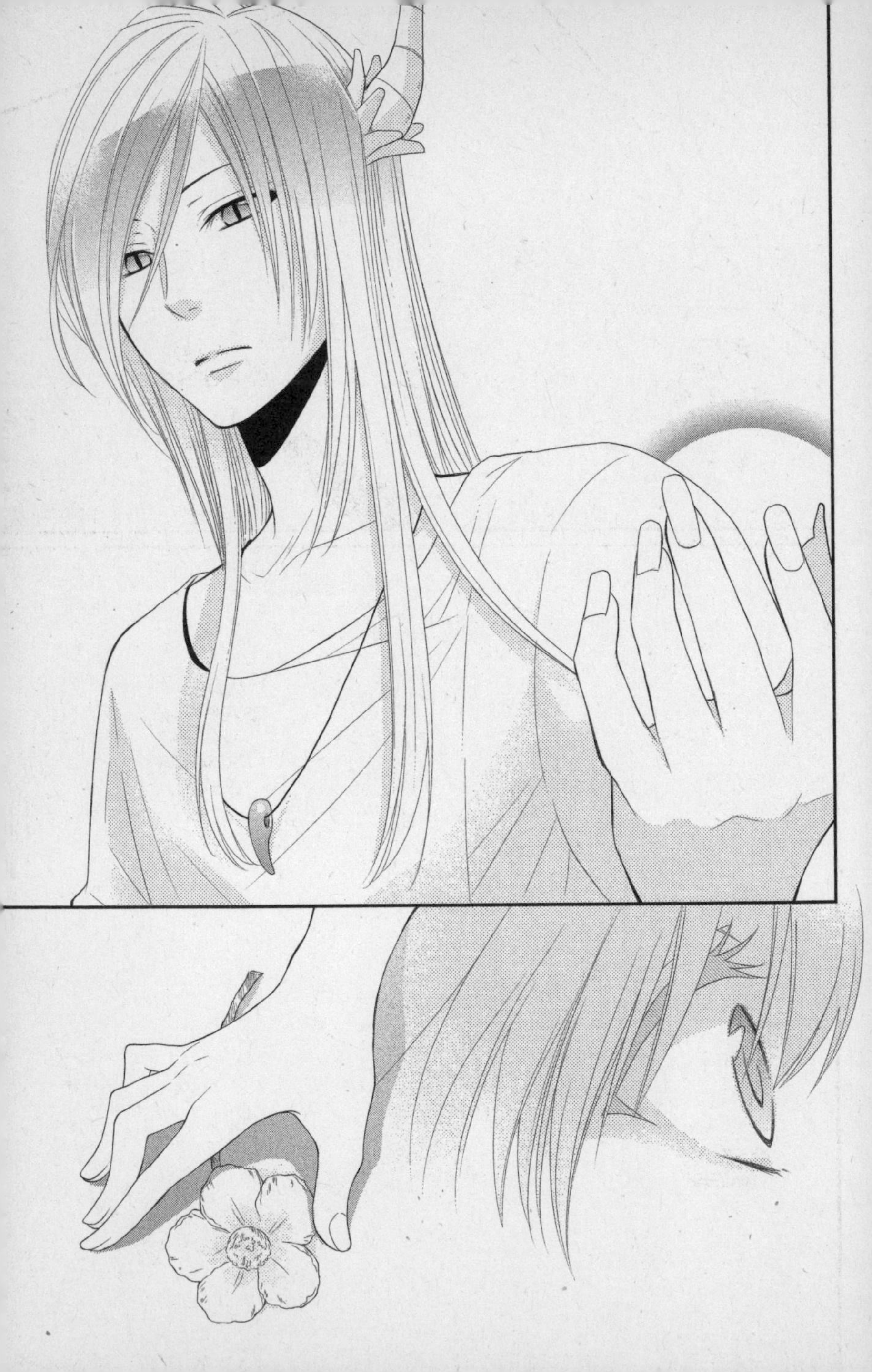

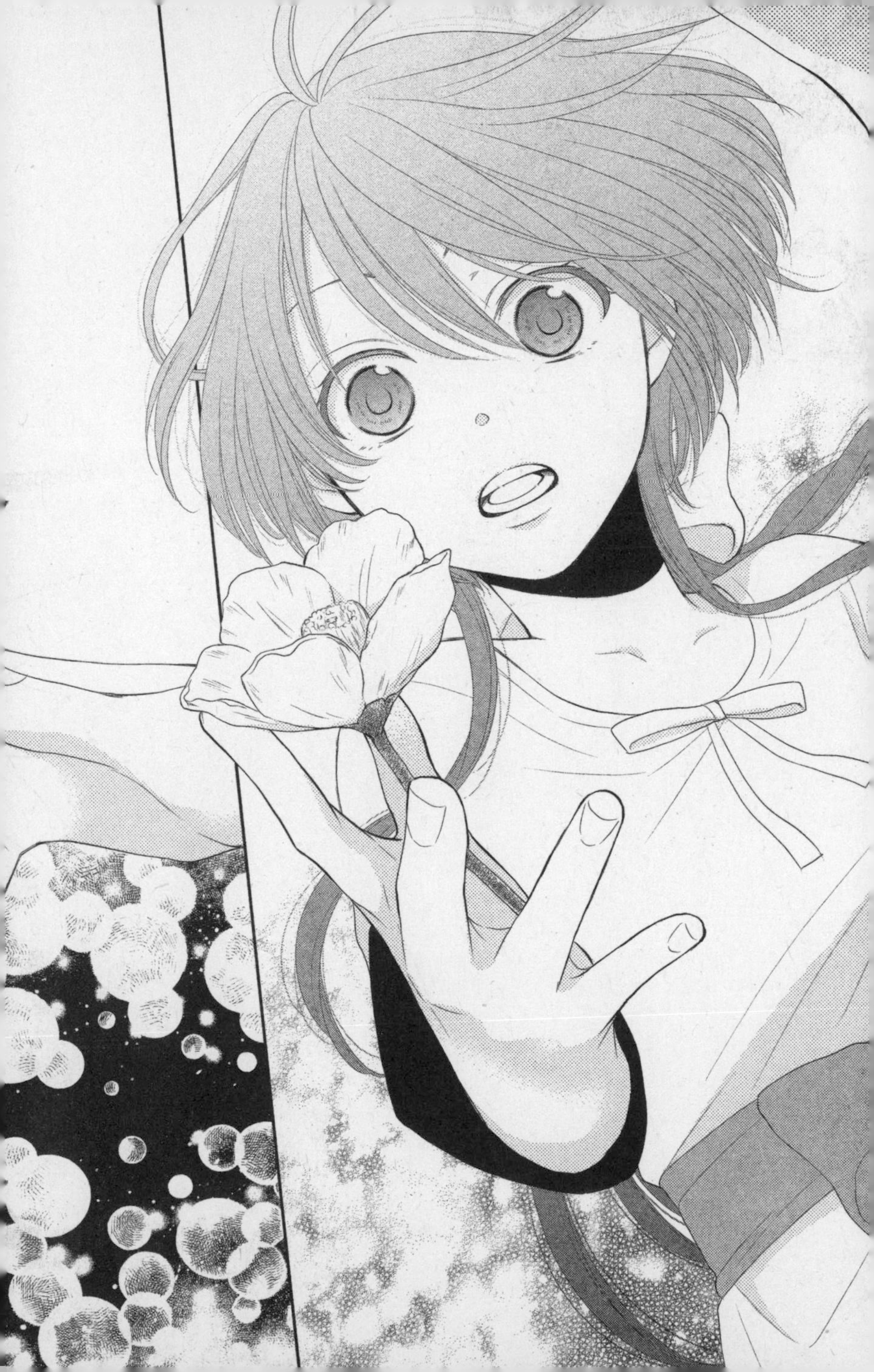

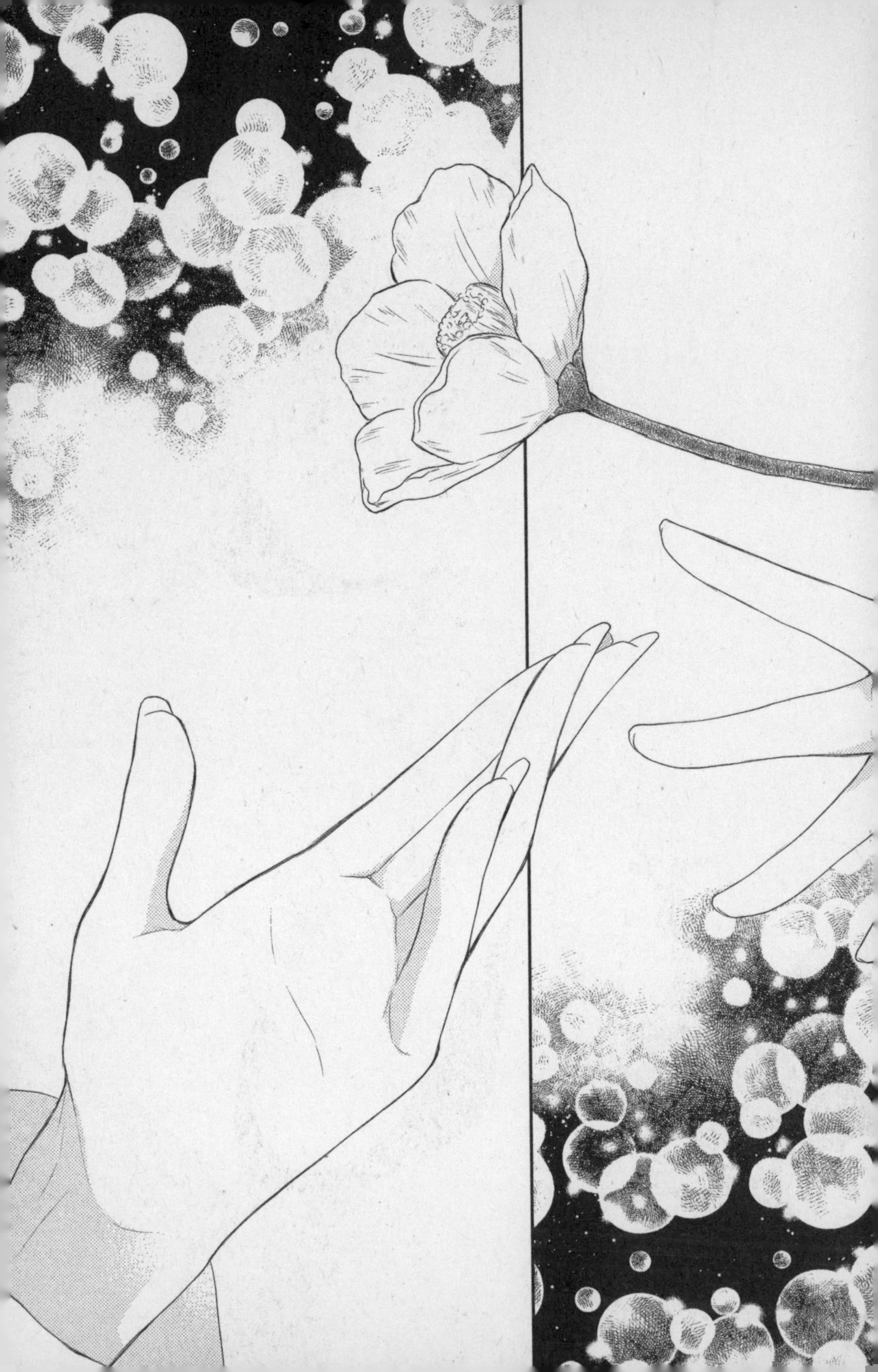

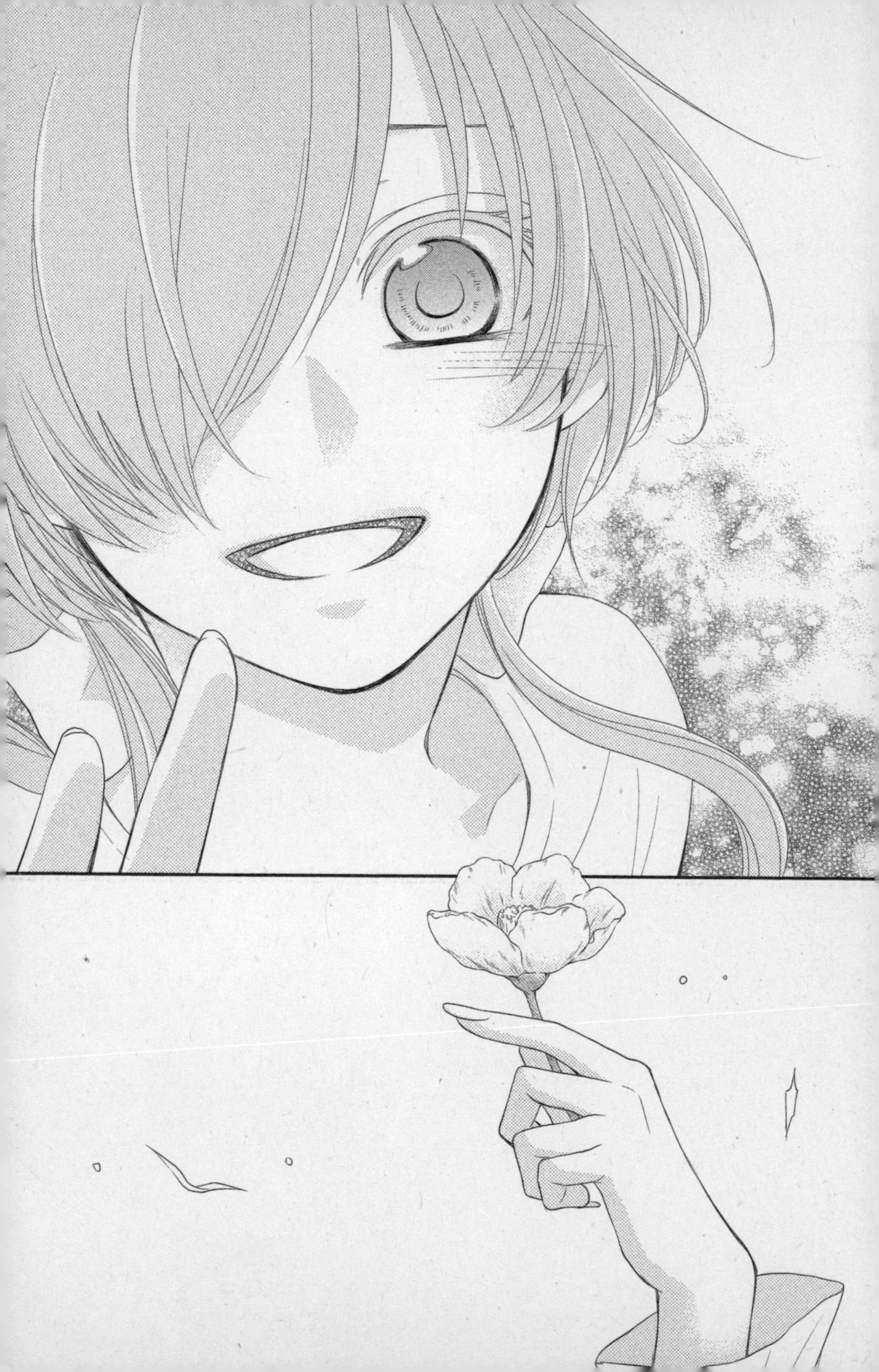

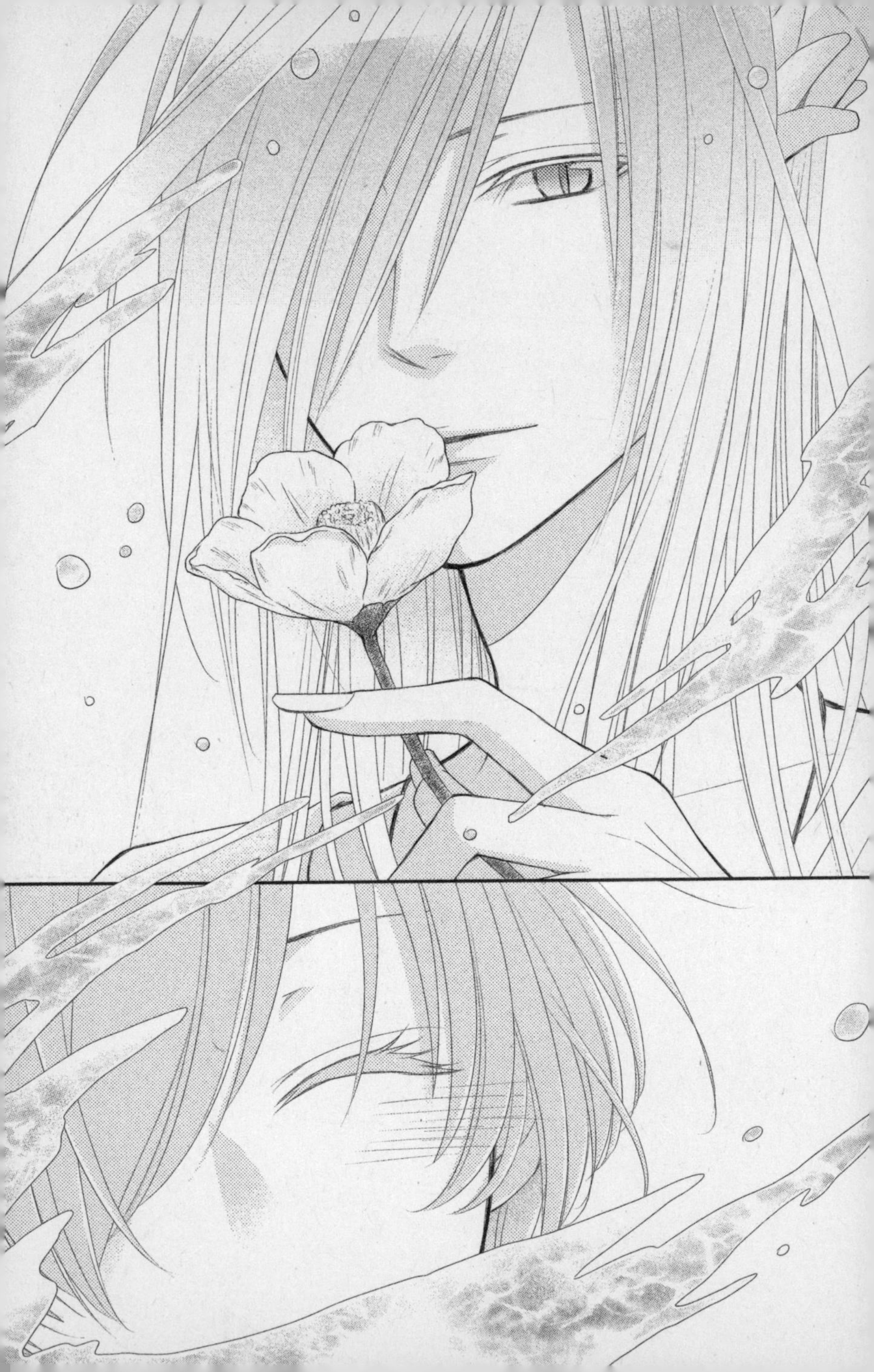

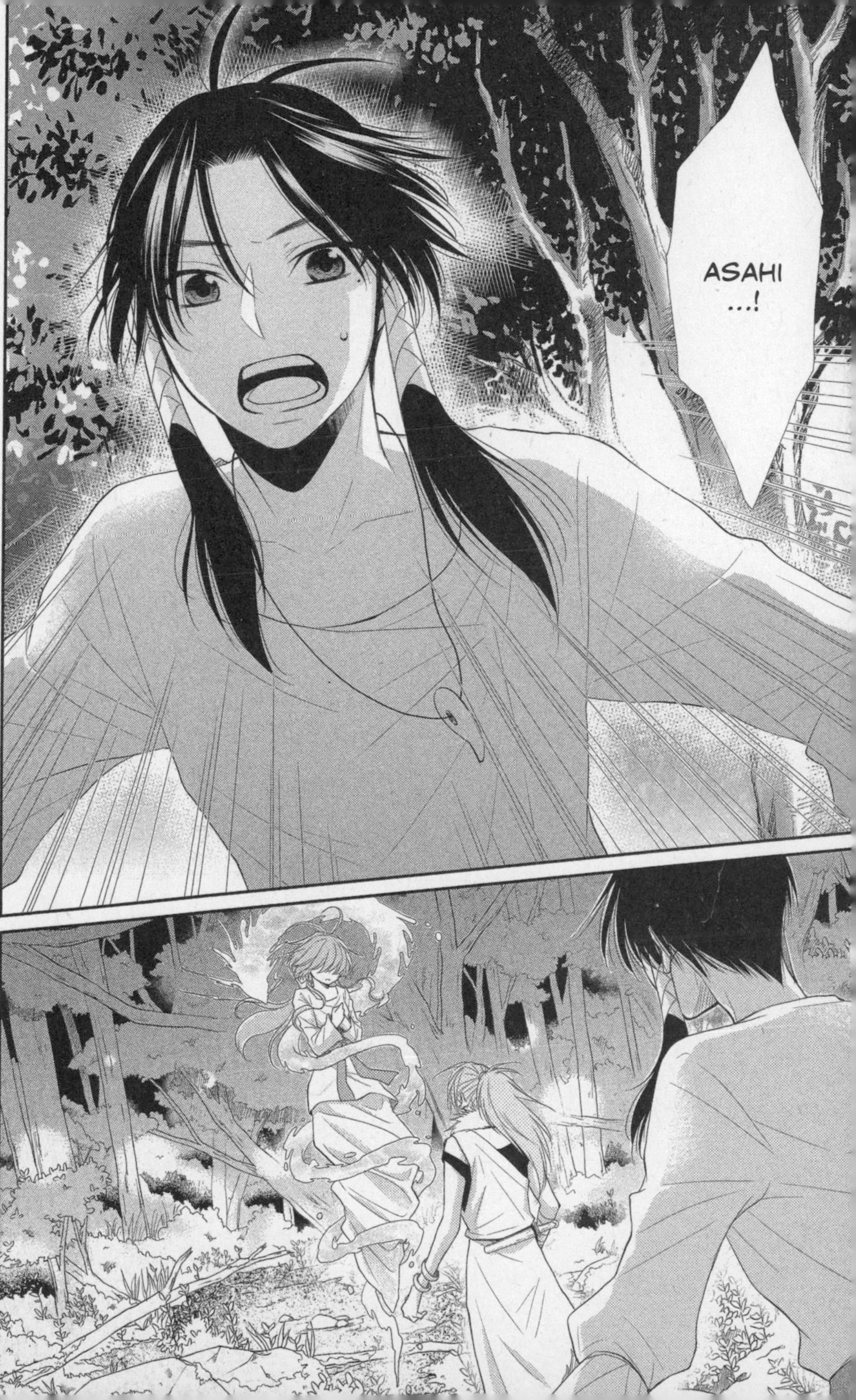
ASAHI ...!

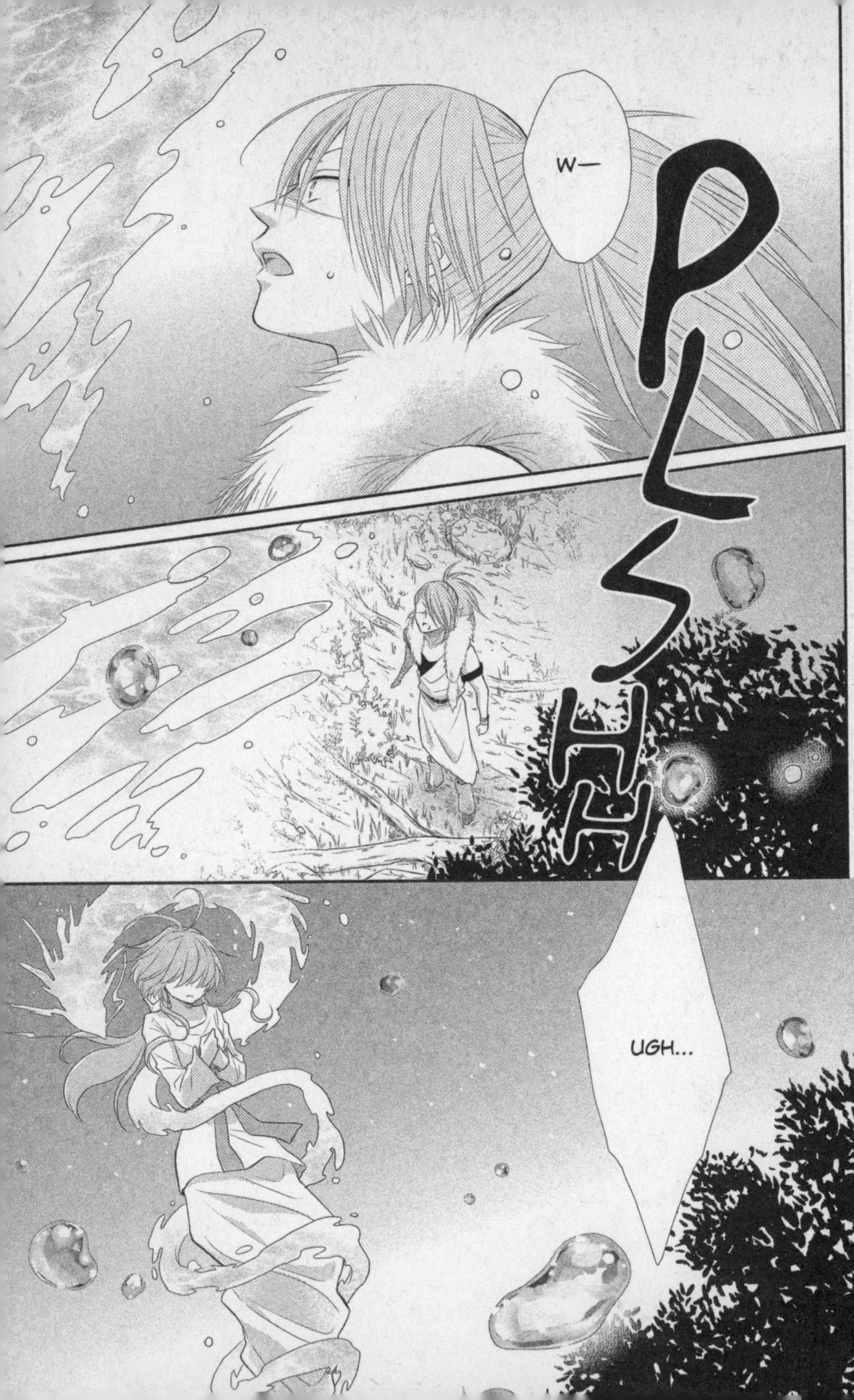
W—
PLSHH
UGH...

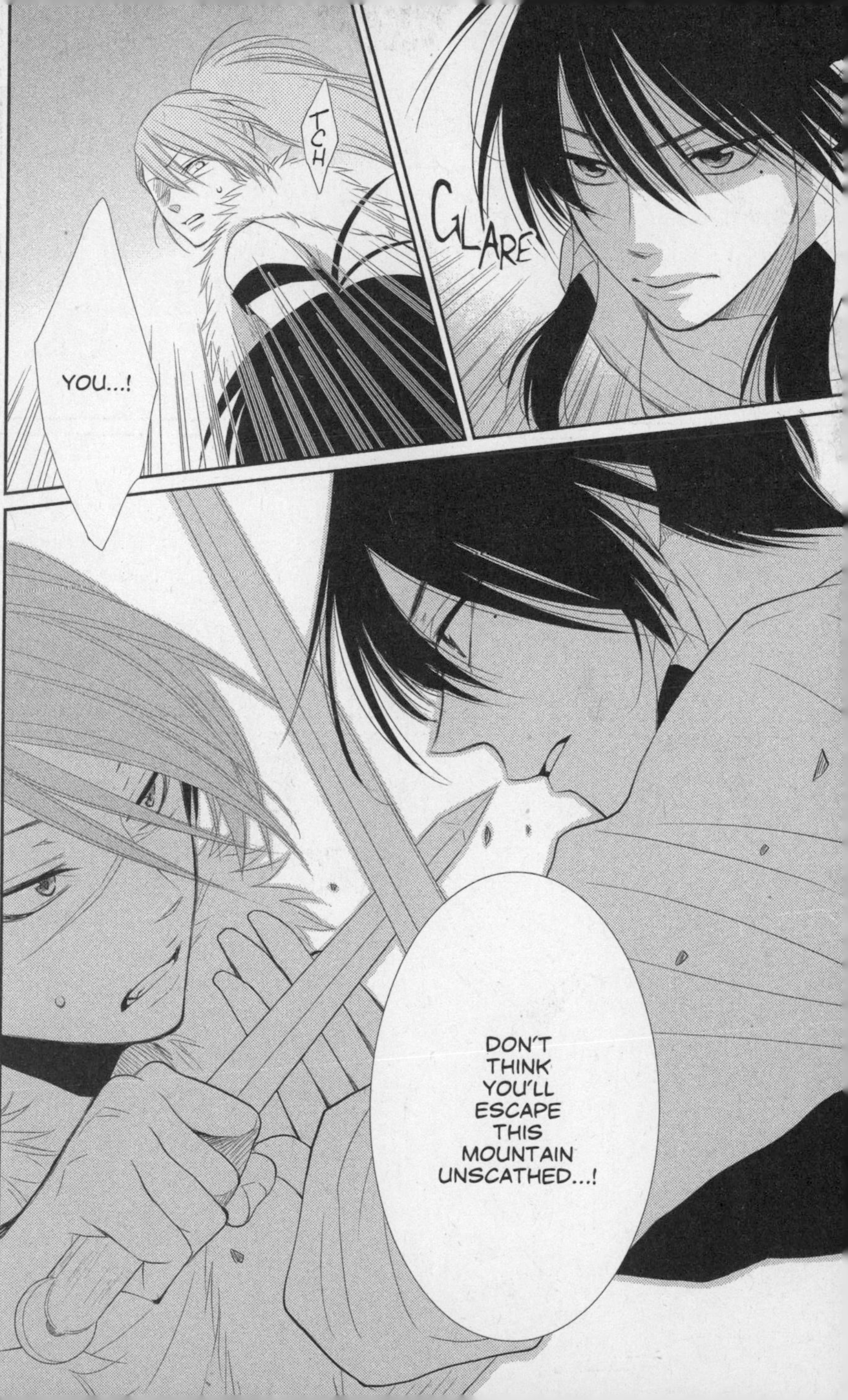
GLARE
TCH
YOU...!
DON'T THINK YOU'LL ESCAPE THIS MOUNTAIN UNSCATHED...!

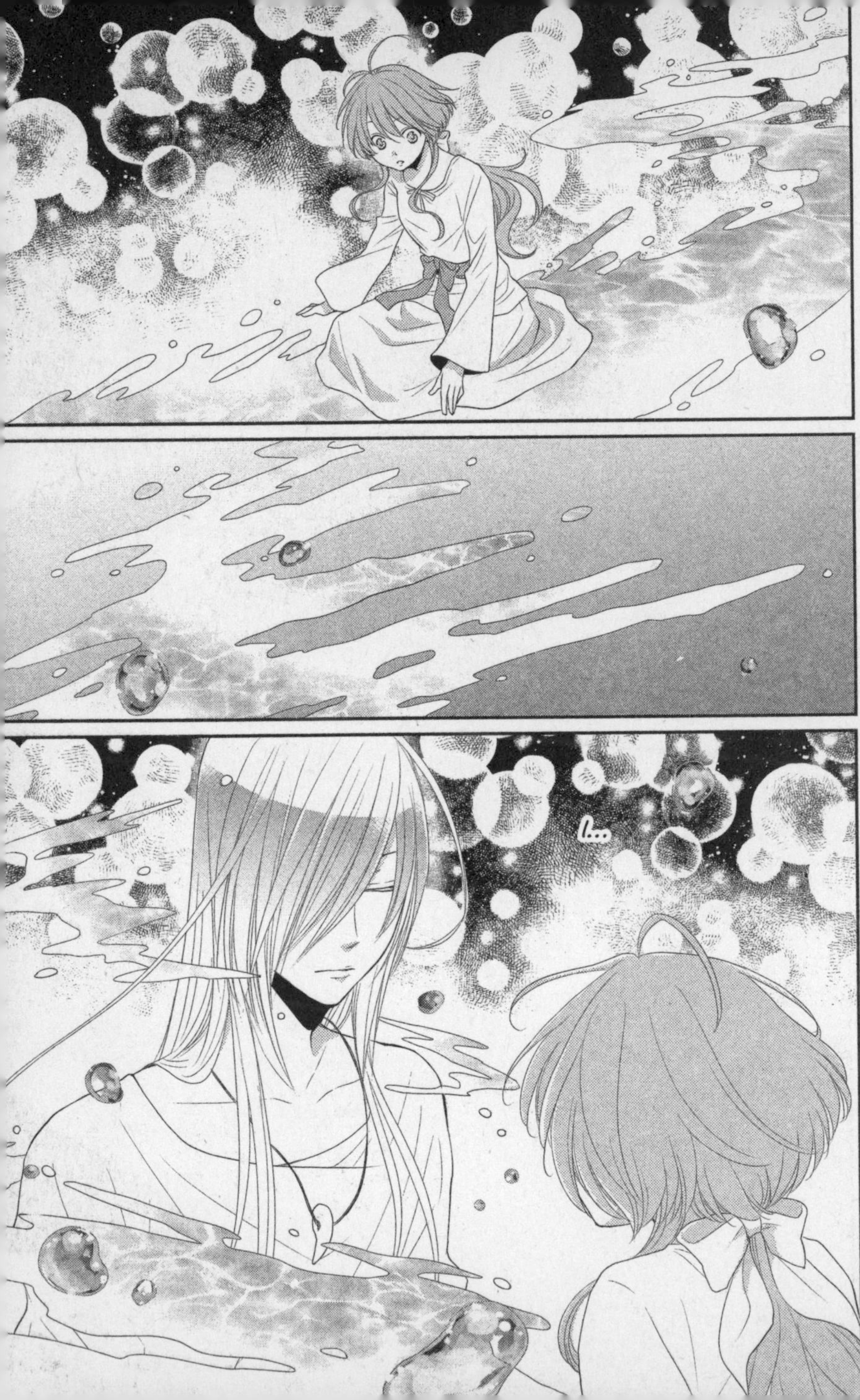
I...

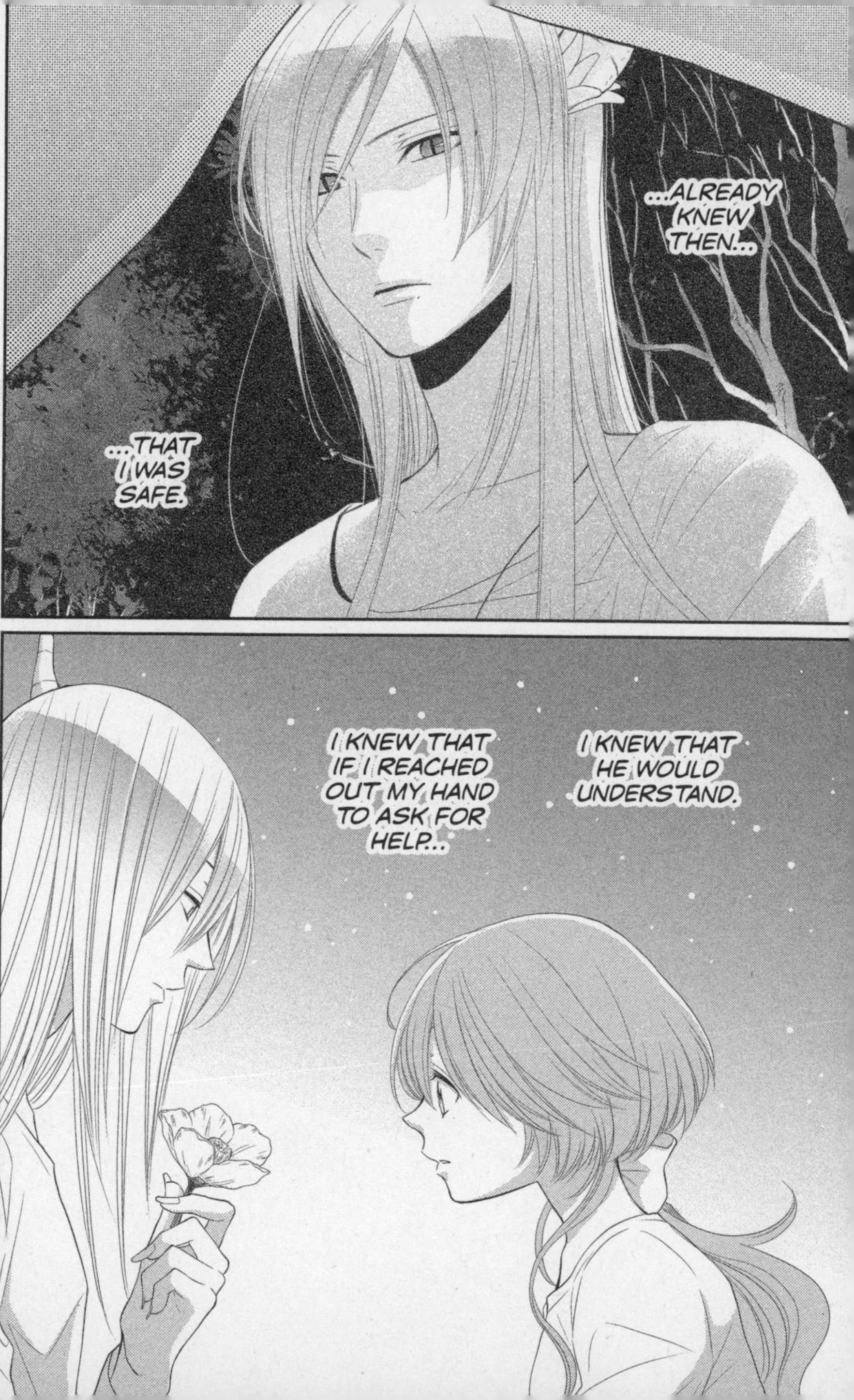
...ALREADY KNEW THEN...
...THAT I WAS SAFE.
I KNEW THAT HE WOULD UNDERSTAND.
I KNEW THAT IF I REACHED OUT MY HAND TO ASK FOR HELP...

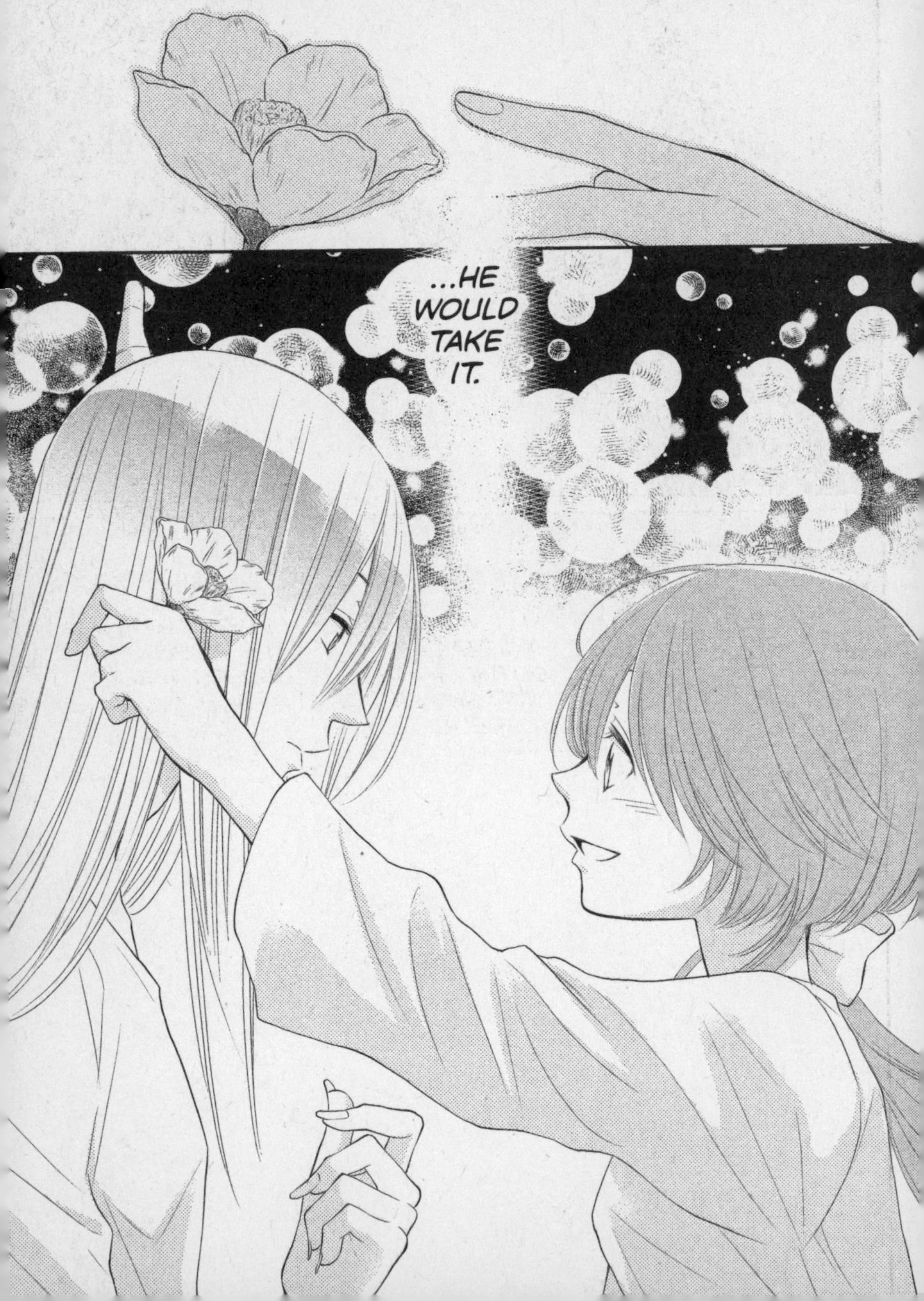
...HE WOULD TAKE IT.

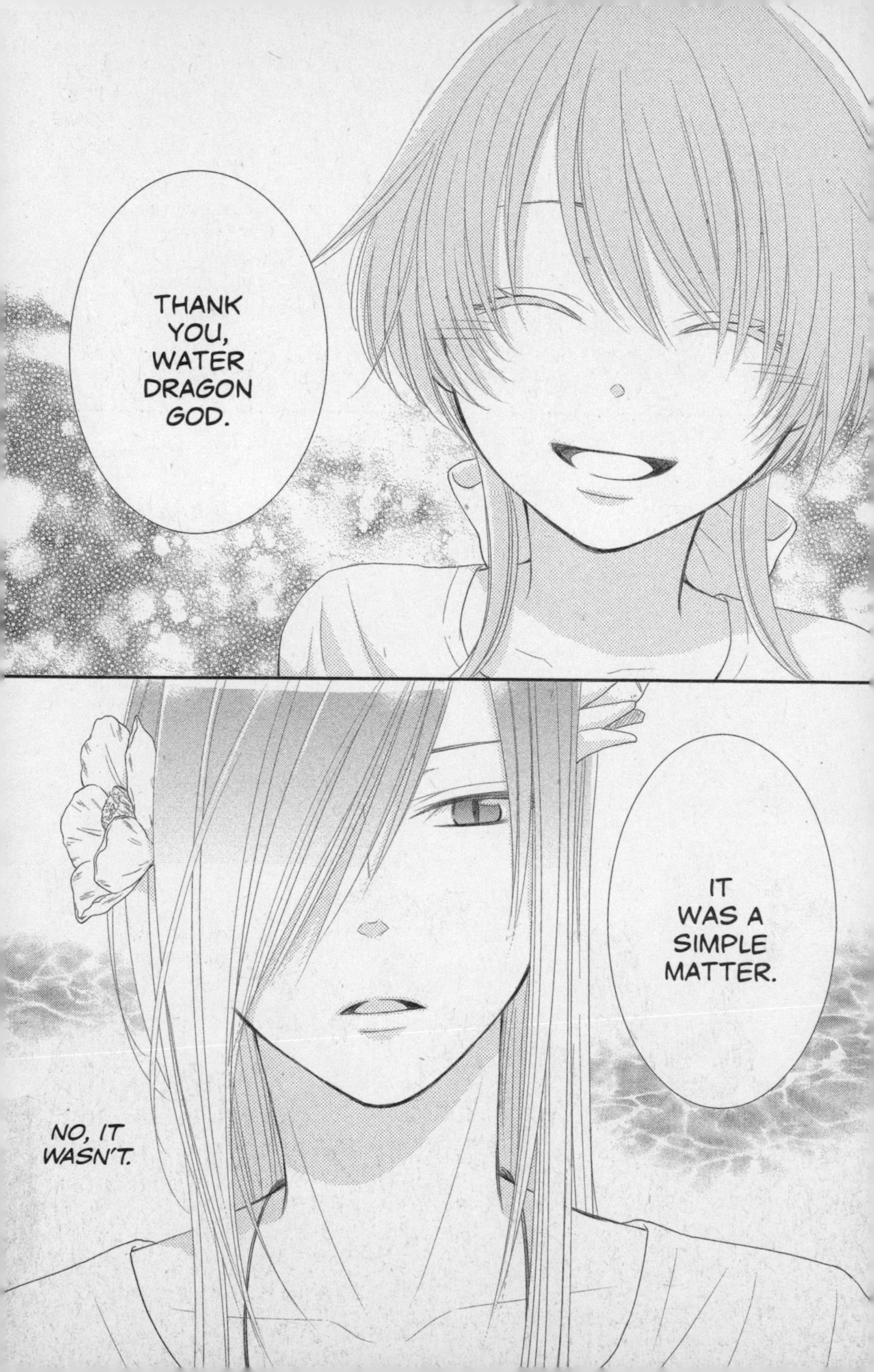
THANK YOU, WATER DRAGON GOD.
IT WAS A SIMPLE MATTER.
NO, IT WASN'T.

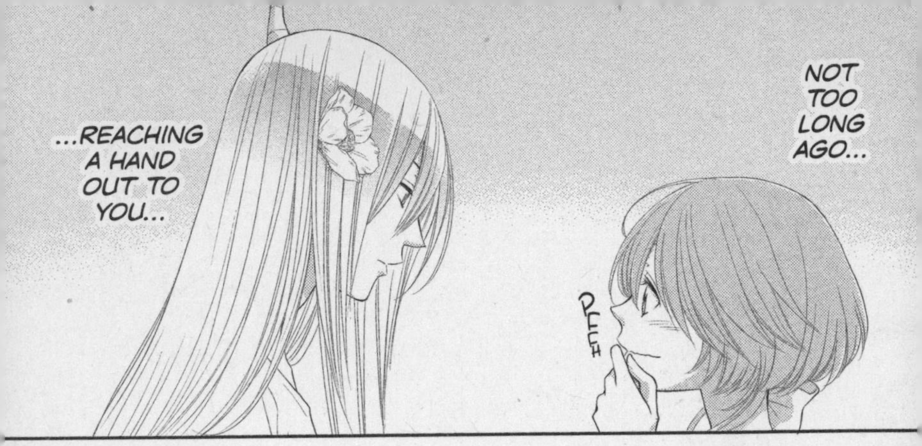
NOT TOO LONG AGO...
...REACHING A HAND OUT TO YOU...
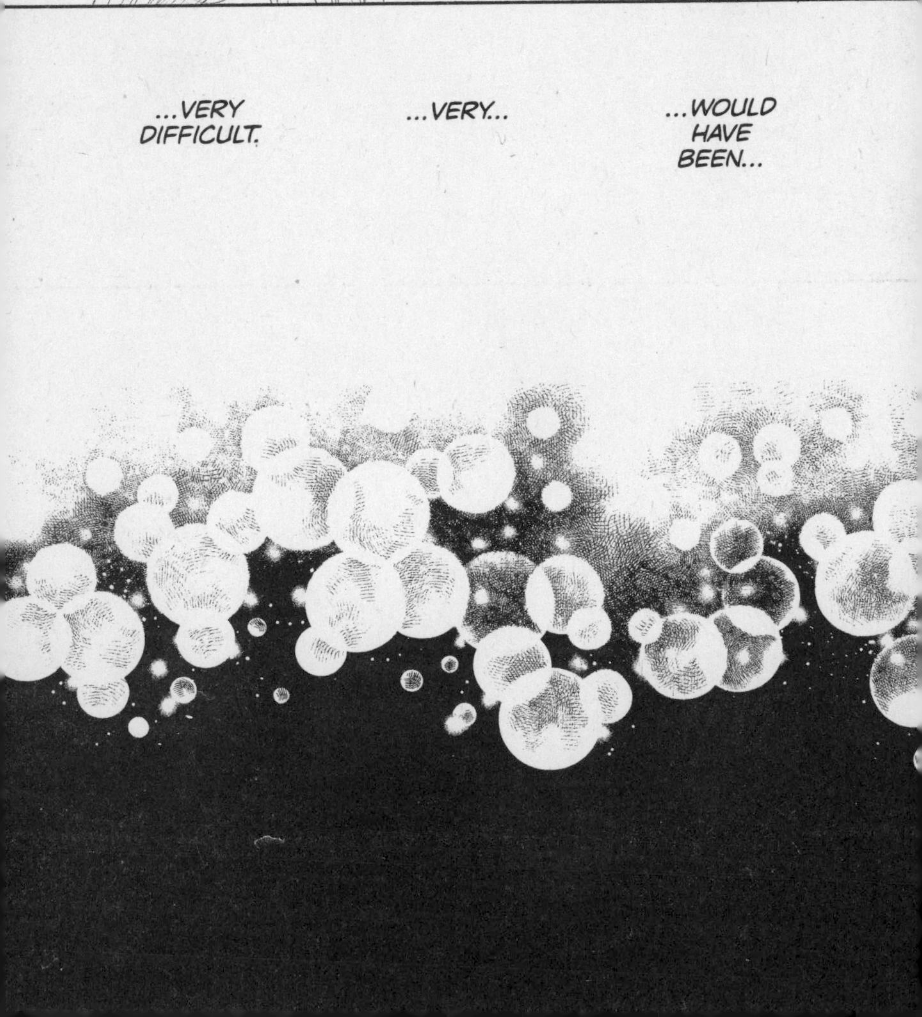
...WOULD HAVE BEEN...
...VERY...
...VERY DIFFICULT.

I racked my brain to figure out how I'd color Tsukihiko if I ever got the chance. "Tsuki means 'moon,' so some yellow? But something dark for his hair, so brown. Hmm... It doesn't seem like it would suit him... Hmmm..." For a while I just left it at that, but then the opportunity to draw him in color came up. At first, I tried his hair in brown, but it really did look weird, so in the end I went with purple because it expressed the mood I wanted. Digital art really is great when it comes to tweaking colors later on.

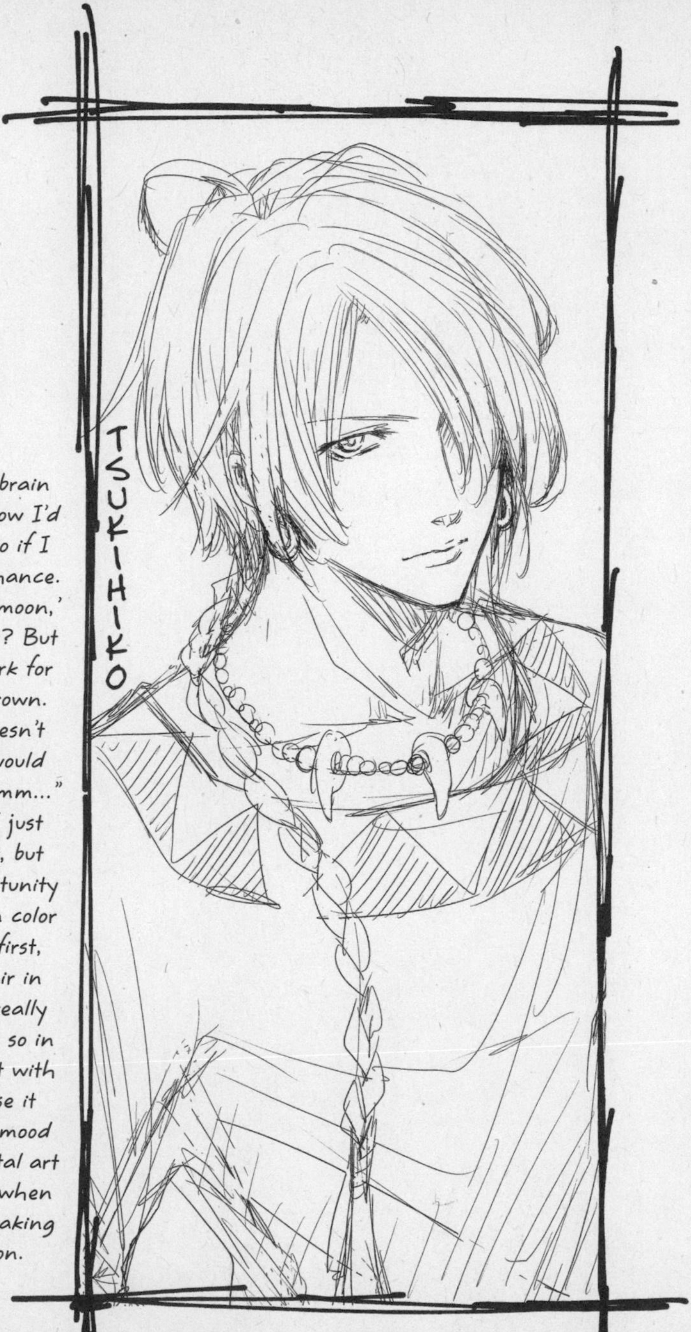
TSUKIHIKO

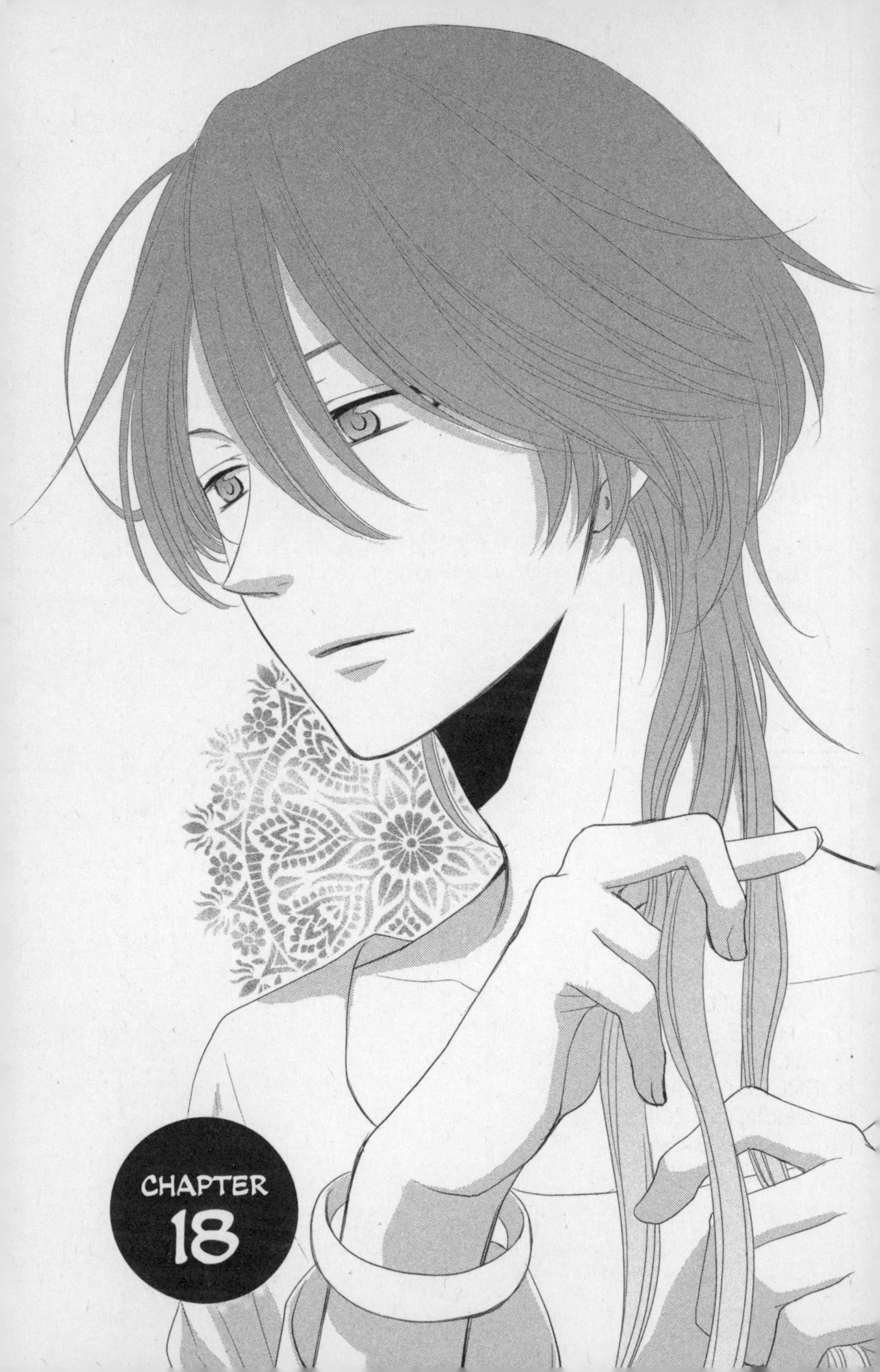
CHAPTER
18

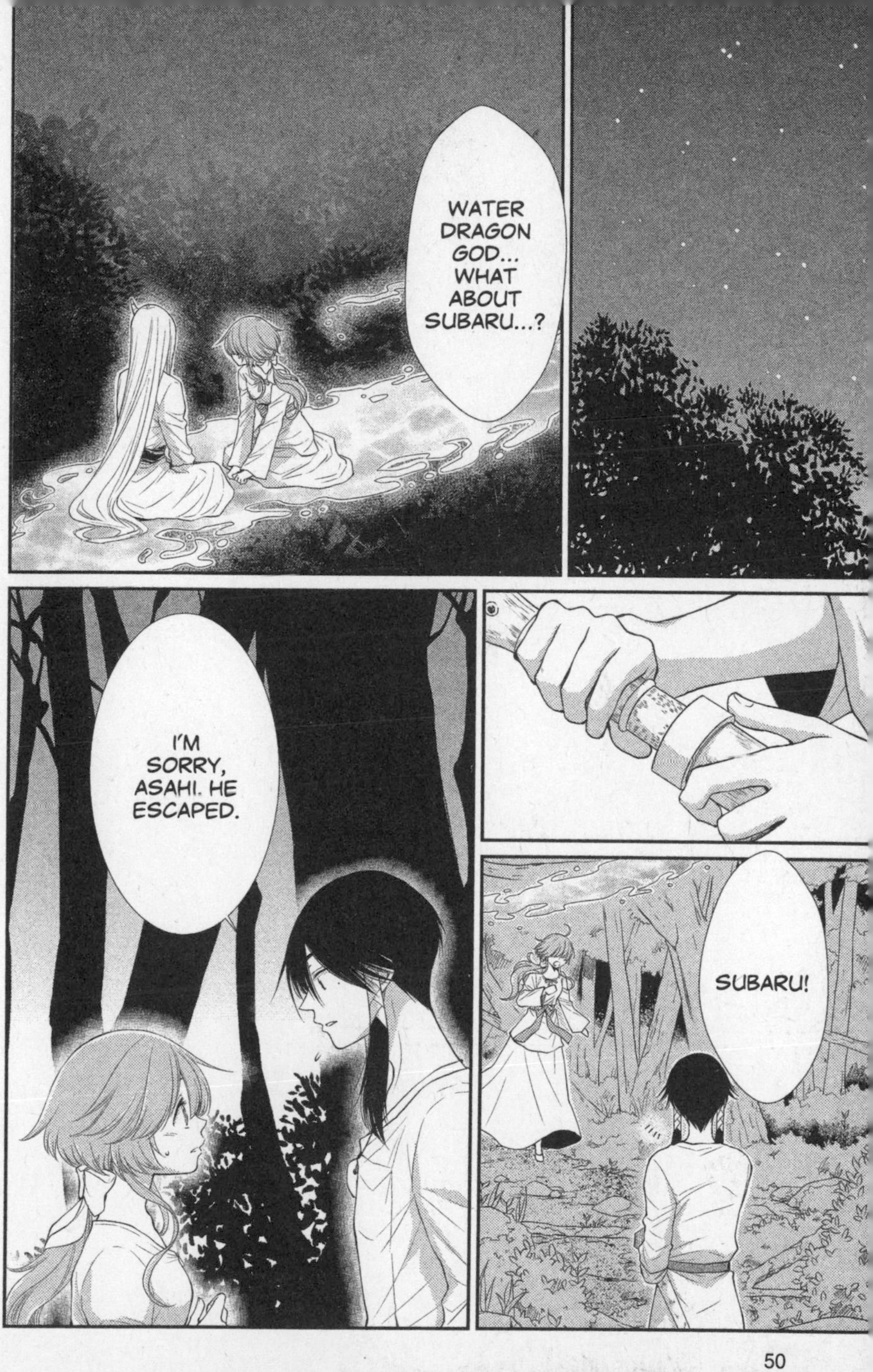
WATER DRAGON GOD... WHAT ABOUT SUBARU...?
SUBARU!
I'M SORRY, ASAHI. HE ESCAPED.

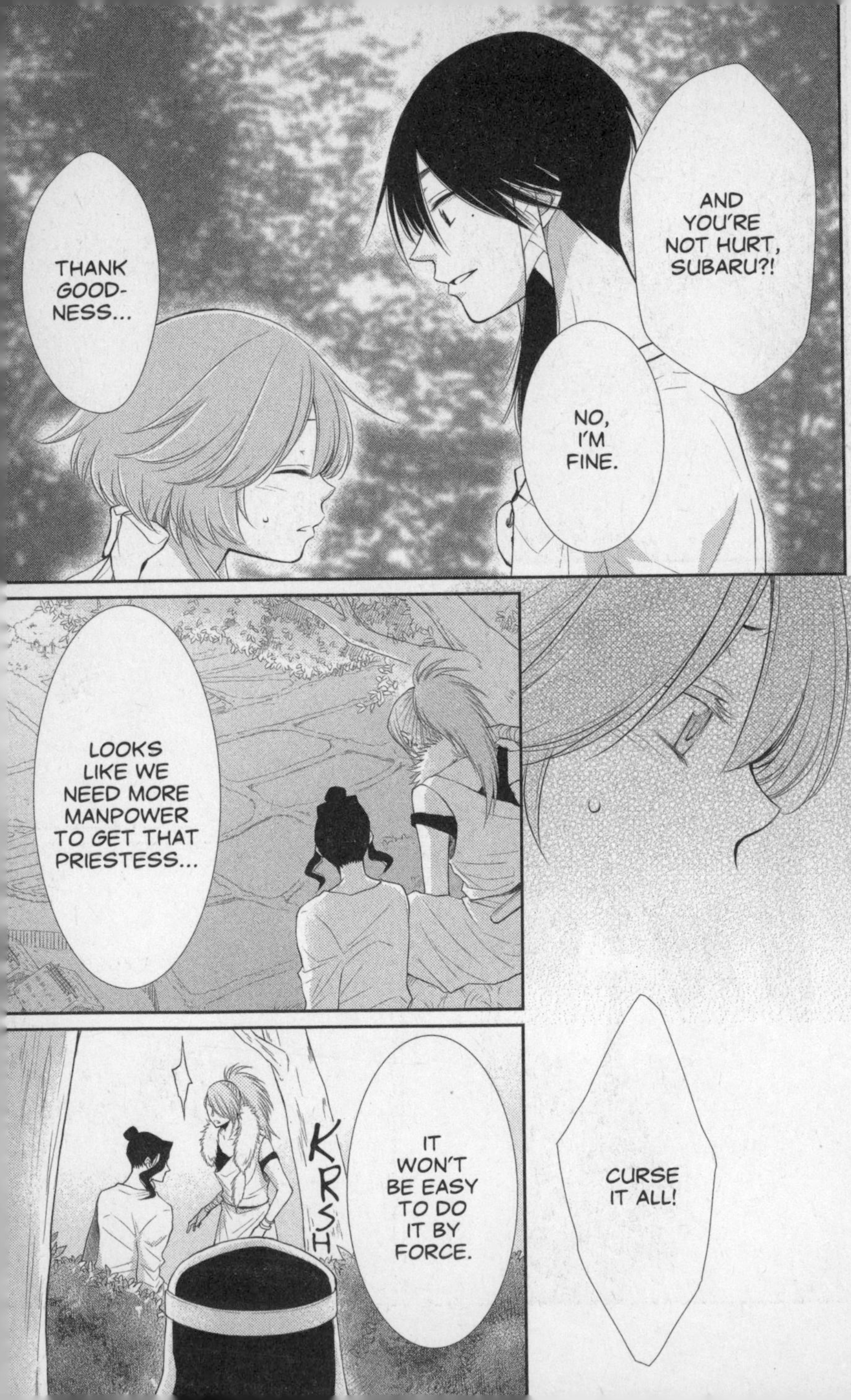
AND YOU'RE NOT HURT, SUBARU?!
NO, I'M FINE.
THANK GOODNESS...
CURSE IT ALL!
LOOKS LIKE WE NEED MORE MANPOWER TO GET THAT PRIESTESS...
KRSH
IT WON'T BE EASY TO DO IT BY FORCE.

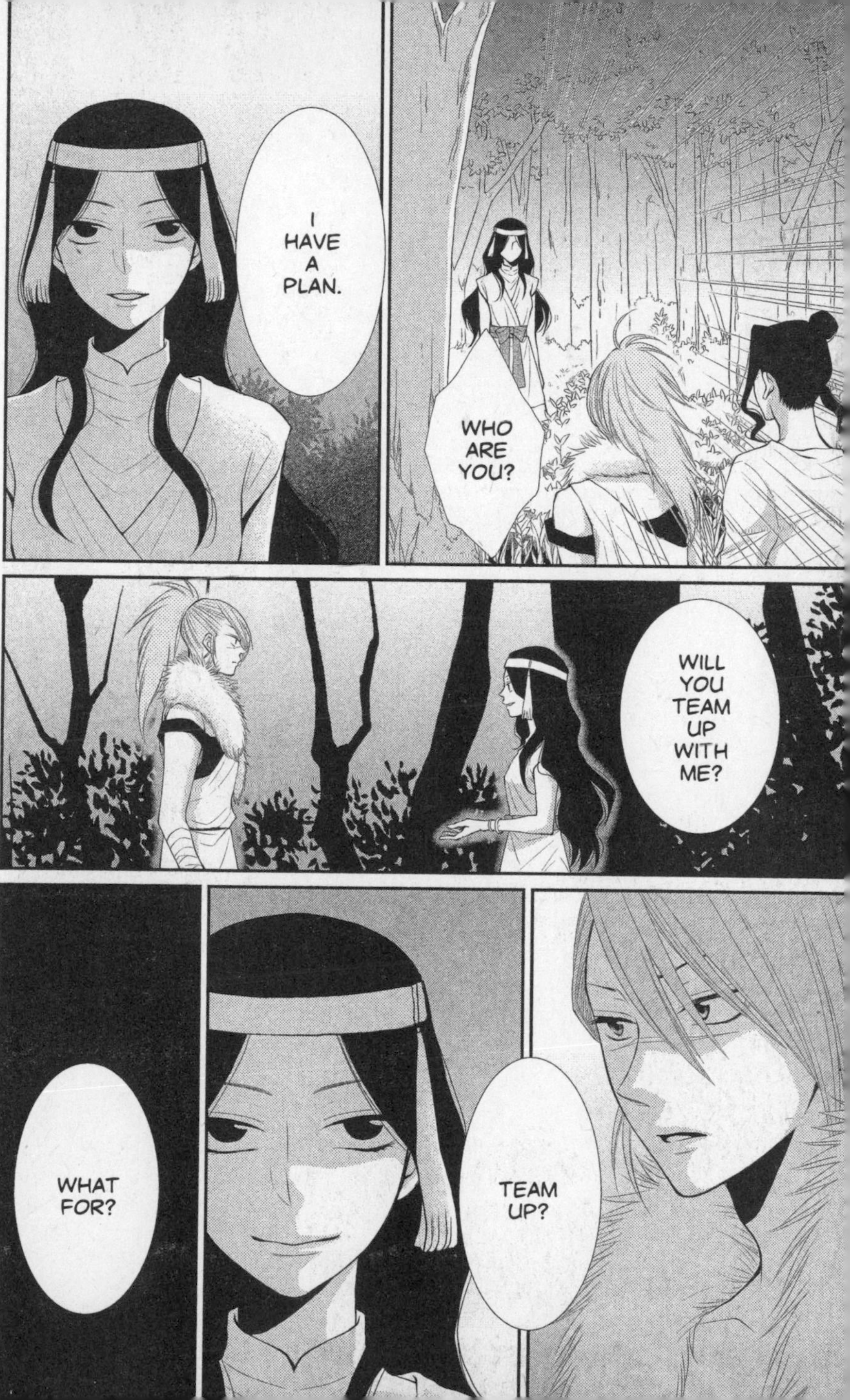
WHO ARE YOU?
I HAVE A PLAN.
WILL YOU TEAM UP WITH ME?
TEAM UP?
WHAT FOR?

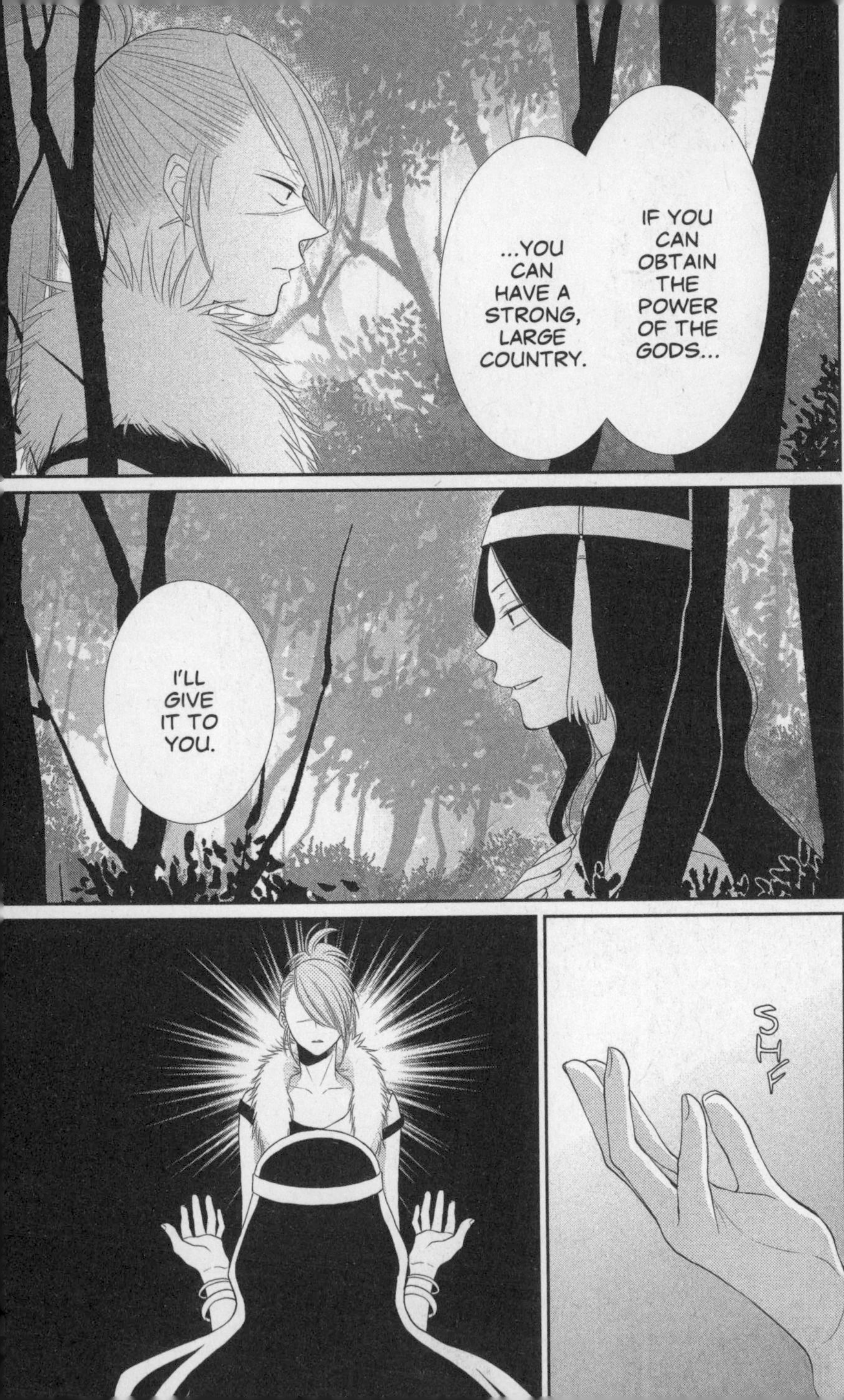
IF YOU CAN OBTAIN THE POWER OF THE GODS...
...YOU CAN HAVE A STRONG, LARGE COUNTRY.
I'LL GIVE IT TO YOU.
SHH

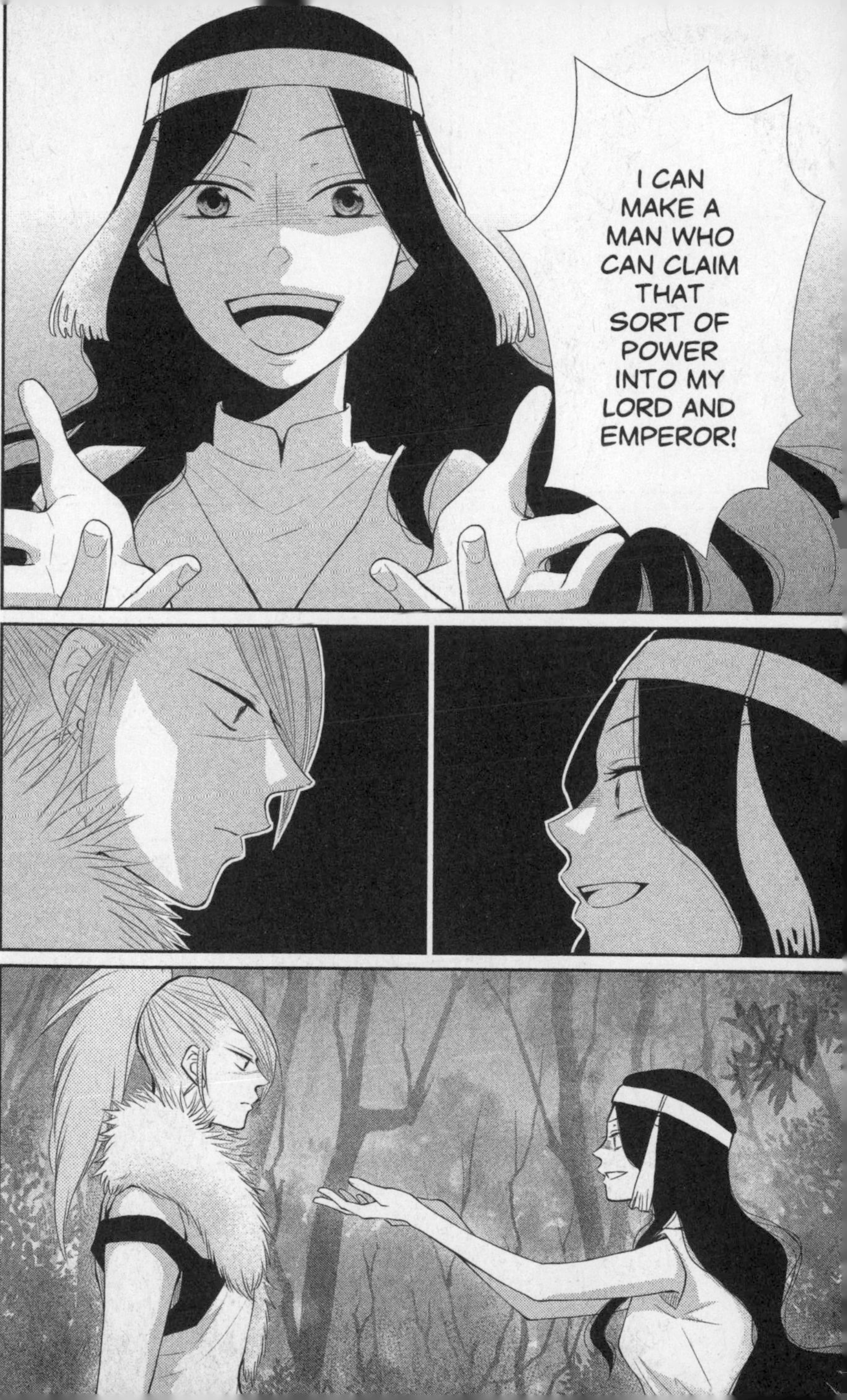
I CAN MAKE A MAN WHO CAN CLAIM THAT SORT OF POWER INTO MY LORD AND EMPEROR!

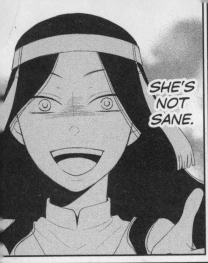

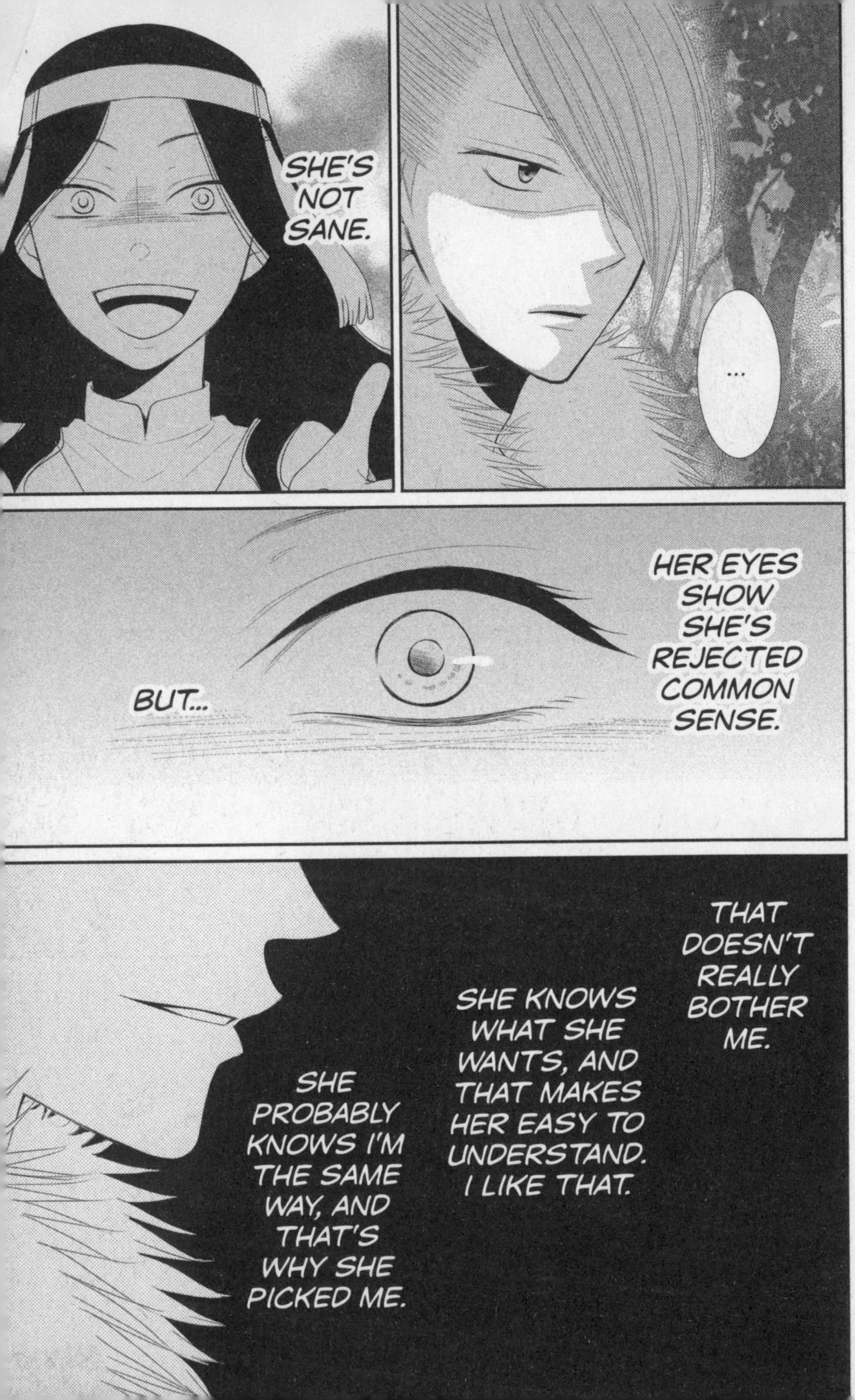

SHE'S NOT SANE.

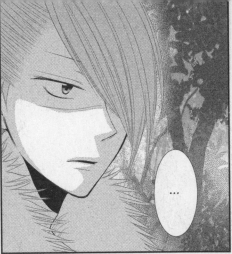

...

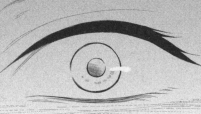

BUT...

HER EYES SHOW SHE'S REJECTED COMMON SENSE.

THAT DOESN'T REALLY BOTHER ME.

SHE KNOWS WHAT SHE WANTS, AND THAT MAKES HER EASY TO UNDERSTAND. I LIKE THAT.

SHE PROBABLY KNOWS I'M THE SAME WAY, AND THAT'S WHY SHE PICKED ME.

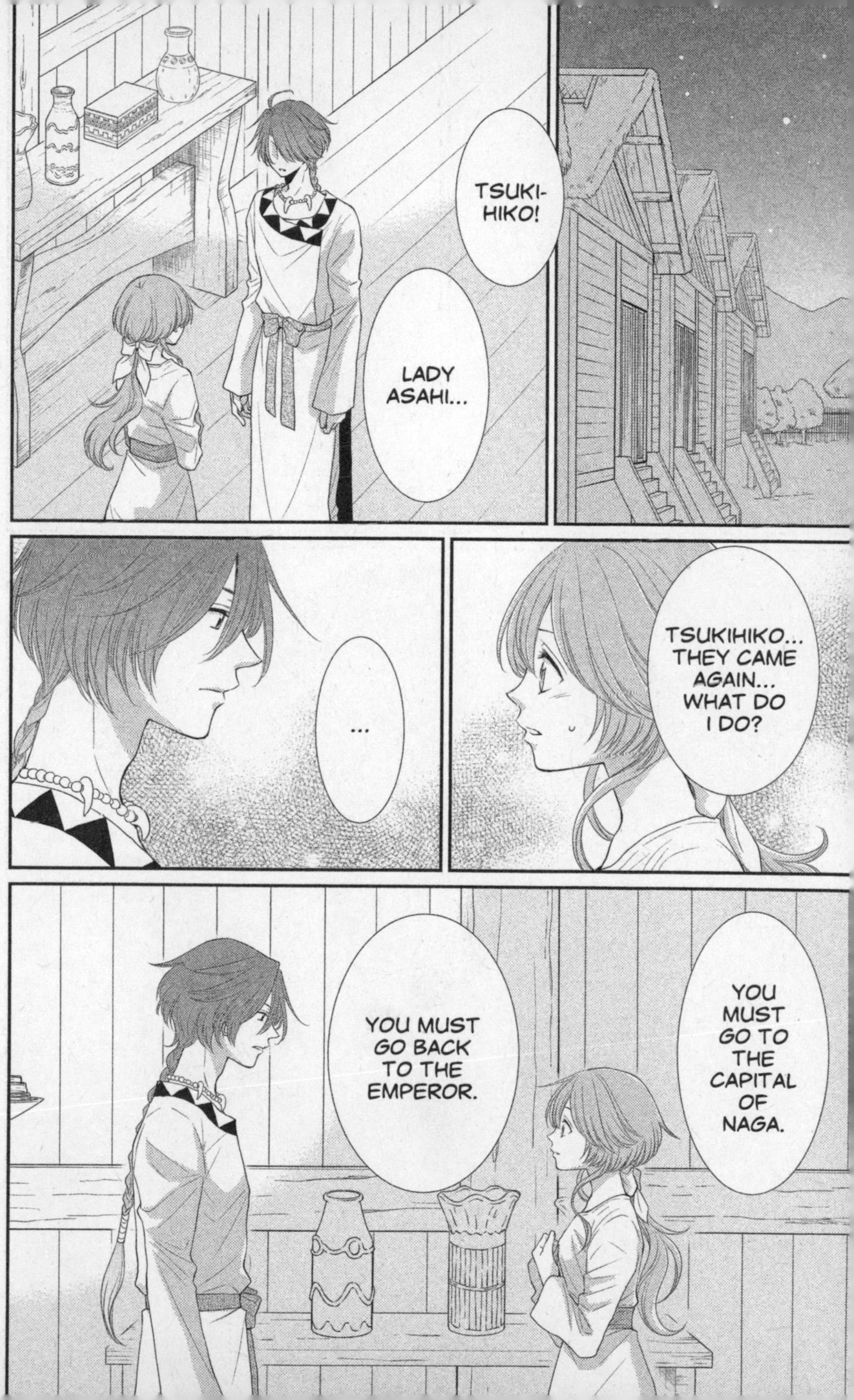
TSUKI-HIKO!
LADY ASAHI...
TSUKIHIKO... THEY CAME AGAIN... WHAT DO I DO?
...
YOU MUST GO TO THE CAPITAL OF NAGA.
YOU MUST GO BACK TO THE EMPEROR.

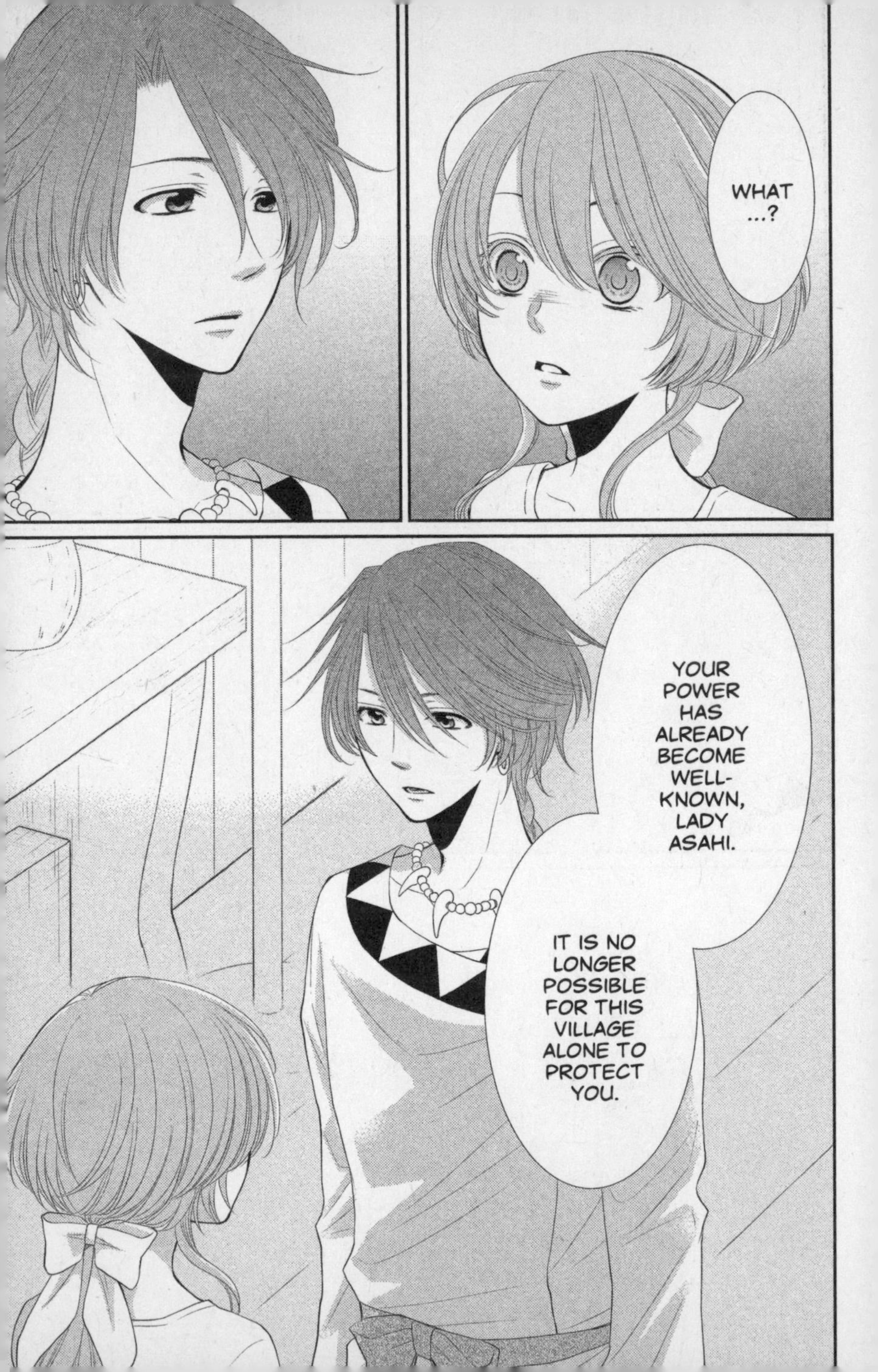
WHAT ...?
YOUR POWER HAS ALREADY BECOME WELL-KNOWN, LADY ASAHI.
IT IS NO LONGER POSSIBLE FOR THIS VILLAGE ALONE TO PROTECT YOU.

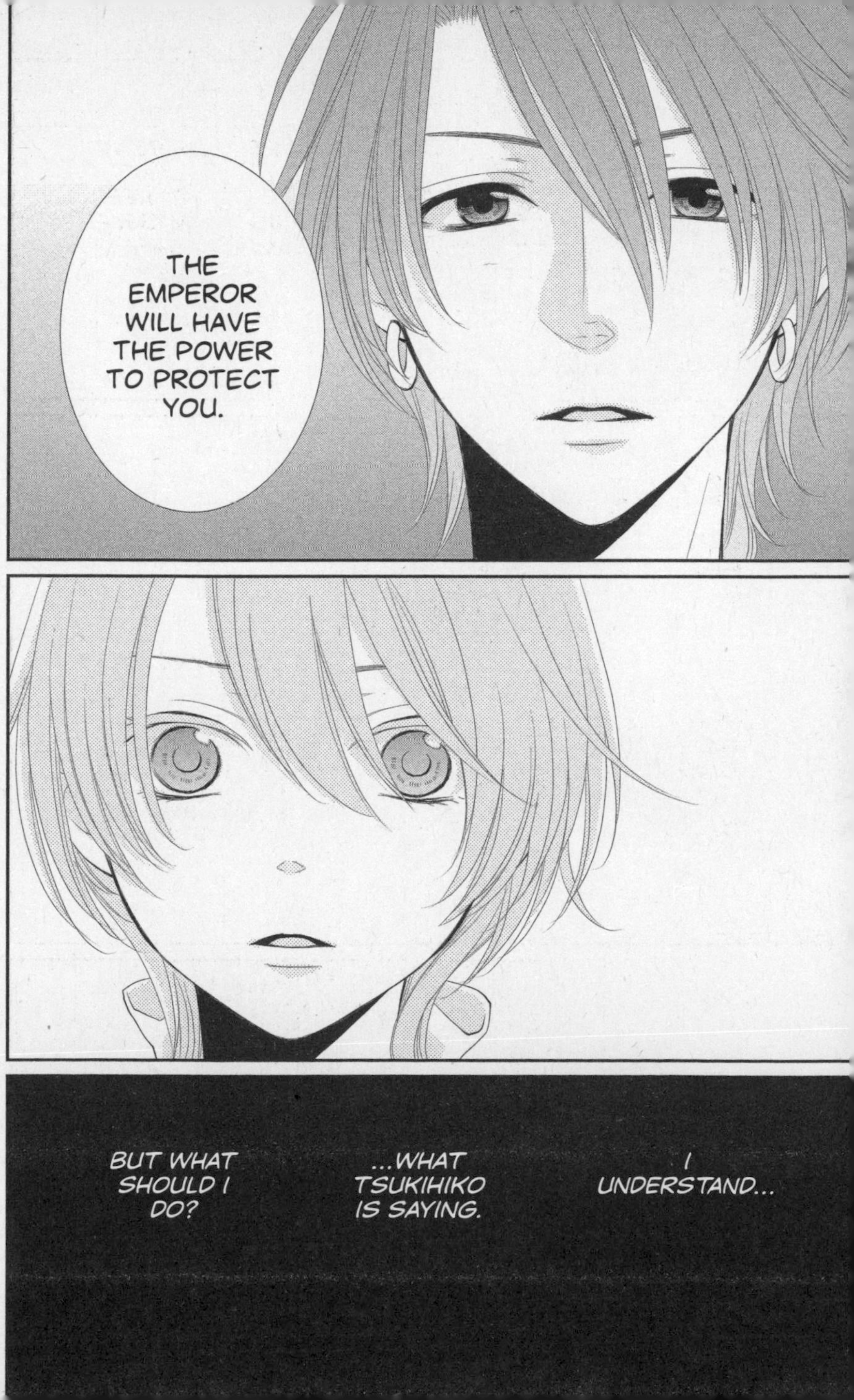
THE EMPEROR WILL HAVE THE POWER TO PROTECT YOU.
I UNDERSTAND...
...WHAT TSUKIHIKO IS SAYING.
BUT WHAT SHOULD I DO?

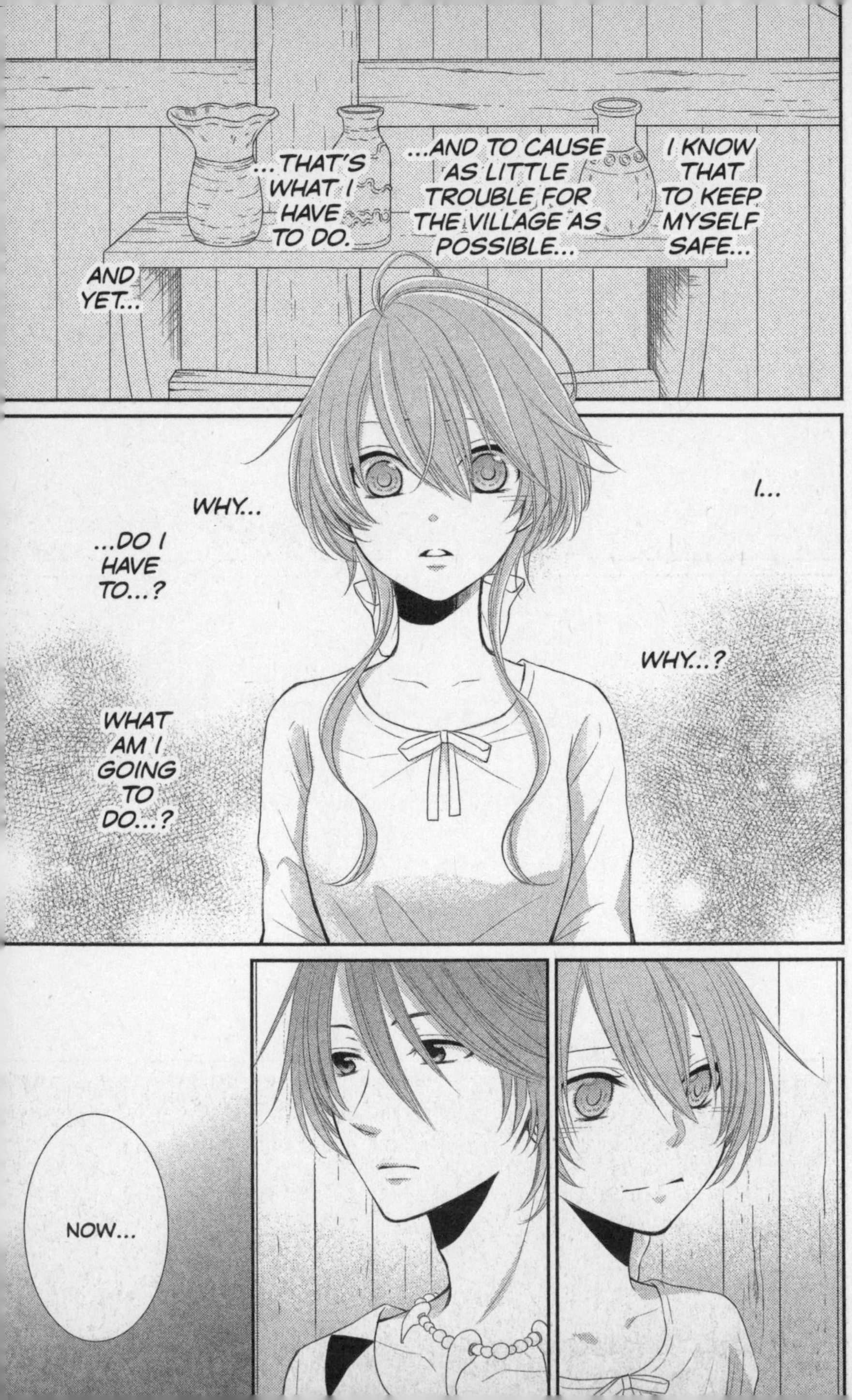
I KNOW THAT TO KEEP MYSELF SAFE...
...AND TO CAUSE AS LITTLE TROUBLE FOR THE VILLAGE AS POSSIBLE...
...THAT'S WHAT I HAVE TO DO.
AND YET...
I...
WHY...
...DO I HAVE TO...?
WHY...?
WHAT AM I GOING TO DO...?
NOW...

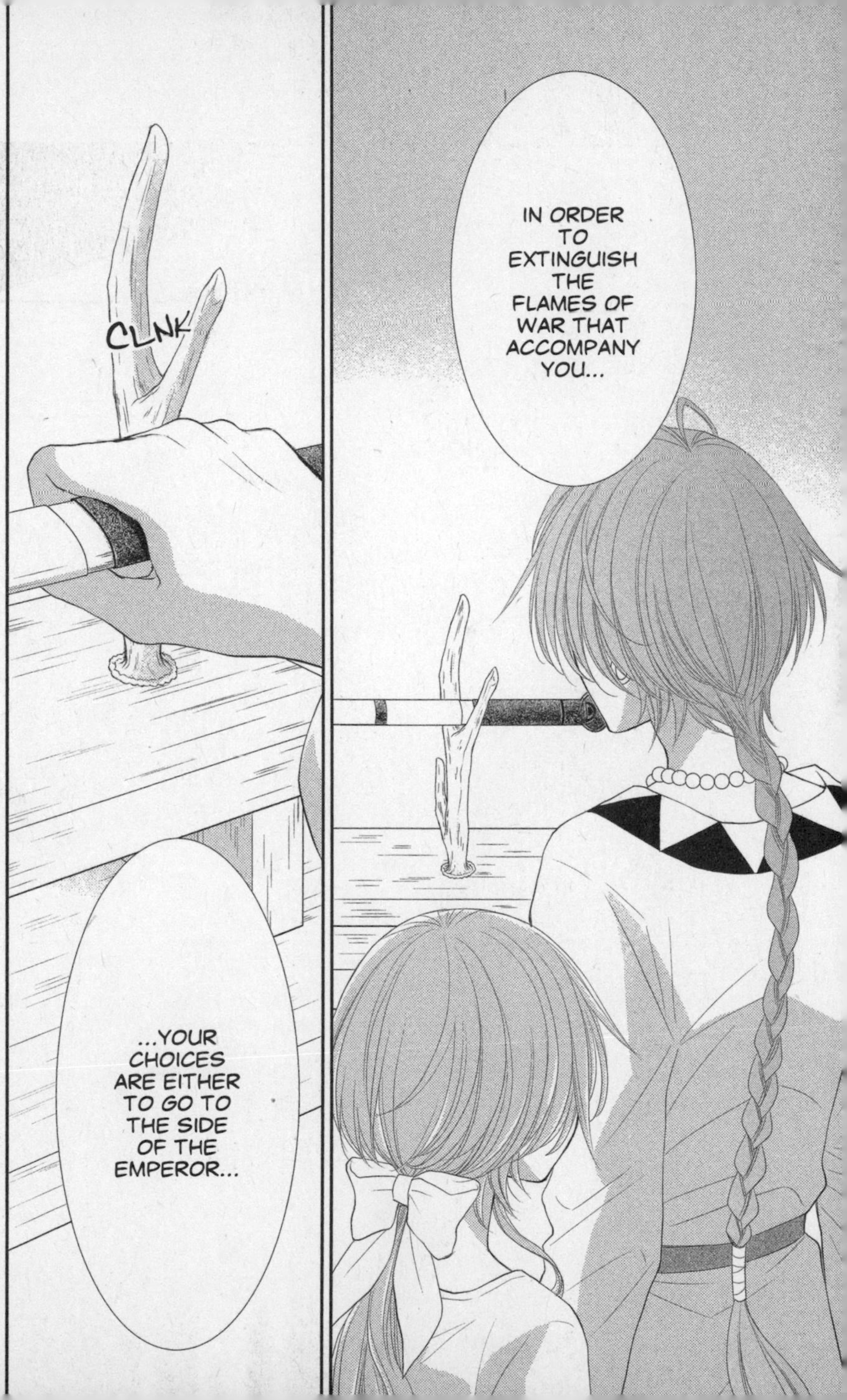
IN ORDER TO EXTINGUISH THE FLAMES OF WAR THAT ACCOMPANY YOU...
CLNK
...YOUR CHOICES ARE EITHER TO GO TO THE SIDE OF THE EMPEROR...

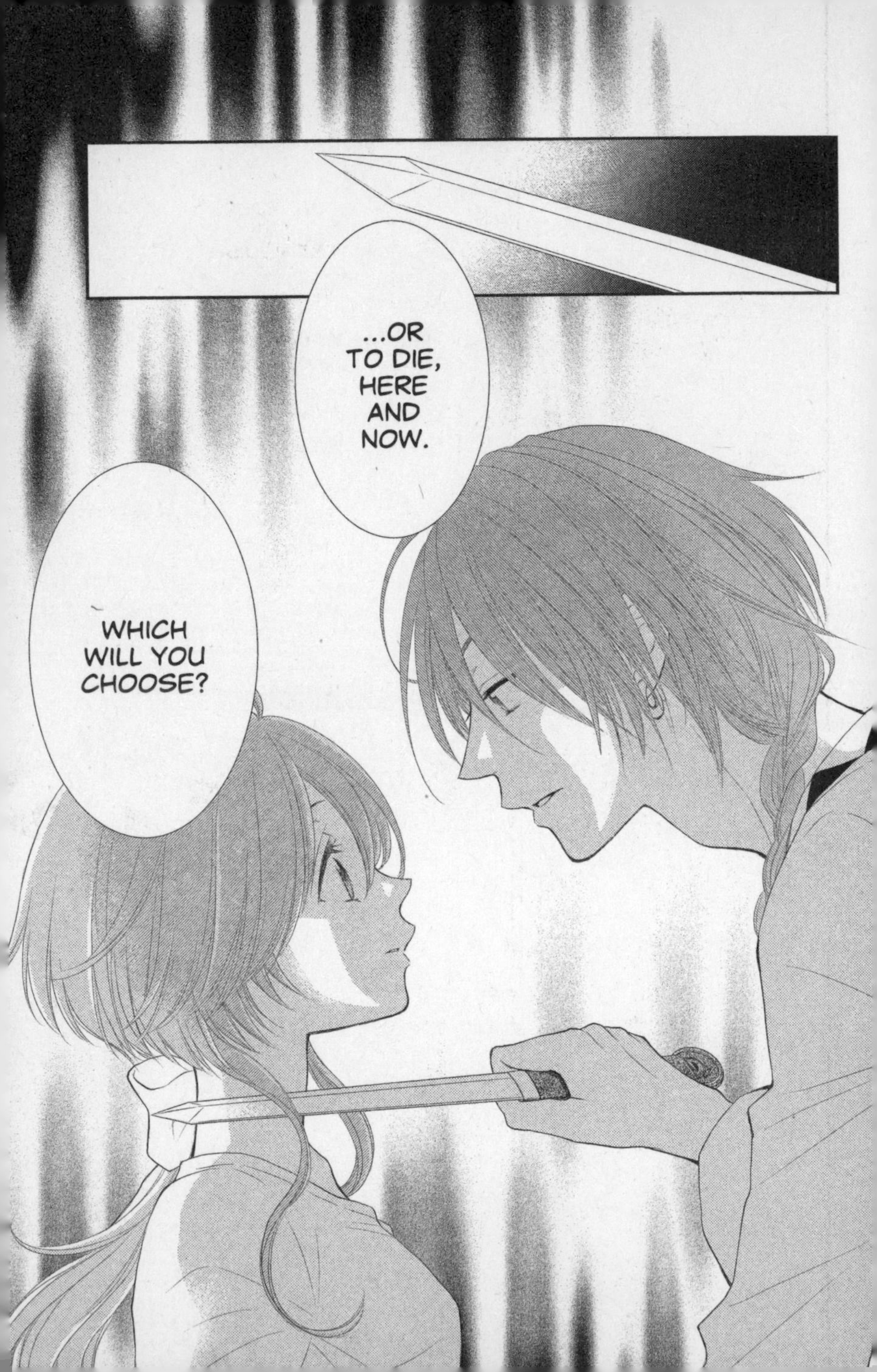
...OR TO DIE, HERE AND NOW.
WHICH WILL YOU CHOOSE?

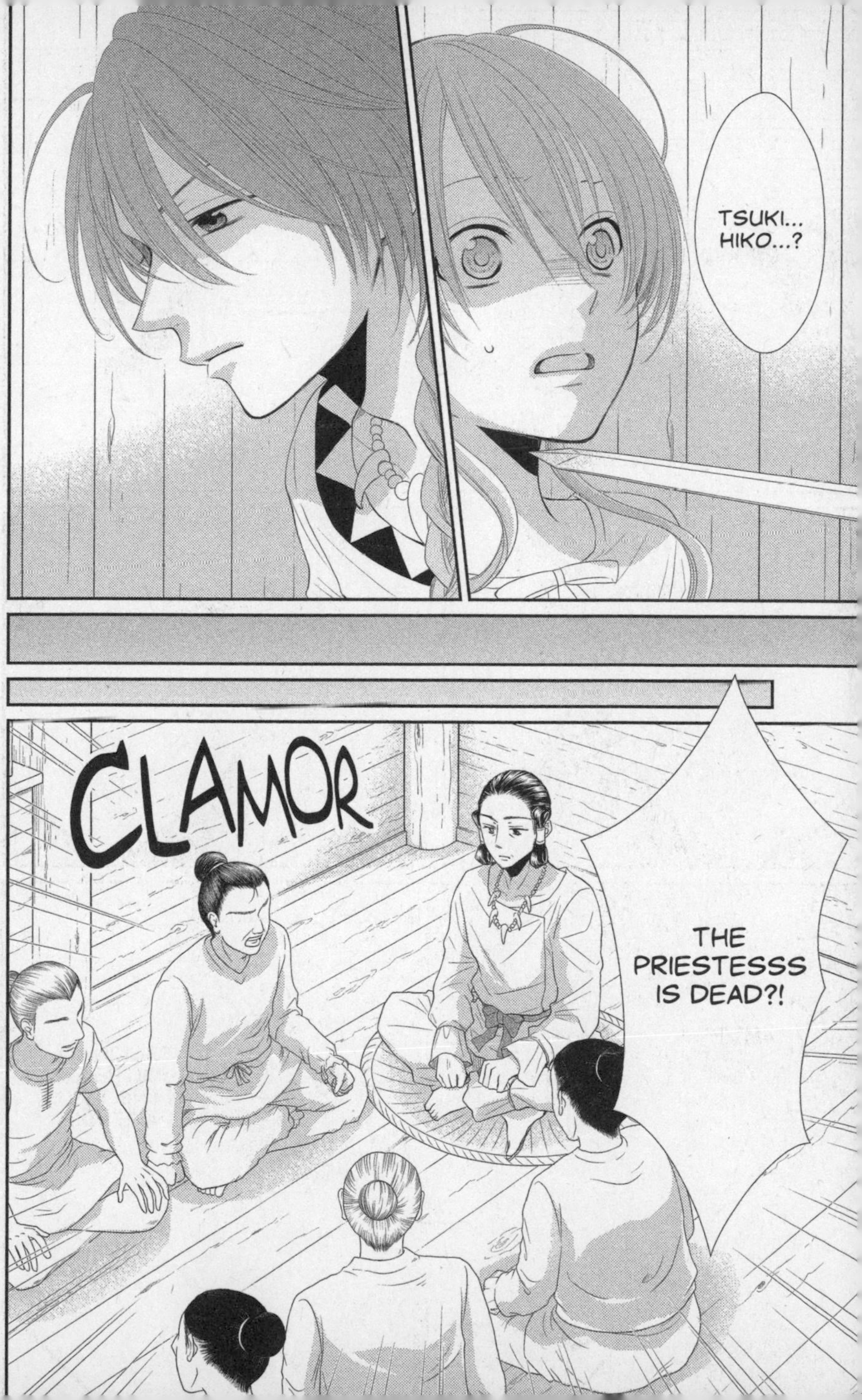
TSUKI... HIKO...?
THE PRIESTESSS IS DEAD?!
CLAMOR

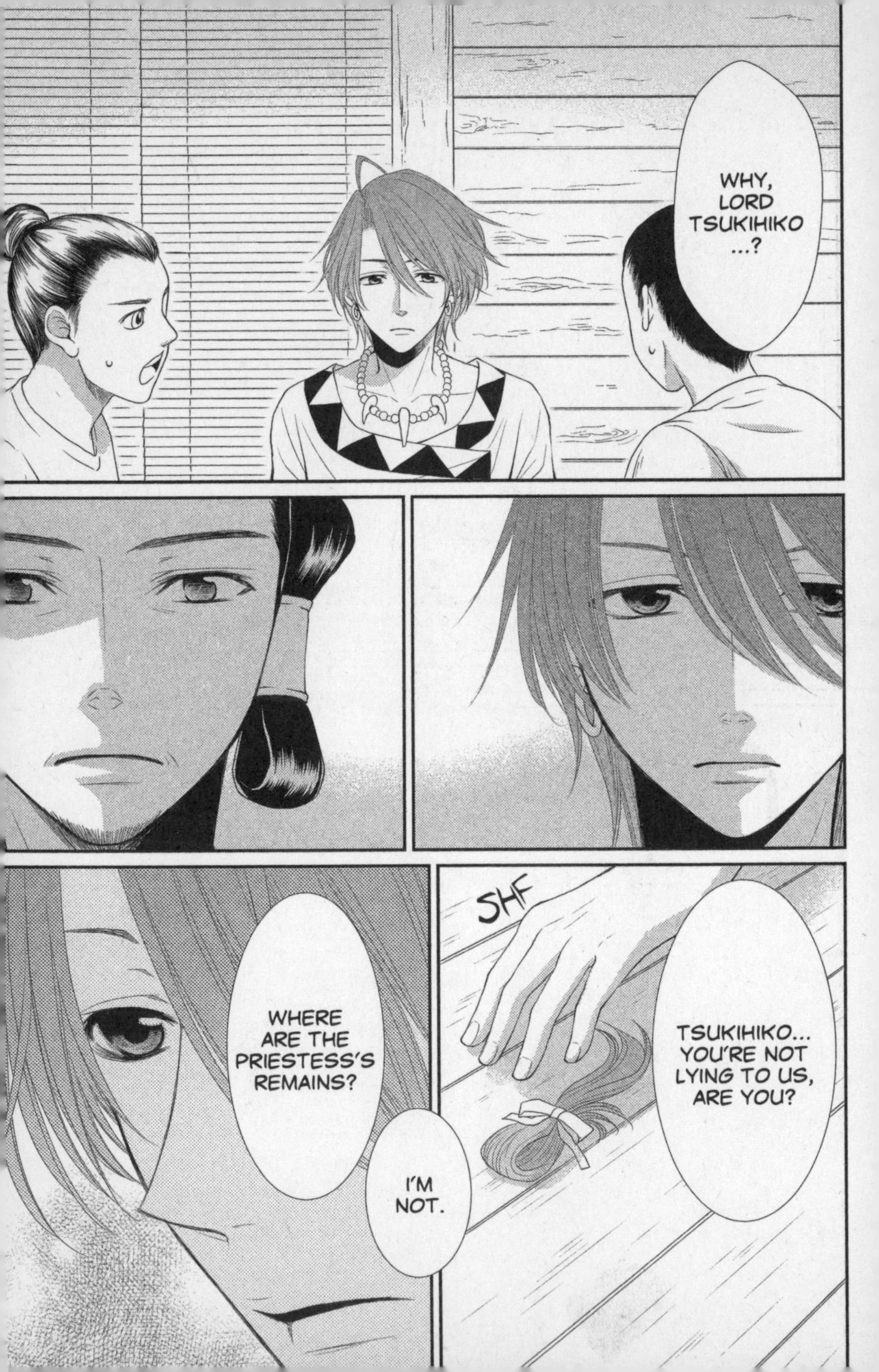
WHY, LORD TSUKIHIKO ...?
SHF
TSUKIHIKO... YOU'RE NOT LYING TO US, ARE YOU?
I'M NOT.
WHERE ARE THE PRIESTESS'S REMAINS?

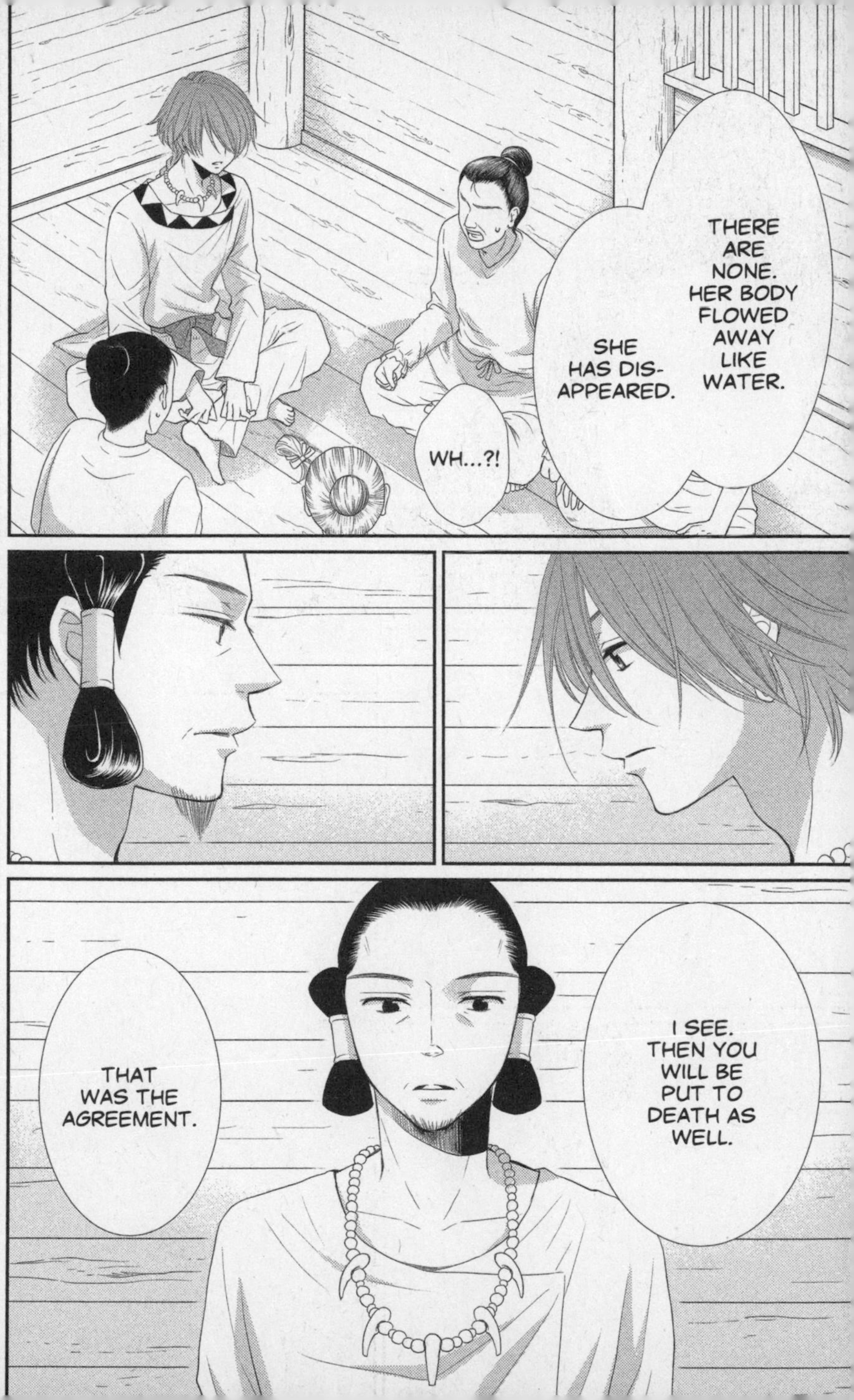
THERE ARE NONE. HER BODY FLOWED AWAY LIKE WATER.
SHE HAS DIS-APPEARED.
WH...?!
I SEE. THEN YOU WILL BE PUT TO DEATH AS WELL.
THAT WAS THE AGREEMENT.

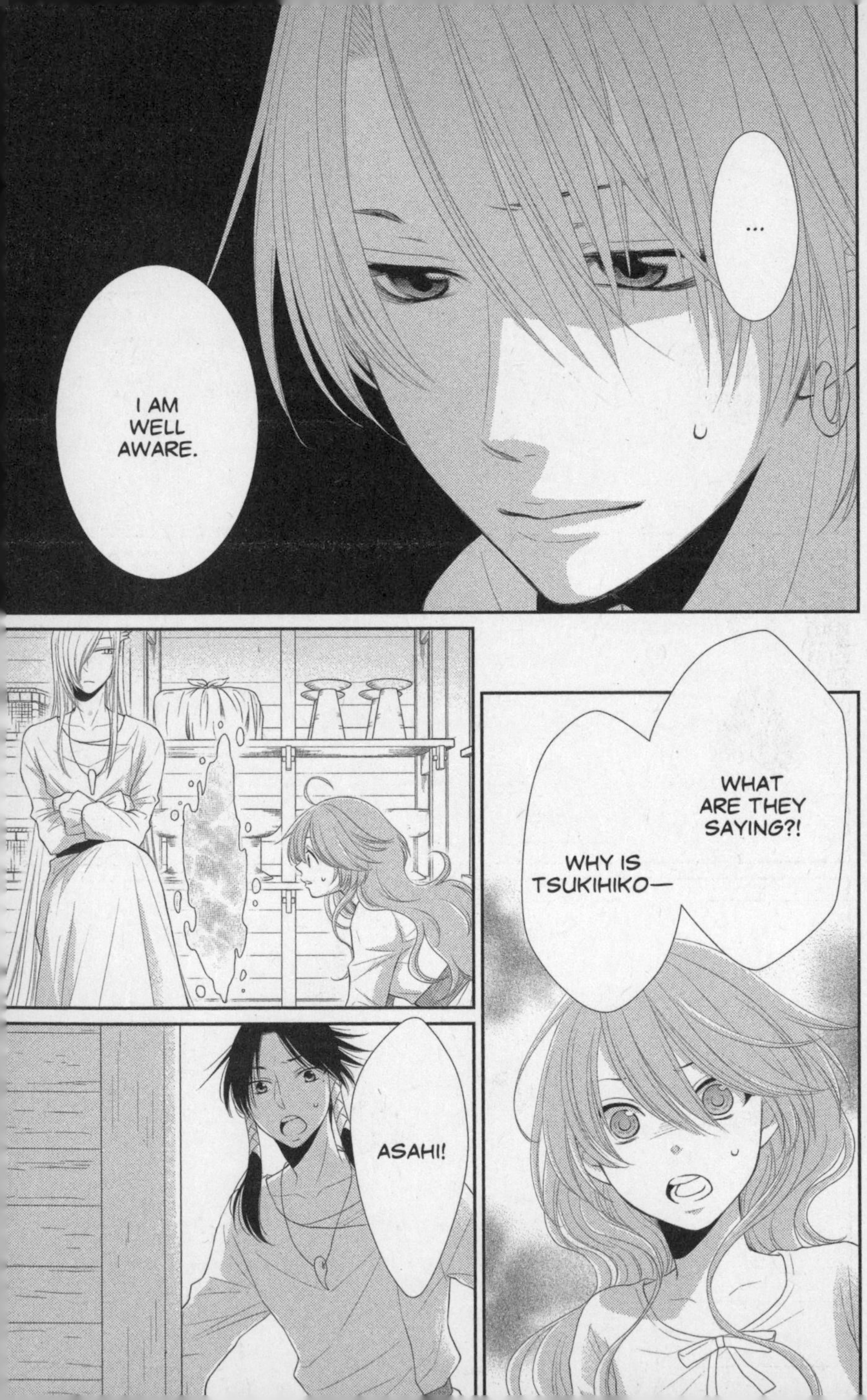
...
I AM WELL AWARE.
WHAT ARE THEY SAYING?!
WHY IS TSUKIHIKO—
ASAHI!

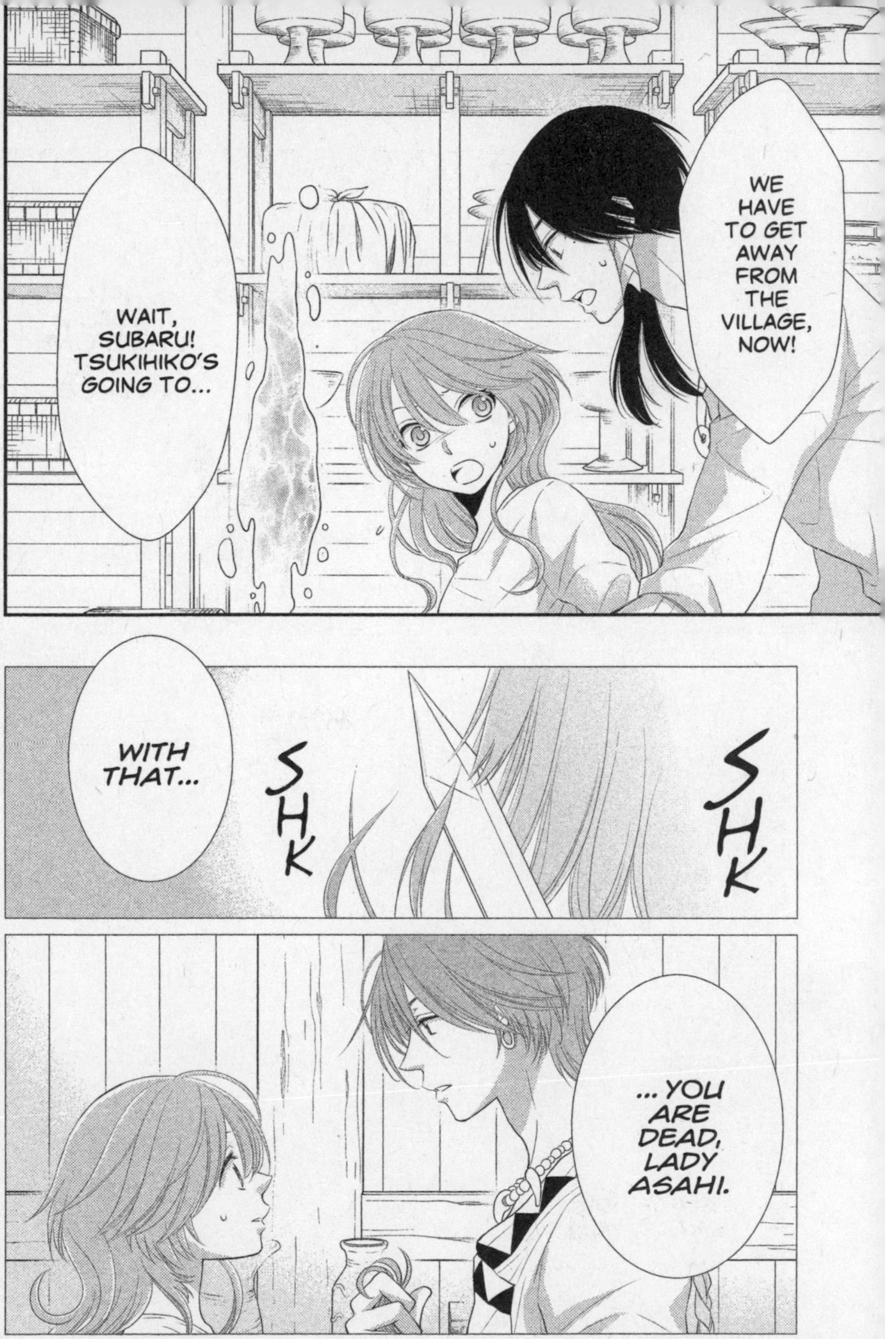
WE HAVE TO GET AWAY FROM THE VILLAGE, NOW!
WAIT, SUBARU! TSUKIHIKO'S GOING TO...
SHK
WITH THAT...
SHK
...YOU ARE DEAD, LADY ASAHI.

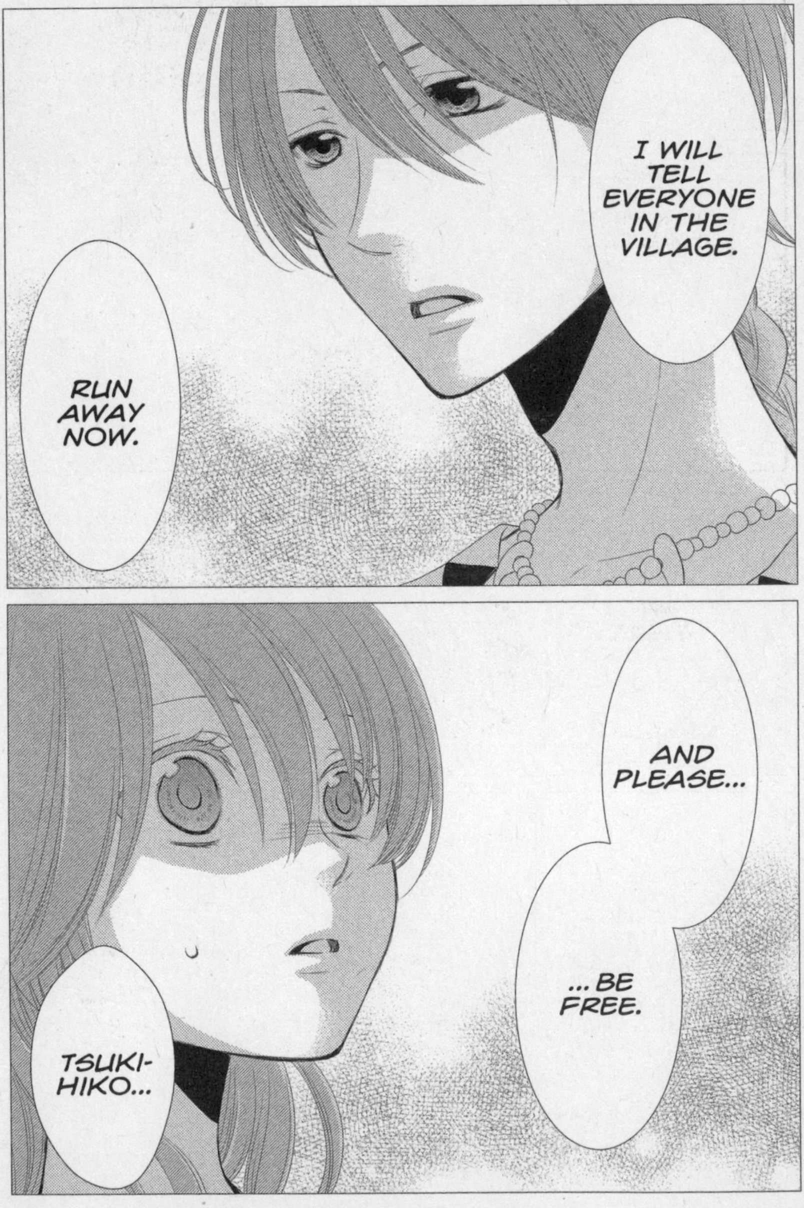
I WILL TELL EVERYONE IN THE VILLAGE.
RUN AWAY NOW.
AND PLEASE...
... BE FREE.
TSUKI-HIKO...

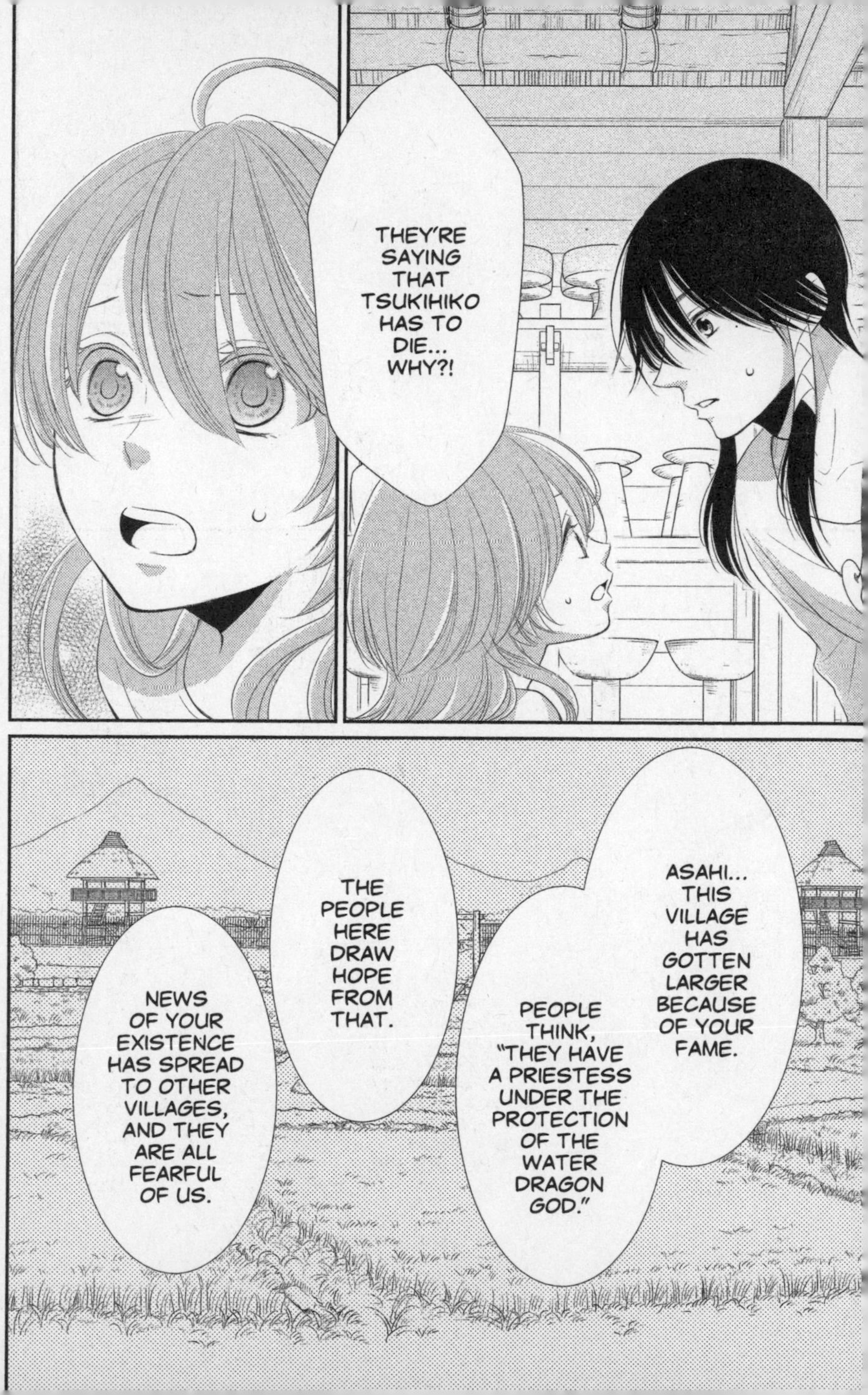
THEY'RE SAYING THAT TSUKIHIKO HAS TO DIE... WHY?!
ASAHI... THIS VILLAGE HAS GOTTEN LARGER BECAUSE OF YOUR FAME.
PEOPLE THINK, "THEY HAVE A PRIESTESS UNDER THE PROTECTION OF THE WATER DRAGON GOD."
THE PEOPLE HERE DRAW HOPE FROM THAT.
NEWS OF YOUR EXISTENCE HAS SPREAD TO OTHER VILLAGES, AND THEY ARE ALL FEARFUL OF US.

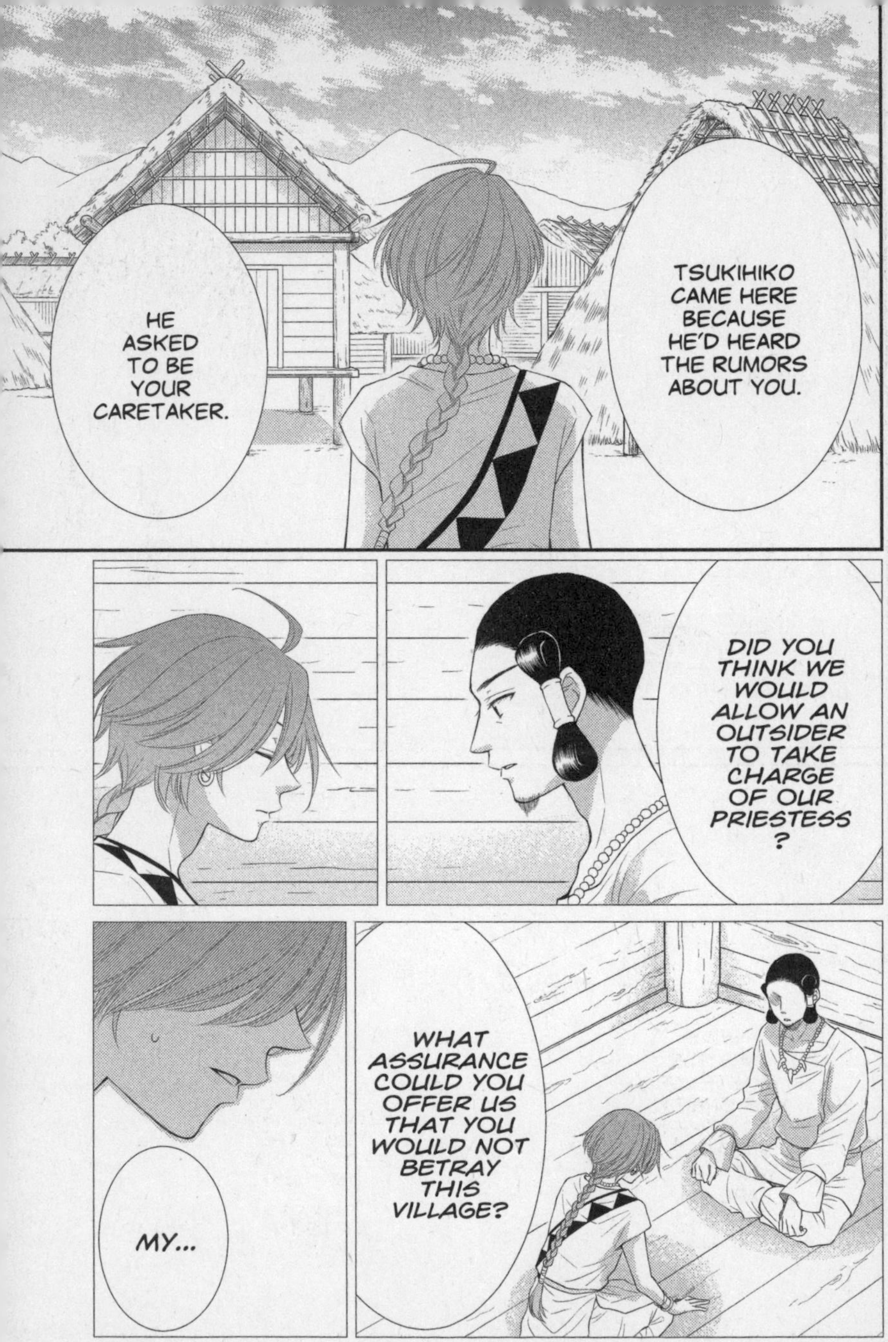
TSUKIHIKO CAME HERE BECAUSE HE'D HEARD THE RUMORS ABOUT YOU.
HE ASKED TO BE YOUR CARETAKER.
DID YOU THINK WE WOULD ALLOW AN OUTSIDER TO TAKE CHARGE OF OUR PRIESTESS?
WHAT ASSURANCE COULD YOU OFFER US THAT YOU WOULD NOT BETRAY THIS VILLAGE?
MY...

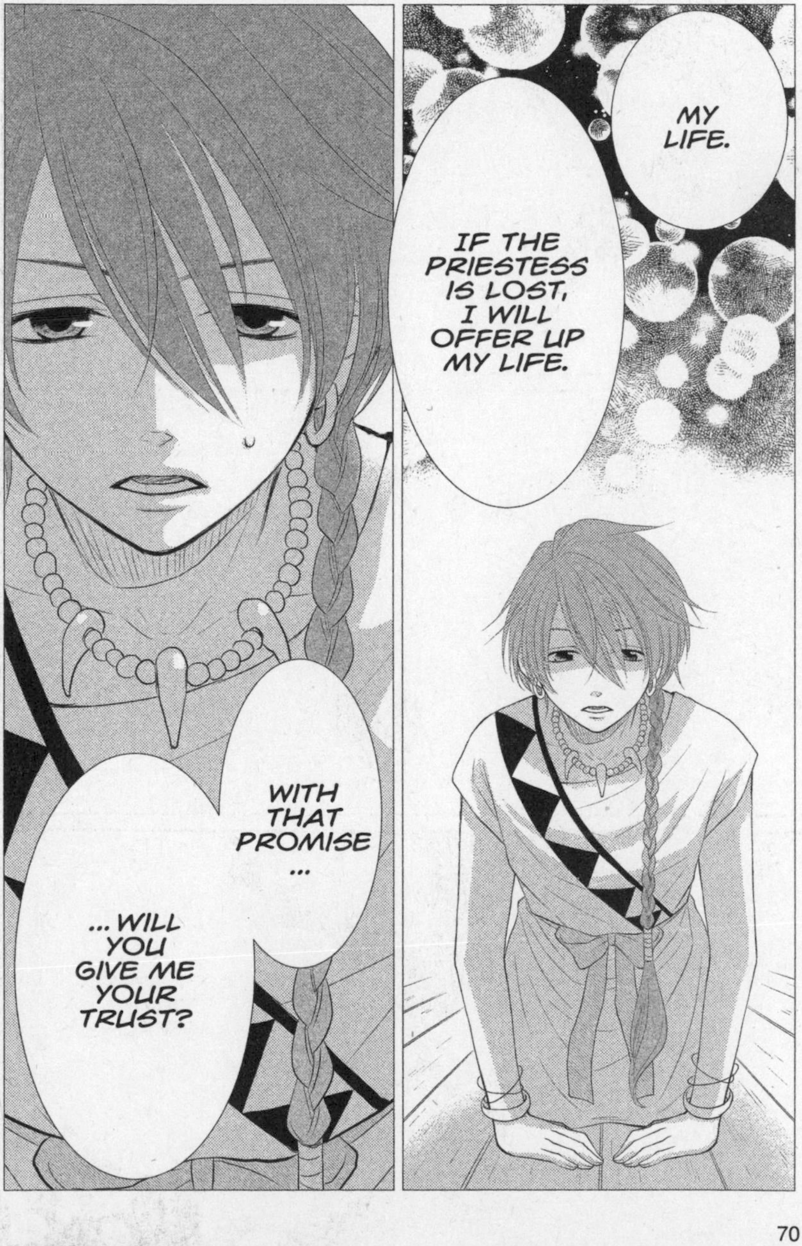
MY LIFE.
IF THE PRIESTESS IS LOST, I WILL OFFER UP MY LIFE.
WITH THAT PROMISE ...
...WILL YOU GIVE ME YOUR TRUST?

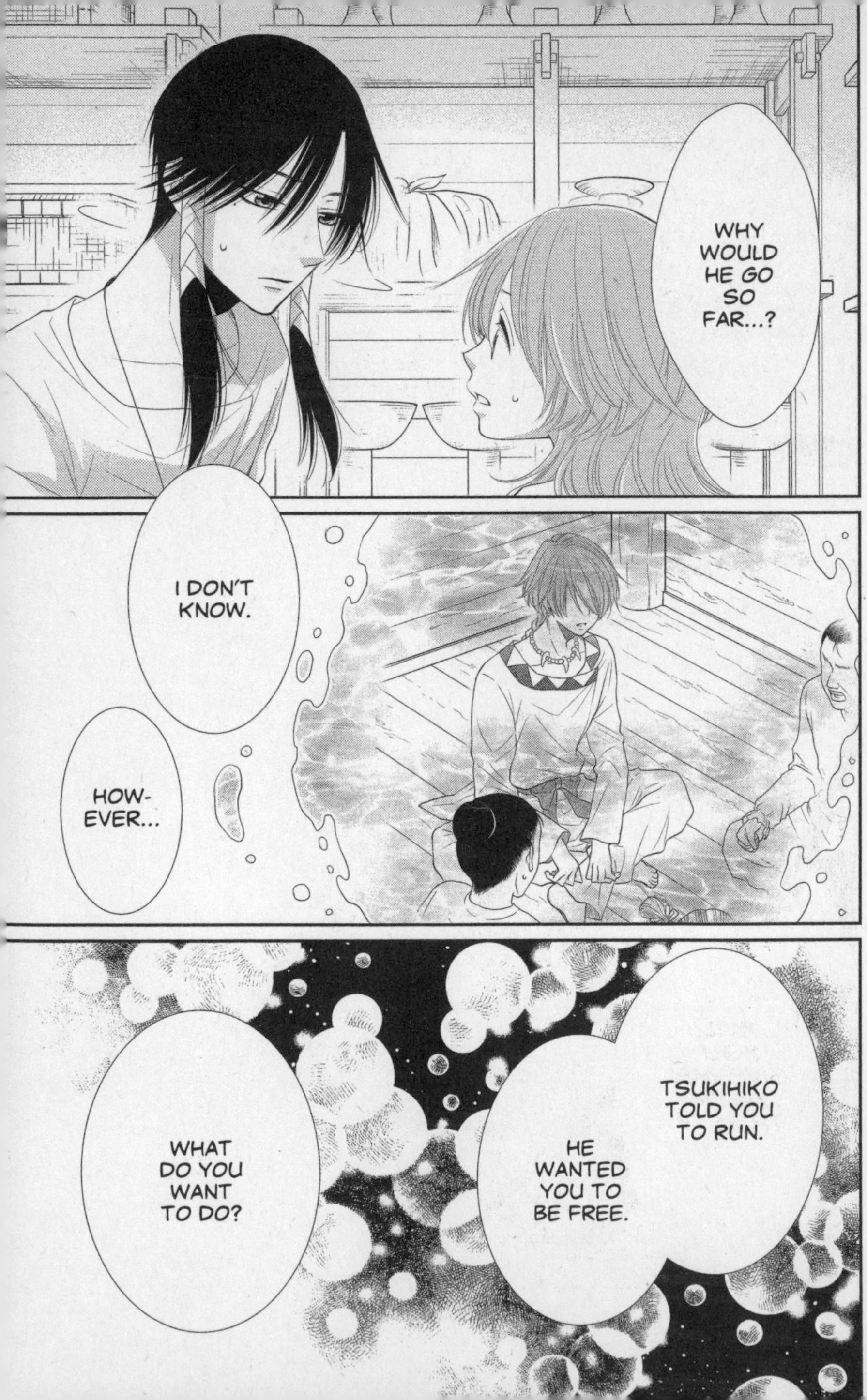
WHY WOULD HE GO SO FAR...?
I DON'T KNOW.
HOW-EVER...
TSUKIHIKO TOLD YOU TO RUN.
HE WANTED YOU TO BE FREE.
WHAT DO YOU WANT TO DO?

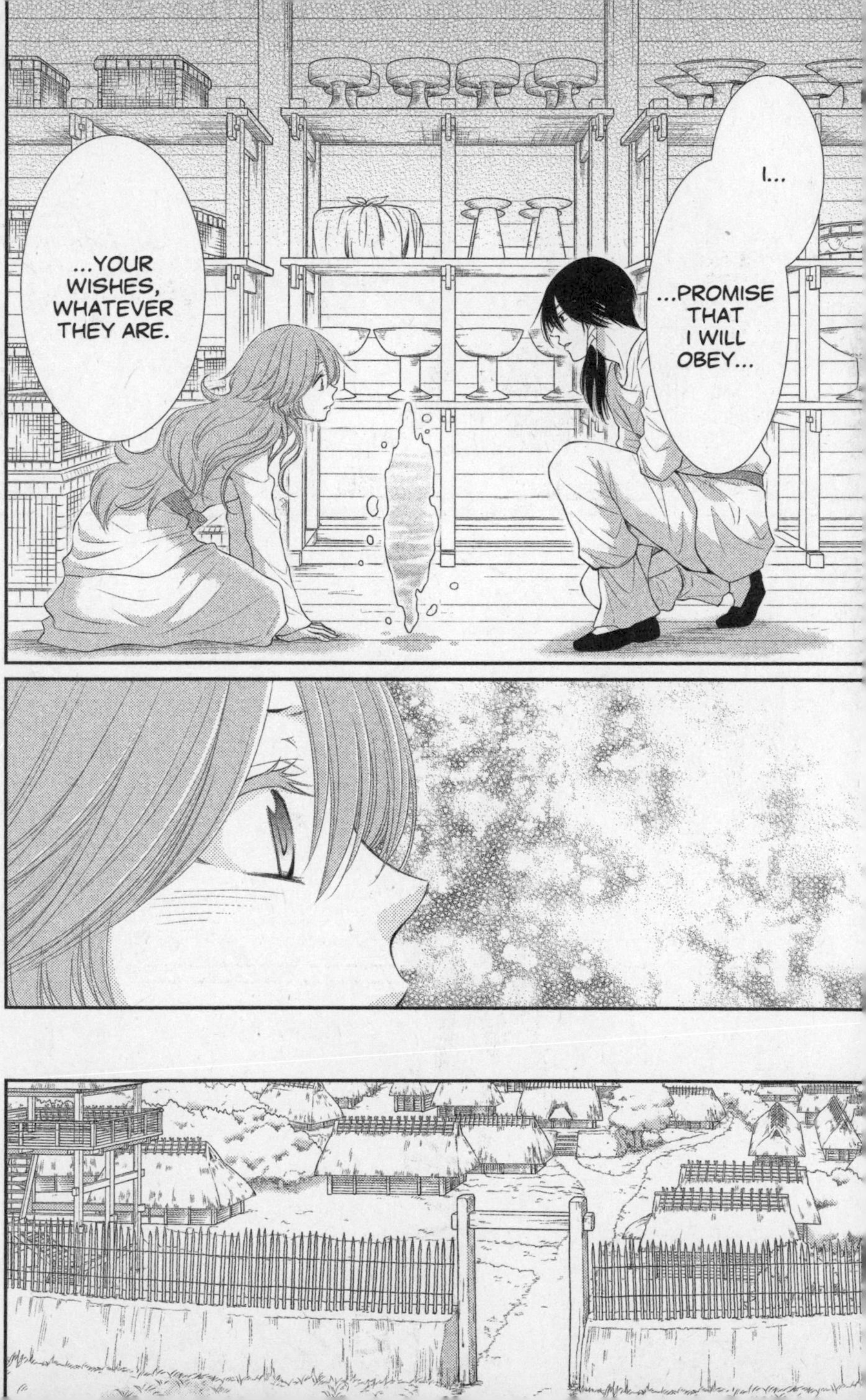
I...
...PROMISE THAT I WILL OBEY...
...YOUR WISHES, WHATEVER THEY ARE.

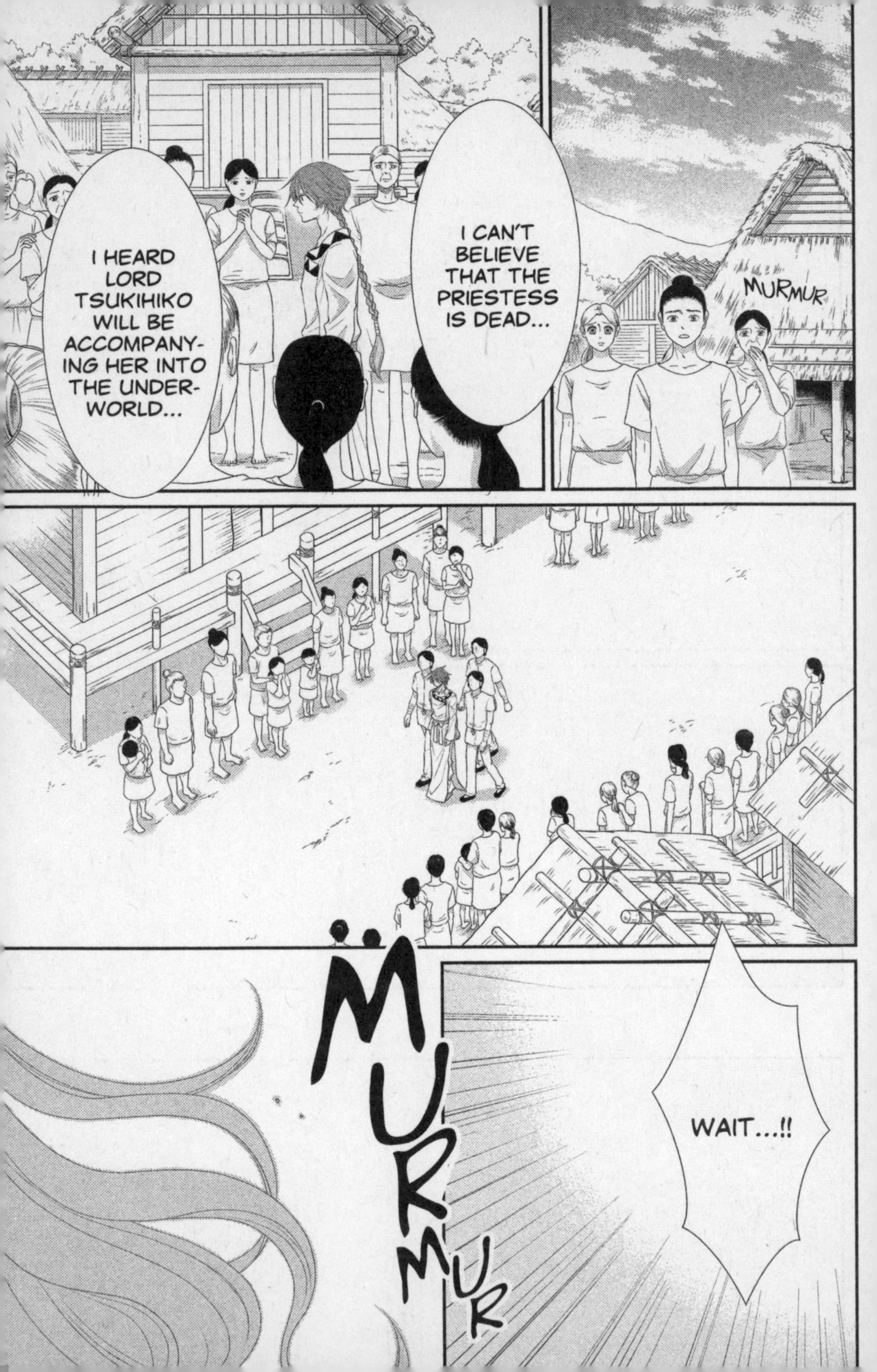
MURMUR
I CAN'T BELIEVE THAT THE PRIESTESS IS DEAD...
I HEARD LORD TSUKIHIKO WILL BE ACCOMPANY-ING HER INTO THE UNDER-WORLD...
WAIT...!!
MURMUR

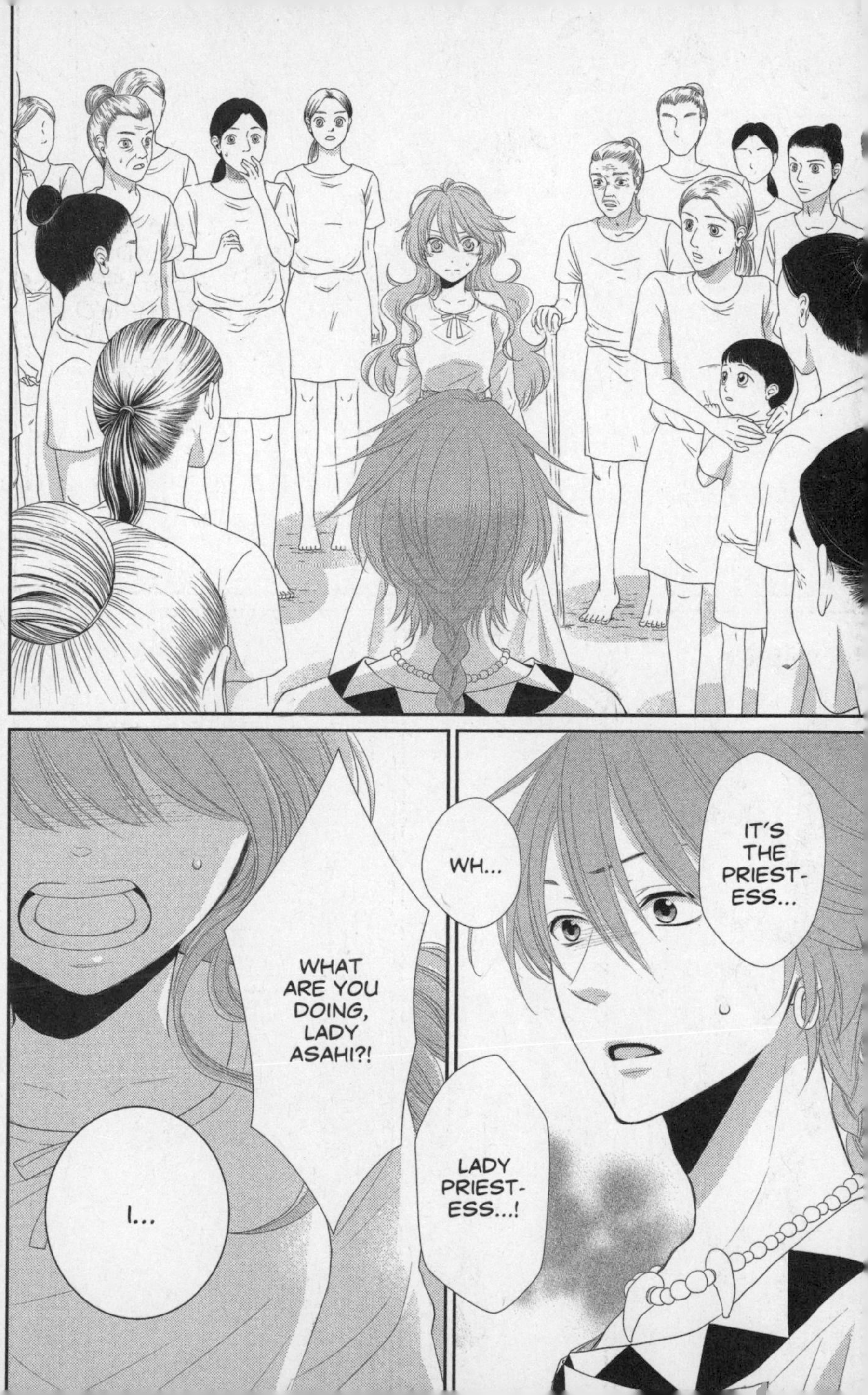
IT'S THE PRIEST-ESS...
WH...
LADY PRIEST-ESS...!
WHAT ARE YOU DOING, LADY ASAHI?!
I...

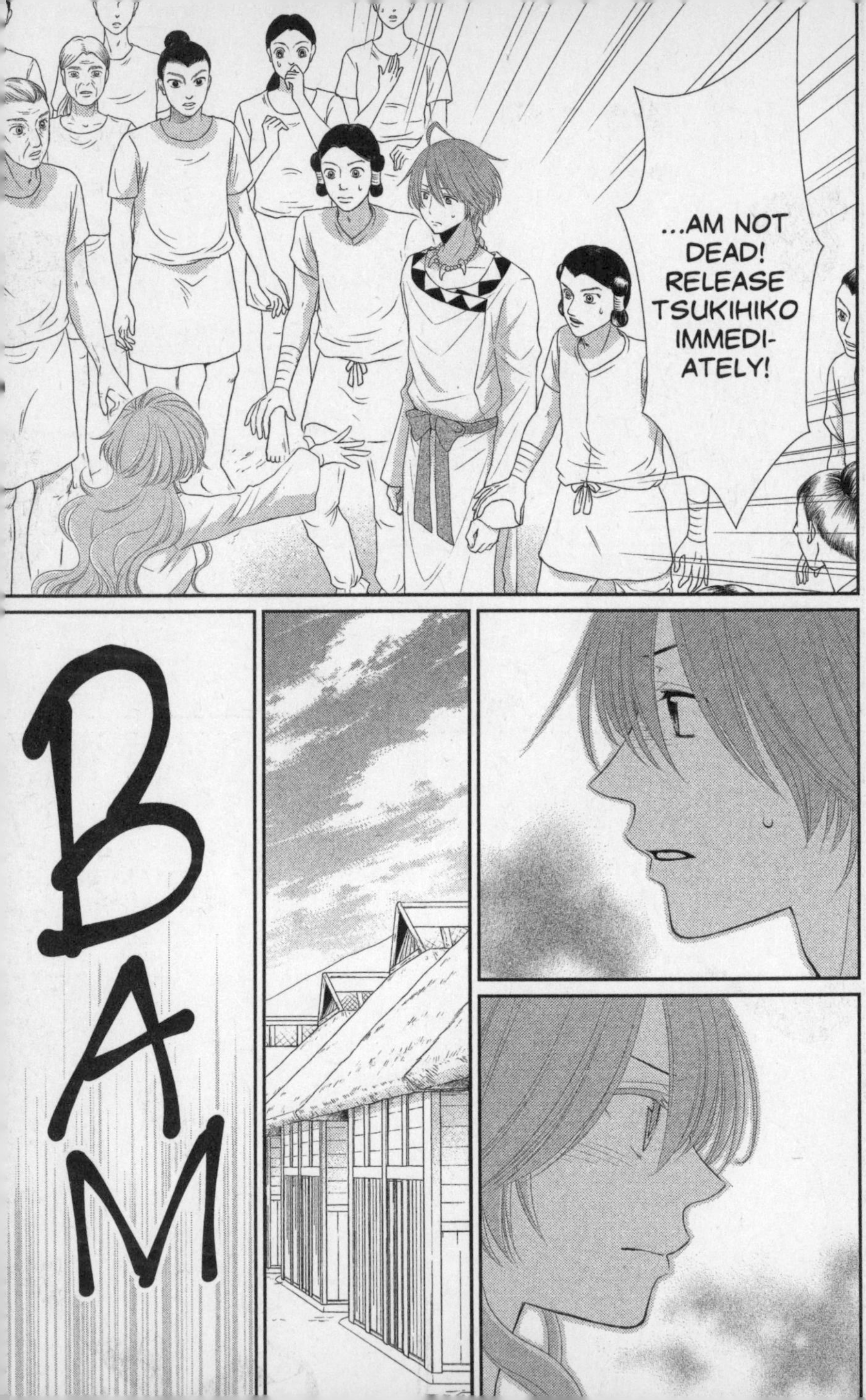
...AM NOT DEAD! RELEASE TSUKIHIKO IMMEDI-ATELY!
BAM

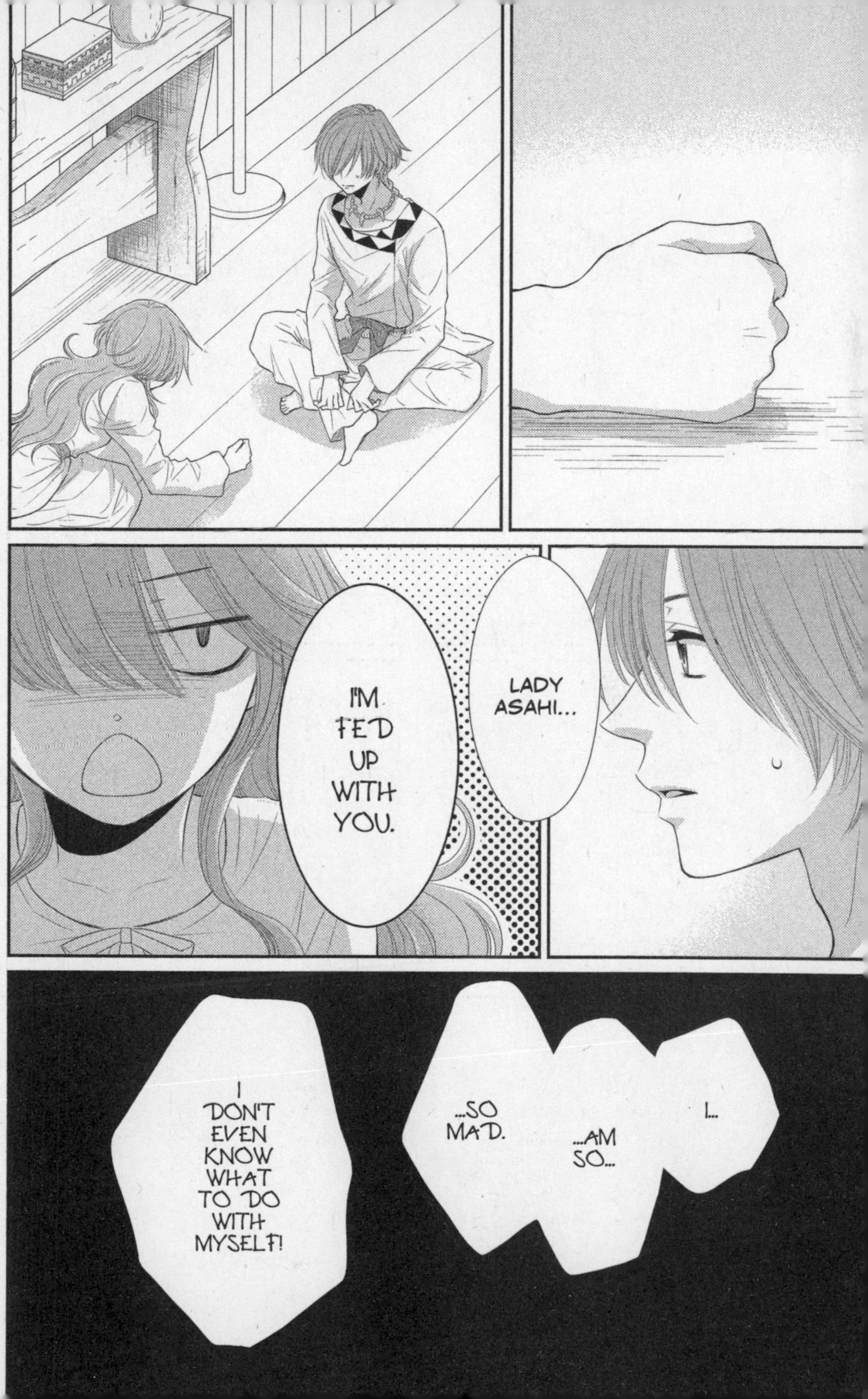
LADY ASAHI...
I'M FED UP WITH YOU.
I...
...AM SO...
...SO MAD.
I DON'T EVEN KNOW WHAT TO DO WITH MYSELF!

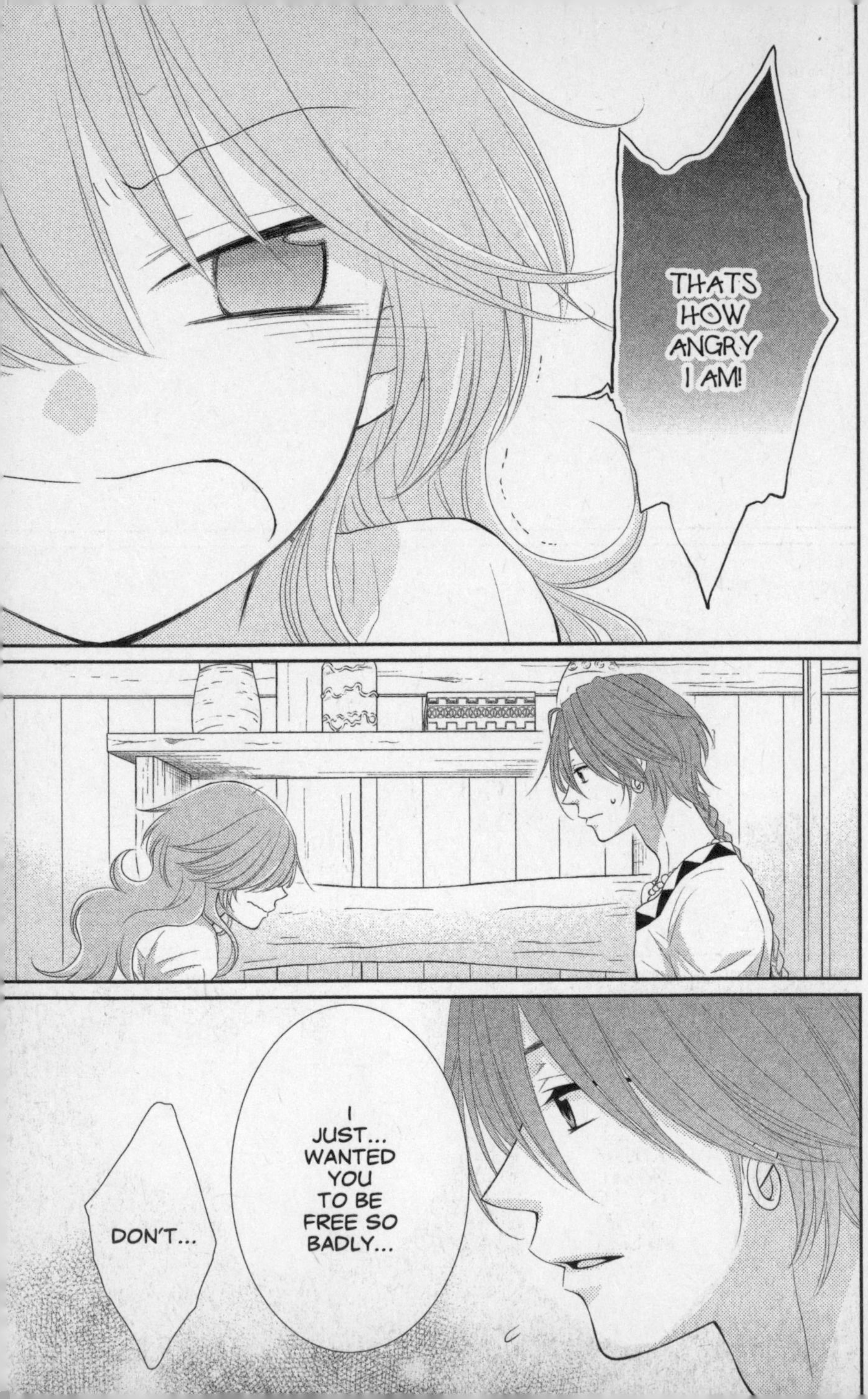
THATS HOW ANGRY I AM!
I JUST... WANTED YOU TO BE FREE SO BADLY...
DON'T...

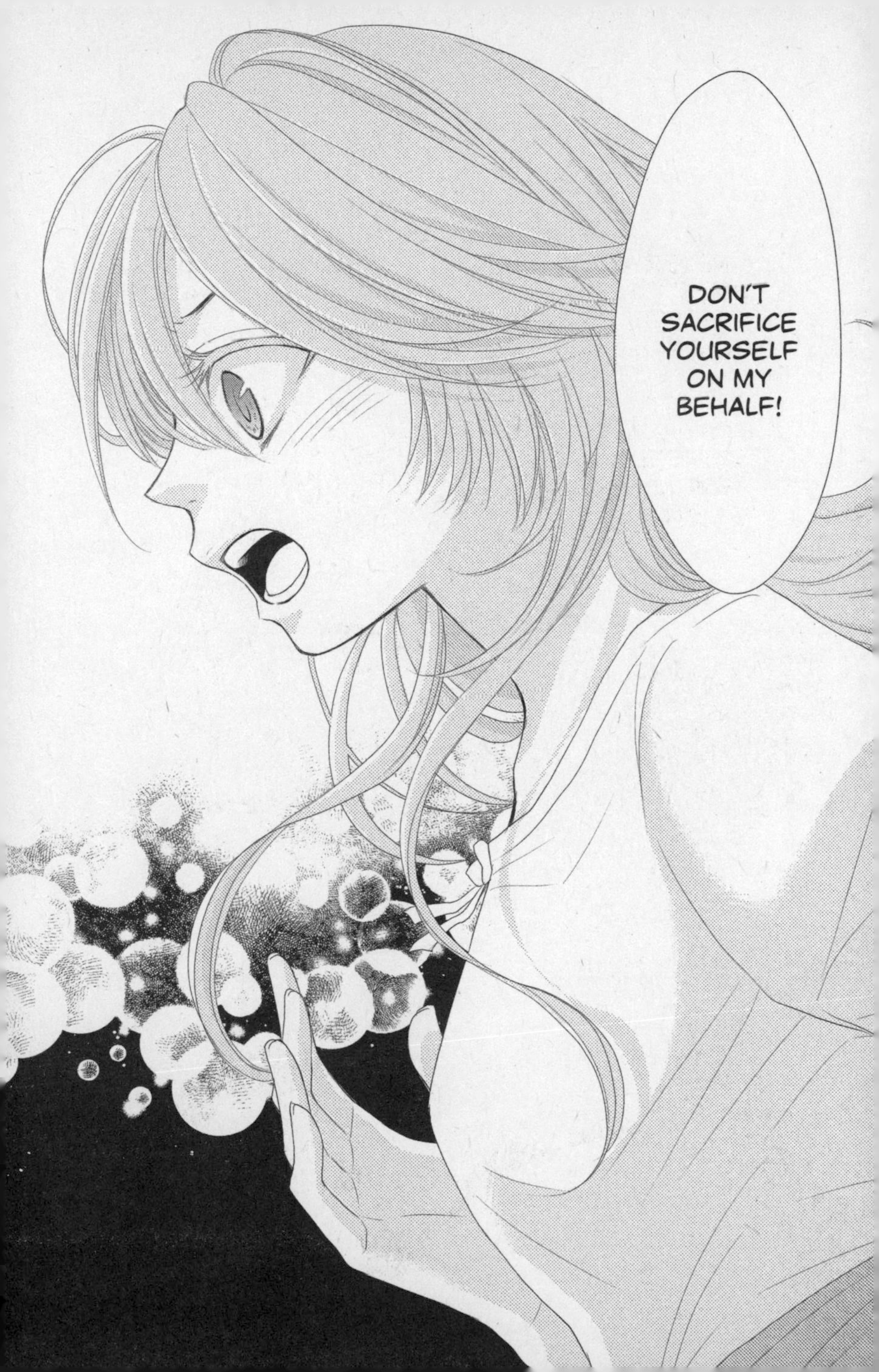
DON'T SACRIFICE YOURSELF ON MY BEHALF!

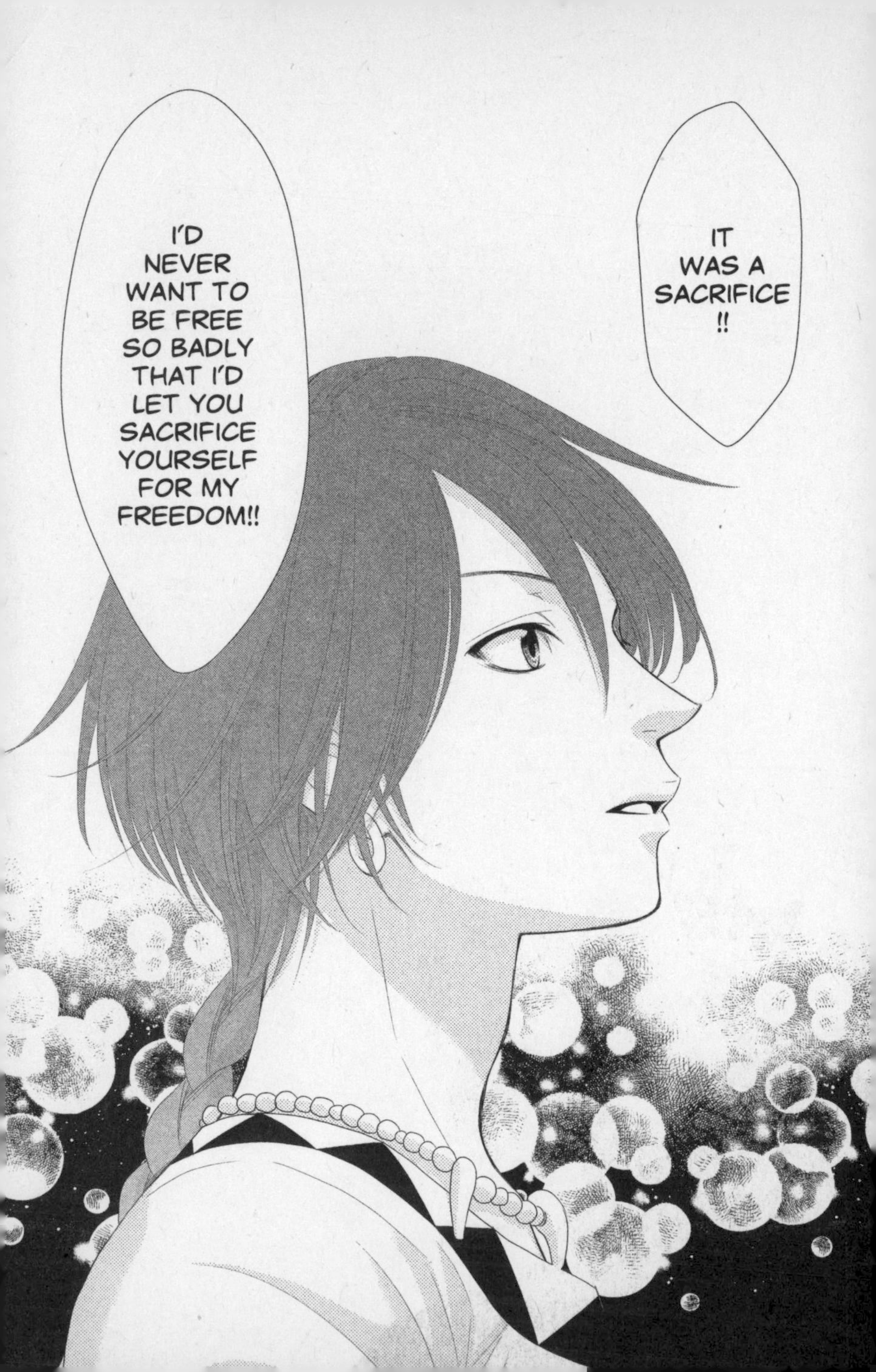
IT WAS A SACRIFICE !!
I'D NEVER WANT TO BE FREE SO BADLY THAT I'D LET YOU SACRIFICE YOURSELF FOR MY FREEDOM!!

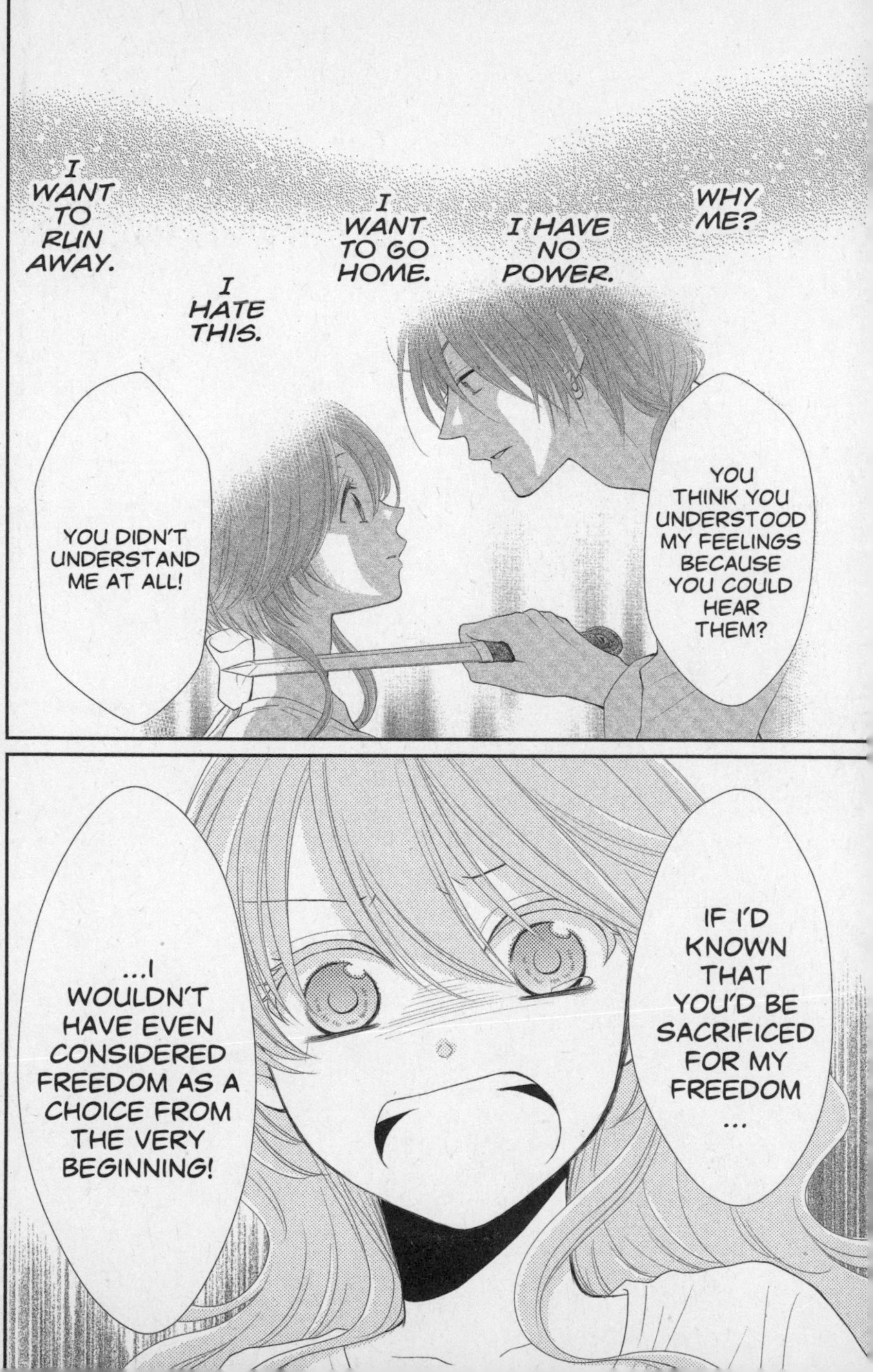
WHY ME?
I HAVE NO POWER.
I WANT TO GO HOME.
I HATE THIS.
I WANT TO RUN AWAY.
YOU THINK YOU UNDERSTOOD MY FEELINGS BECAUSE YOU COULD HEAR THEM?
YOU DIDN'T UNDERSTAND ME AT ALL!
IF I'D KNOWN THAT YOU'D BE SACRIFICED FOR MY FREEDOM...
...I WOULDN'T HAVE EVEN CONSIDERED FREEDOM AS A CHOICE FROM THE VERY BEGINNING!

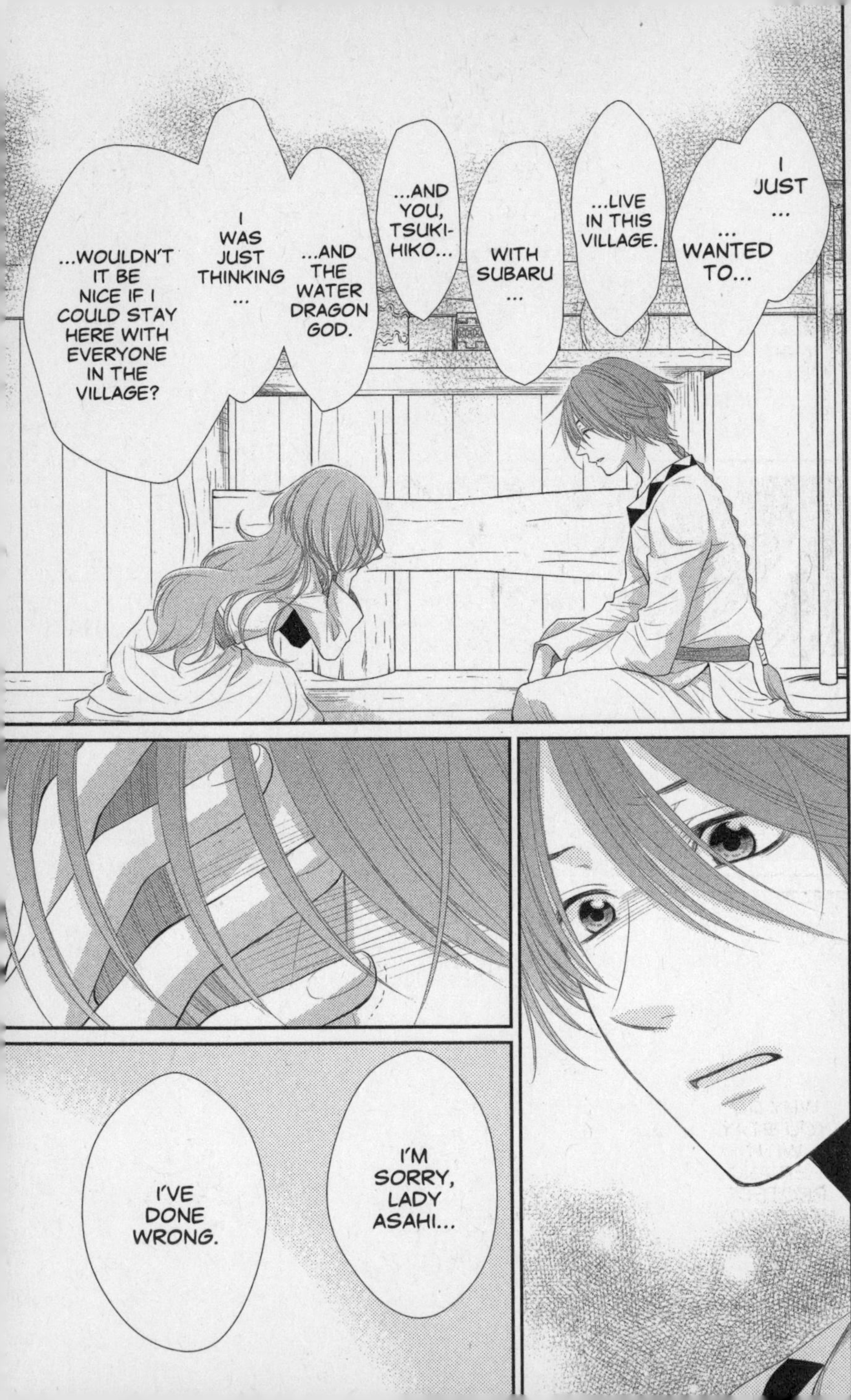
I JUST ... WANTED TO...
...LIVE IN THIS VILLAGE.
WITH SUBARU ...
...AND YOU, TSUKI-HIKO...
...AND THE WATER DRAGON GOD.
I WAS JUST THINKING ...
...WOULDN'T IT BE NICE IF I COULD STAY HERE WITH EVERYONE IN THE VILLAGE?
I'M SORRY, LADY ASAHI...
I'VE DONE WRONG.

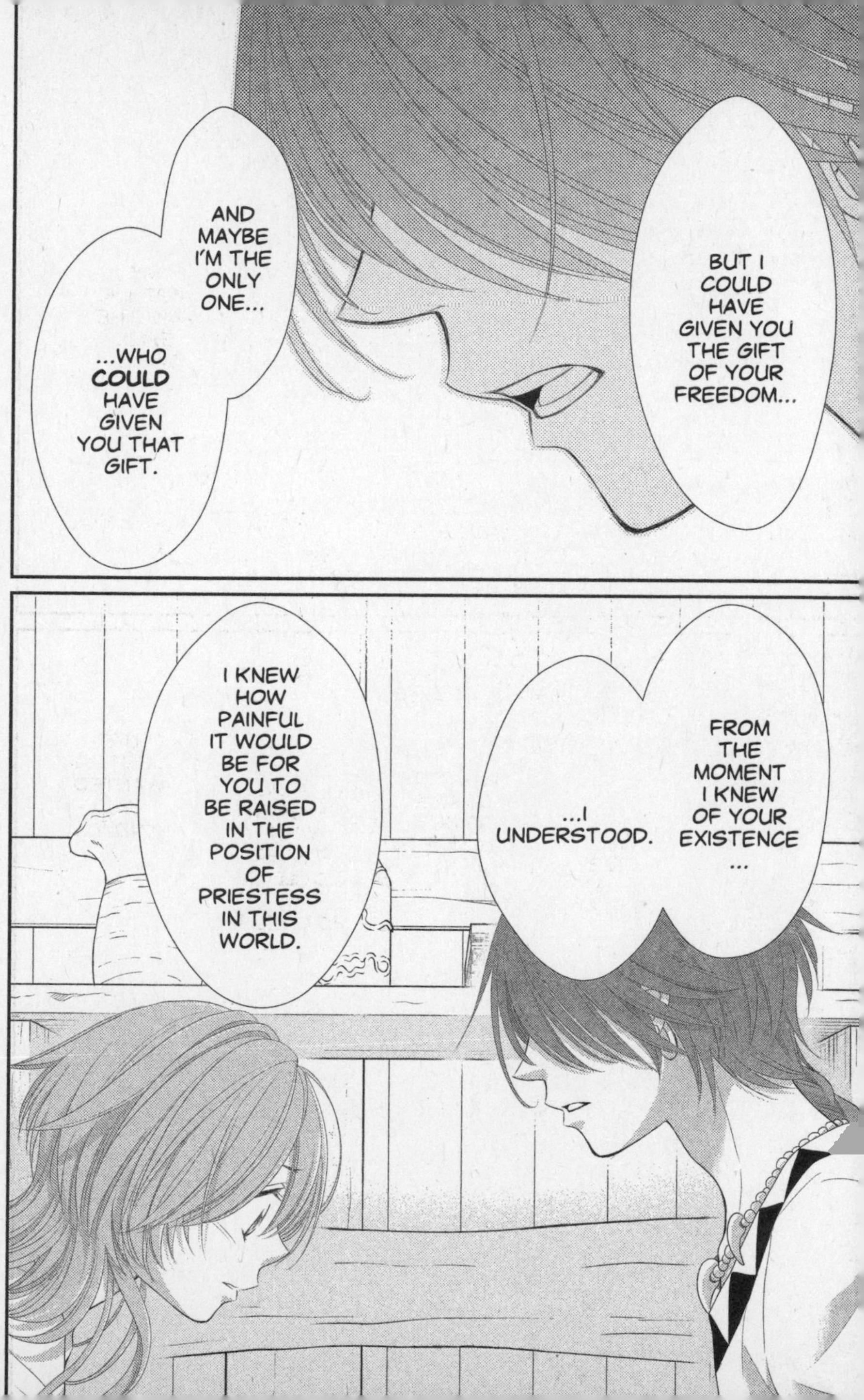
BUT I COULD HAVE GIVEN YOU THE GIFT OF YOUR FREEDOM...
AND MAYBE I'M THE ONLY ONE...
...WHO **COULD** HAVE GIVEN YOU THAT GIFT.
FROM THE MOMENT I KNEW OF YOUR EXISTENCE...
...I UNDERSTOOD.
I KNEW HOW PAINFUL IT WOULD BE FOR YOU TO BE RAISED IN THE POSITION OF PRIESTESS IN THIS WORLD.

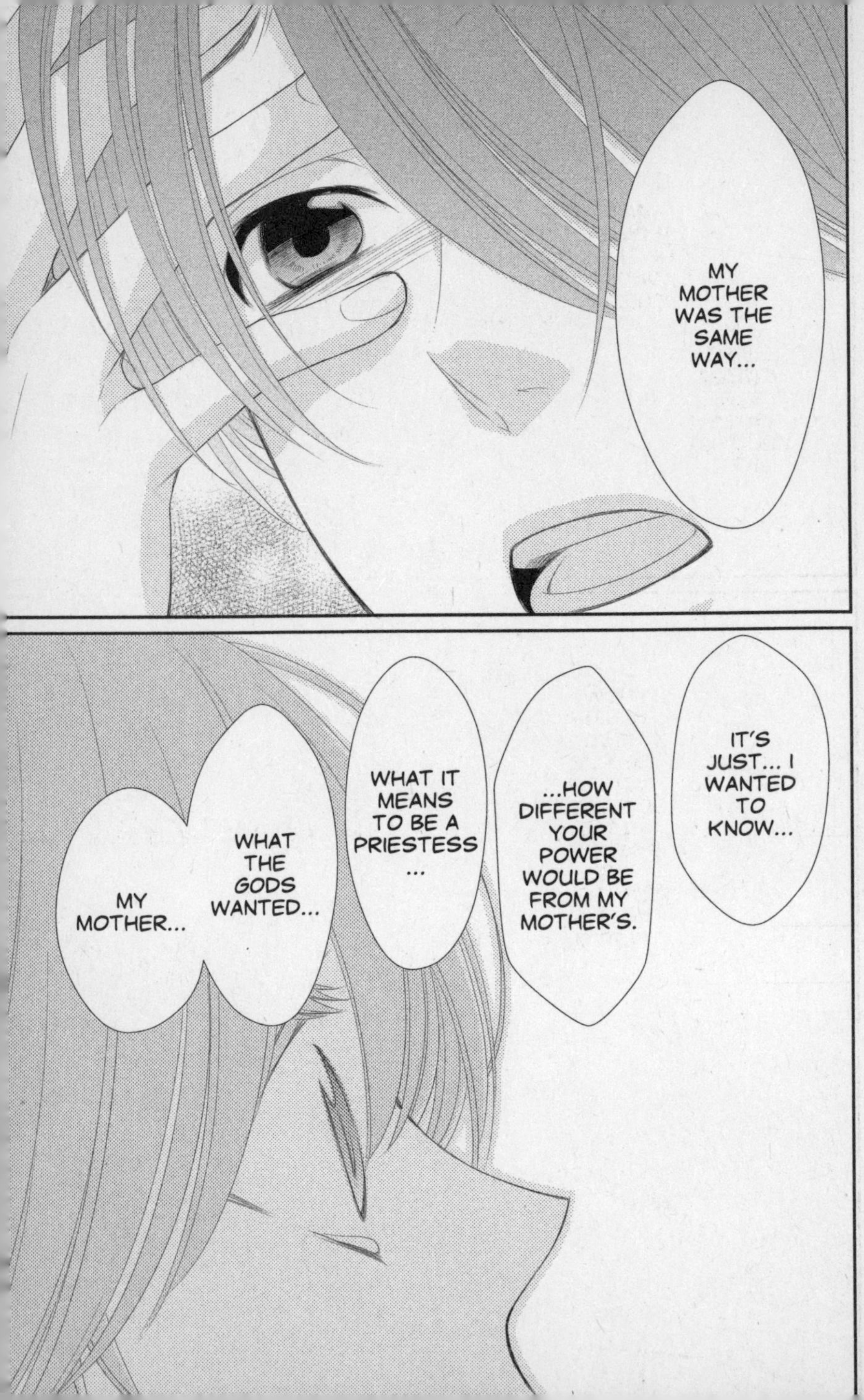
MY MOTHER WAS THE SAME WAY...
IT'S JUST... I WANTED TO KNOW...
...HOW DIFFERENT YOUR POWER WOULD BE FROM MY MOTHER'S.
WHAT IT MEANS TO BE A PRIESTESS ...
WHAT THE GODS WANTED...
MY MOTHER...

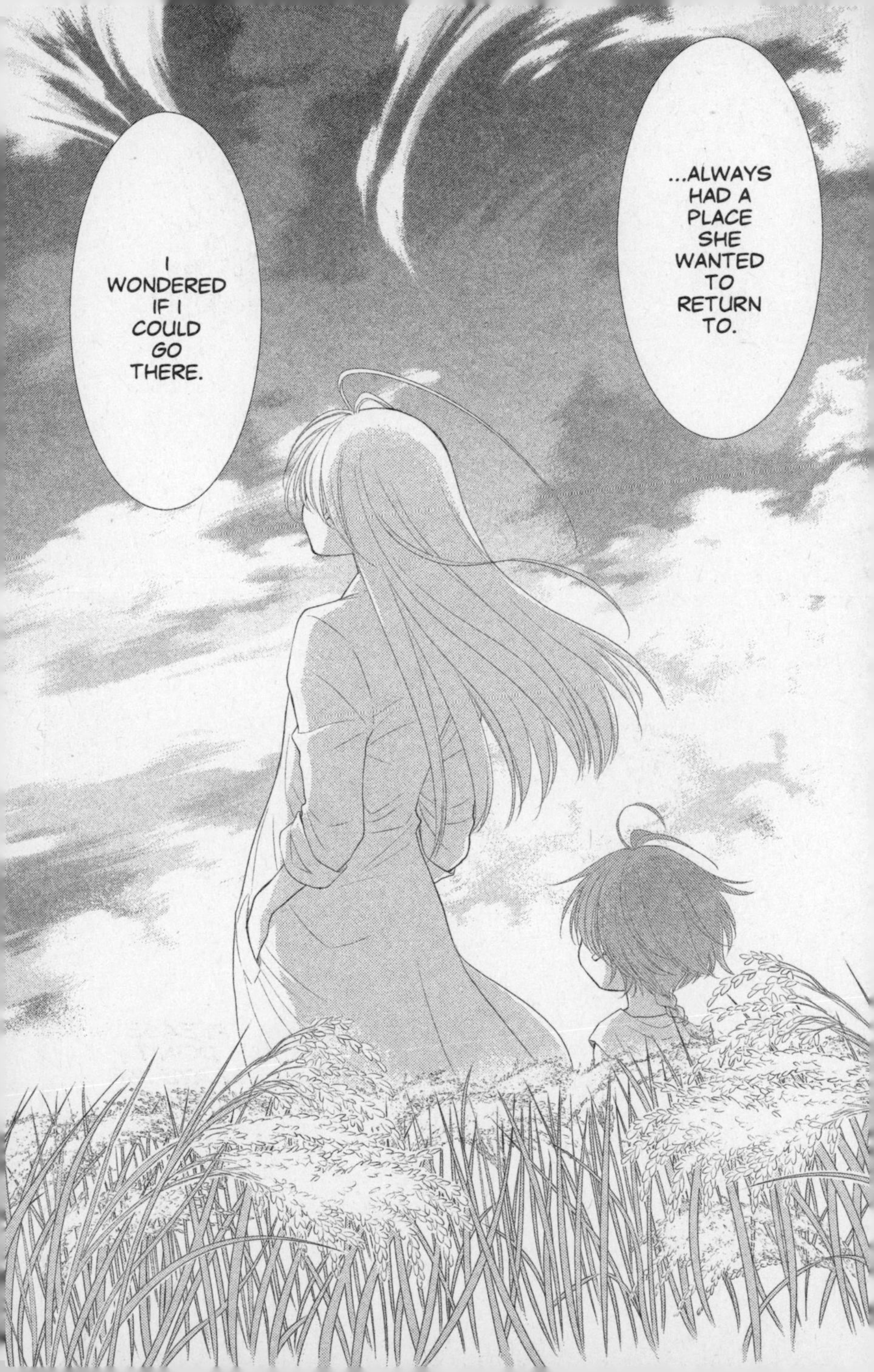
...ALWAYS HAD A PLACE SHE WANTED TO RETURN TO.
I WONDERED IF I COULD GO THERE.

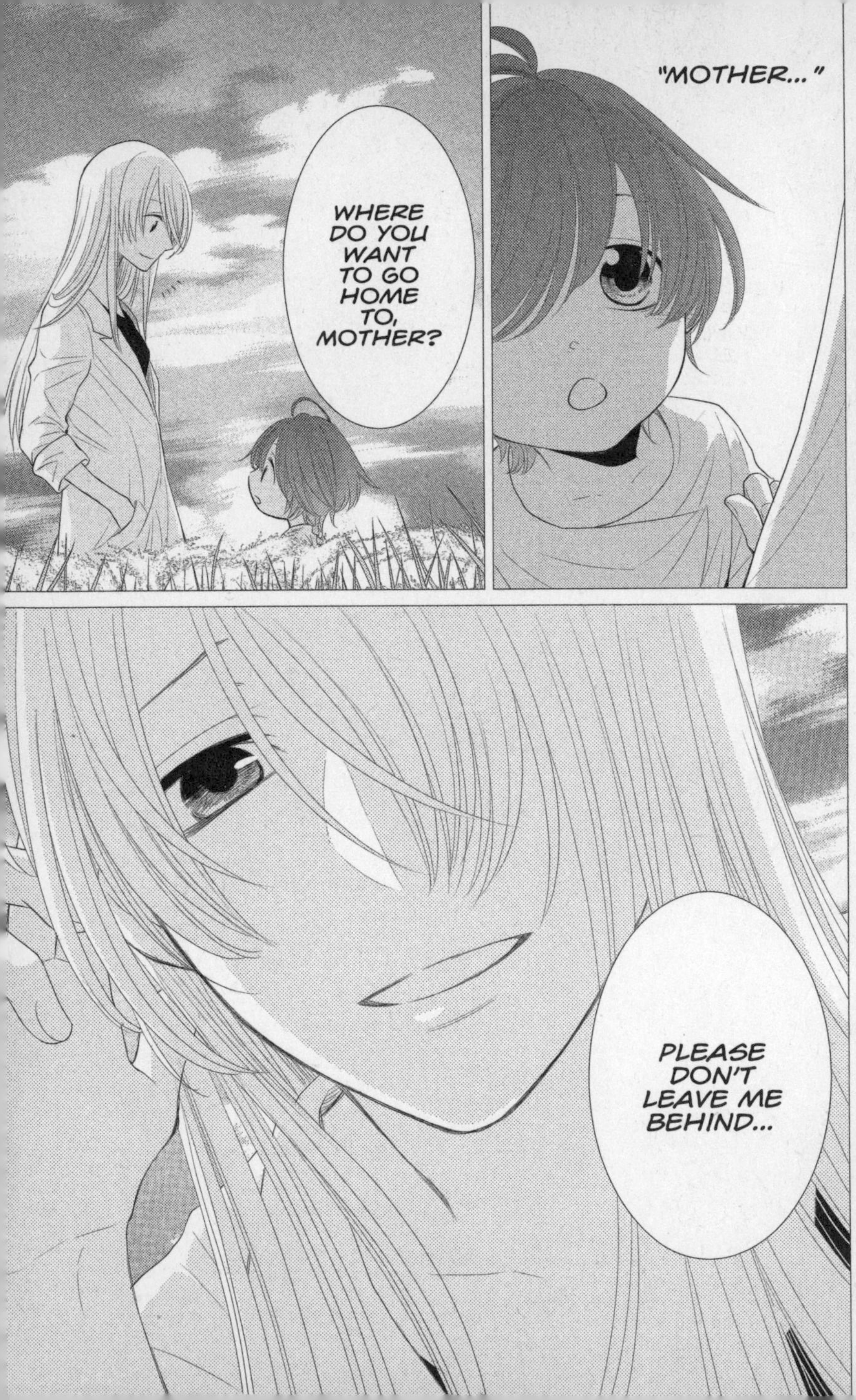
"MOTHER..."
WHERE DO YOU WANT TO GO HOME TO, MOTHER?
PLEASE DON'T LEAVE ME BEHIND...

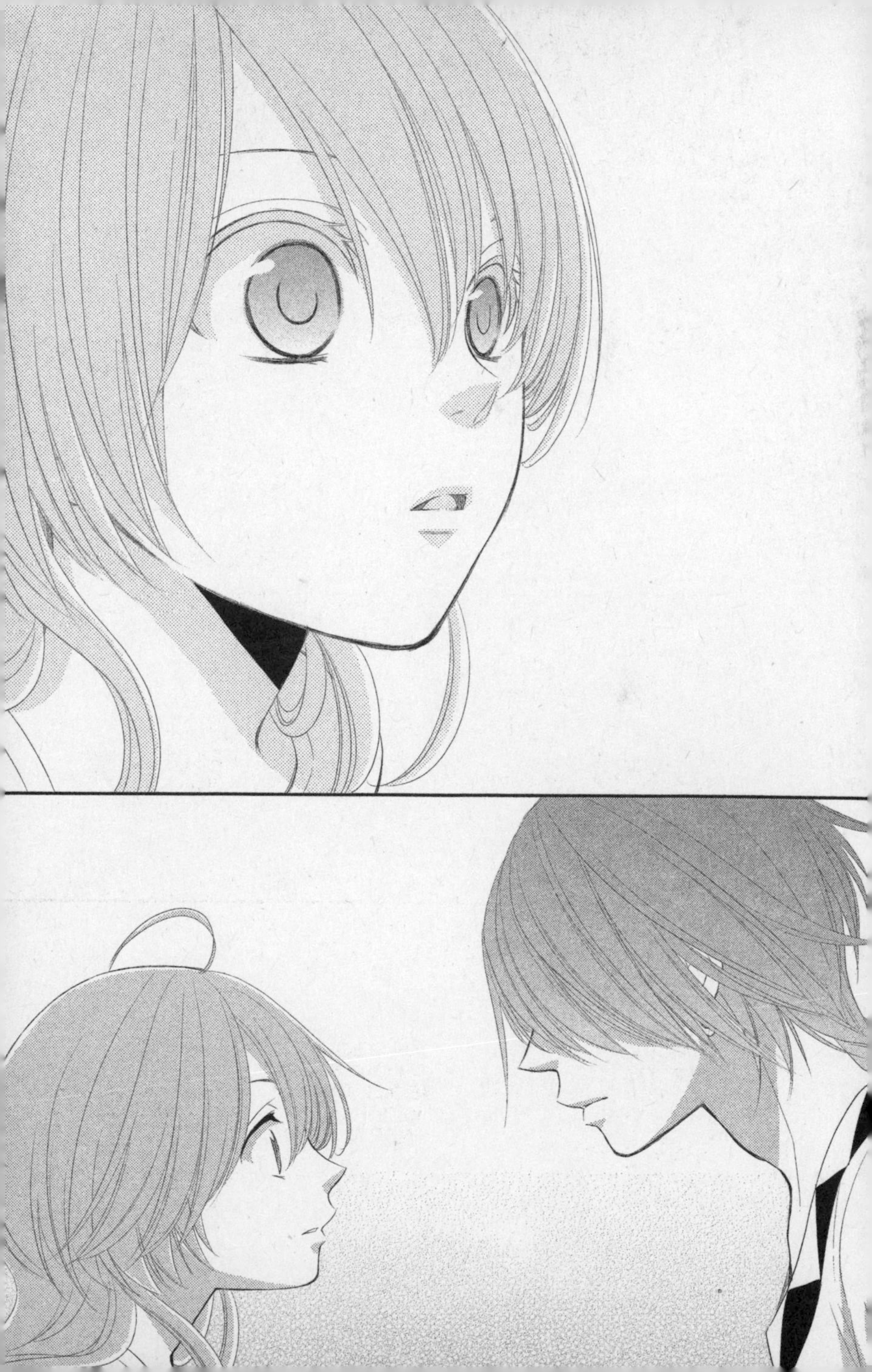

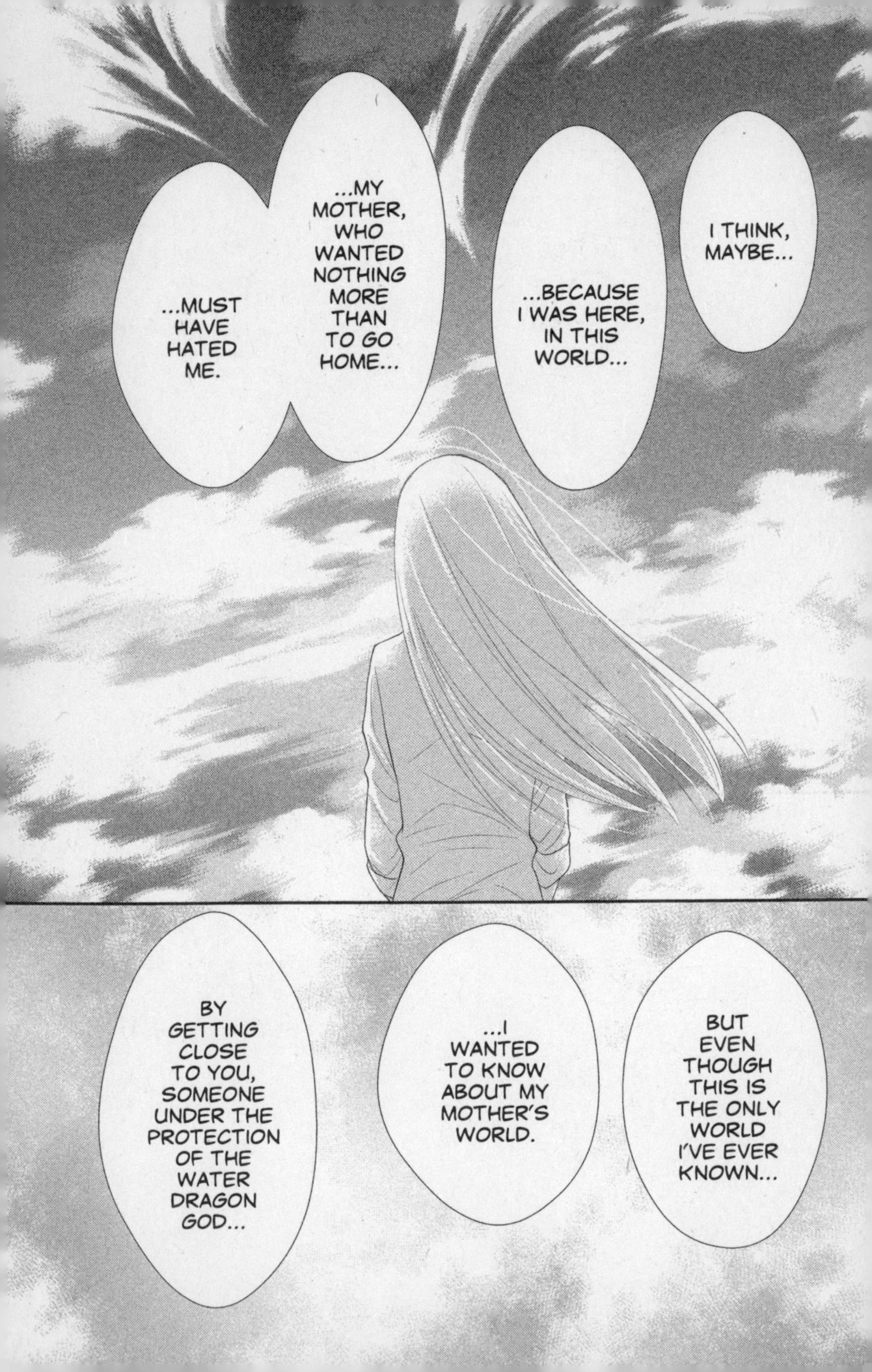
I THINK, MAYBE...
...BECAUSE I WAS HERE, IN THIS WORLD...
...MY MOTHER, WHO WANTED NOTHING MORE THAN TO GO HOME...
...MUST HAVE HATED ME.
BUT EVEN THOUGH THIS IS THE ONLY WORLD I'VE EVER KNOWN...
...I WANTED TO KNOW ABOUT MY MOTHER'S WORLD.
BY GETTING CLOSE TO YOU, SOMEONE UNDER THE PROTECTION OF THE WATER DRAGON GOD...

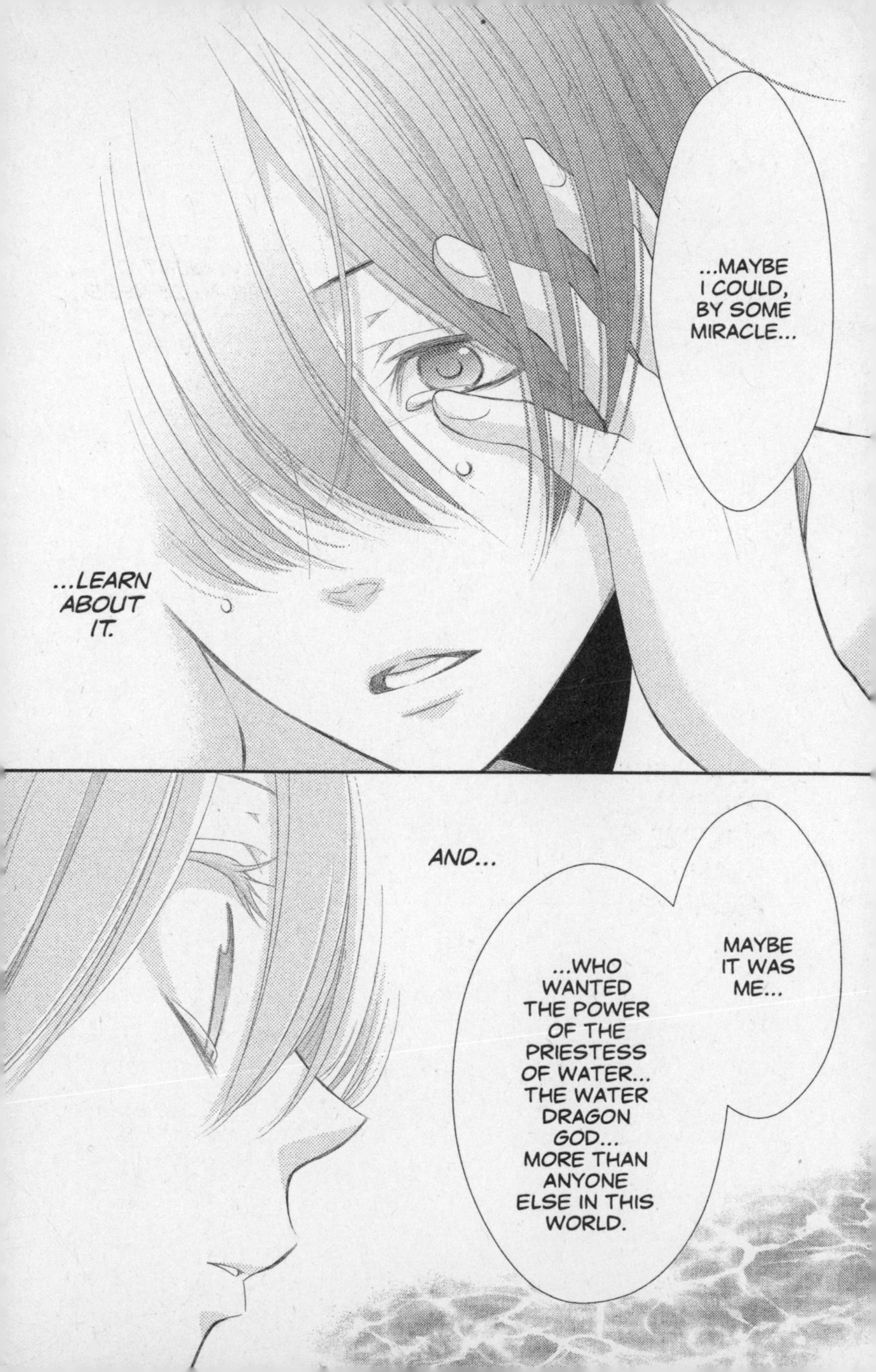
...MAYBE I COULD, BY SOME MIRACLE...
...LEARN ABOUT IT.
AND...
MAYBE IT WAS ME...
...WHO WANTED THE POWER OF THE PRIESTESS OF WATER... THE WATER DRAGON GOD... MORE THAN ANYONE ELSE IN THIS WORLD.

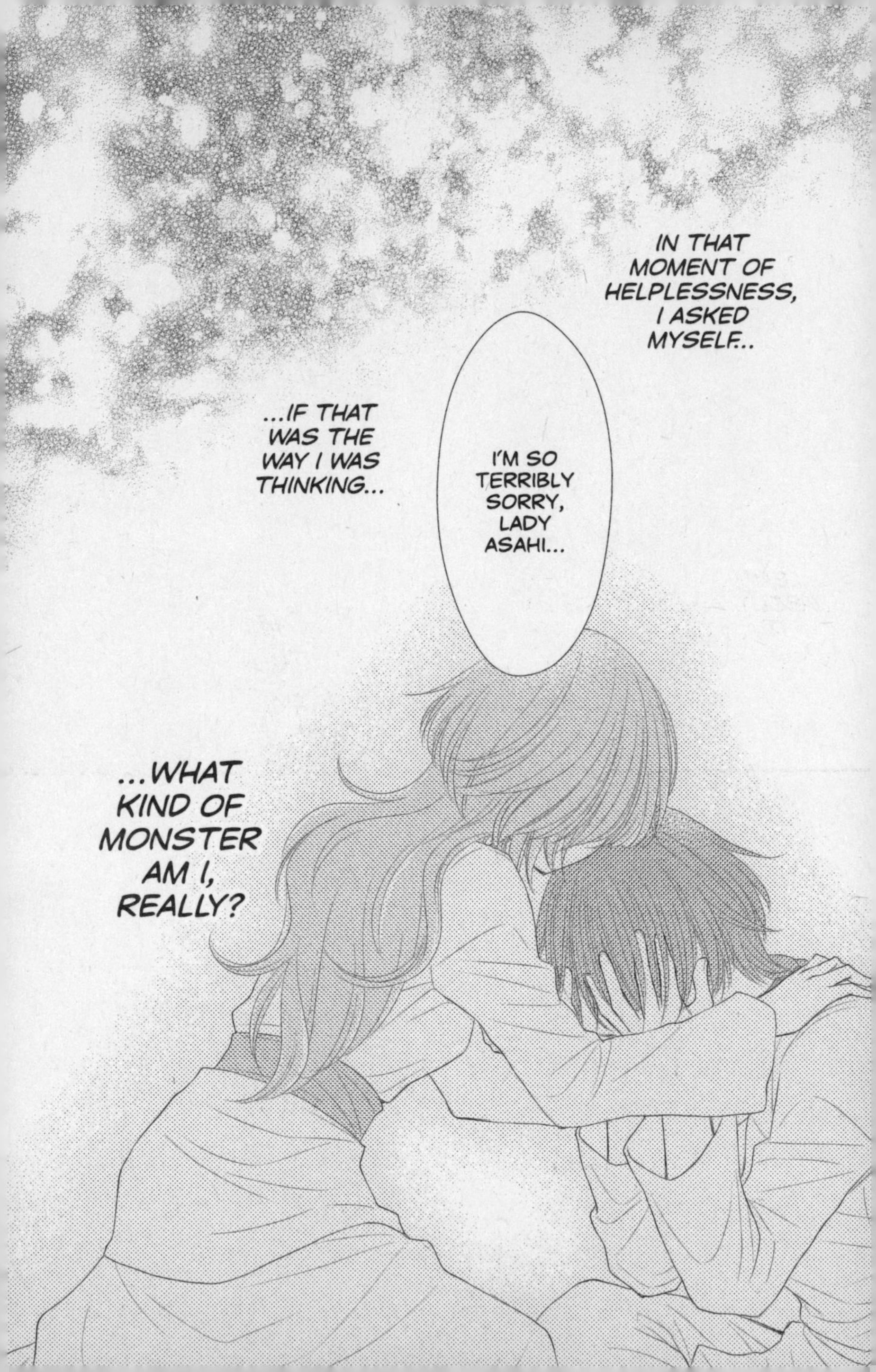
IN THAT MOMENT OF HELPLESSNESS, I ASKED MYSELF...
I'M SO TERRIBLY SORRY, LADY ASAHI...
...IF THAT WAS THE WAY I WAS THINKING...
...WHAT KIND OF MONSTER AM I, REALLY?

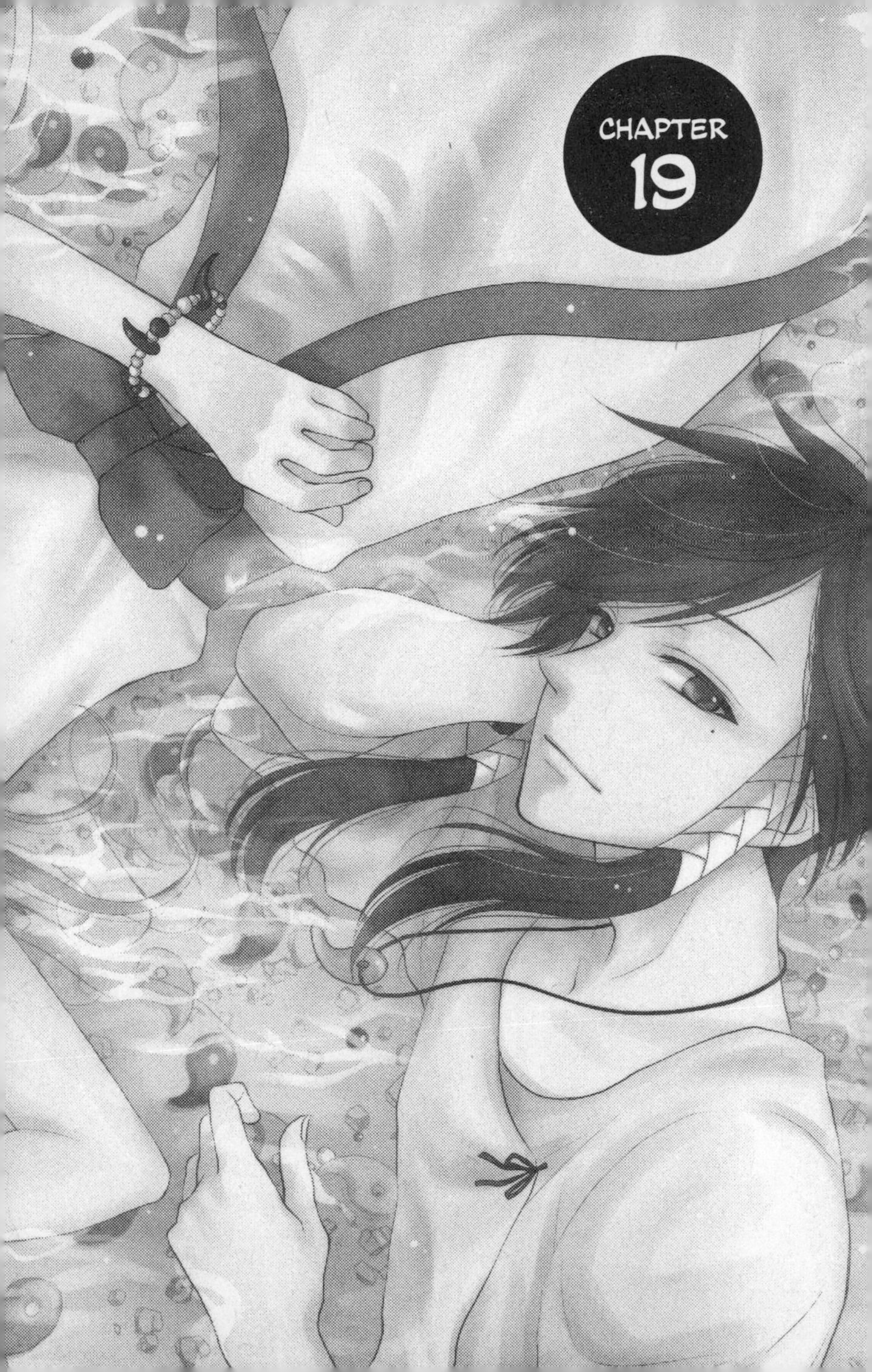
CHAPTER
19

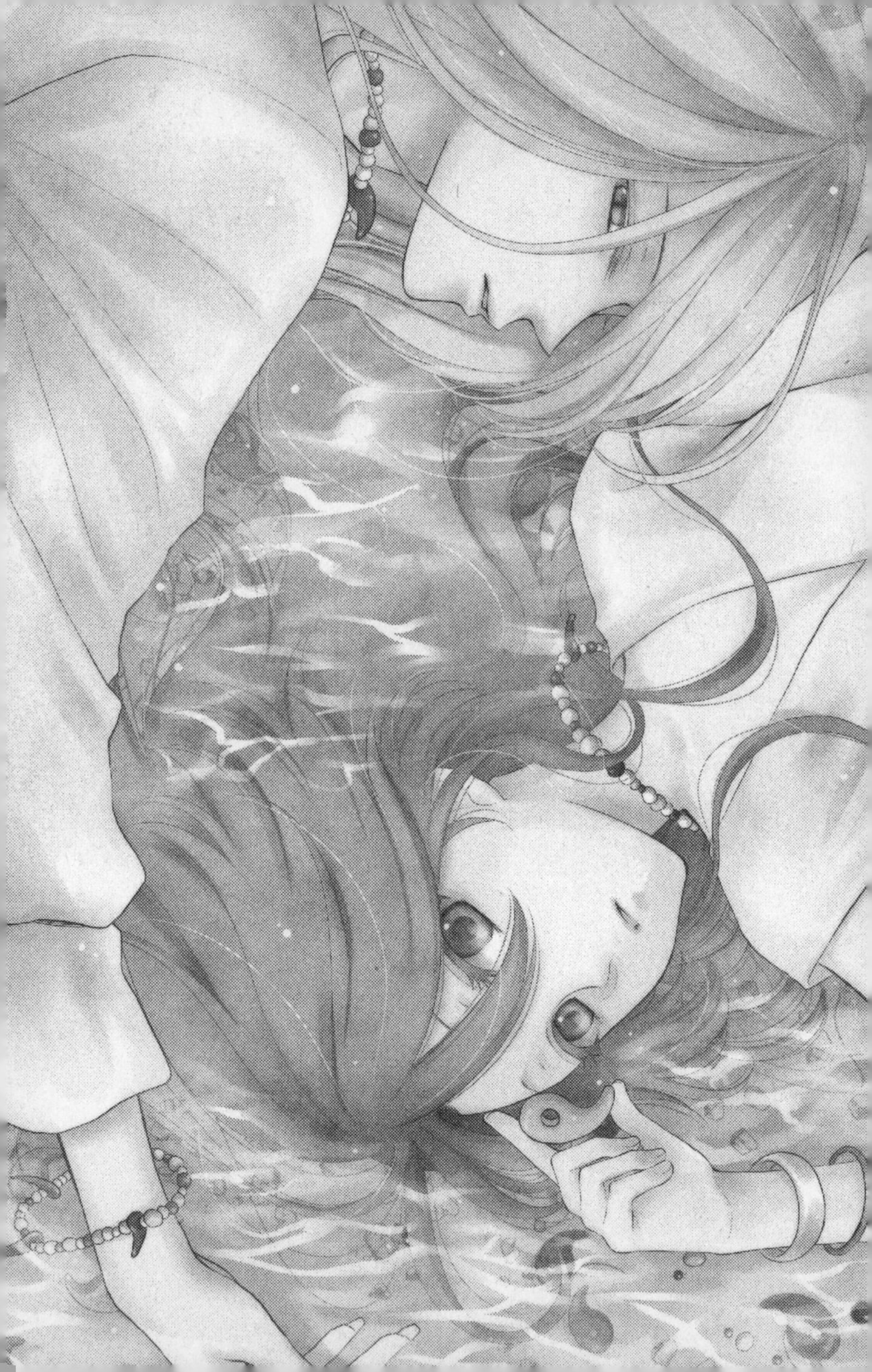

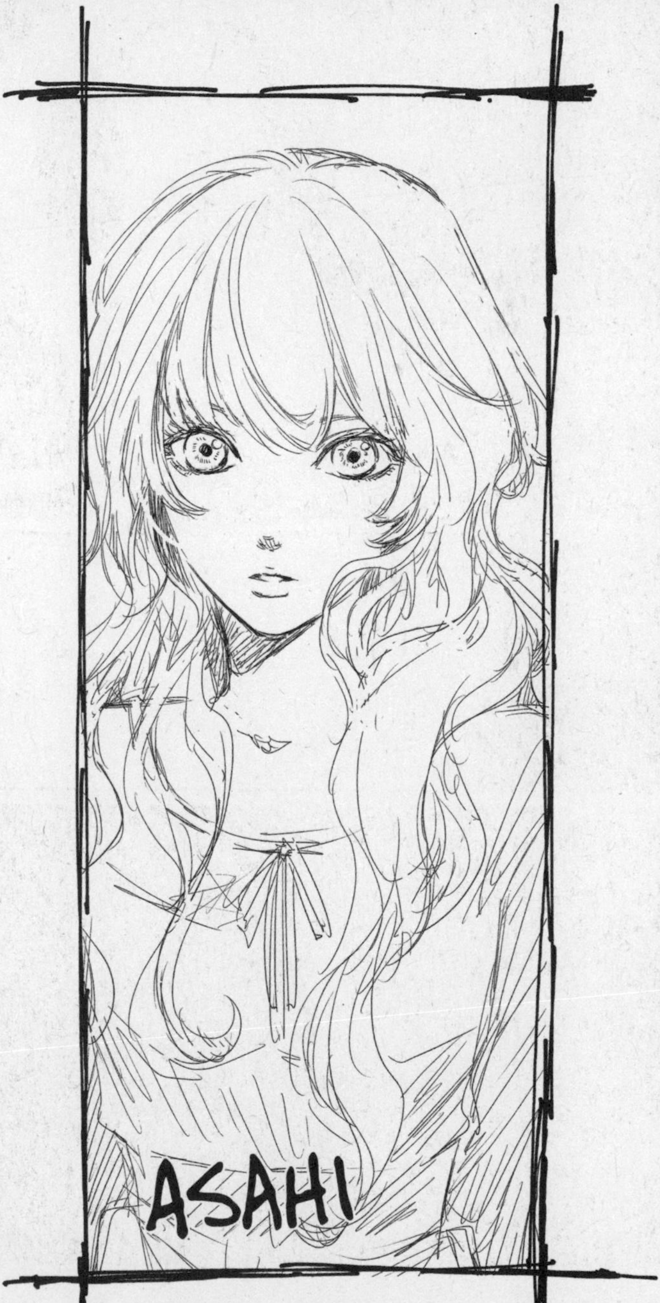
ASAHI

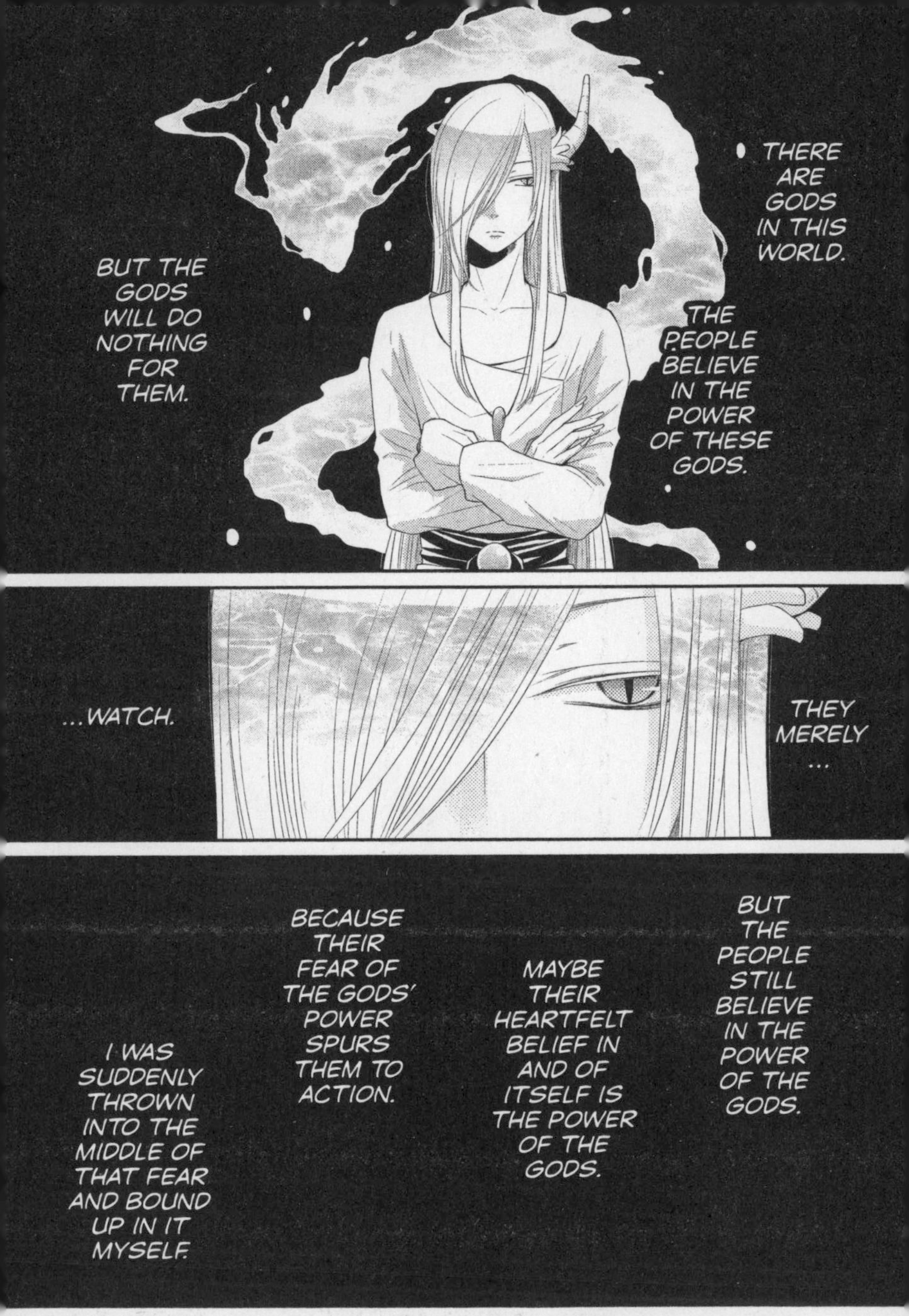
THERE ARE GODS IN THIS WORLD.
THE PEOPLE BELIEVE IN THE POWER OF THESE GODS.
BUT THE GODS WILL DO NOTHING FOR THEM.
THEY MERELY ...
...WATCH.
BUT THE PEOPLE STILL BELIEVE IN THE POWER OF THE GODS.
MAYBE THEIR HEARTFELT BELIEF IN AND OF ITSELF IS THE POWER OF THE GODS.
BECAUSE THEIR FEAR OF THE GODS' POWER SPURS THEM TO ACTION.
I WAS SUDDENLY THROWN INTO THE MIDDLE OF THAT FEAR AND BOUND UP IN IT MYSELF.

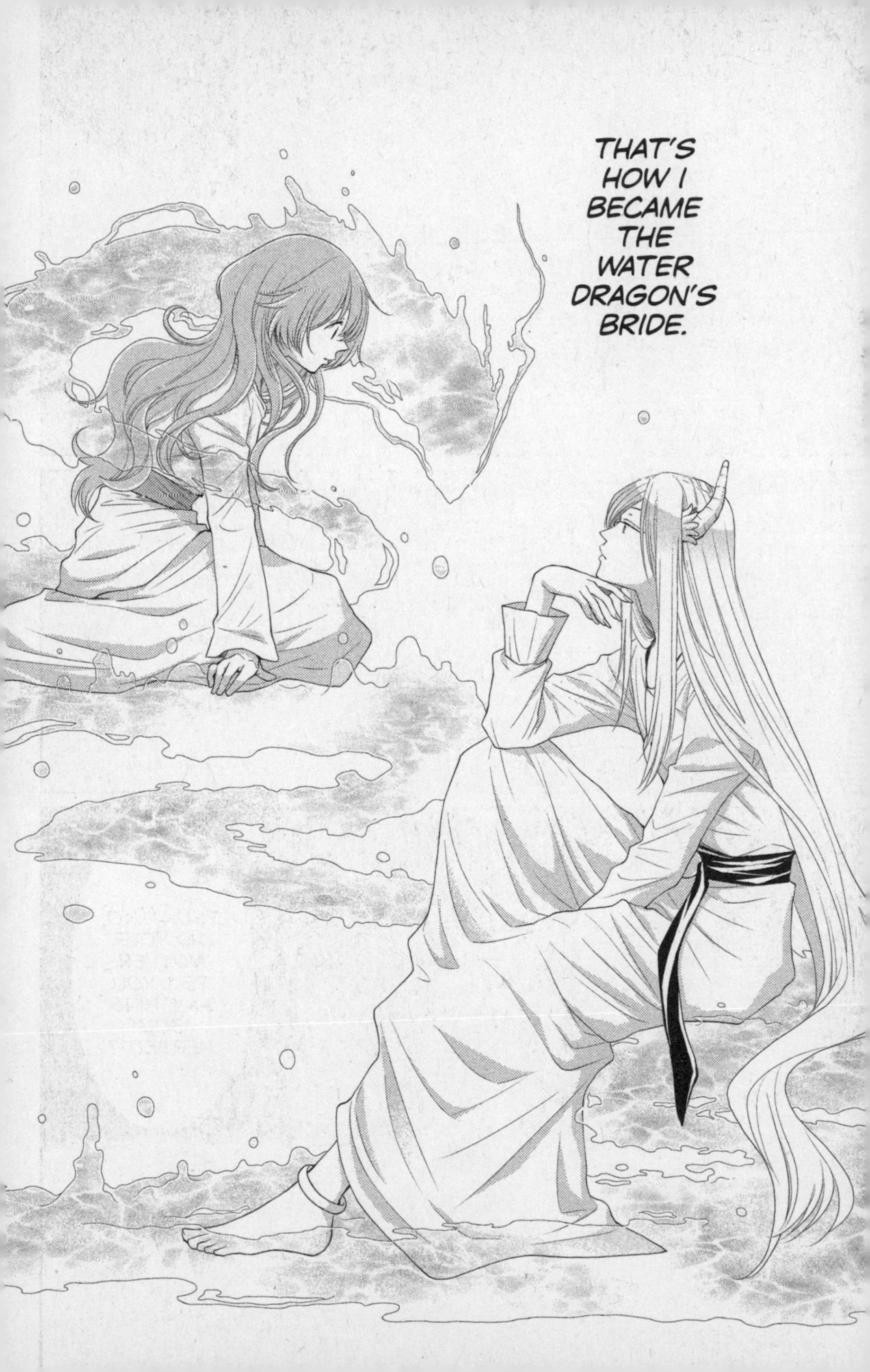
THAT'S HOW I BECAME THE WATER DRAGON'S BRIDE.

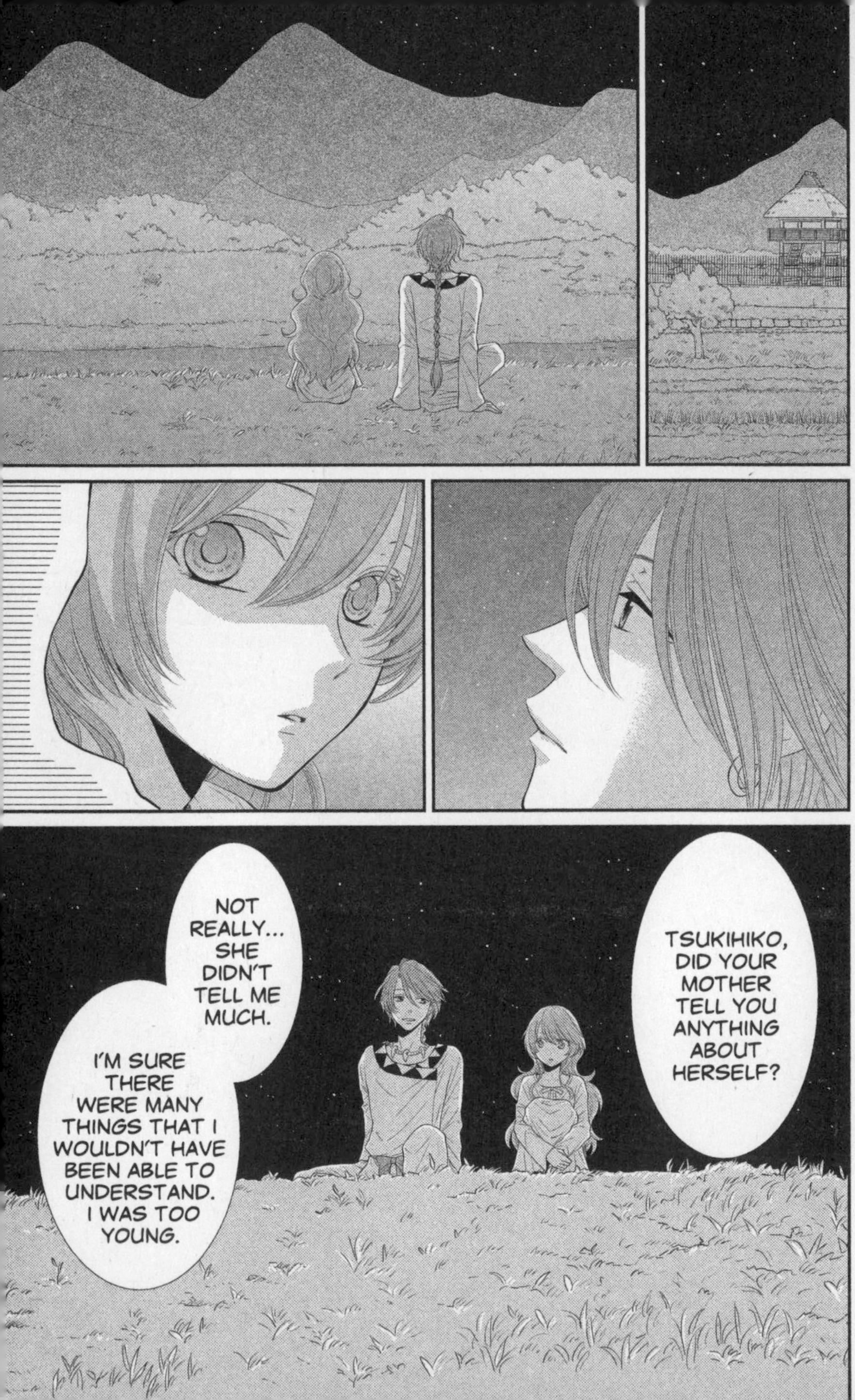
TSUKIHIKO, DID YOUR MOTHER TELL YOU ANYTHING ABOUT HERSELF?
NOT REALLY... SHE DIDN'T TELL ME MUCH.
I'M SURE THERE WERE MANY THINGS THAT I WOULDN'T HAVE BEEN ABLE TO UNDERSTAND. I WAS TOO YOUNG.

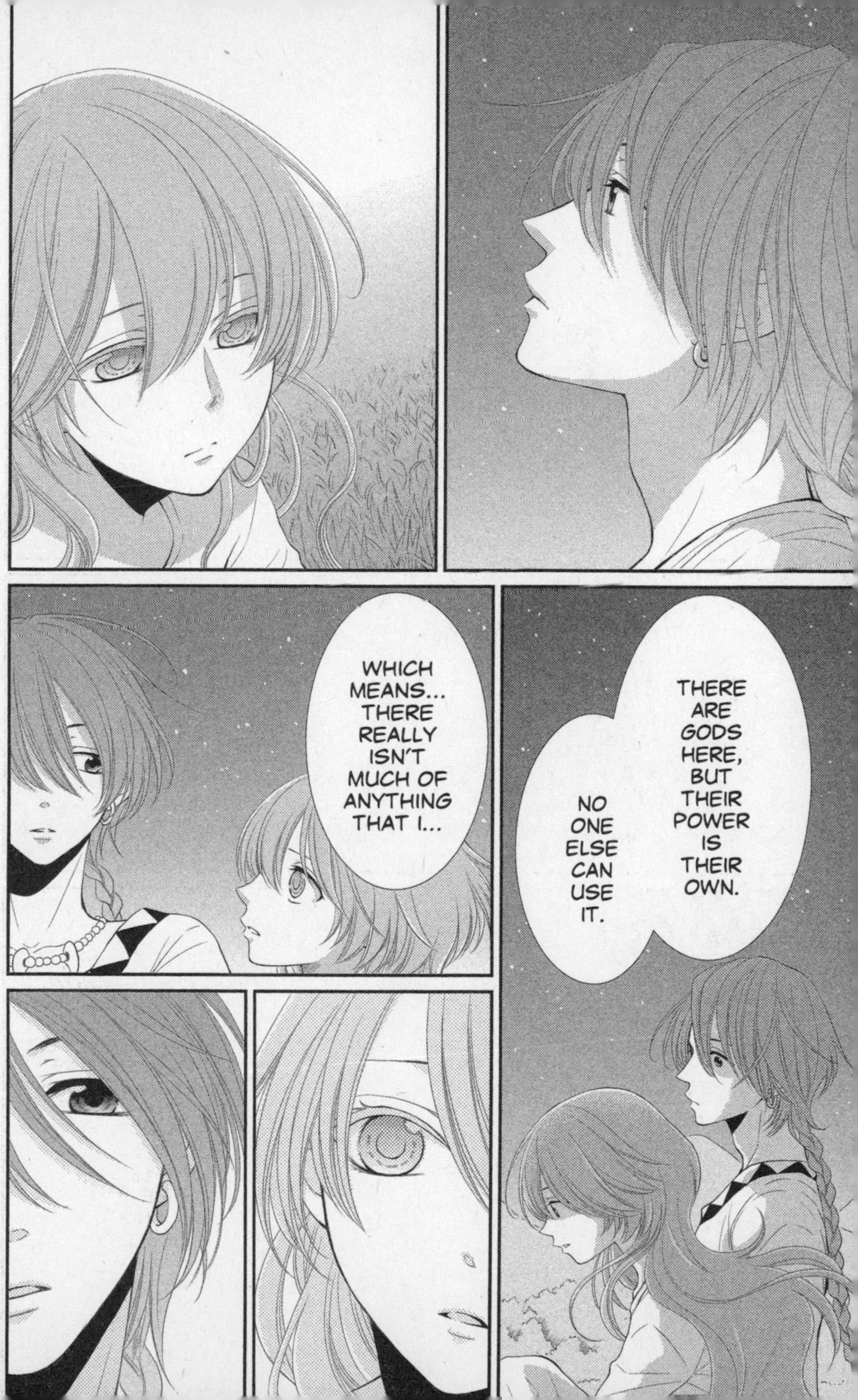
THERE ARE GODS HERE, BUT THEIR POWER IS THEIR OWN.
NO ONE ELSE CAN USE IT.
WHICH MEANS... THERE REALLY ISN'T MUCH OF ANYTHING THAT I...

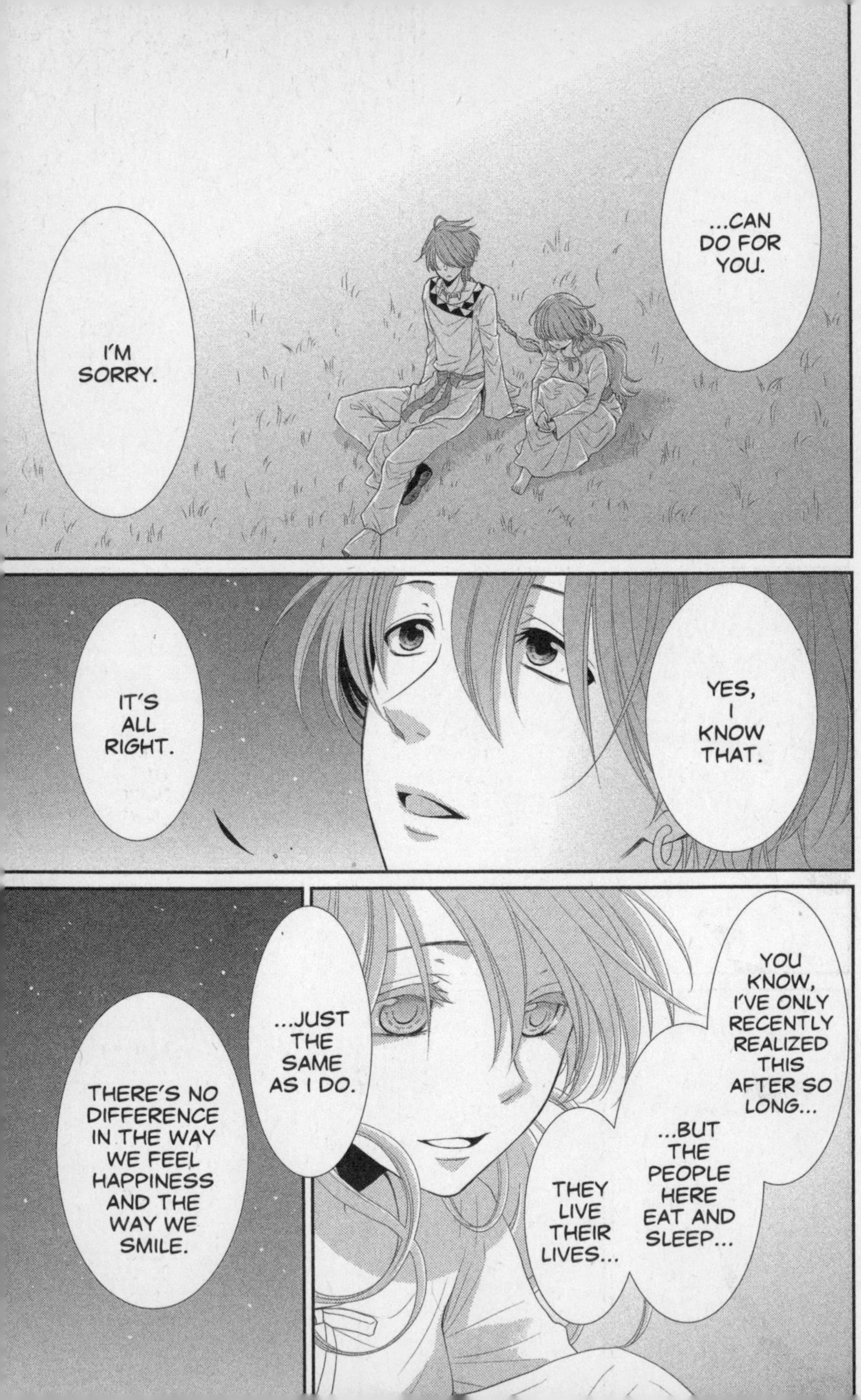
...CAN DO FOR YOU.
I'M SORRY.
YES, I KNOW THAT.
IT'S ALL RIGHT.
YOU KNOW, I'VE ONLY RECENTLY REALIZED THIS AFTER SO LONG...
...BUT THE PEOPLE HERE EAT AND SLEEP...
THEY LIVE THEIR LIVES...
...JUST THE SAME AS I DO.
THERE'S NO DIFFERENCE IN THE WAY WE FEEL HAPPINESS AND THE WAY WE SMILE.

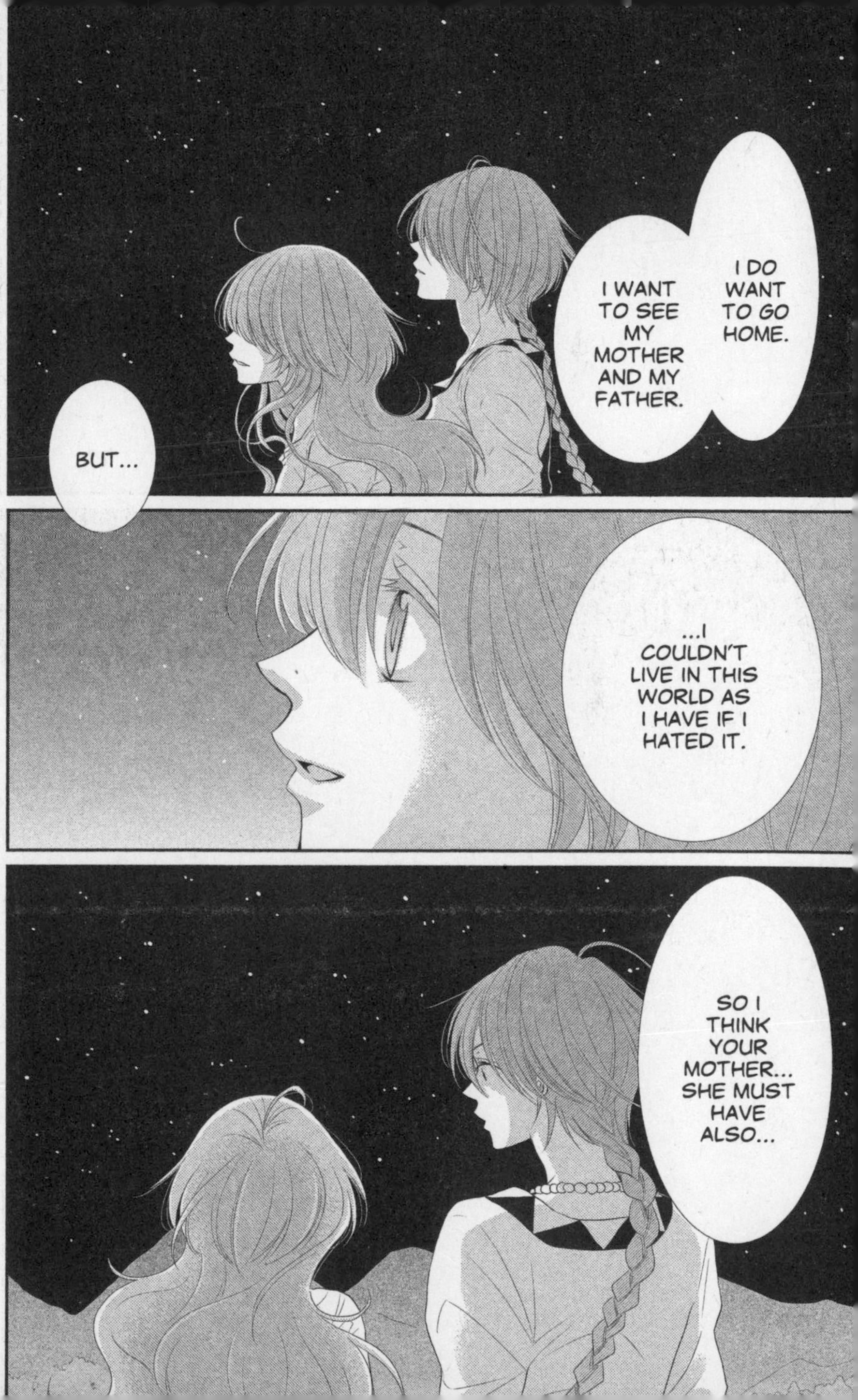
I DO WANT TO GO HOME.
I WANT TO SEE MY MOTHER AND MY FATHER.
BUT...
...I COULDN'T LIVE IN THIS WORLD AS I HAVE IF I HATED IT.
SO I THINK YOUR MOTHER... SHE MUST HAVE ALSO...

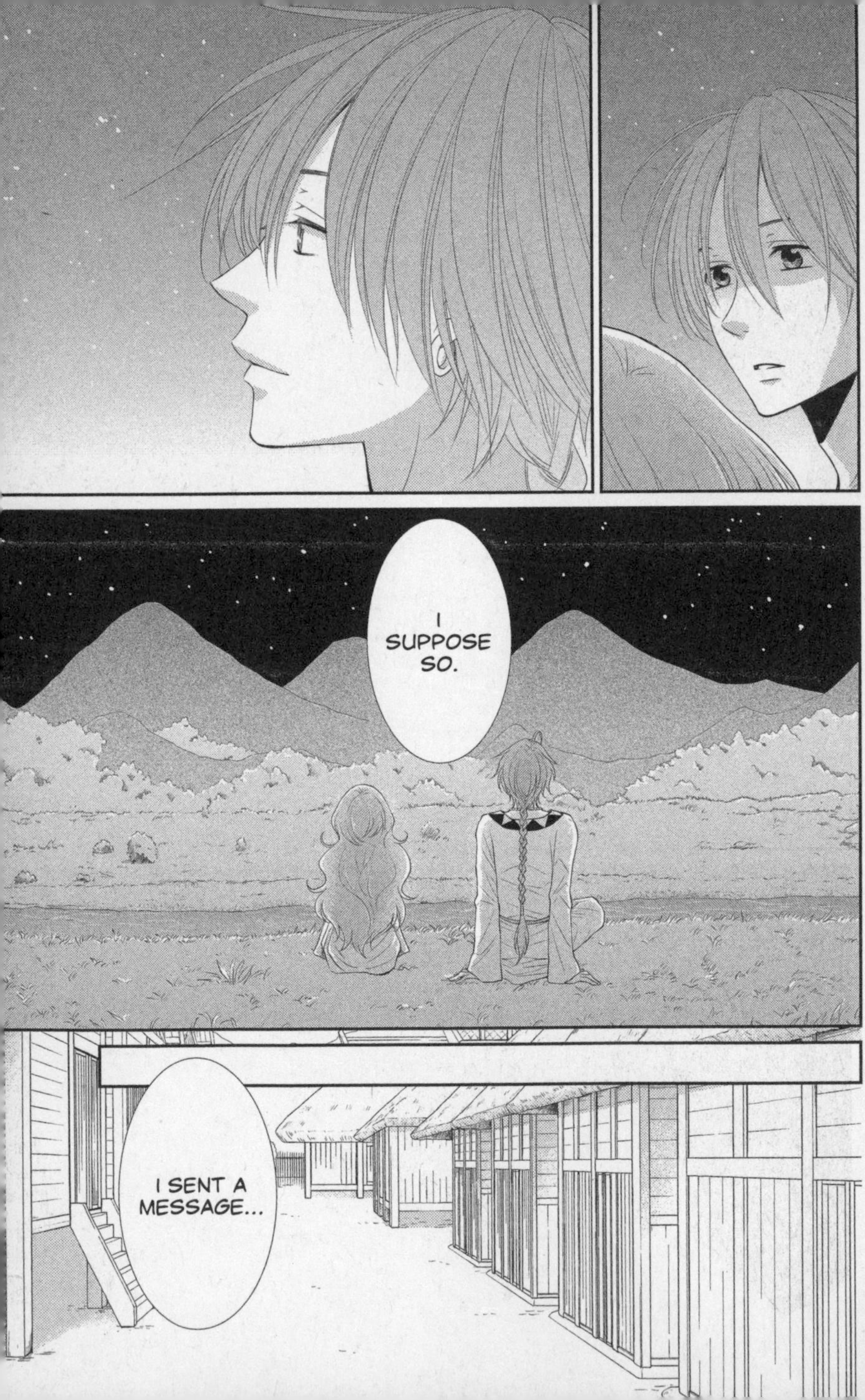
I SUPPOSE SO.
I SENT A MESSAGE...

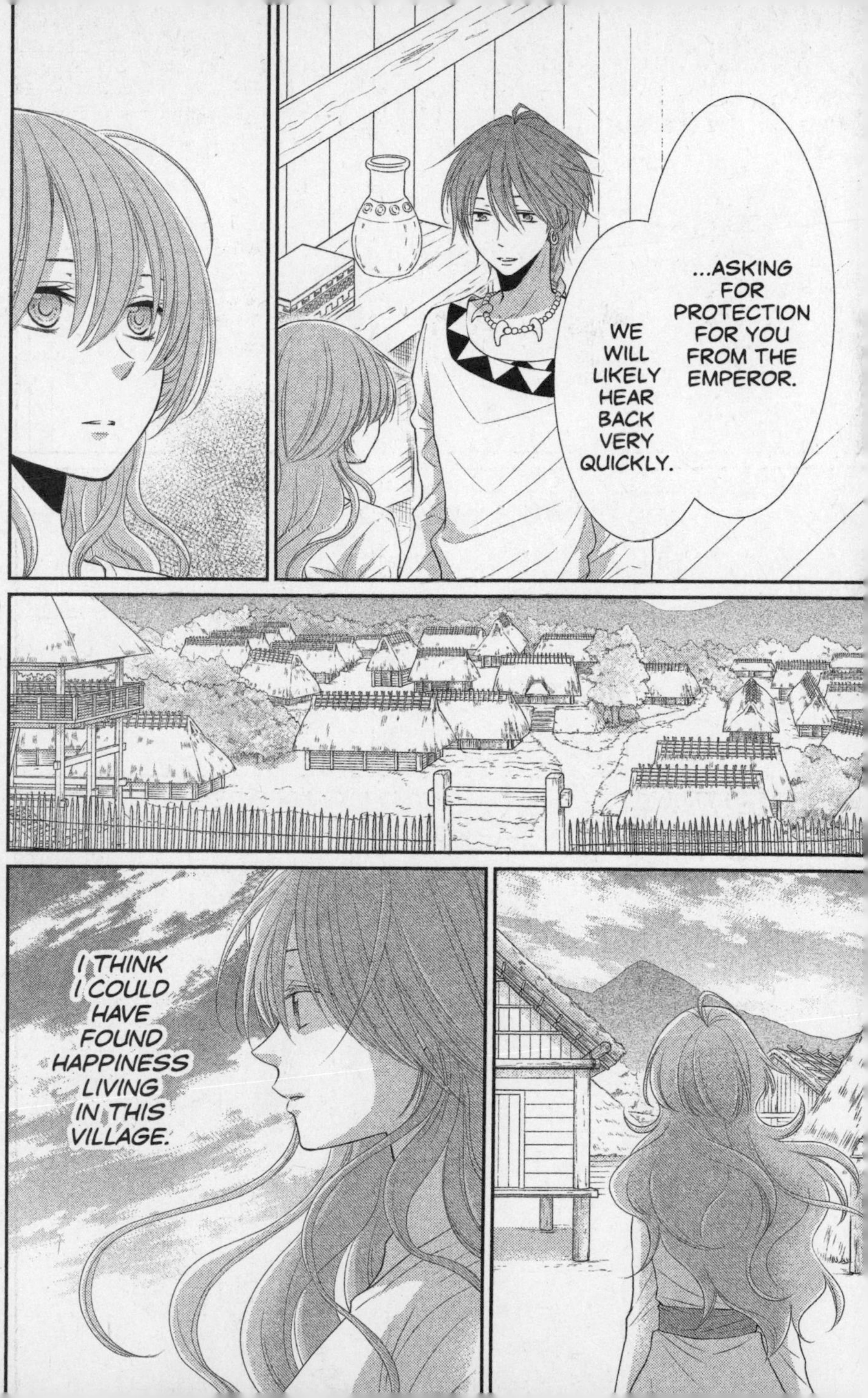
...ASKING FOR PROTECTION FOR YOU FROM THE EMPEROR.
WE WILL LIKELY HEAR BACK VERY QUICKLY.
I THINK I COULD HAVE FOUND HAPPINESS LIVING IN THIS VILLAGE.

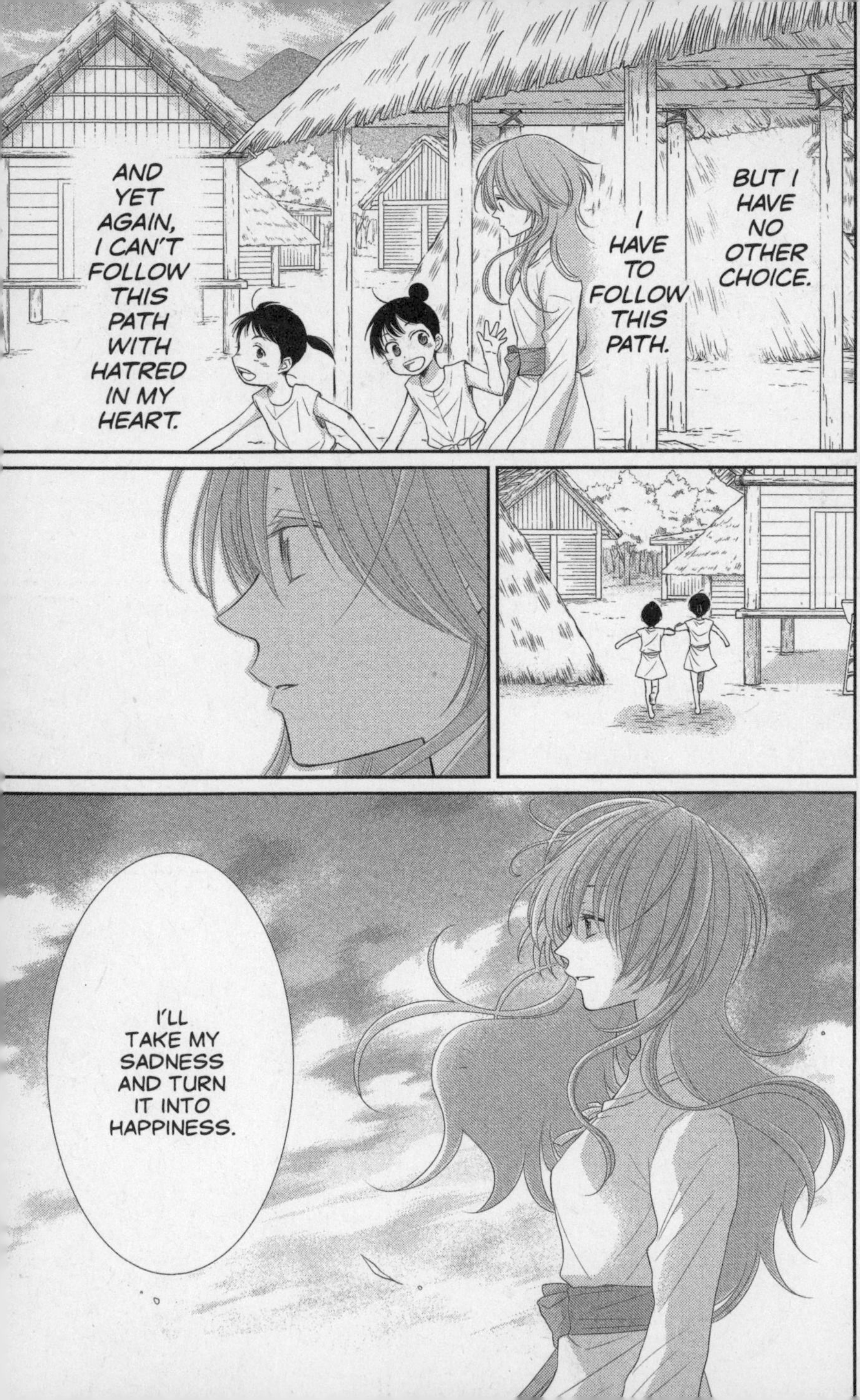
BUT I HAVE NO OTHER CHOICE.
I HAVE TO FOLLOW THIS PATH.
AND YET AGAIN, I CAN'T FOLLOW THIS PATH WITH HATRED IN MY HEART.
I'LL TAKE MY SADNESS AND TURN IT INTO HAPPINESS.

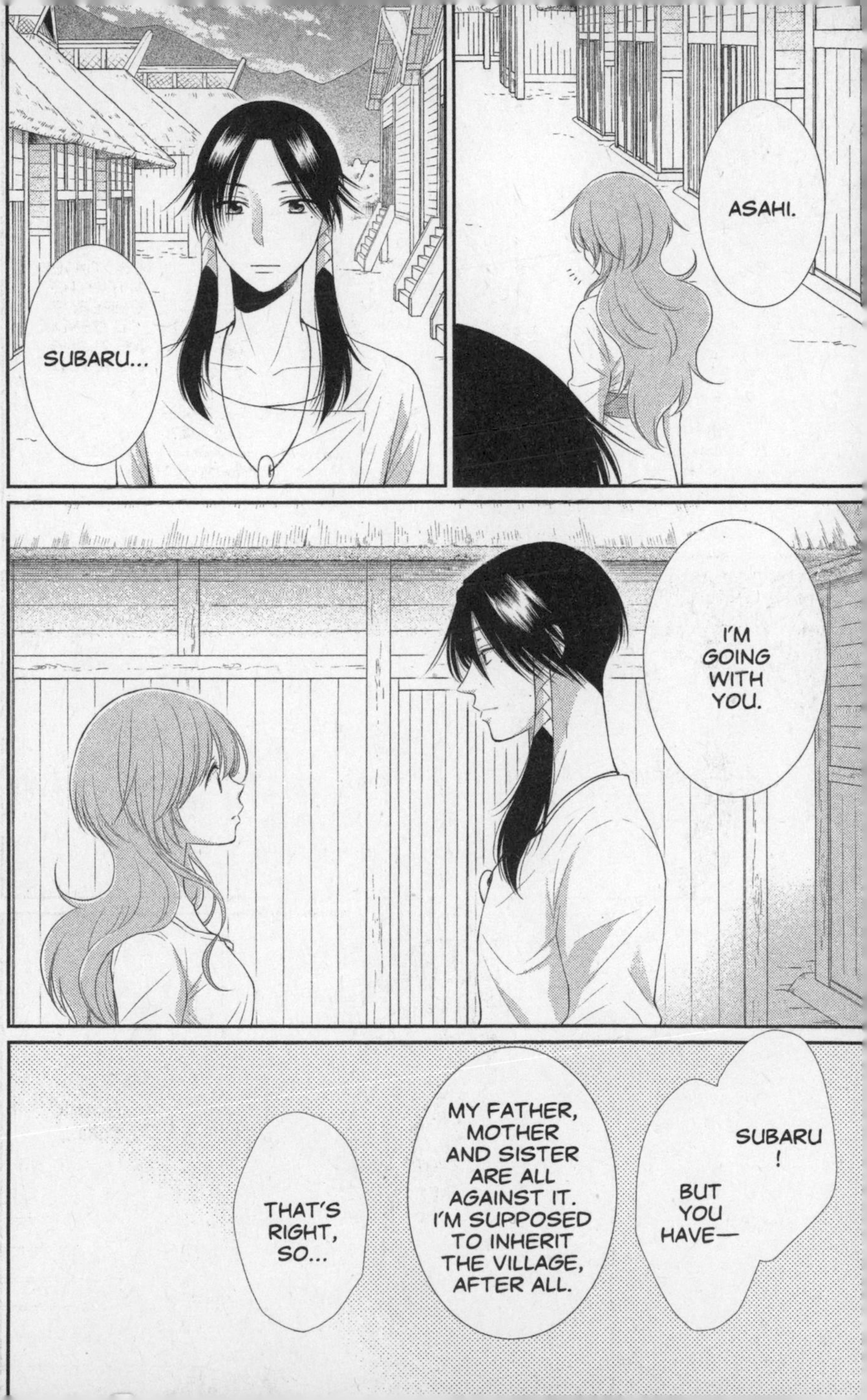
ASAHI.
SUBARU...
I'M GOING WITH YOU.
SUBARU!
BUT YOU HAVE—
MY FATHER, MOTHER AND SISTER ARE ALL AGAINST IT. I'M SUPPOSED TO INHERIT THE VILLAGE, AFTER ALL.
THAT'S RIGHT, SO...

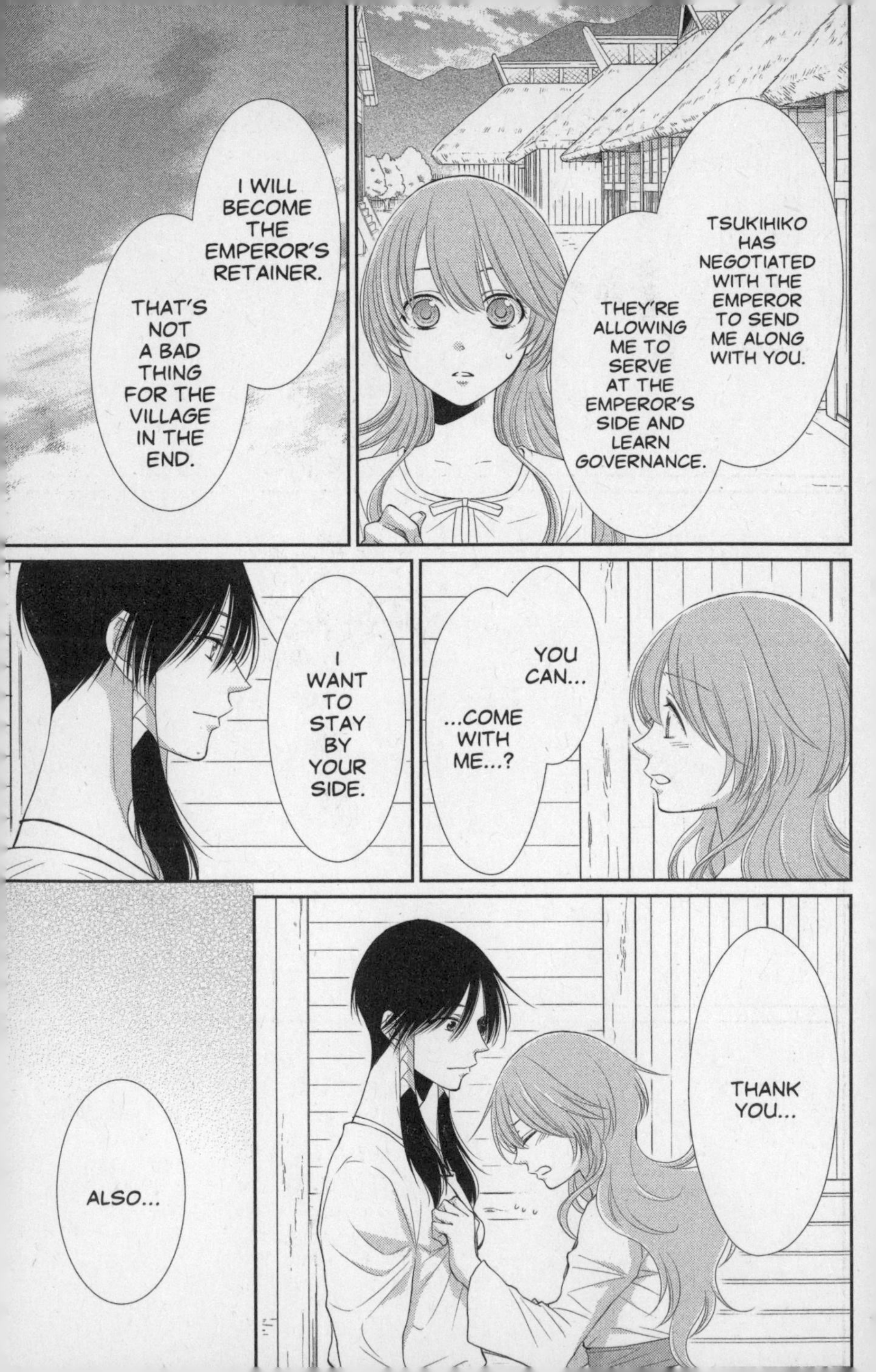
TSUKIHIKO HAS NEGOTIATED WITH THE EMPEROR TO SEND ME ALONG WITH YOU.
THEY'RE ALLOWING ME TO SERVE AT THE EMPEROR'S SIDE AND LEARN GOVERNANCE.
I WILL BECOME THE EMPEROR'S RETAINER.
THAT'S NOT A BAD THING FOR THE VILLAGE IN THE END.
YOU CAN...
...COME WITH ME...?
I WANT TO STAY BY YOUR SIDE.
THANK YOU...
ALSO...

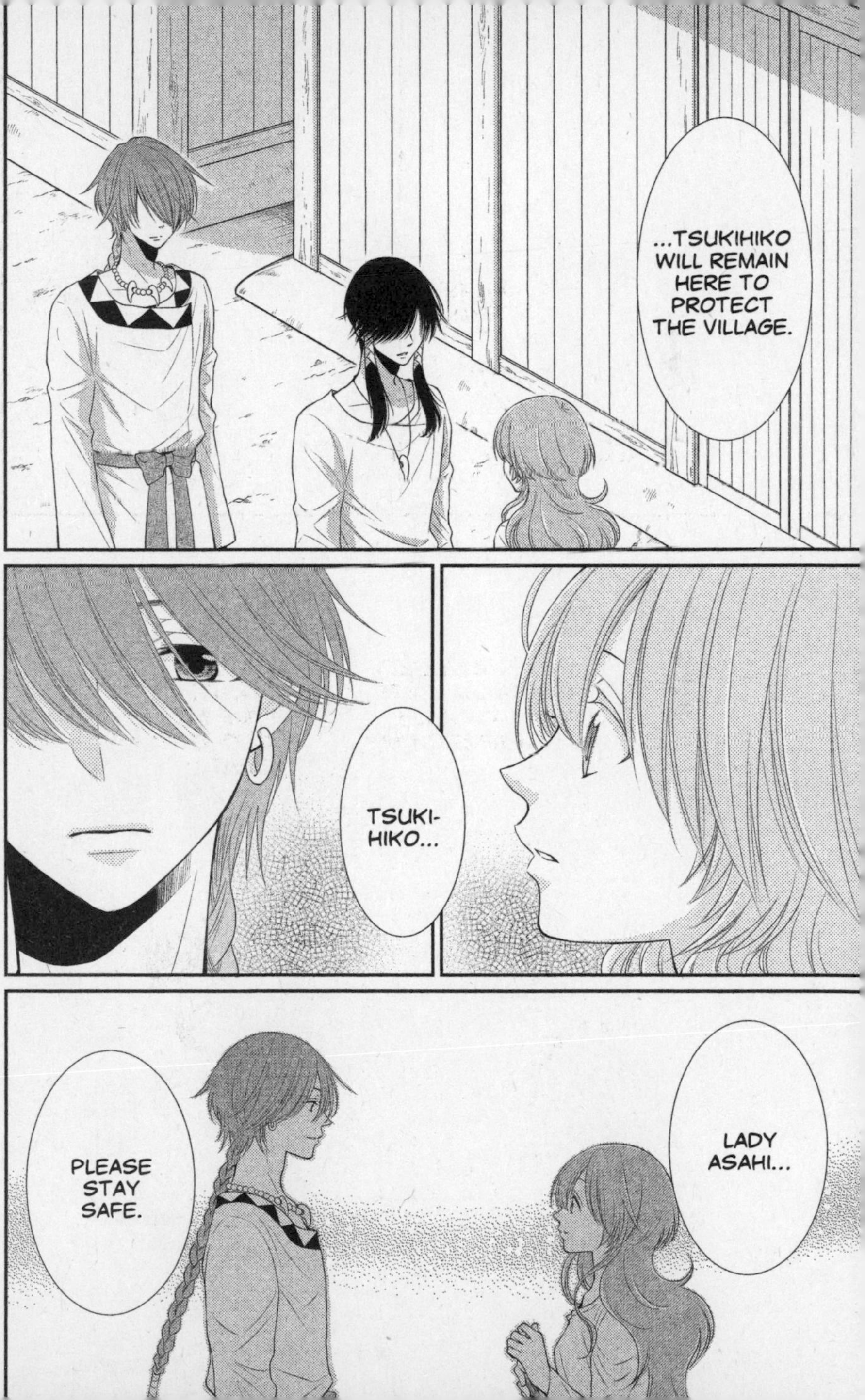
...TSUKIHIKO WILL REMAIN HERE TO PROTECT THE VILLAGE.
TSUKI-HIKO...
LADY ASAHI...
PLEASE STAY SAFE.

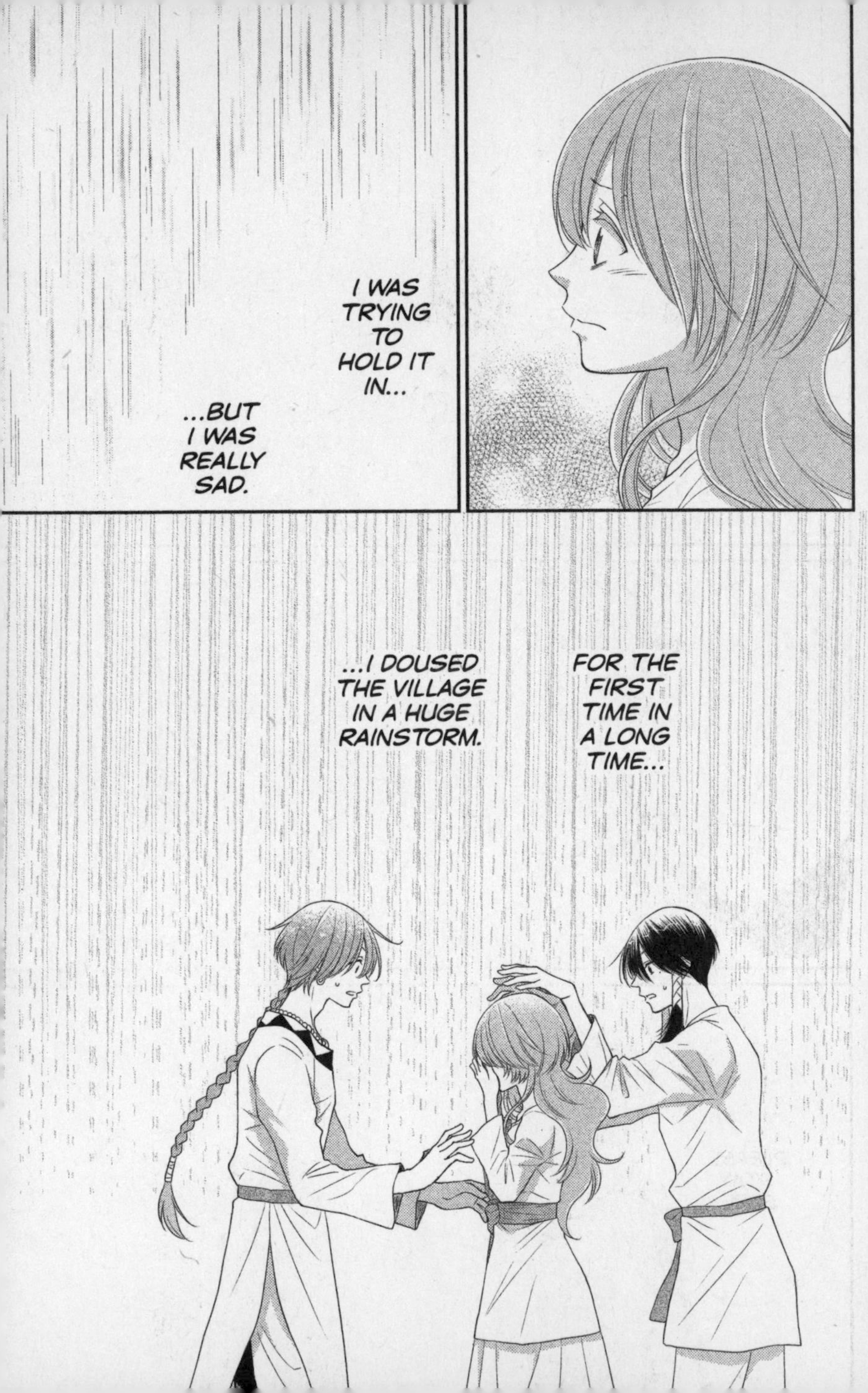
I WAS TRYING TO HOLD IT IN...
...BUT I WAS REALLY SAD.
FOR THE FIRST TIME IN A LONG TIME...
...I DOUSED THE VILLAGE IN A HUGE RAINSTORM.

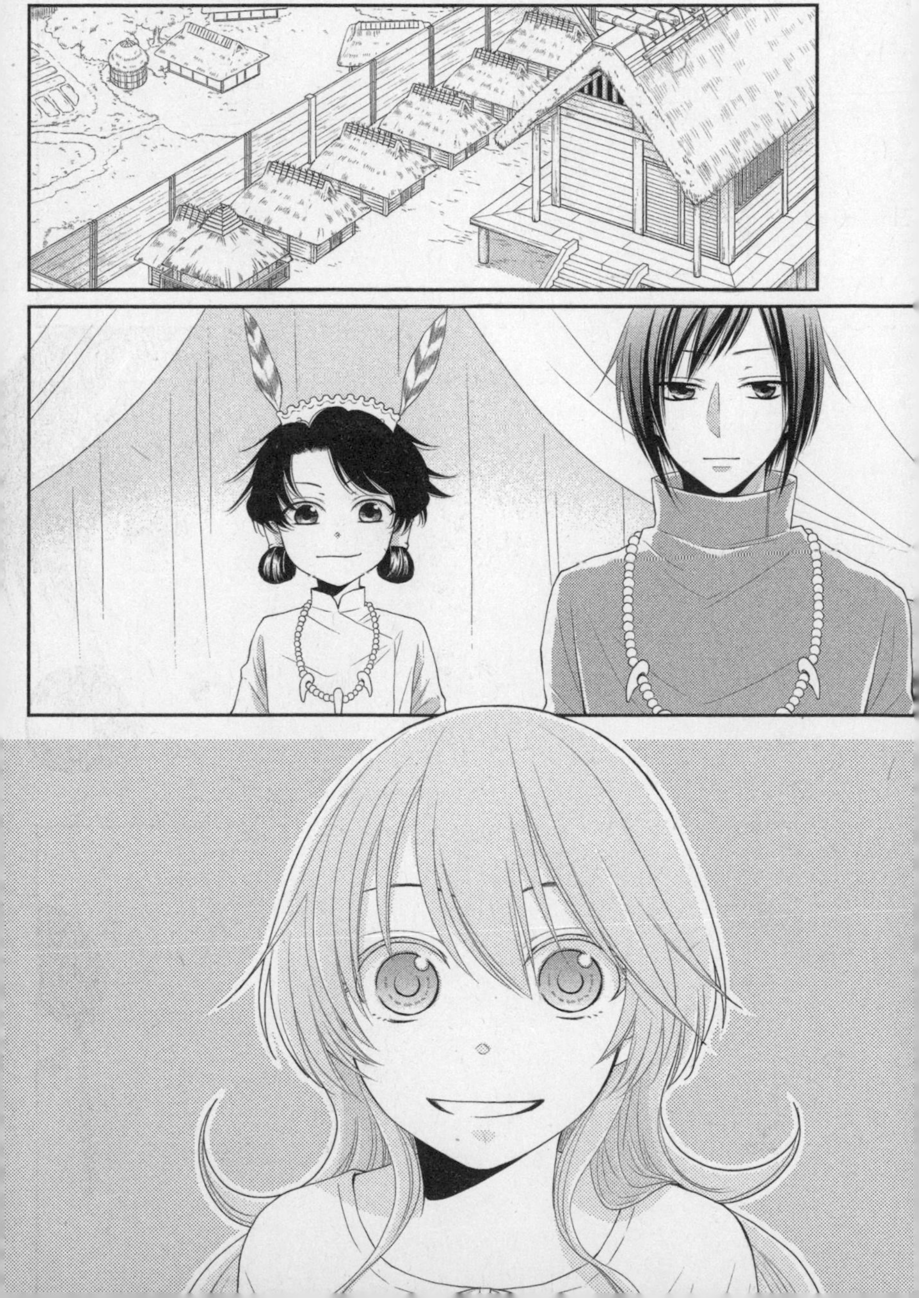

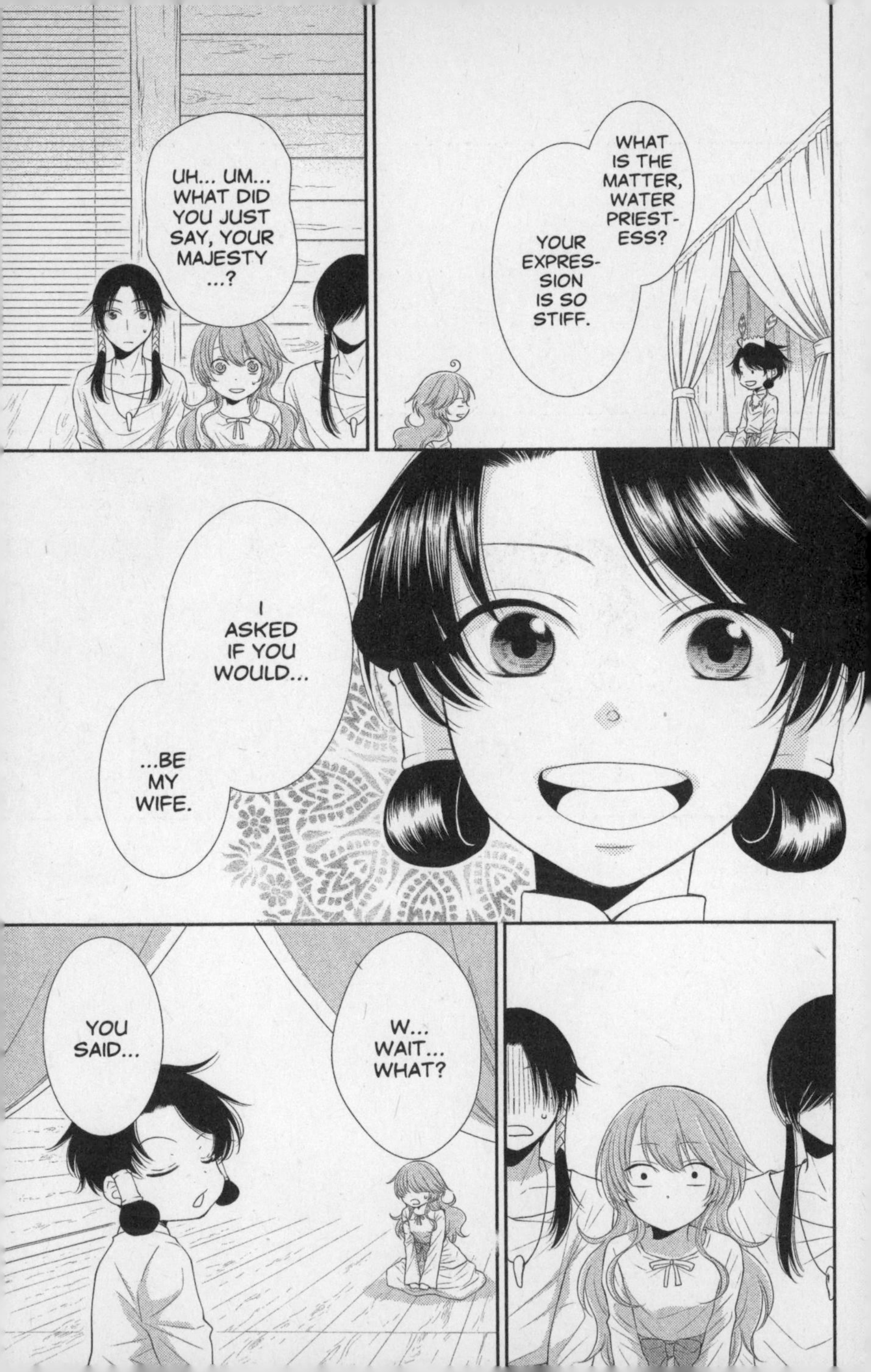
WHAT IS THE MATTER, WATER PRIEST-ESS?
YOUR EXPRES-SION IS SO STIFF.
UH... UM... WHAT DID YOU JUST SAY, YOUR MAJESTY ...?
I ASKED IF YOU WOULD...
...BE MY WIFE.
W... WAIT... WHAT?
YOU SAID...

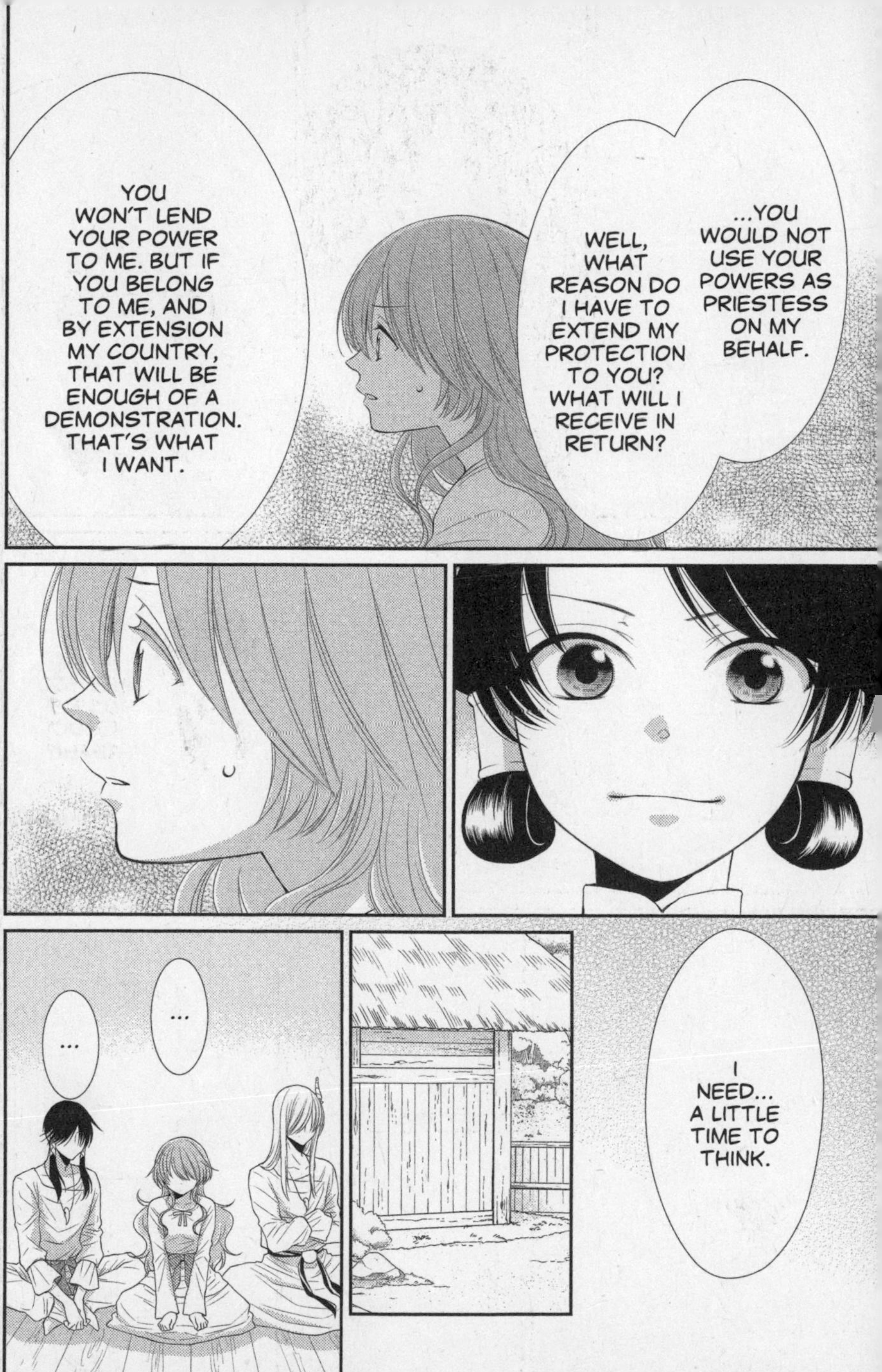
...YOU WOULD NOT USE YOUR POWERS AS PRIESTESS ON MY BEHALF.
WELL, WHAT REASON DO I HAVE TO EXTEND MY PROTECTION TO YOU? WHAT WILL I RECEIVE IN RETURN?
YOU WON'T LEND YOUR POWER TO ME. BUT IF YOU BELONG TO ME, AND BY EXTENSION MY COUNTRY, THAT WILL BE ENOUGH OF A DEMONSTRATION. THAT'S WHAT I WANT.
I NEED... A LITTLE TIME TO THINK.
...
...

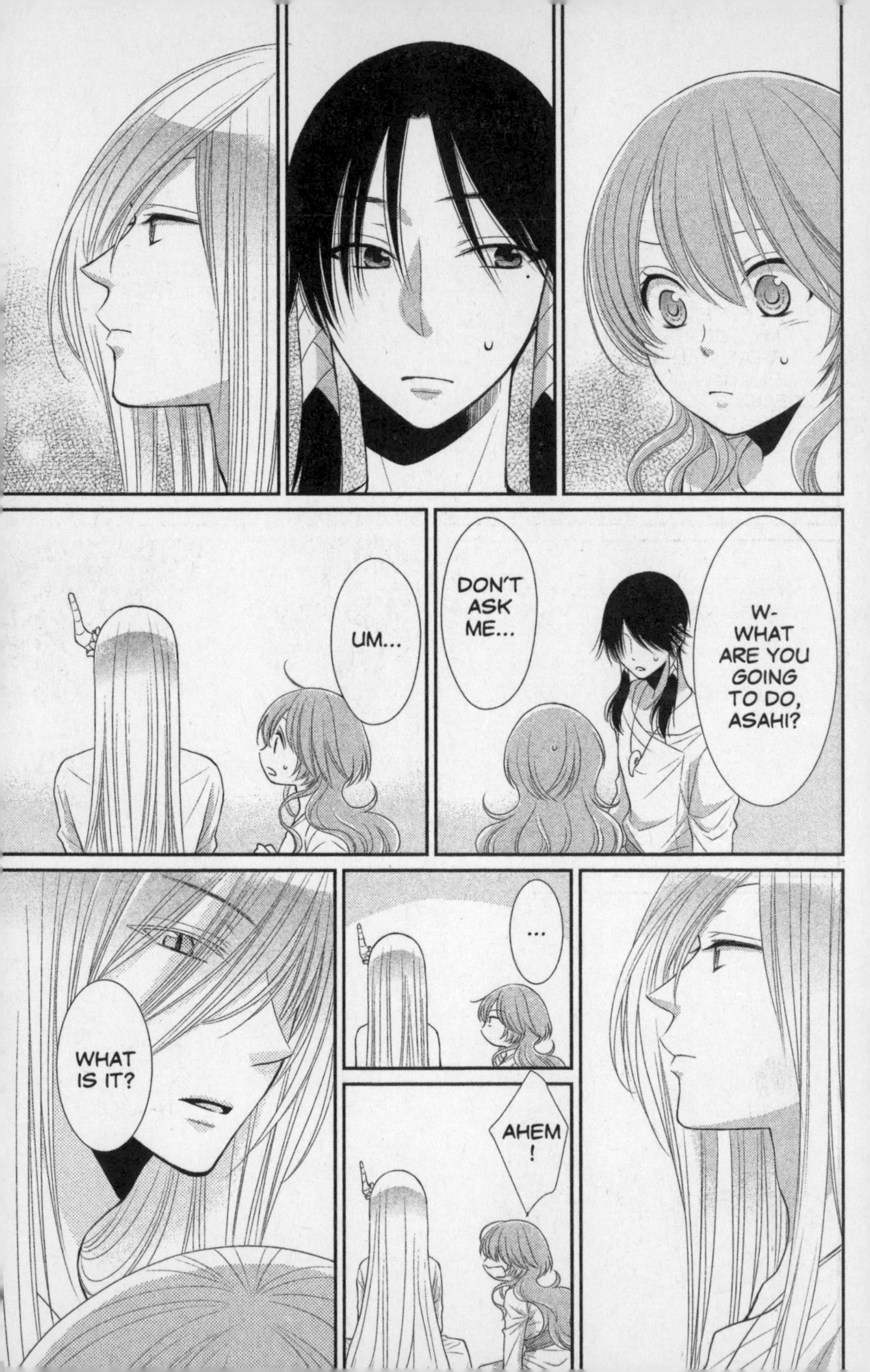
W- WHAT ARE YOU GOING TO DO, ASAHI?
DON'T ASK ME...
UM...
...
AHEM!
WHAT IS IT?

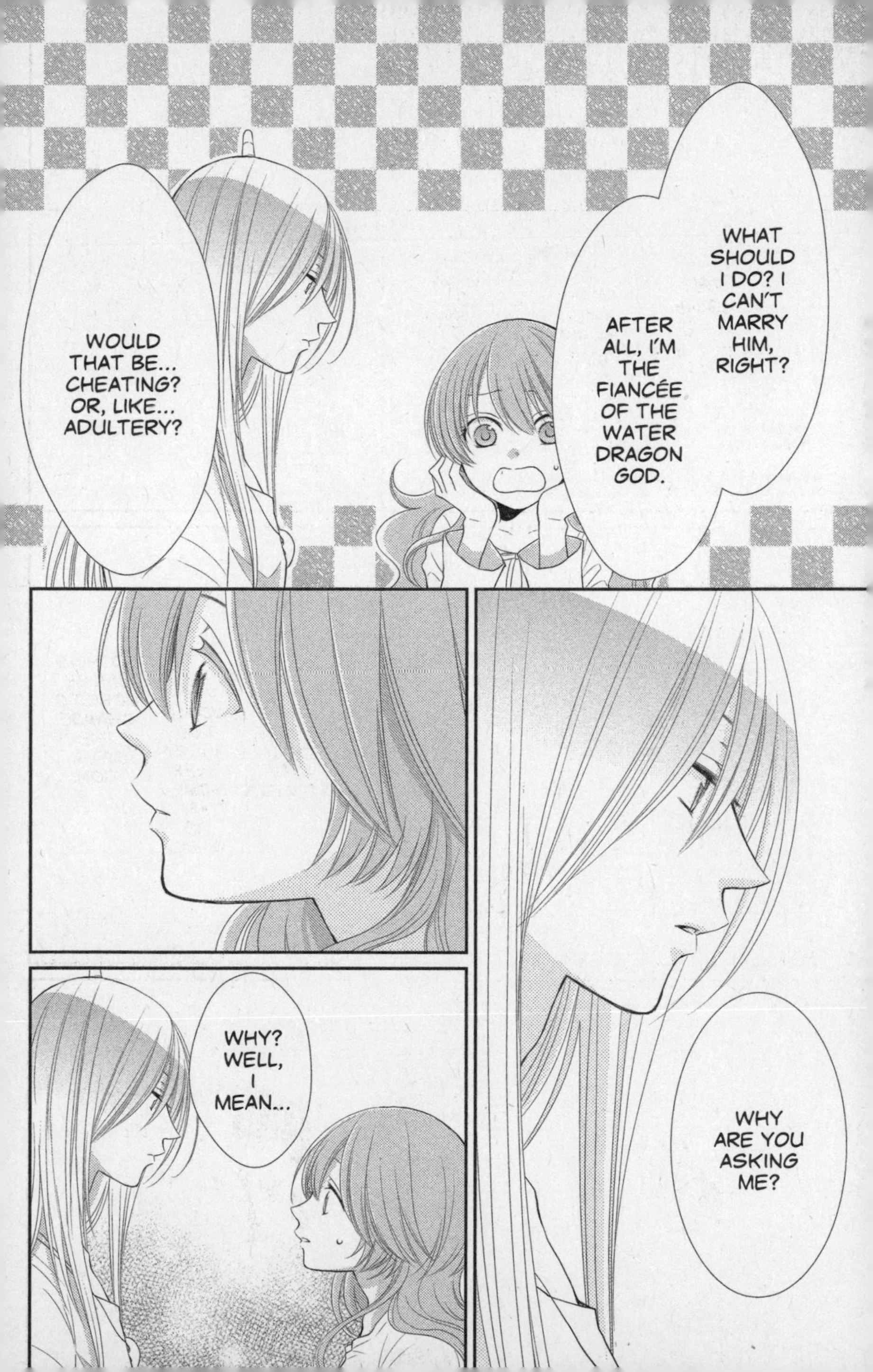
WHAT SHOULD I DO? I CAN'T MARRY HIM, RIGHT?
AFTER ALL, I'M THE FIANCÉE OF THE WATER DRAGON GOD.
WOULD THAT BE... CHEATING? OR, LIKE... ADULTERY?
WHY ARE YOU ASKING ME?
WHY? WELL, I MEAN...

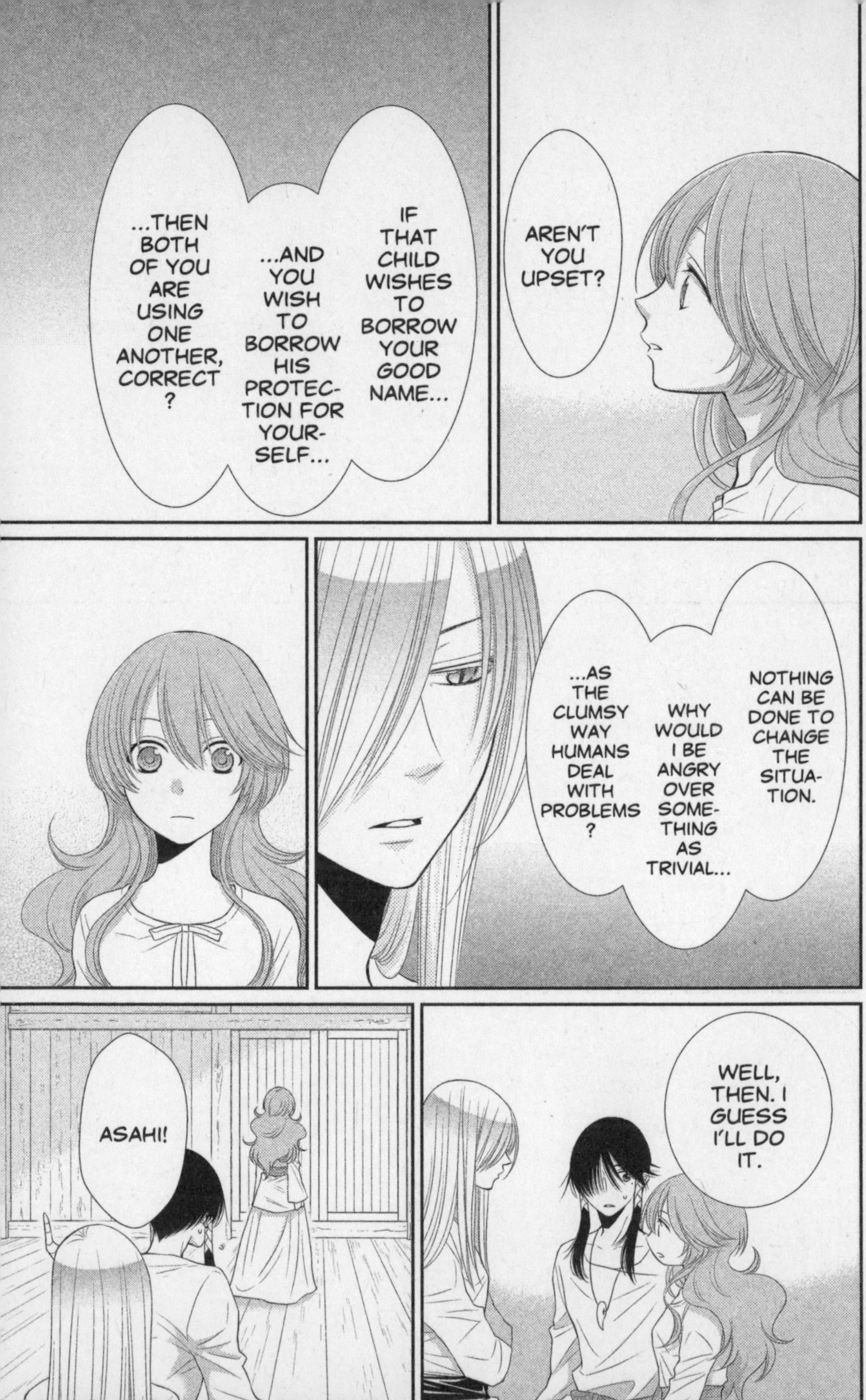
AREN'T YOU UPSET?
IF THAT CHILD WISHES TO BORROW YOUR GOOD NAME...
...AND YOU WISH TO BORROW HIS PROTECTION FOR YOURSELF...
...THEN BOTH OF YOU ARE USING ONE ANOTHER, CORRECT?
NOTHING CAN BE DONE TO CHANGE THE SITUATION.
WHY WOULD I BE ANGRY OVER SOMETHING AS TRIVIAL...
...AS THE CLUMSY WAY HUMANS DEAL WITH PROBLEMS?
WELL, THEN. I GUESS I'LL DO IT.
ASAHI!

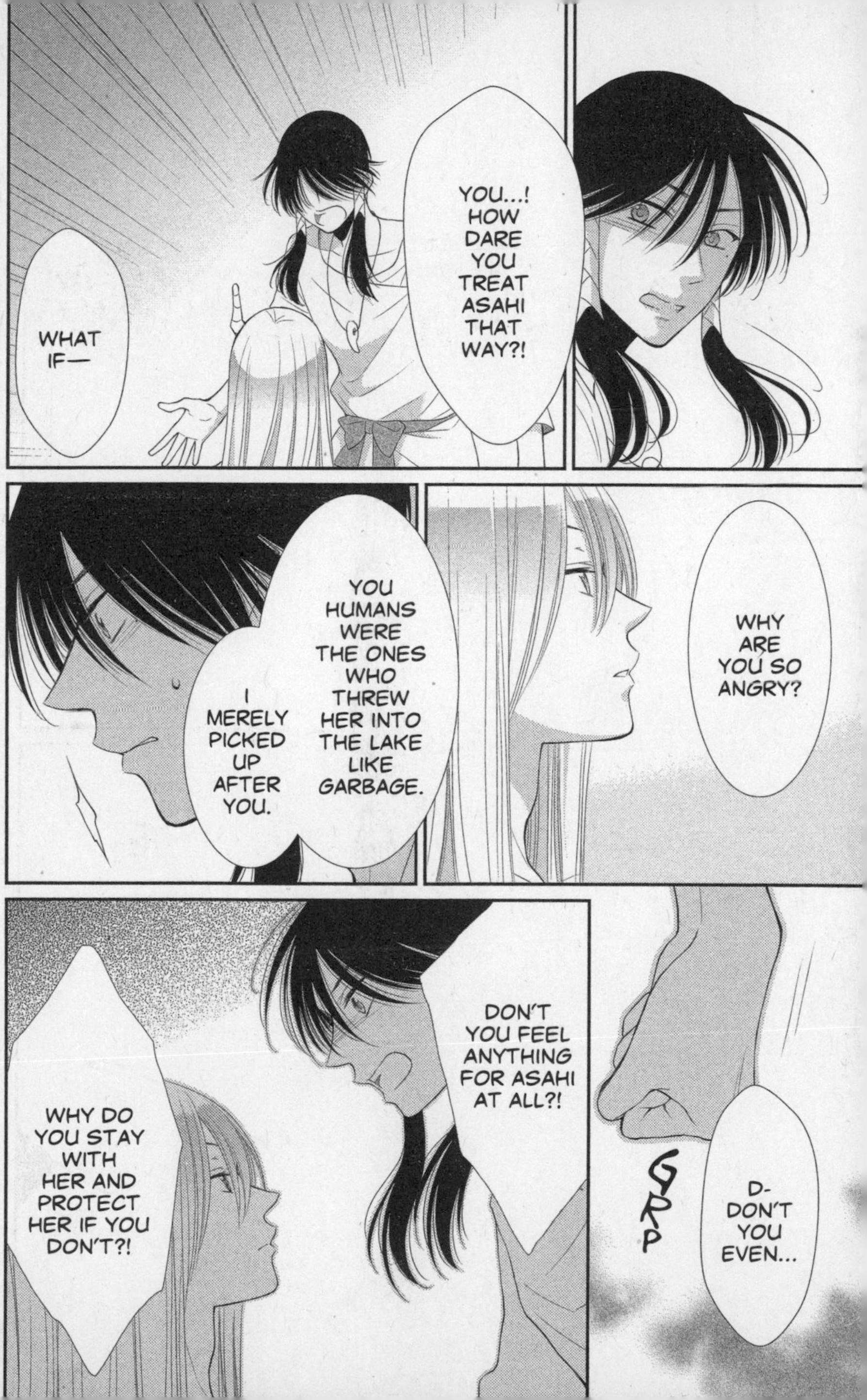
YOU...! HOW DARE YOU TREAT ASAHI THAT WAY?!
WHAT IF—
WHY ARE YOU SO ANGRY?
YOU HUMANS WERE THE ONES WHO THREW HER INTO THE LAKE LIKE GARBAGE.
I MERELY PICKED UP AFTER YOU.
GRP
D-DON'T YOU EVEN...
DON'T YOU FEEL ANYTHING FOR ASAHI AT ALL?!
WHY DO YOU STAY WITH HER AND PROTECT HER IF YOU DON'T?!

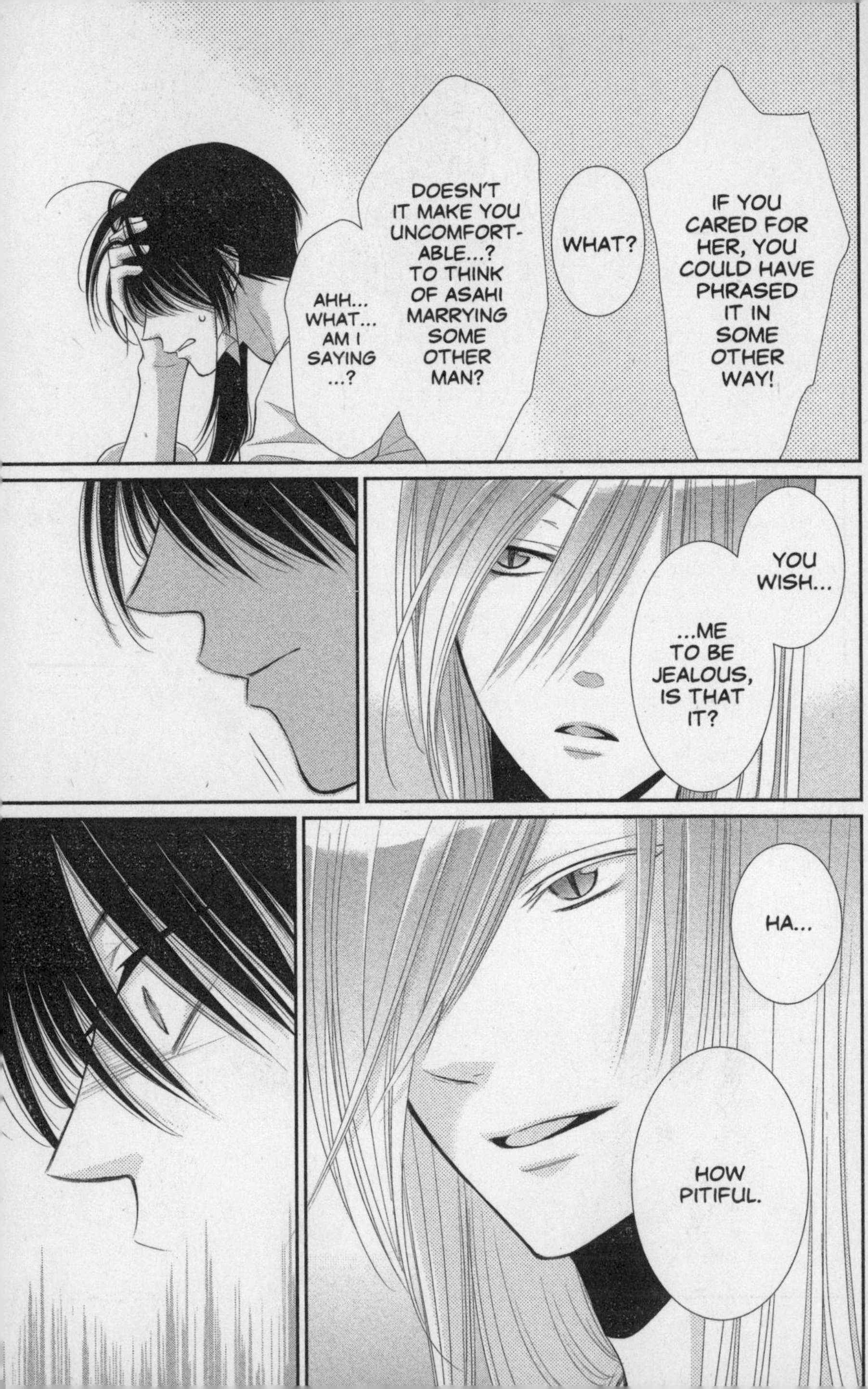
IF YOU CARED FOR HER, YOU COULD HAVE PHRASED IT IN SOME OTHER WAY!
WHAT?
DOESN'T IT MAKE YOU UNCOMFORT-ABLE...? TO THINK OF ASAHI MARRYING SOME OTHER MAN?
AHH... WHAT... AM I SAYING ...?
YOU WISH...
...ME TO BE JEALOUS, IS THAT IT?
HA...
HOW PITIFUL.

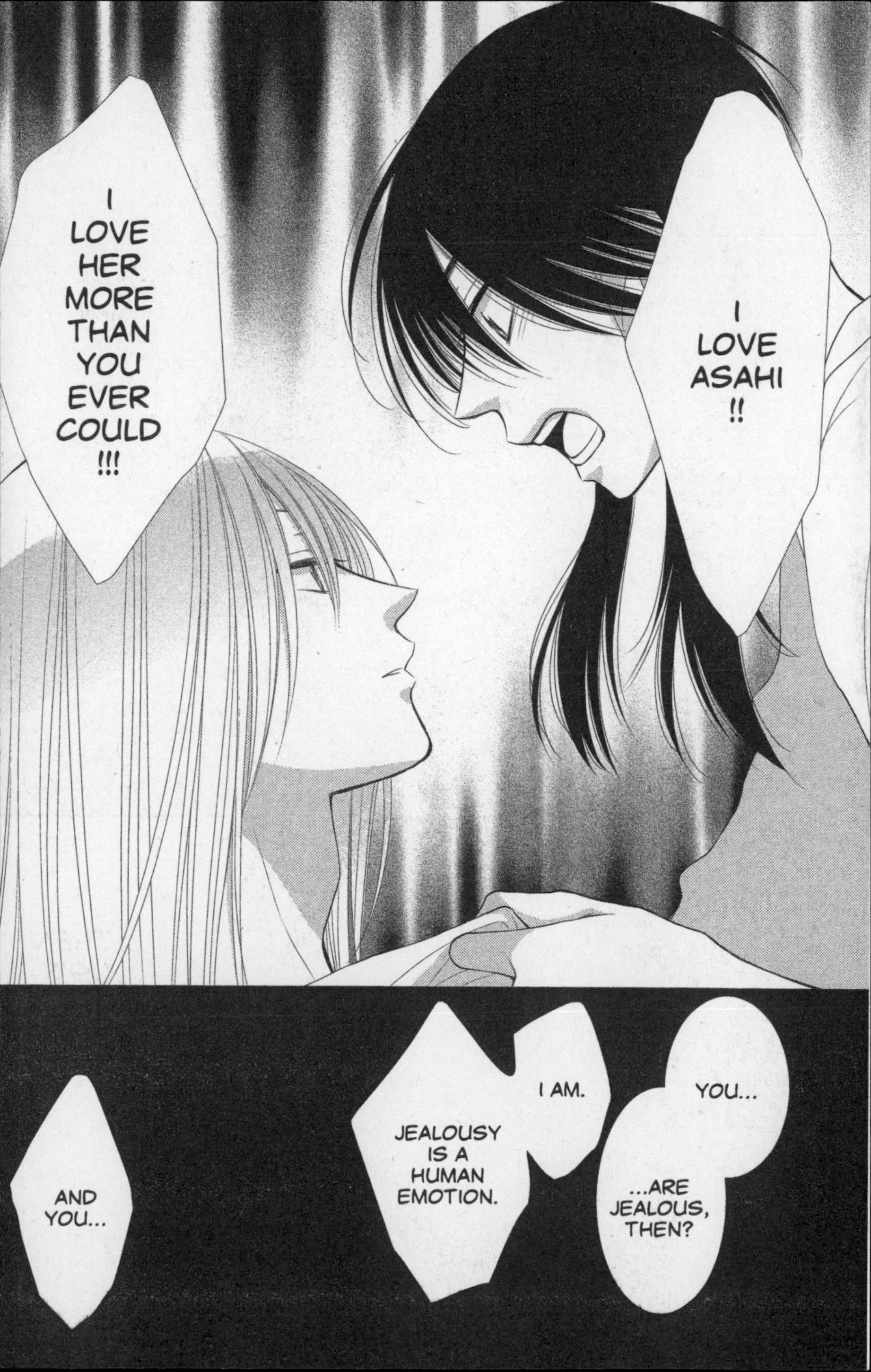
I LOVE ASAHI !!
I LOVE HER MORE THAN YOU EVER COULD !!!
YOU...
...ARE JEALOUS, THEN?
I AM.
JEALOUSY IS A HUMAN EMOTION.
AND YOU...

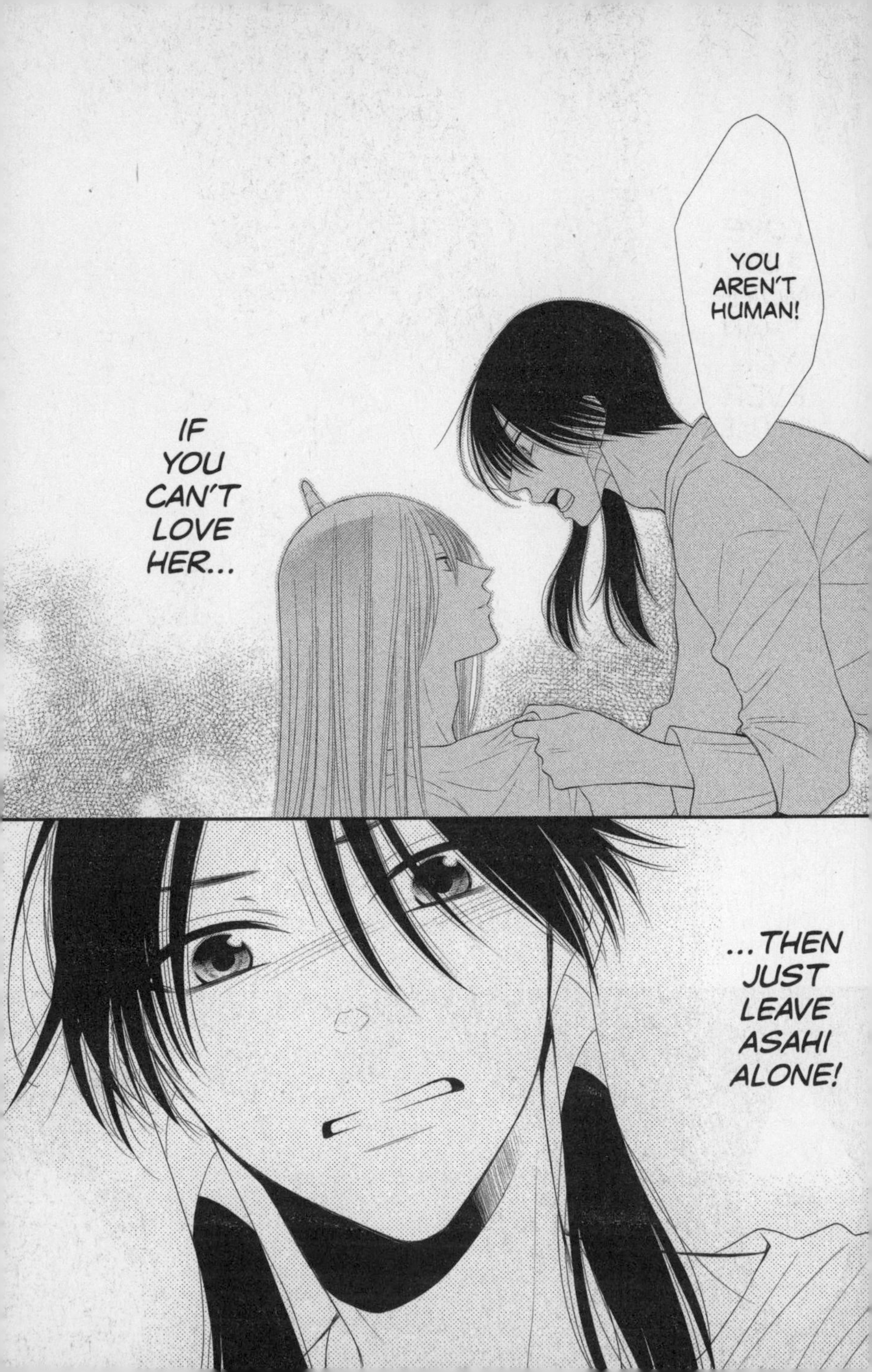
YOU AREN'T HUMAN!
IF YOU CAN'T LOVE HER...
...THEN JUST LEAVE ASAHI ALONE!

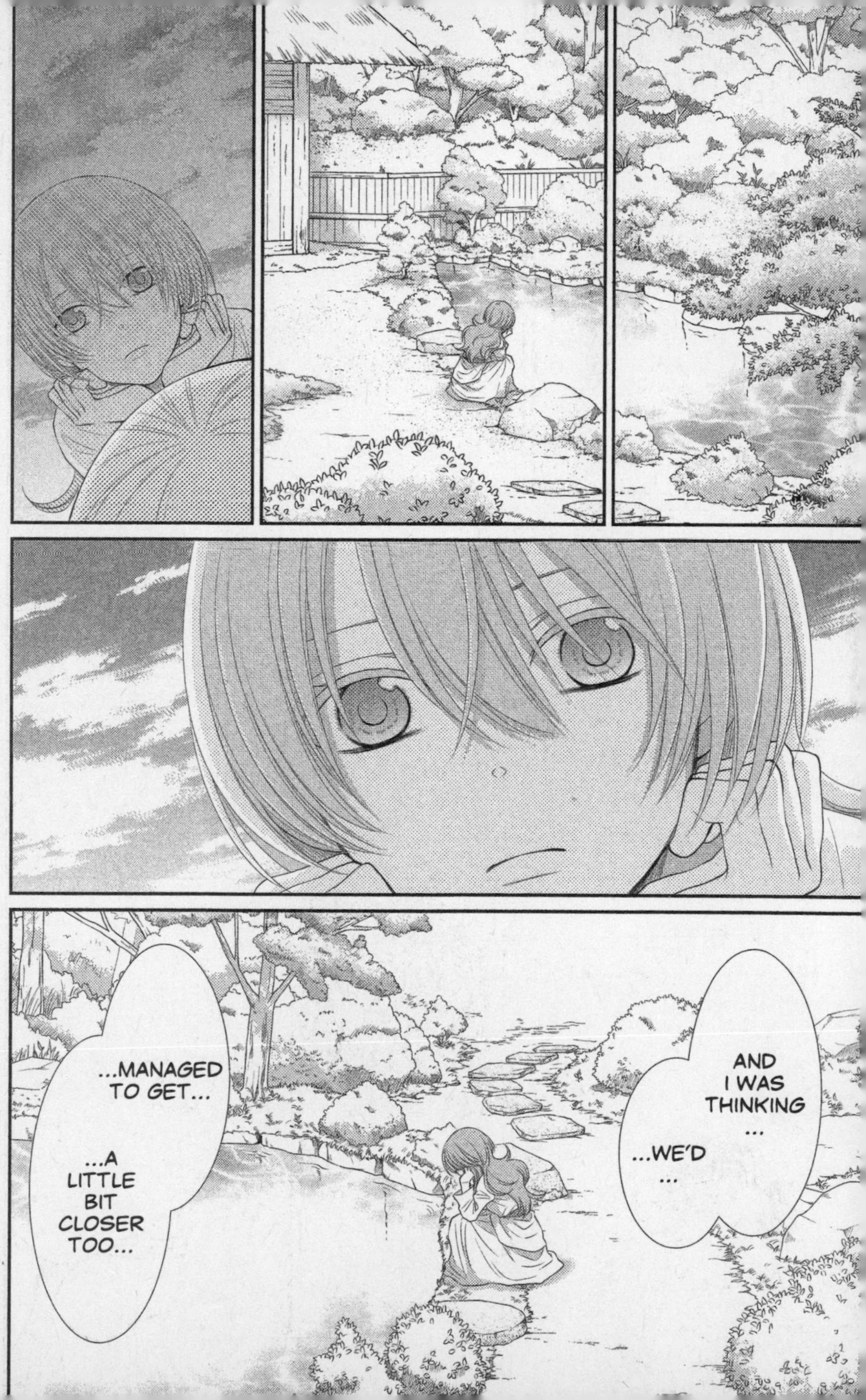
AND I WAS THINKING ...
...WE'D ...
...MANAGED TO GET...
...A LITTLE BIT CLOSER TOO...

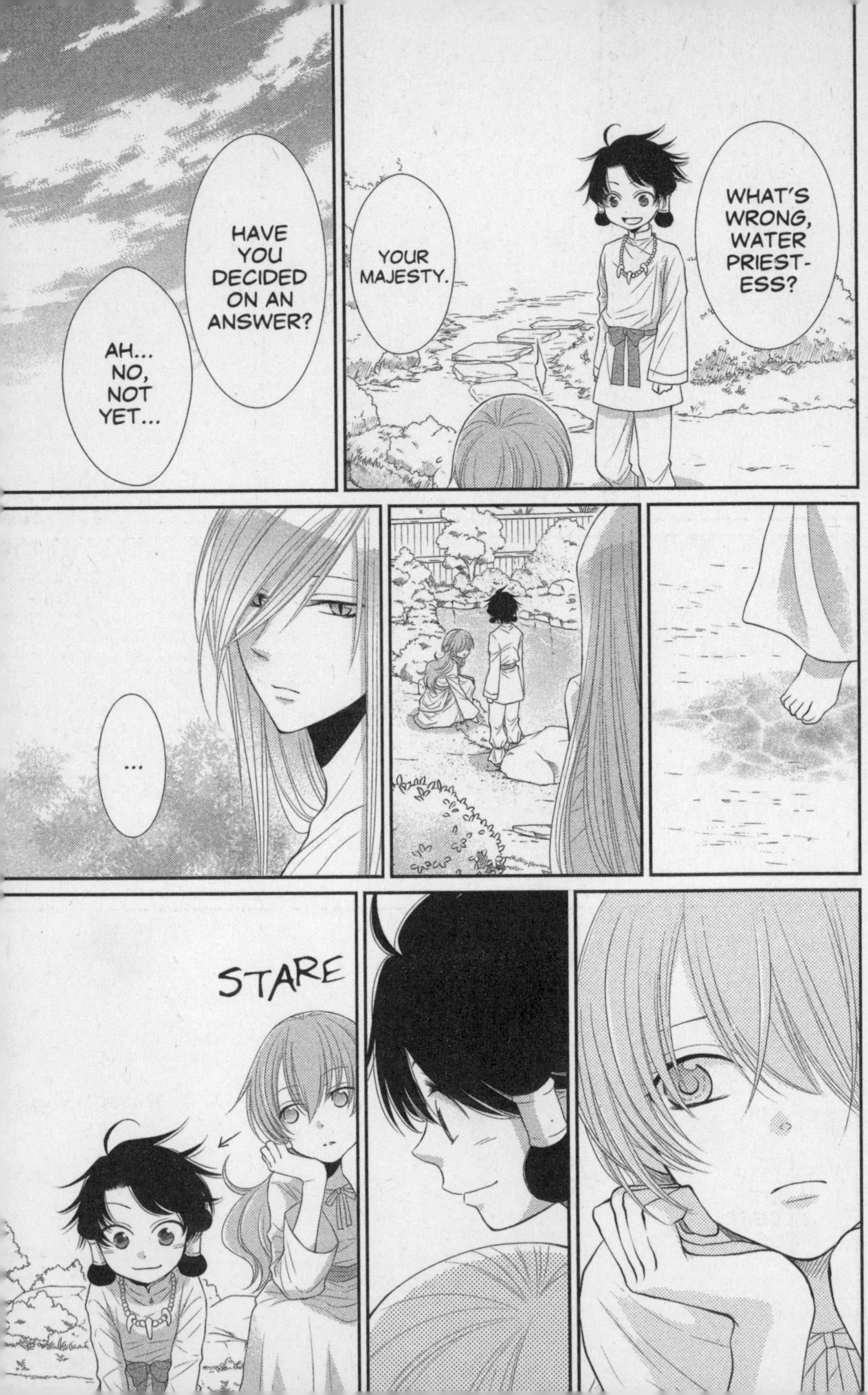
WHAT'S WRONG, WATER PRIEST-ESS?
YOUR MAJESTY.
HAVE YOU DECIDED ON AN ANSWER?
AH... NO, NOT YET...
...
STARE

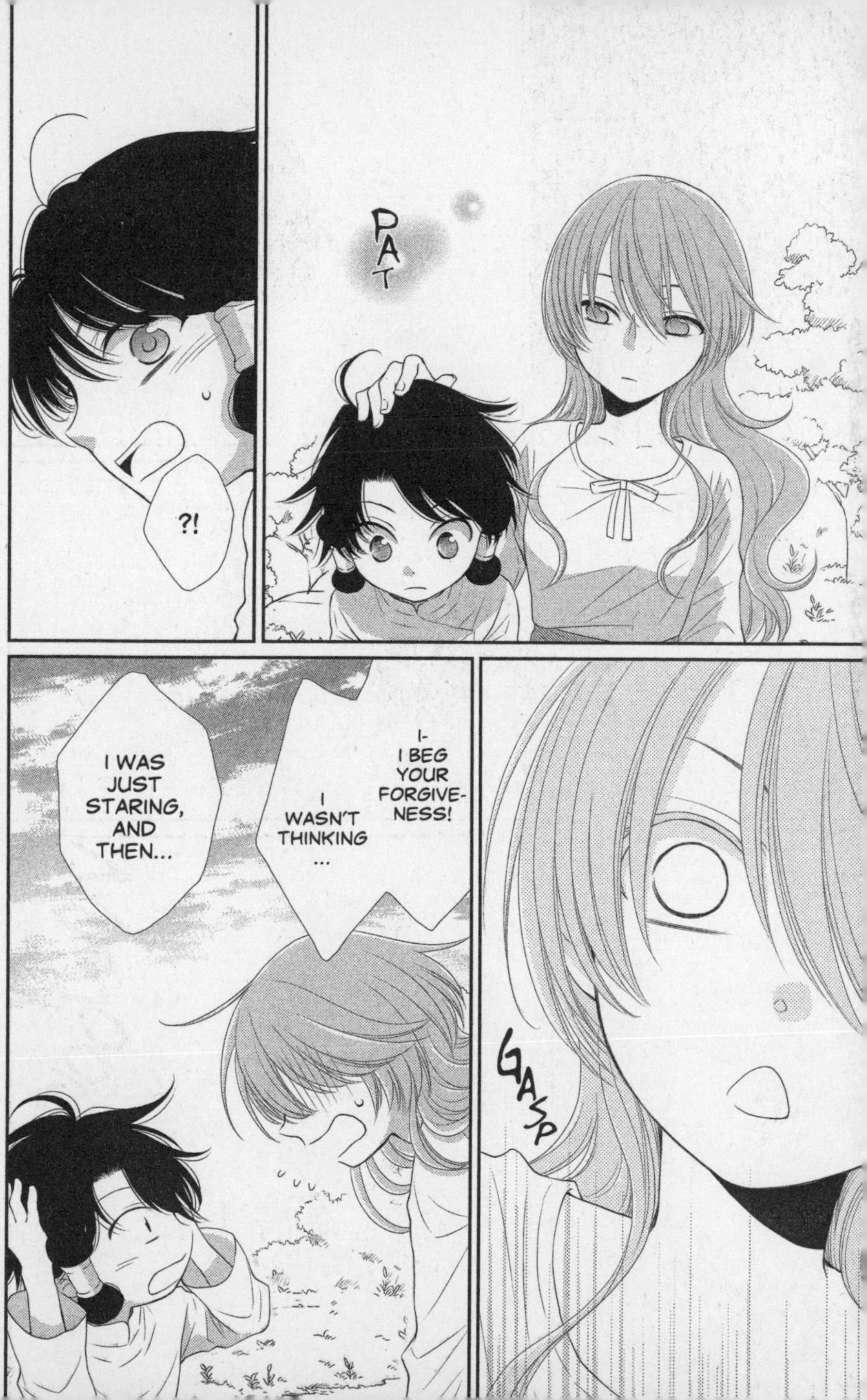
PAT
?!
GASP
I- I BEG YOUR FORGIVE-NESS!
I WASN'T THINKING ...
I WAS JUST STARING, AND THEN...

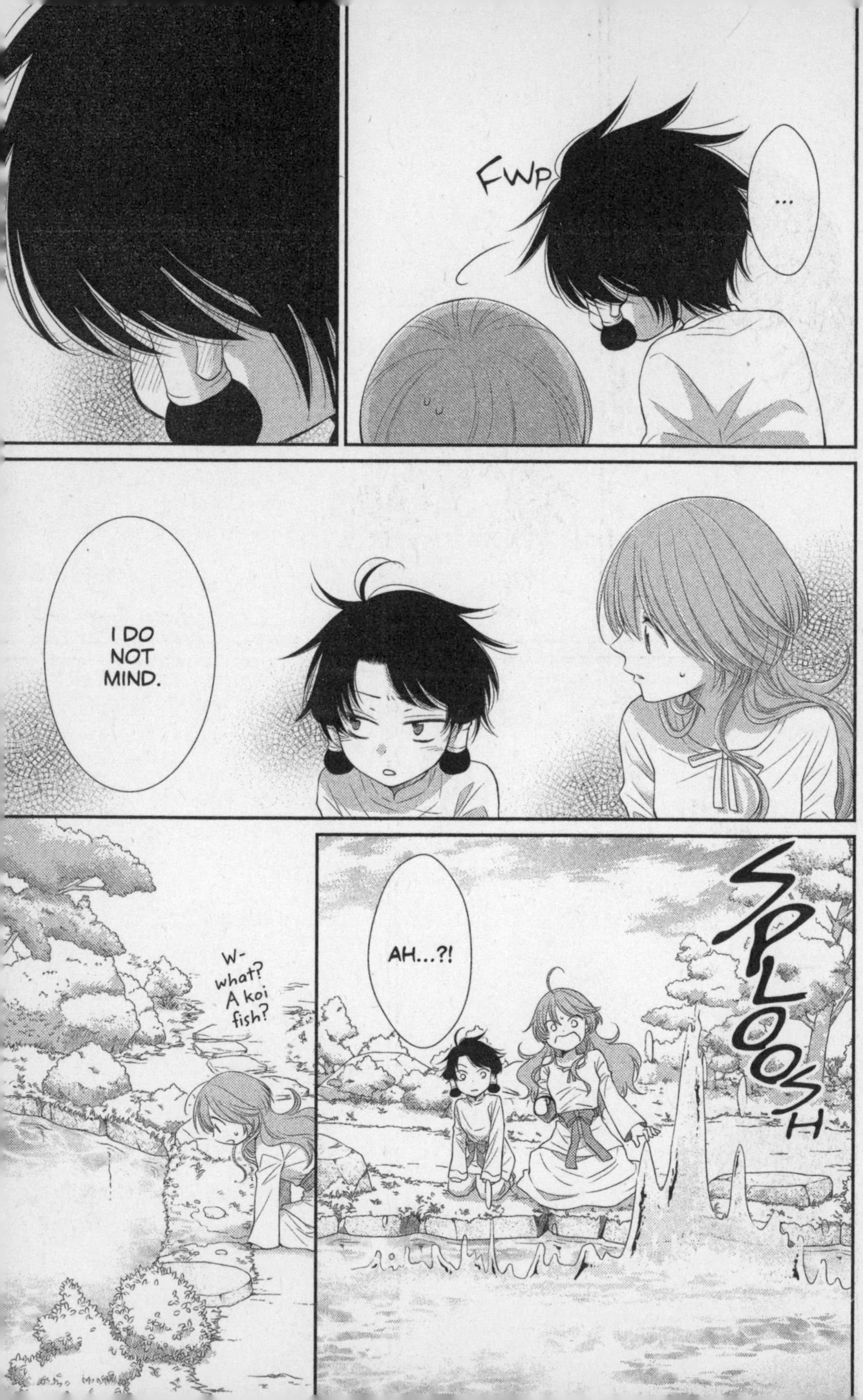
FWP
...
I DO NOT MIND.
SPLOOSH
AH...?!
W-what? A koi fish?

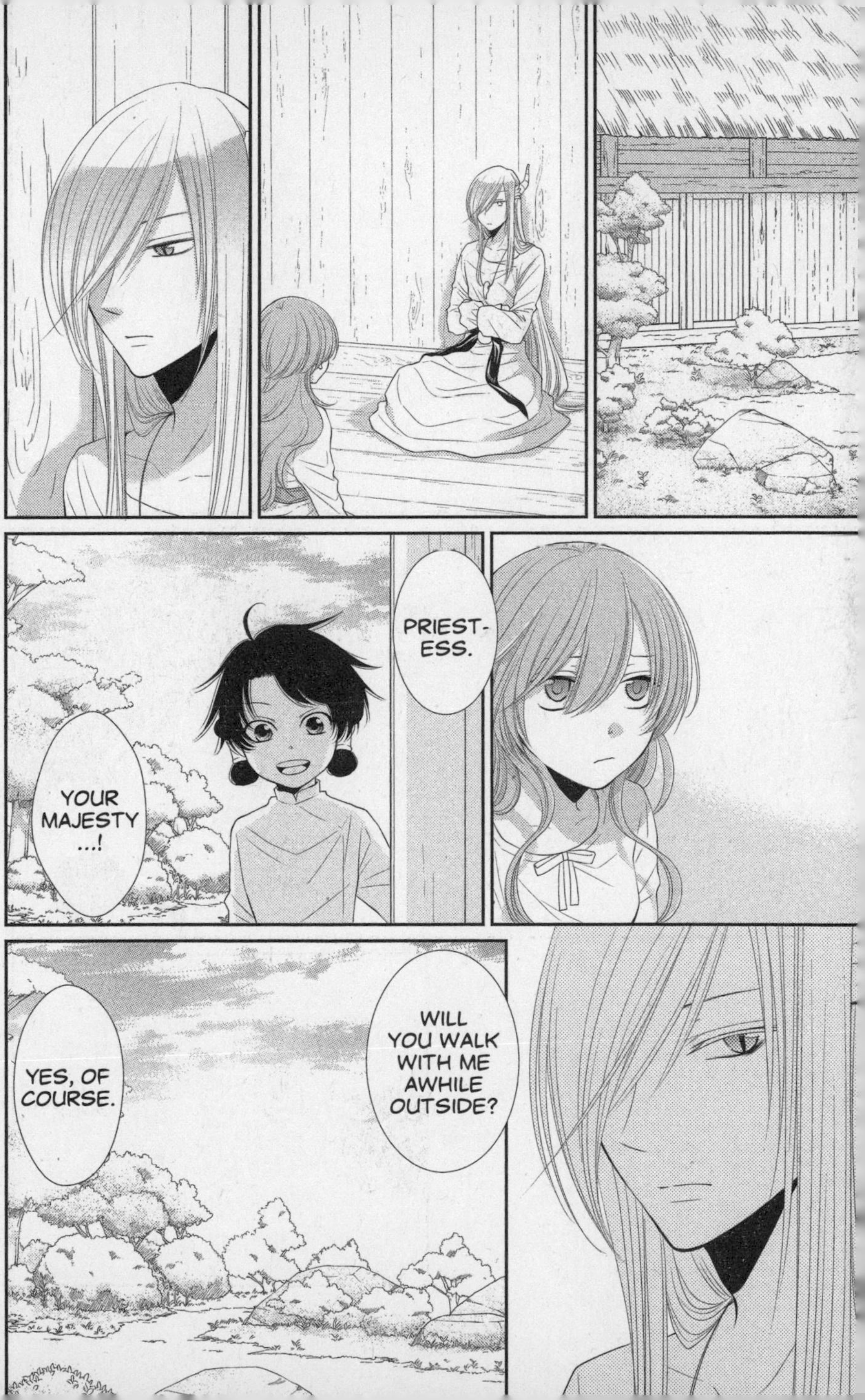
PRIEST-ESS.
YOUR MAJESTY ...!
WILL YOU WALK WITH ME AWHILE OUTSIDE?
YES, OF COURSE.

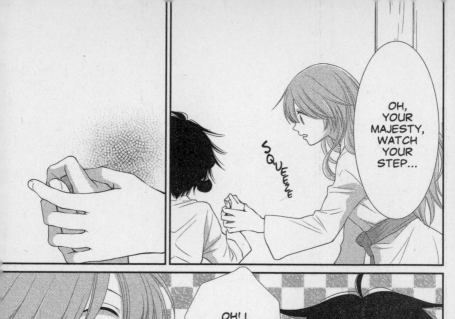

OH, YOUR MAJESTY, WATCH YOUR STEP...

SQUEEZE

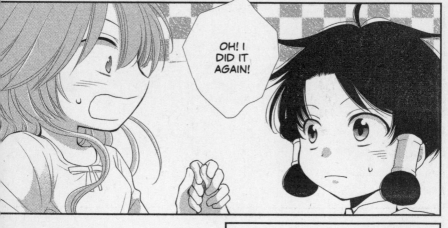

OH! I DID IT AGAIN!

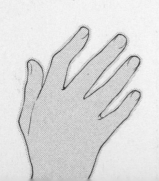

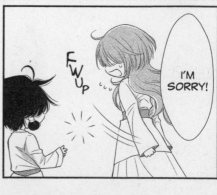

FWUP

I'M SORRY!

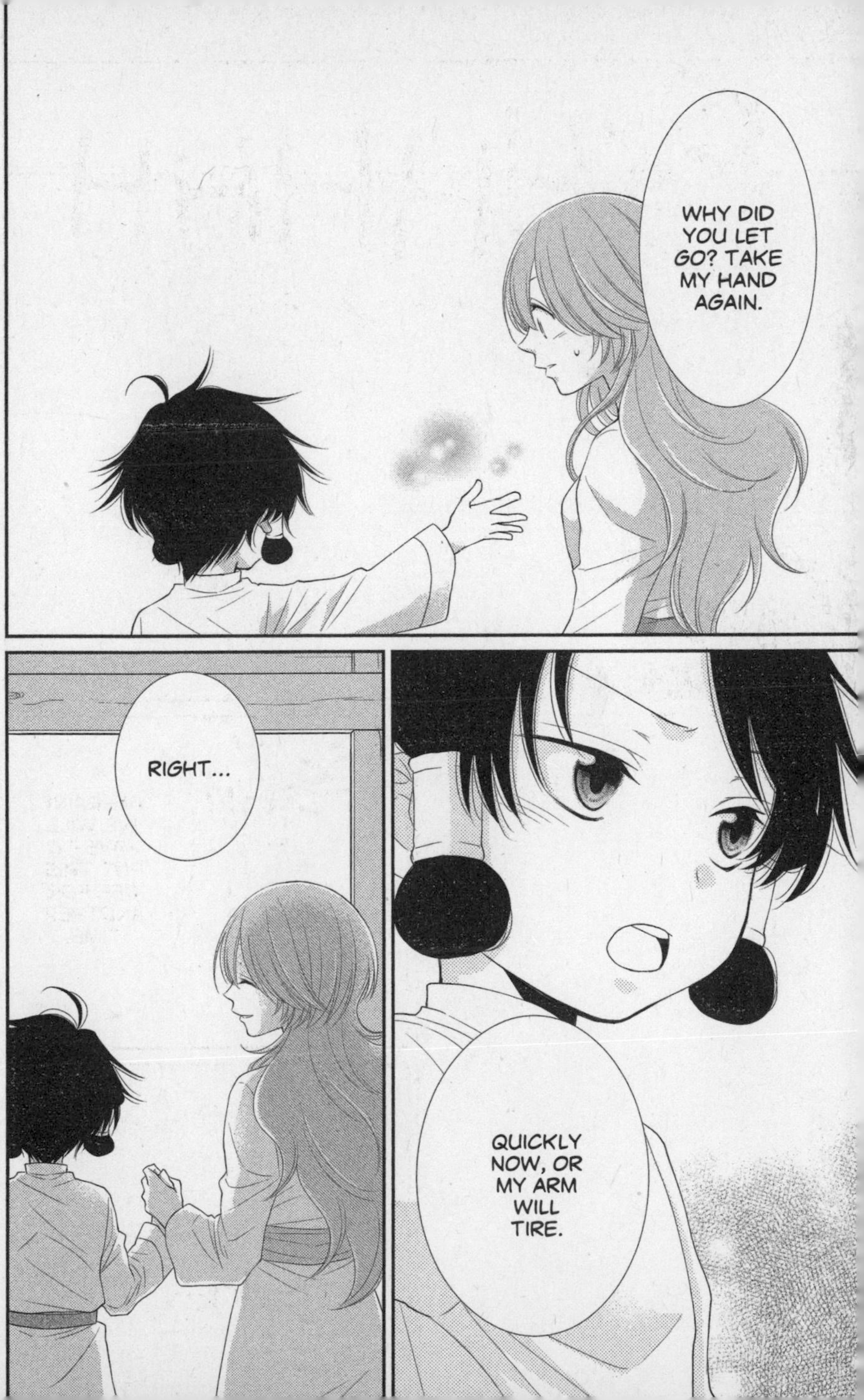
WHY DID YOU LET GO? TAKE MY HAND AGAIN.
QUICKLY NOW, OR MY ARM WILL TIRE.
RIGHT...

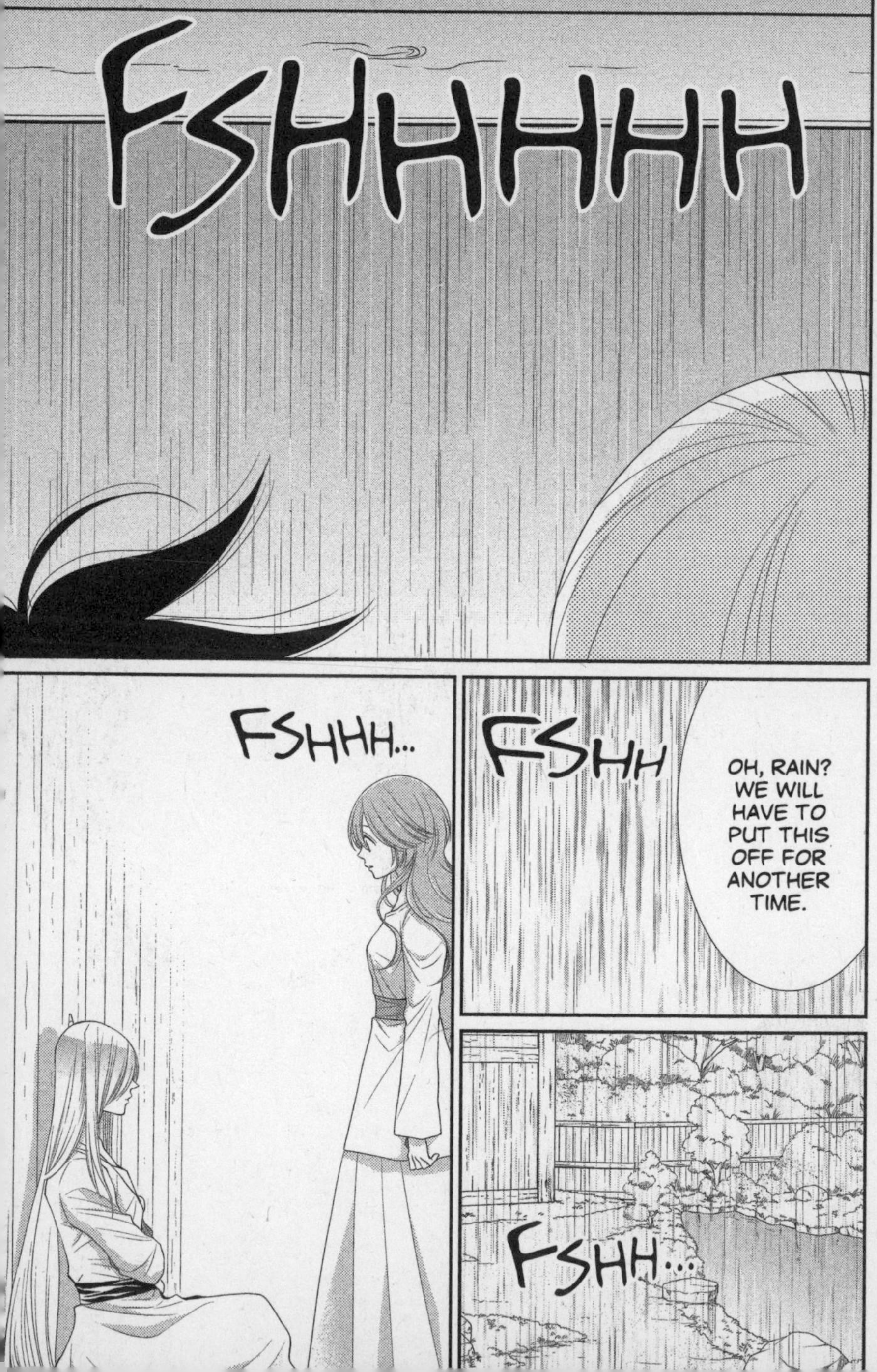
FSHHHHH
FSHH
OH, RAIN? WE WILL HAVE TO PUT THIS OFF FOR ANOTHER TIME.
FSHH...
FSHHH...

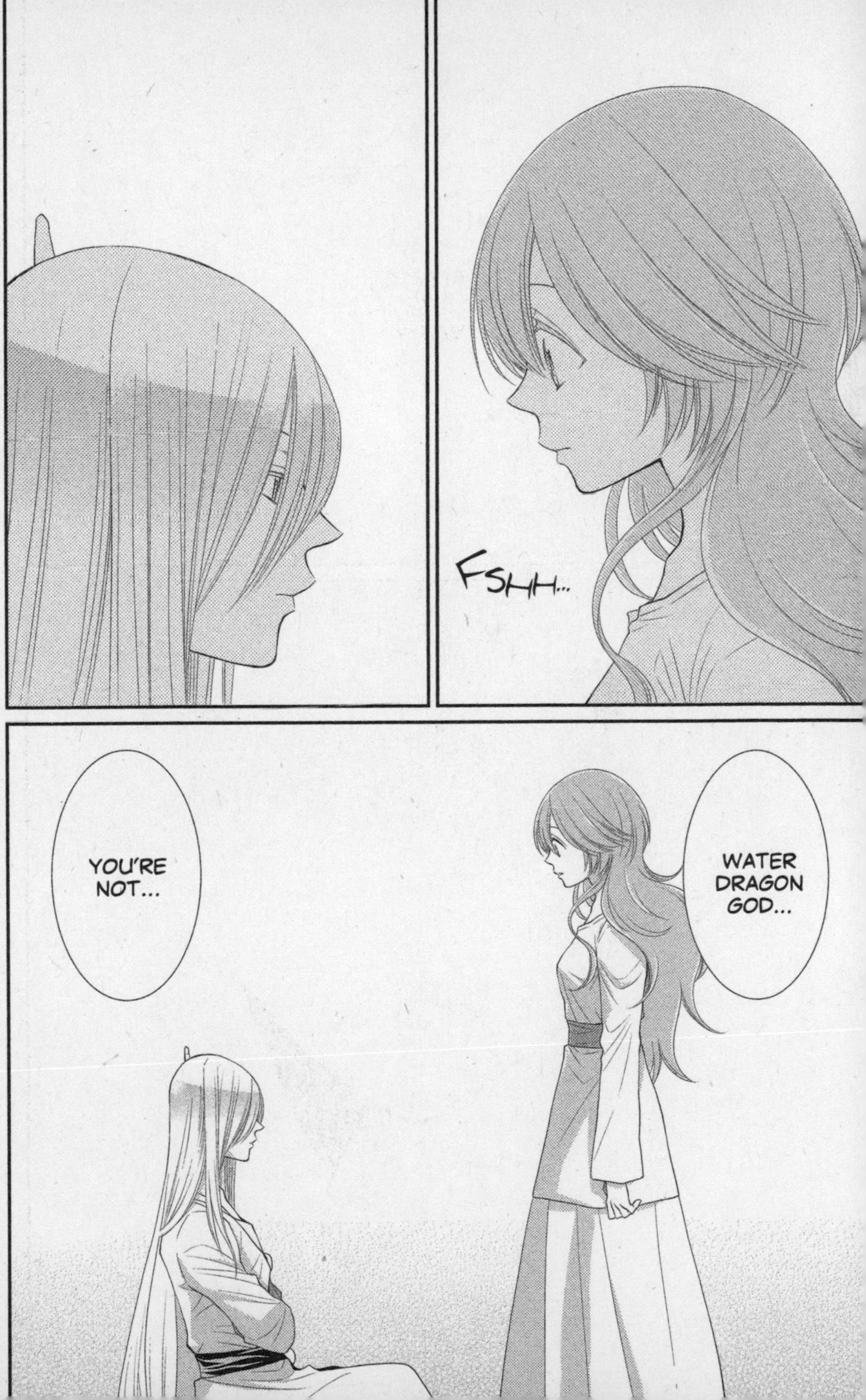
FSHH...
WATER DRAGON GOD...
YOU'RE NOT...

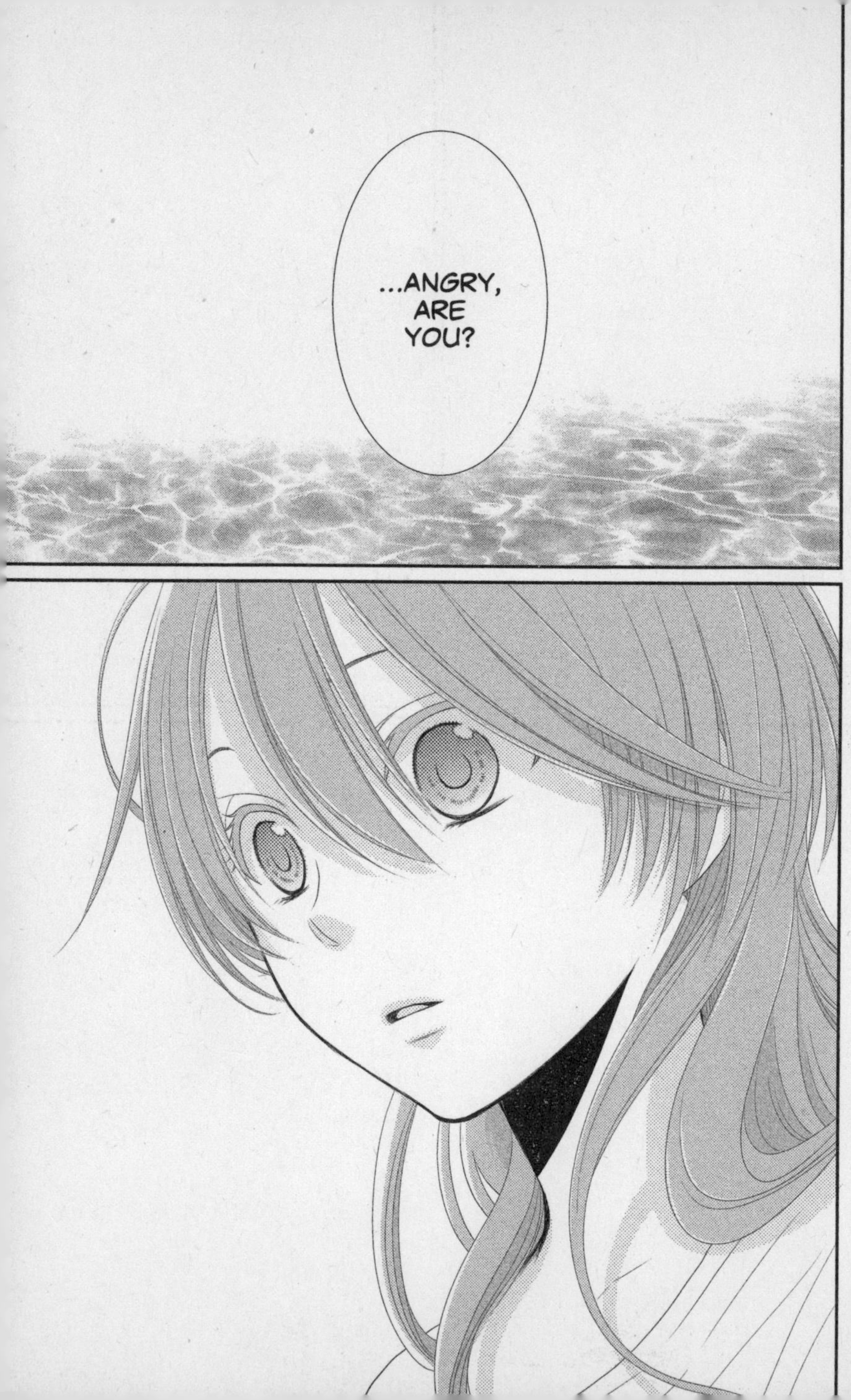
...ANGRY,
ARE
YOU?

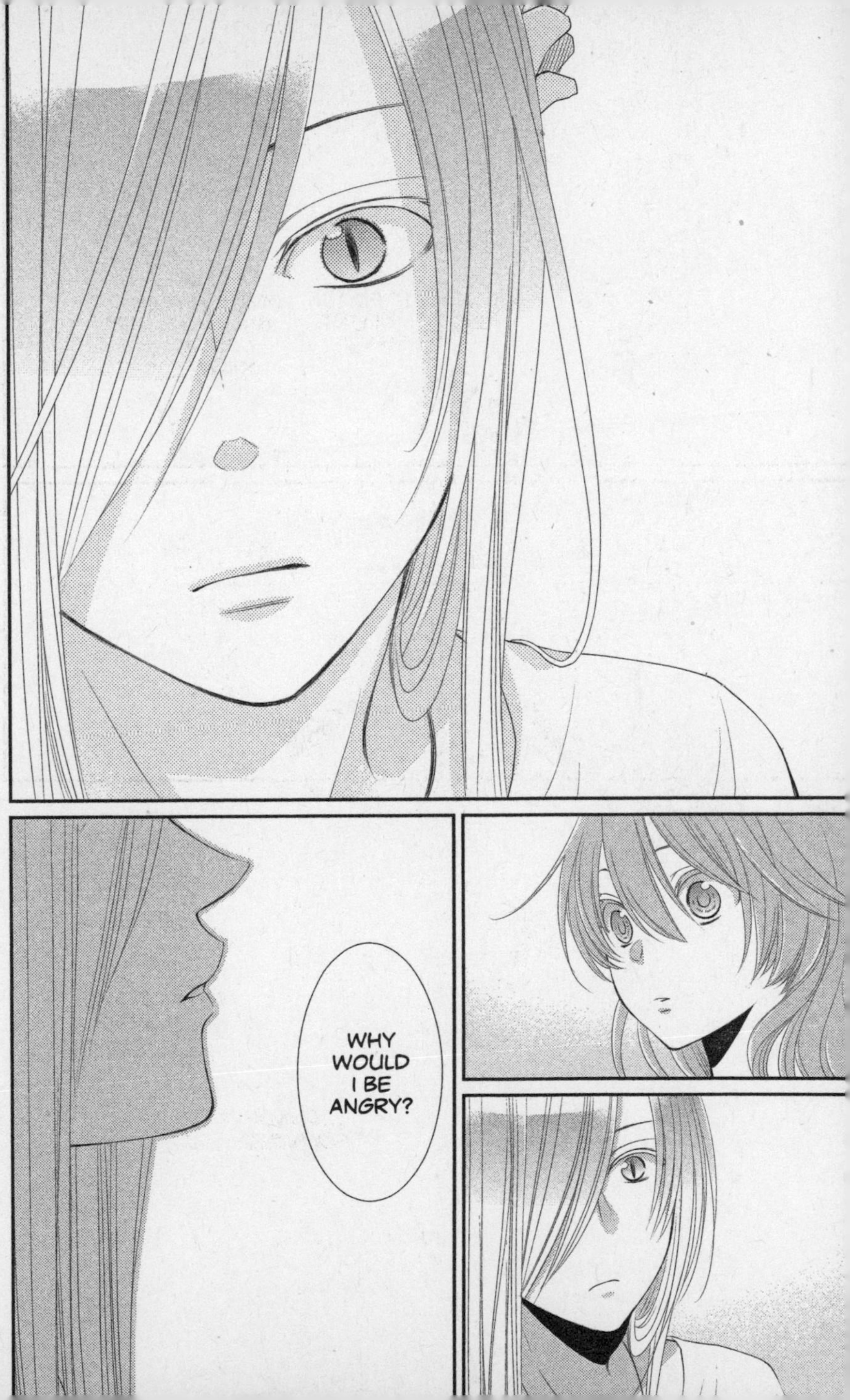
WHY WOULD I BE ANGRY?

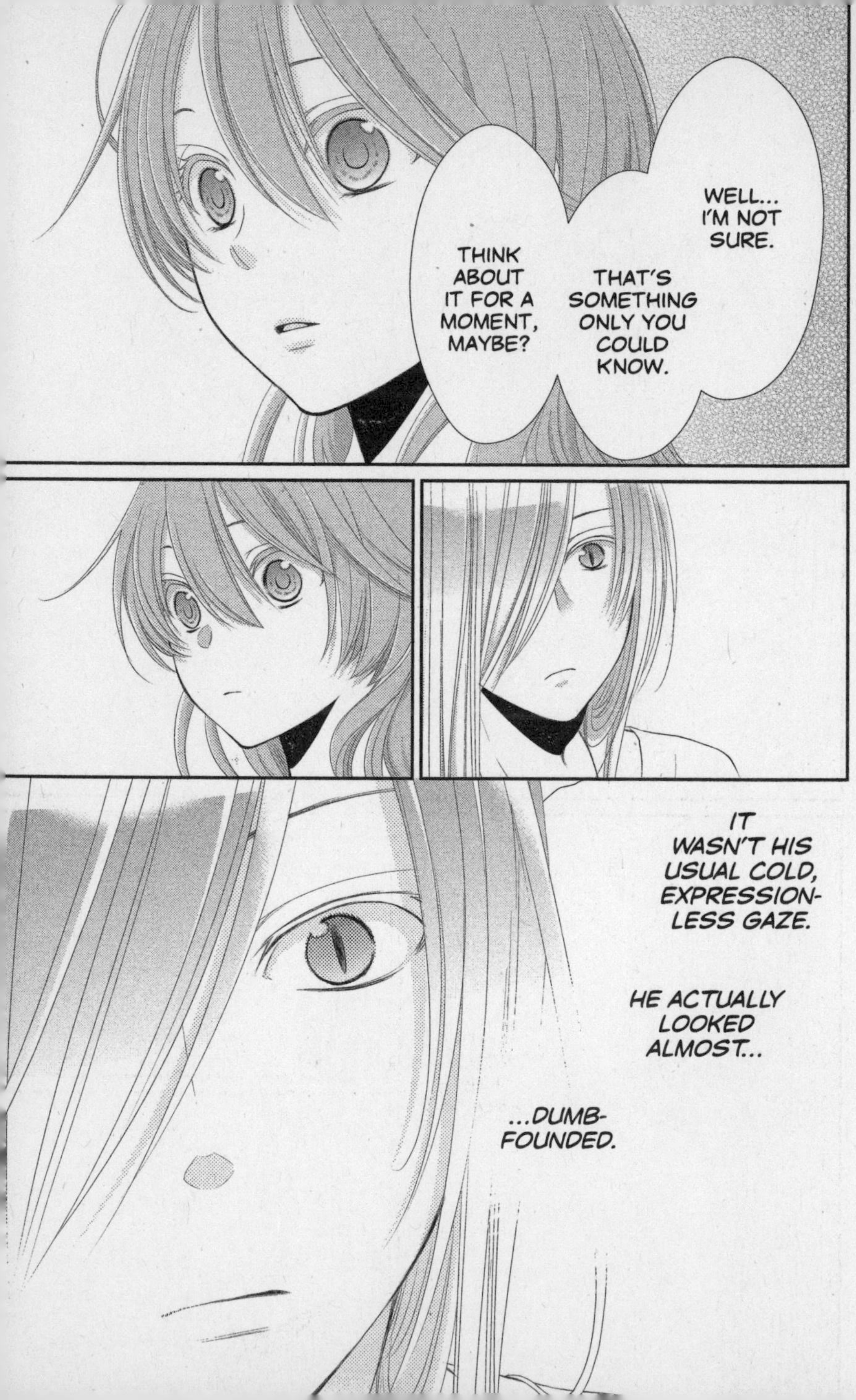
WELL... I'M NOT SURE.
THAT'S SOMETHING ONLY YOU COULD KNOW.
THINK ABOUT IT FOR A MOMENT, MAYBE?
IT WASN'T HIS USUAL COLD, EXPRESSION-LESS GAZE.
HE ACTUALLY LOOKED ALMOST...
...DUMB-FOUNDED.

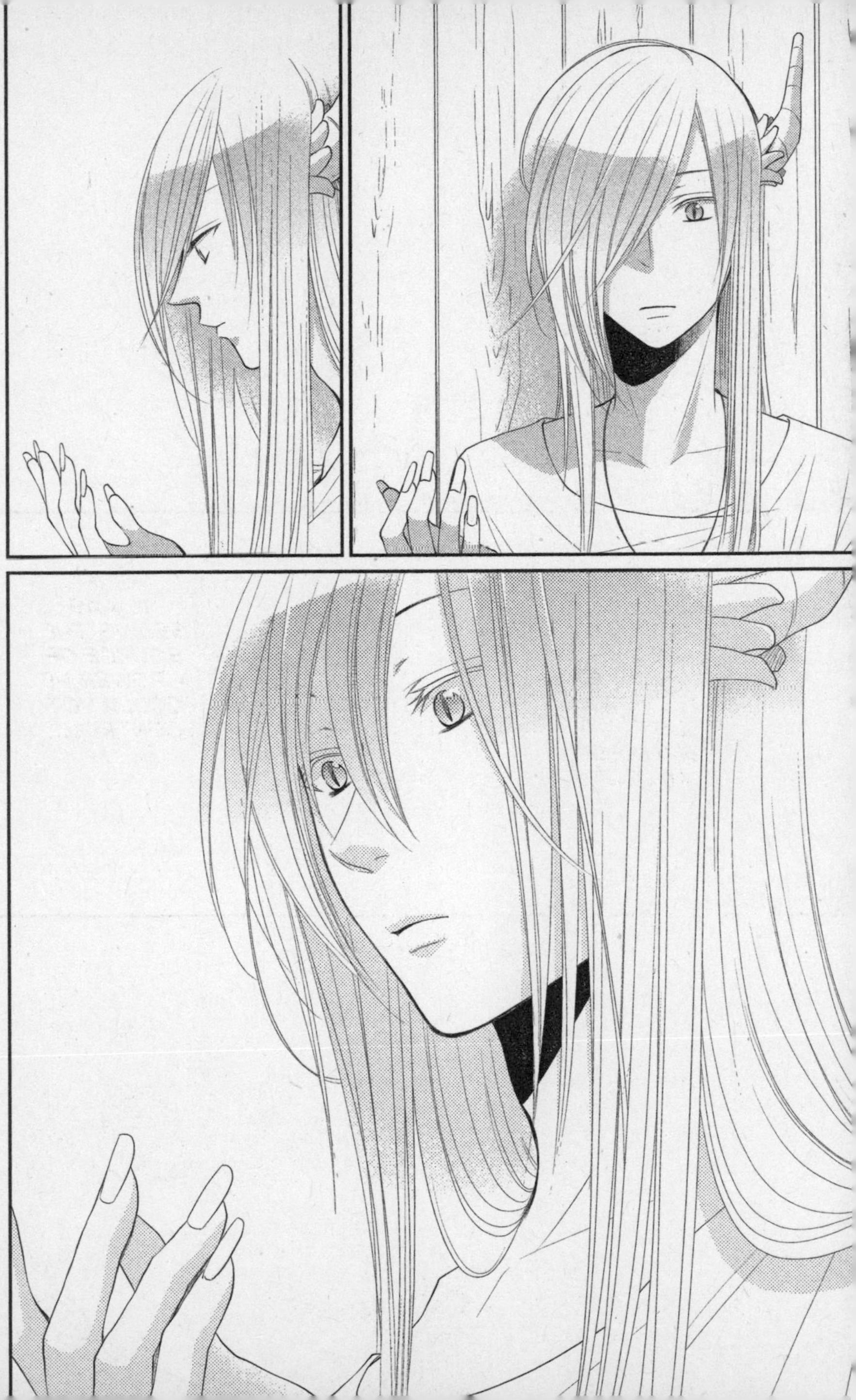

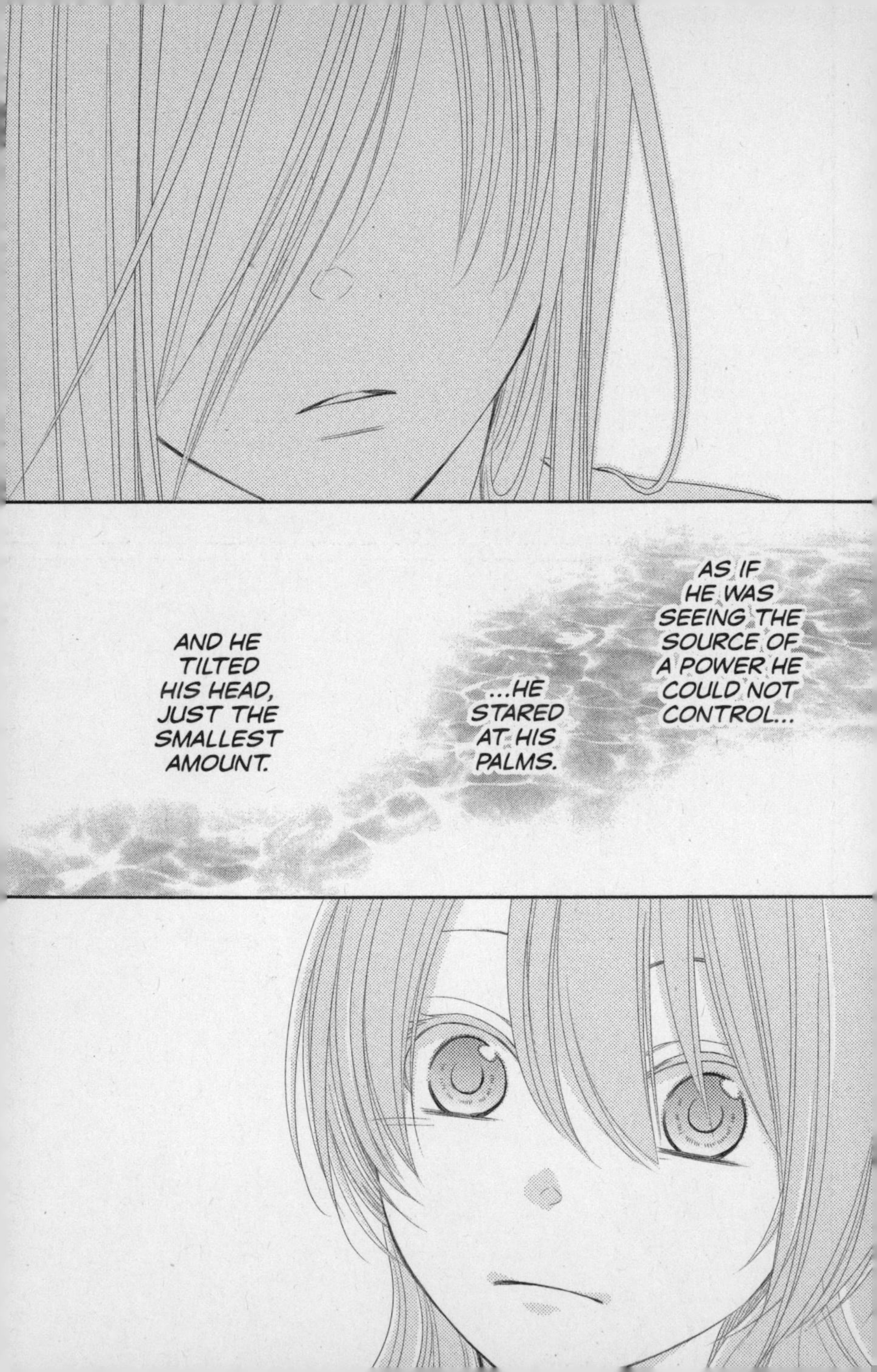
AS IF HE WAS SEEING THE SOURCE OF A POWER HE COULD NOT CONTROL...
...HE STARED AT HIS PALMS.
AND HE TILTED HIS HEAD, JUST THE SMALLEST AMOUNT.

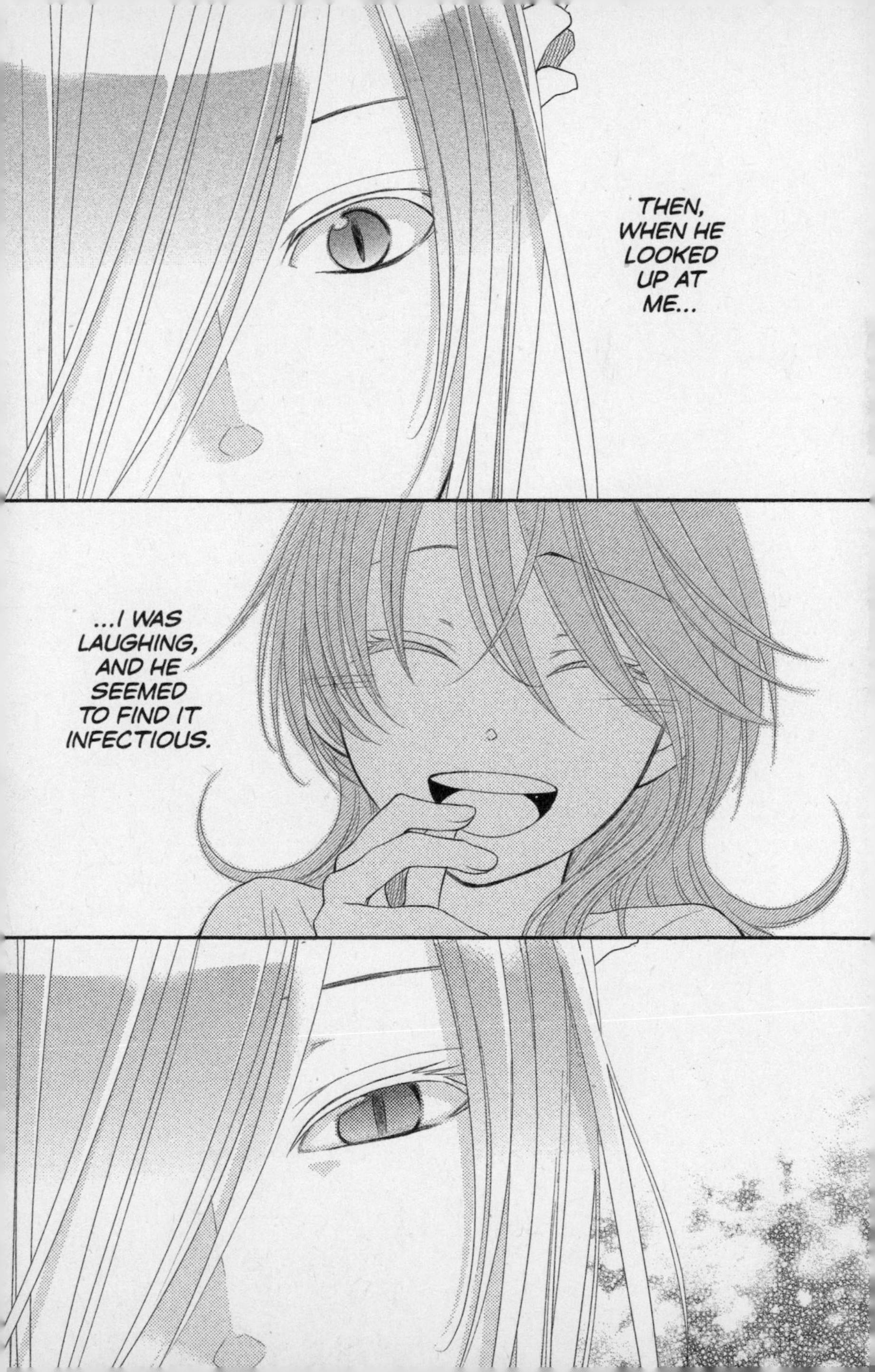
THEN, WHEN HE LOOKED UP AT ME...
...I WAS LAUGHING, AND HE SEEMED TO FIND IT INFECTIOUS.

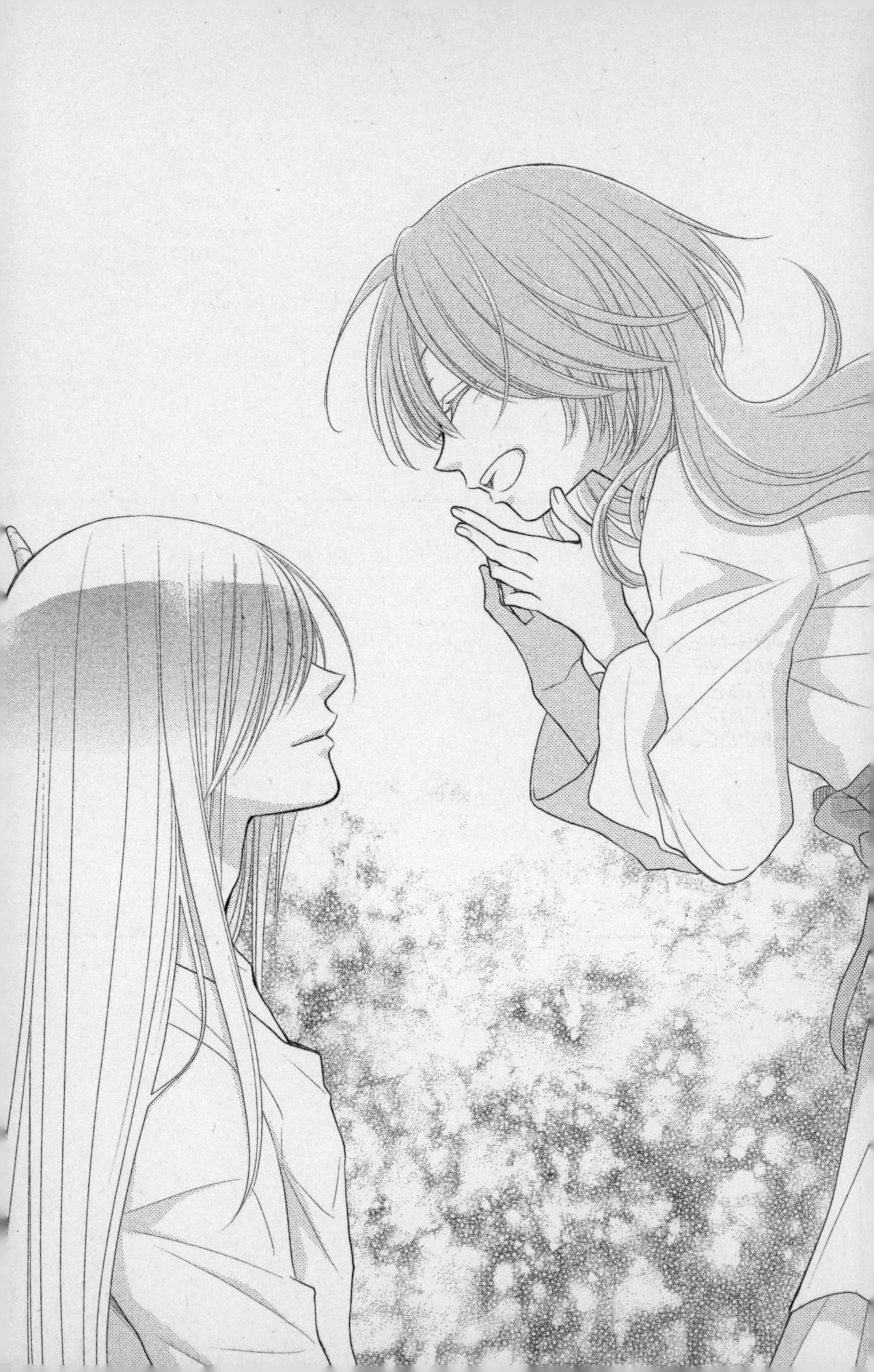

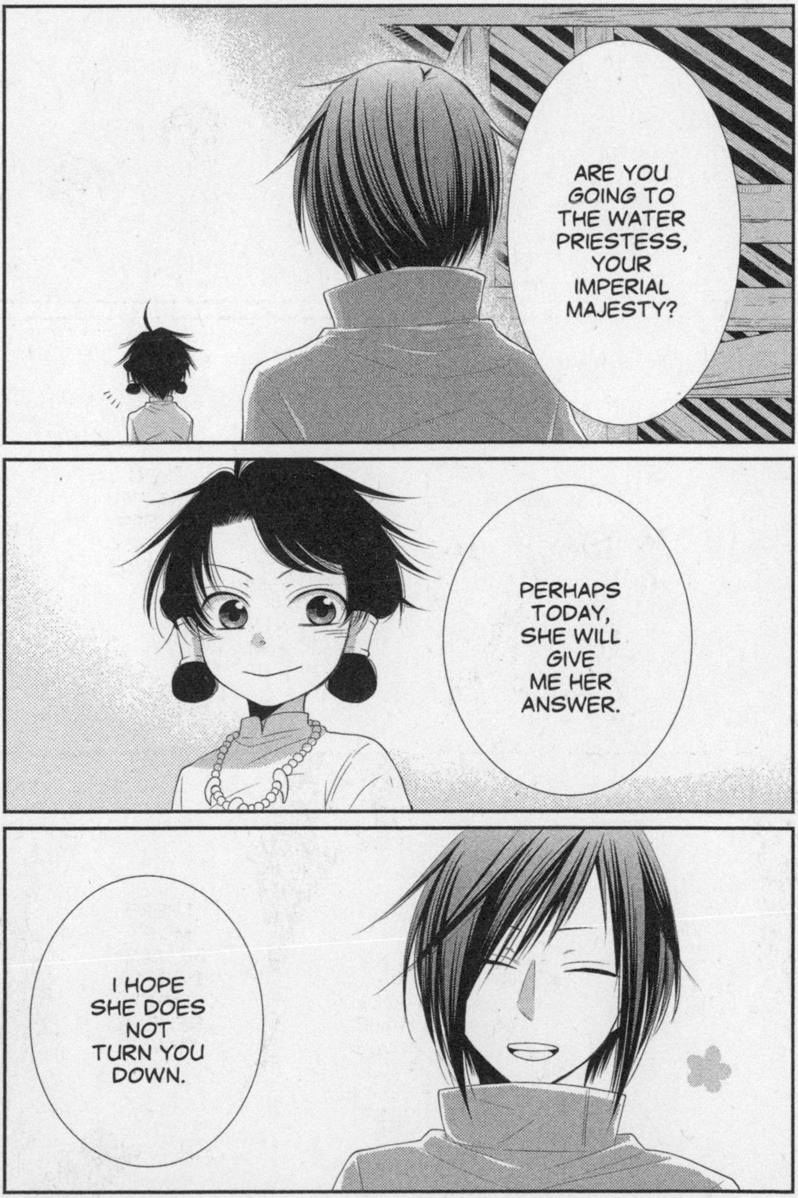
ARE YOU GOING TO THE WATER PRIESTESS, YOUR IMPERIAL MAJESTY?
PERHAPS TODAY, SHE WILL GIVE ME HER ANSWER.
I HOPE SHE DOES NOT TURN YOU DOWN.

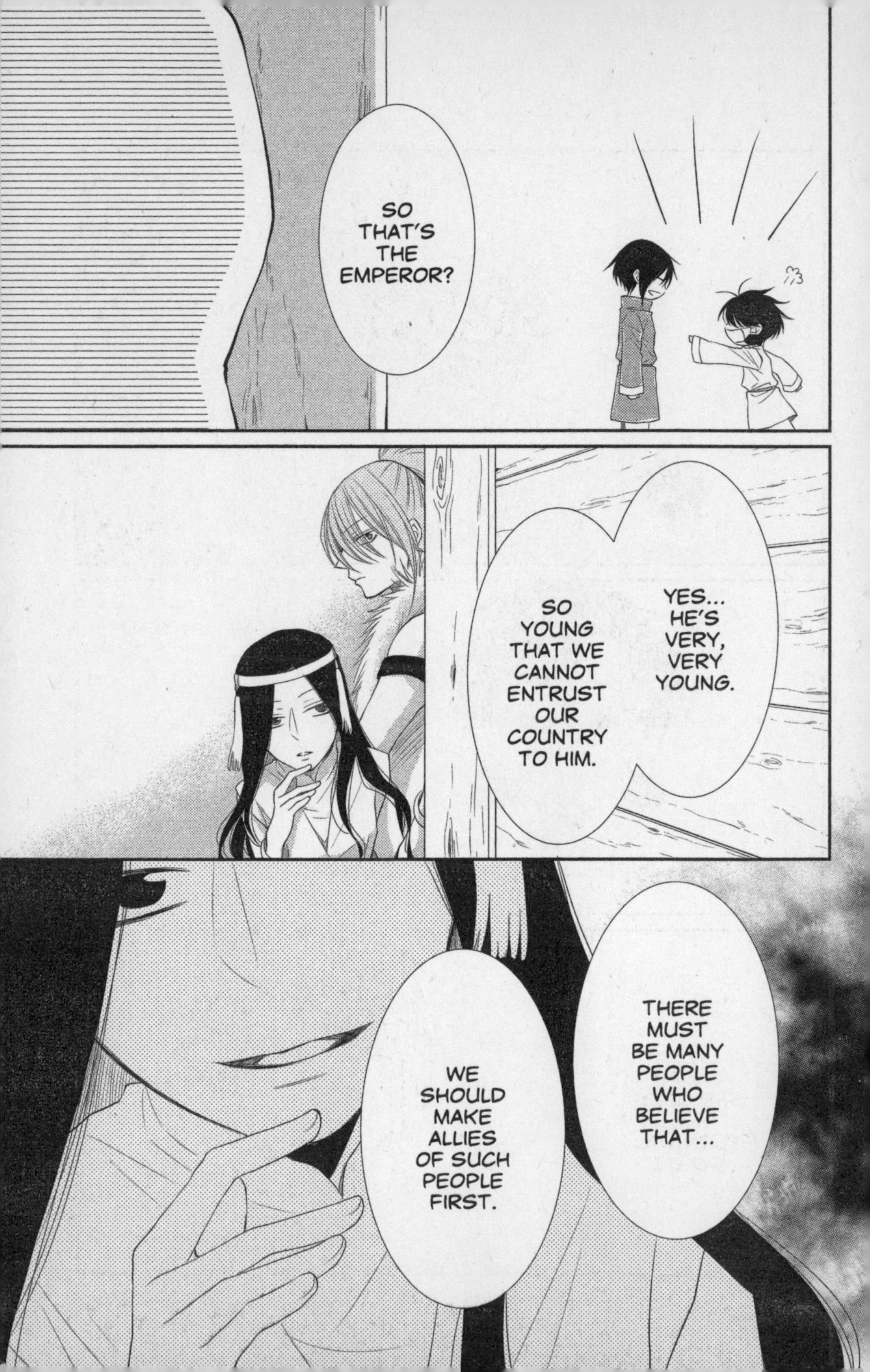
SO THAT'S THE EMPEROR?
YES... HE'S VERY, VERY YOUNG.
SO YOUNG THAT WE CANNOT ENTRUST OUR COUNTRY TO HIM.
THERE MUST BE MANY PEOPLE WHO BELIEVE THAT...
WE SHOULD MAKE ALLIES OF SUCH PEOPLE FIRST.

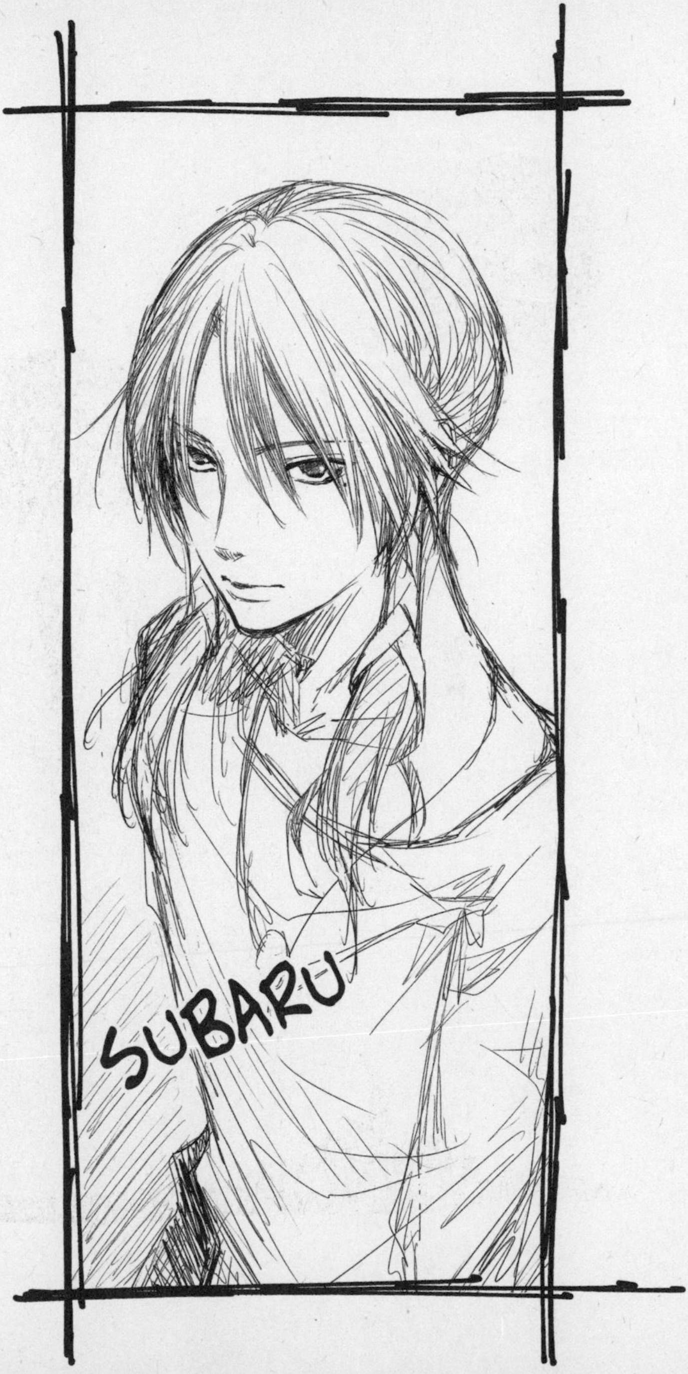
SUBARU

CHAPTER 20

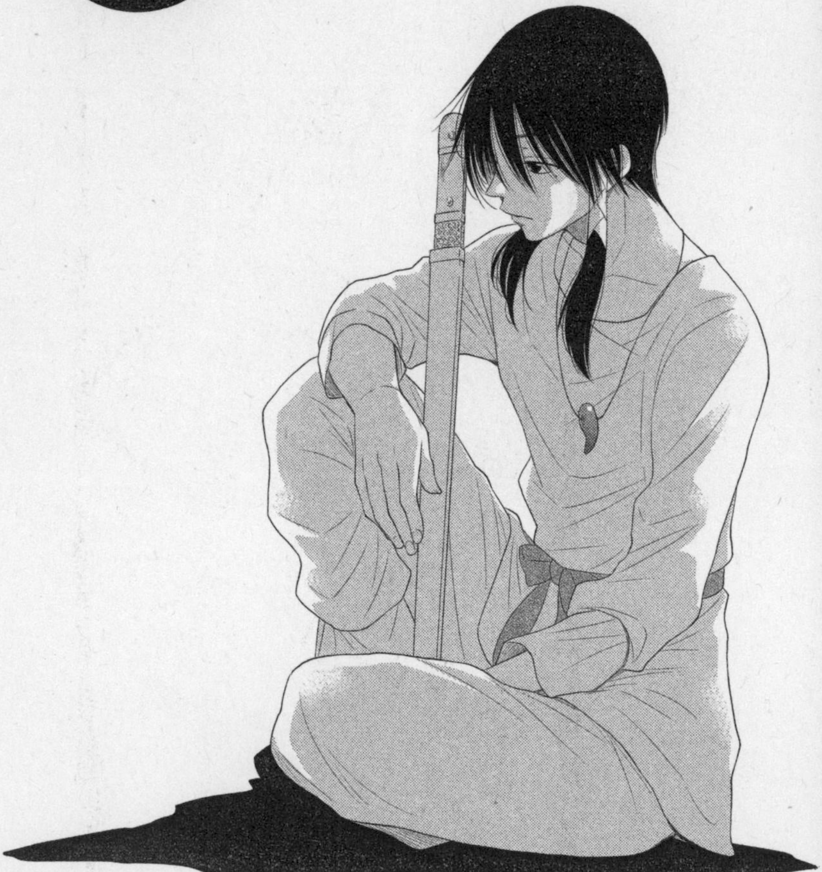

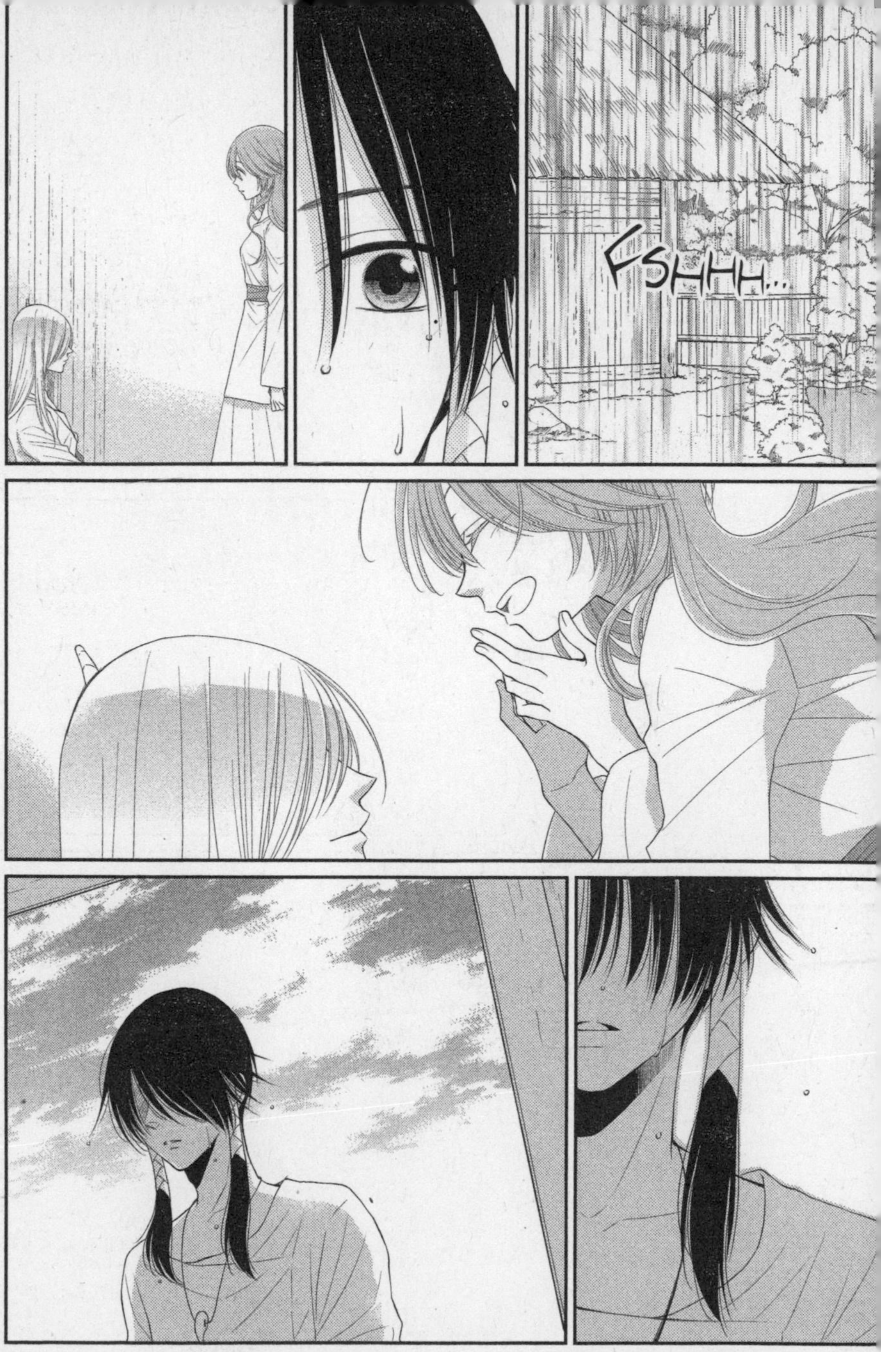
FSHHH...

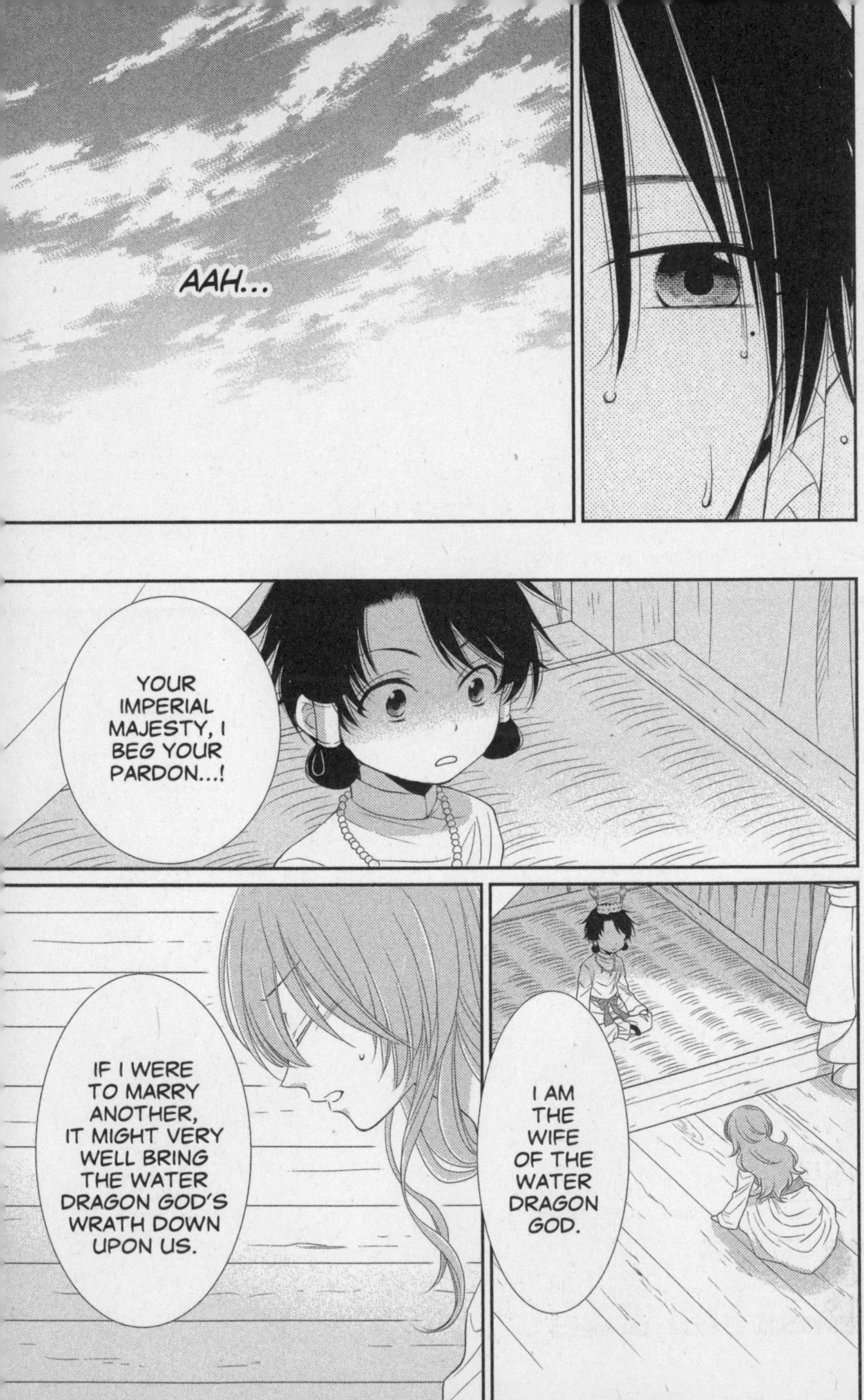
AAH...
YOUR IMPERIAL MAJESTY, I BEG YOUR PARDON...!
I AM THE WIFE OF THE WATER DRAGON GOD.
IF I WERE TO MARRY ANOTHER, IT MIGHT VERY WELL BRING THE WATER DRAGON GOD'S WRATH DOWN UPON US.

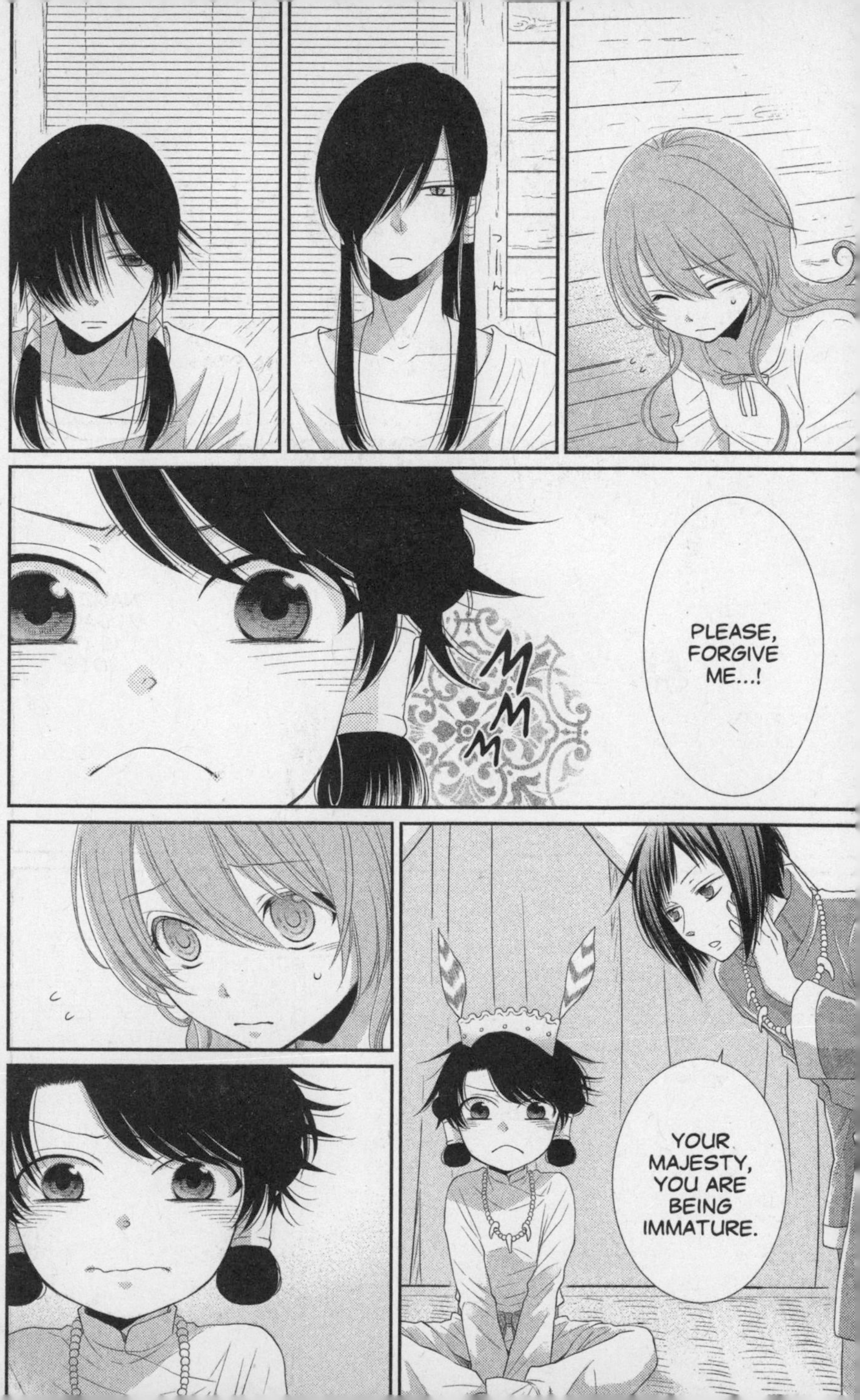
PLEASE, FORGIVE ME...!
MMMM
YOUR MAJESTY, YOU ARE BEING IMMATURE.

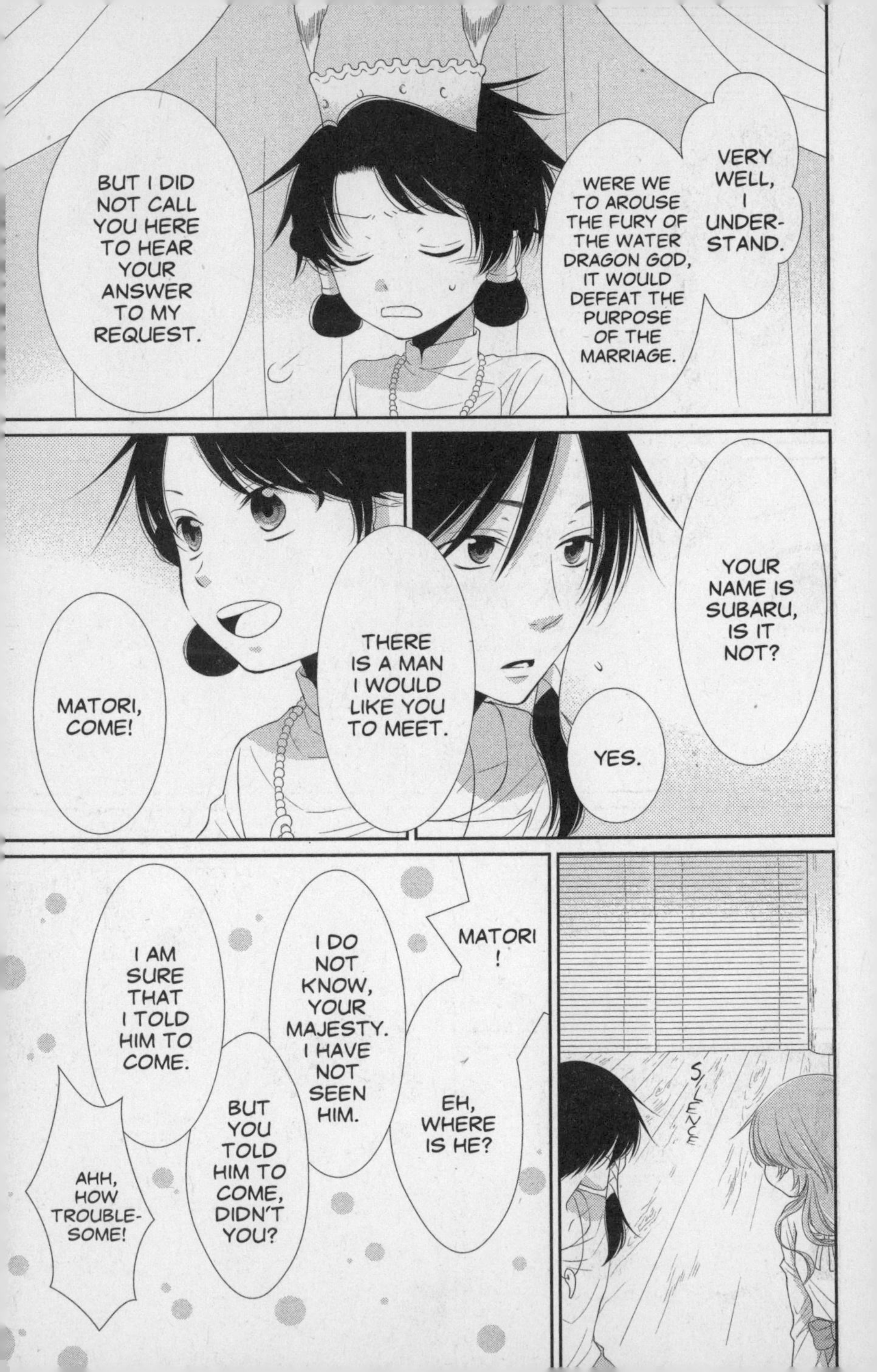
VERY WELL, I UNDER-STAND.
WERE WE TO AROUSE THE FURY OF THE WATER DRAGON GOD, IT WOULD DEFEAT THE PURPOSE OF THE MARRIAGE.
BUT I DID NOT CALL YOU HERE TO HEAR YOUR ANSWER TO MY REQUEST.
YOUR NAME IS SUBARU, IS IT NOT?
YES.
THERE IS A MAN I WOULD LIKE YOU TO MEET.
MATORI, COME!
SILENCE
MATORI!
EH, WHERE IS HE?
I DO NOT KNOW, YOUR MAJESTY. I HAVE NOT SEEN HIM.
BUT YOU TOLD HIM TO COME, DIDN'T YOU?
I AM SURE THAT I TOLD HIM TO COME.
AHH, HOW TROUBLE-SOME!

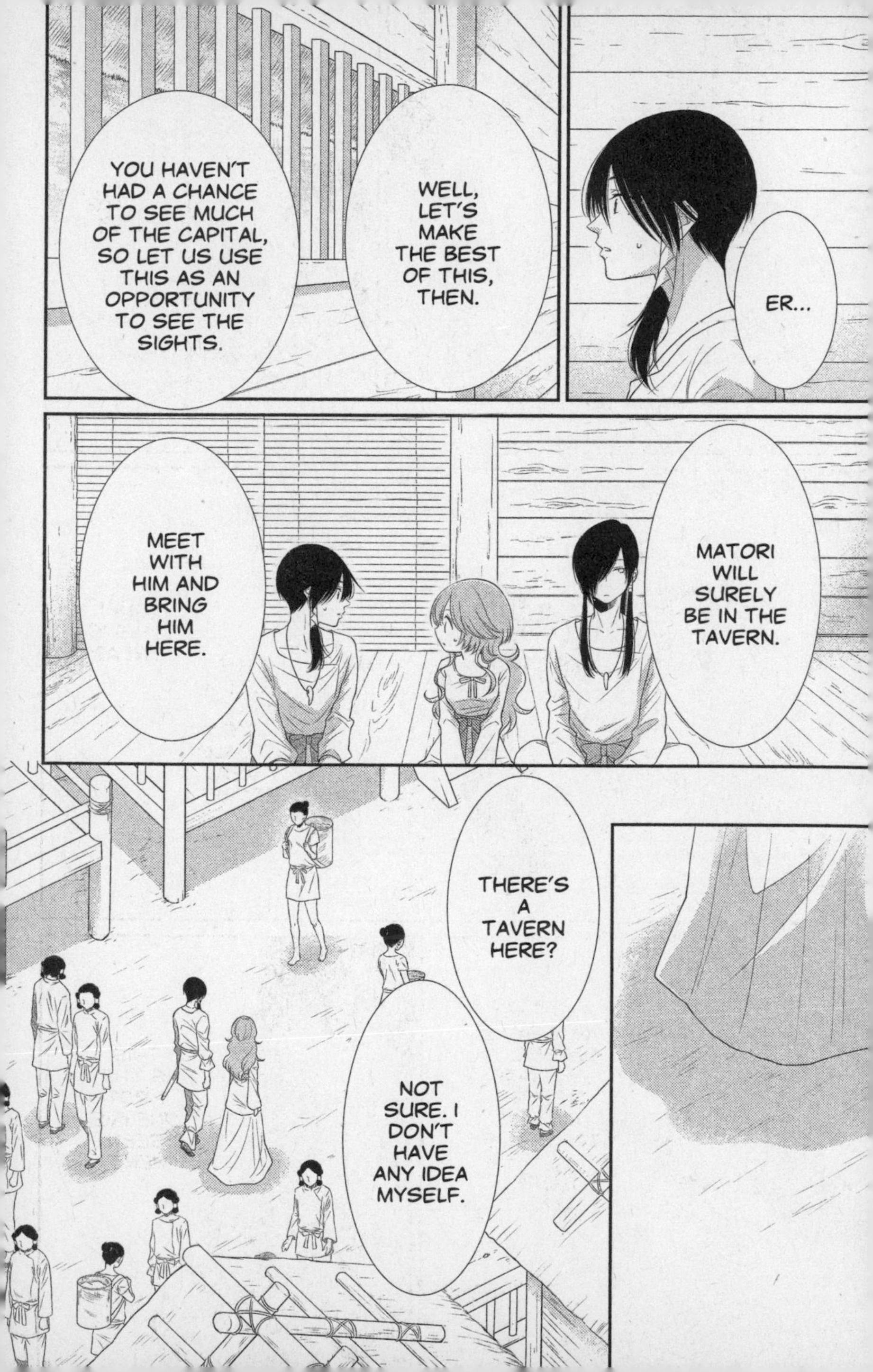
ER...
WELL, LET'S MAKE THE BEST OF THIS, THEN.
YOU HAVEN'T HAD A CHANCE TO SEE MUCH OF THE CAPITAL, SO LET US USE THIS AS AN OPPORTUNITY TO SEE THE SIGHTS.
MATORI WILL SURELY BE IN THE TAVERN.
MEET WITH HIM AND BRING HIM HERE.
THERE'S A TAVERN HERE?
NOT SURE. I DON'T HAVE ANY IDEA MYSELF.

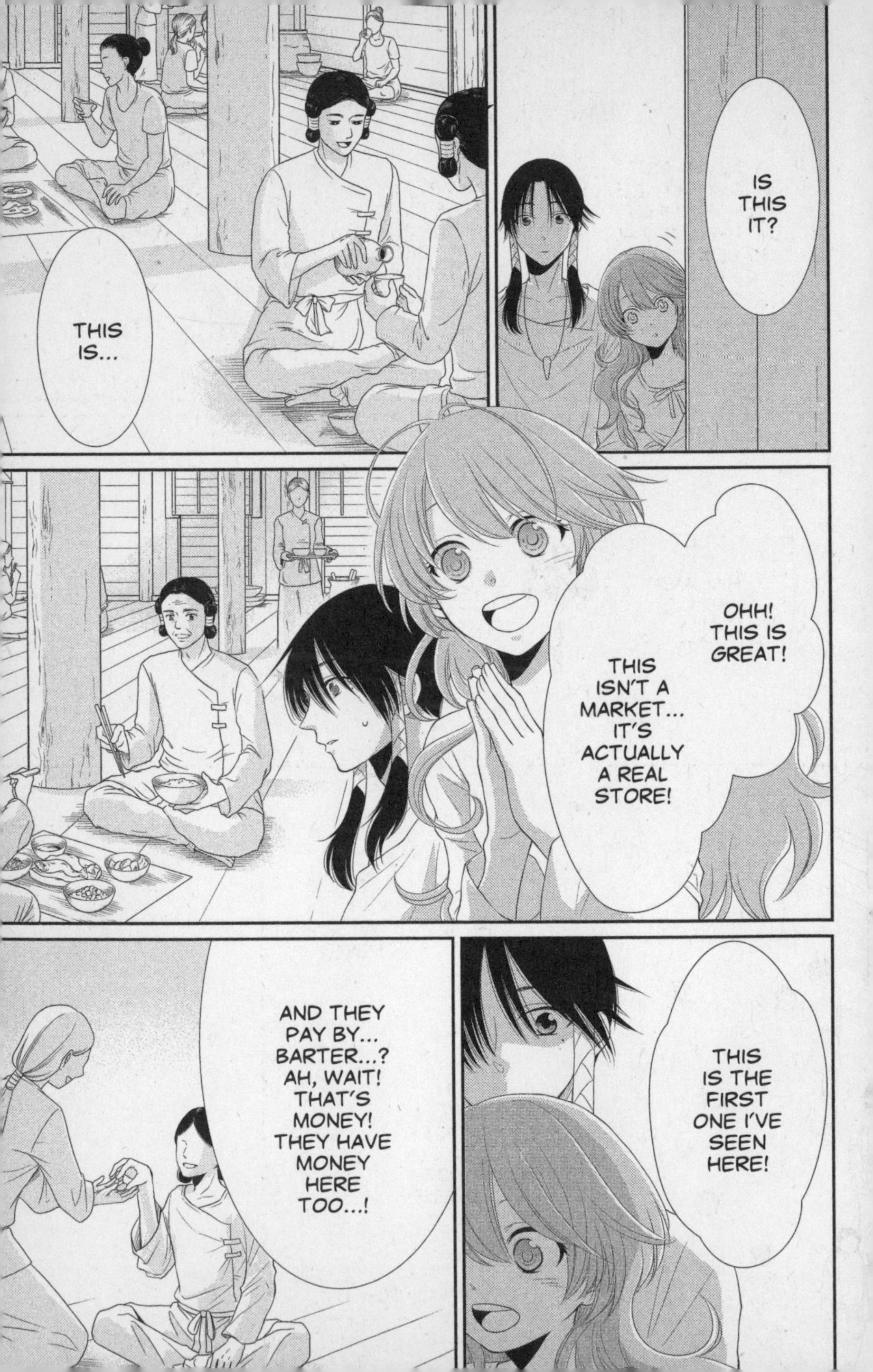
IS THIS IT?
THIS IS...
OHH! THIS IS GREAT!
THIS ISN'T A MARKET... IT'S ACTUALLY A REAL STORE!
THIS IS THE FIRST ONE I'VE SEEN HERE!
AND THEY PAY BY... BARTER...? AH, WAIT! THAT'S MONEY! THEY HAVE MONEY HERE TOO...!

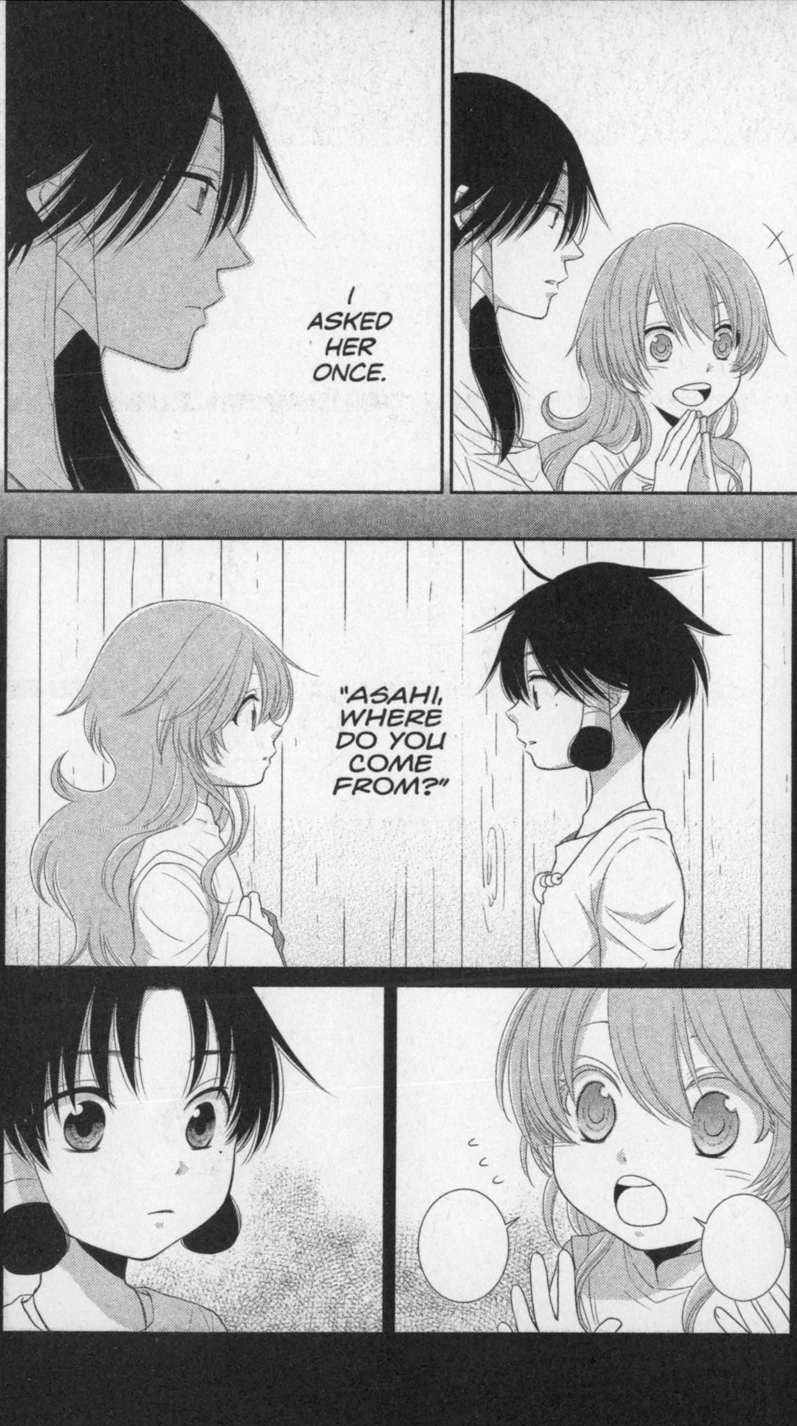
I ASKED HER ONCE.
"ASAHI, WHERE DO YOU COME FROM?"

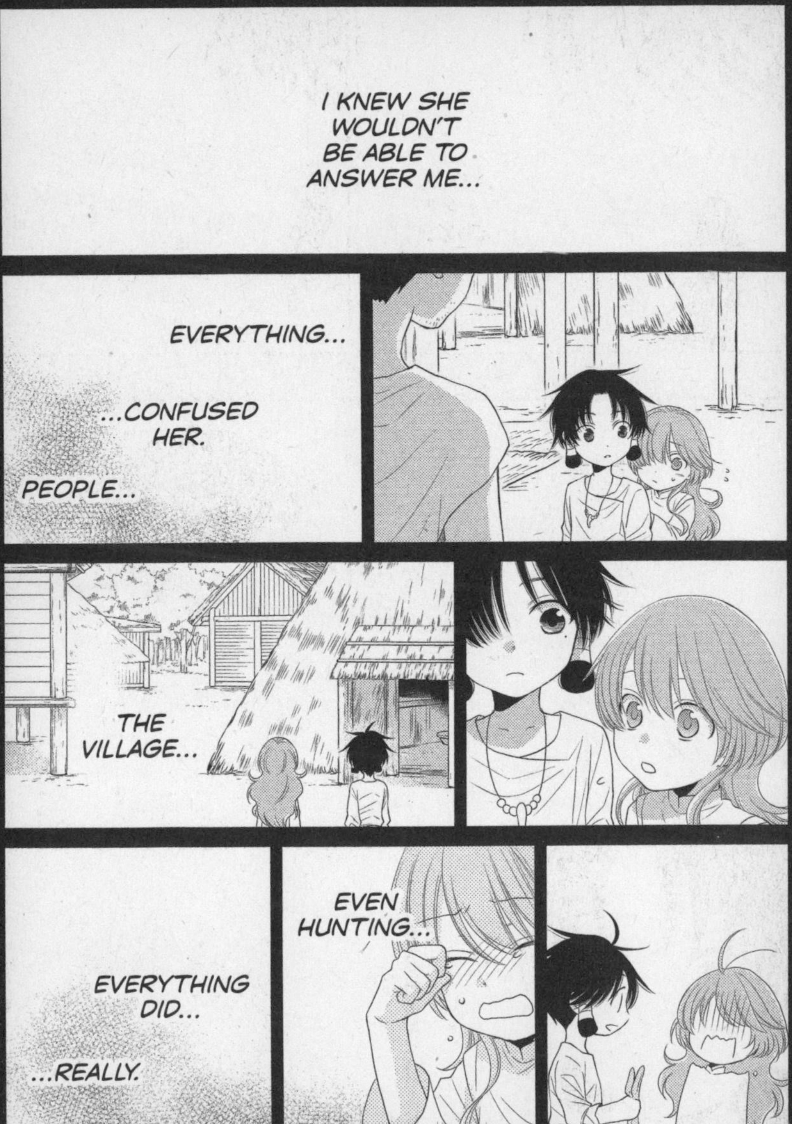
I KNEW SHE WOULDN'T BE ABLE TO ANSWER ME...
EVERYTHING...
...CONFUSED HER.
PEOPLE...
THE VILLAGE...
EVEN HUNTING...
EVERYTHING DID...
...REALLY.

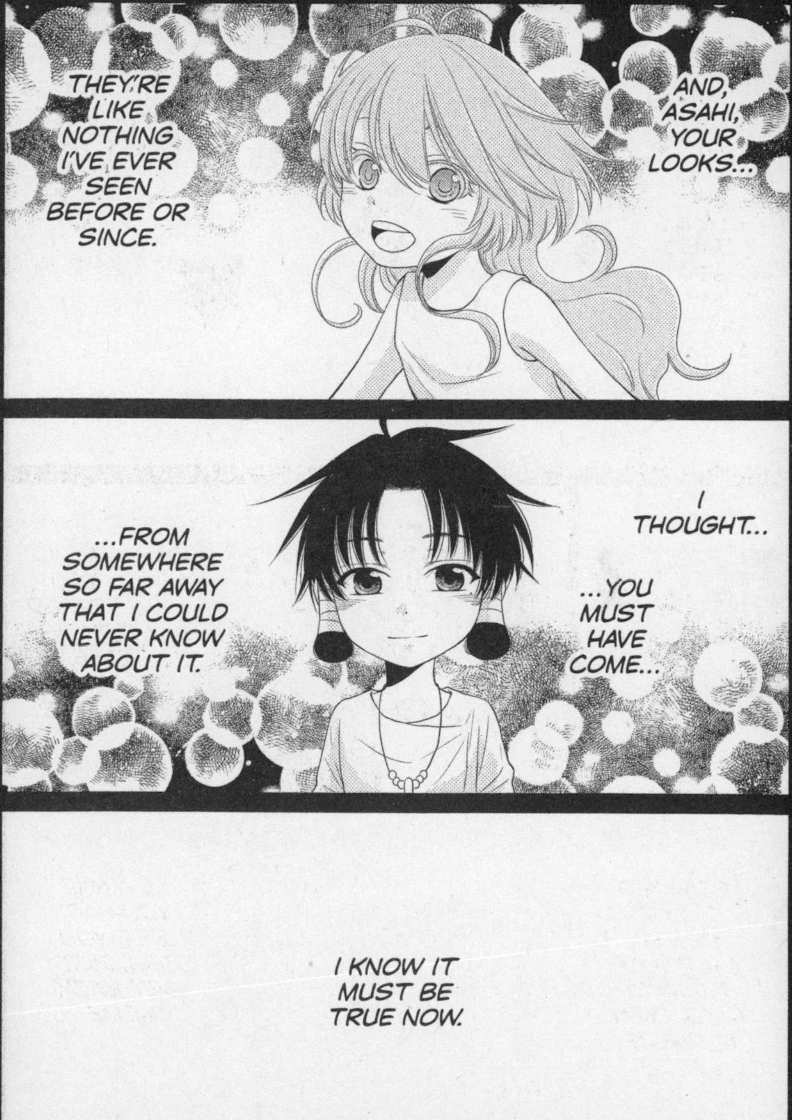
AND, ASAHI, YOUR LOOKS...
THEY'RE LIKE NOTHING I'VE EVER SEEN BEFORE OR SINCE.
I THOUGHT...
...YOU MUST HAVE COME...
...FROM SOMEWHERE SO FAR AWAY THAT I COULD NEVER KNOW ABOUT IT.
I KNOW IT MUST BE TRUE NOW.

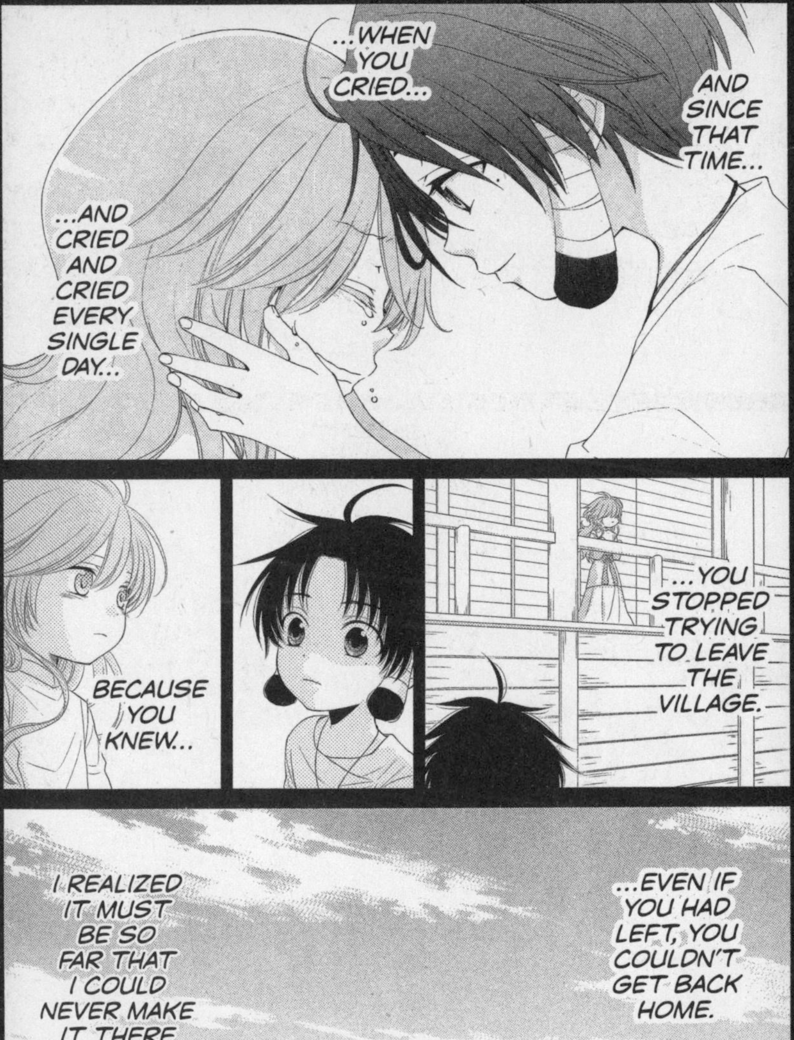
...WHEN YOU CRIED...
...AND CRIED AND CRIED EVERY SINGLE DAY...
AND SINCE THAT TIME...
...YOU STOPPED TRYING TO LEAVE THE VILLAGE.
BECAUSE YOU KNEW...
...EVEN IF YOU HAD LEFT, YOU COULDN'T GET BACK HOME.
I REALIZED IT MUST BE SO FAR THAT I COULD NEVER MAKE IT THERE MYSELF.

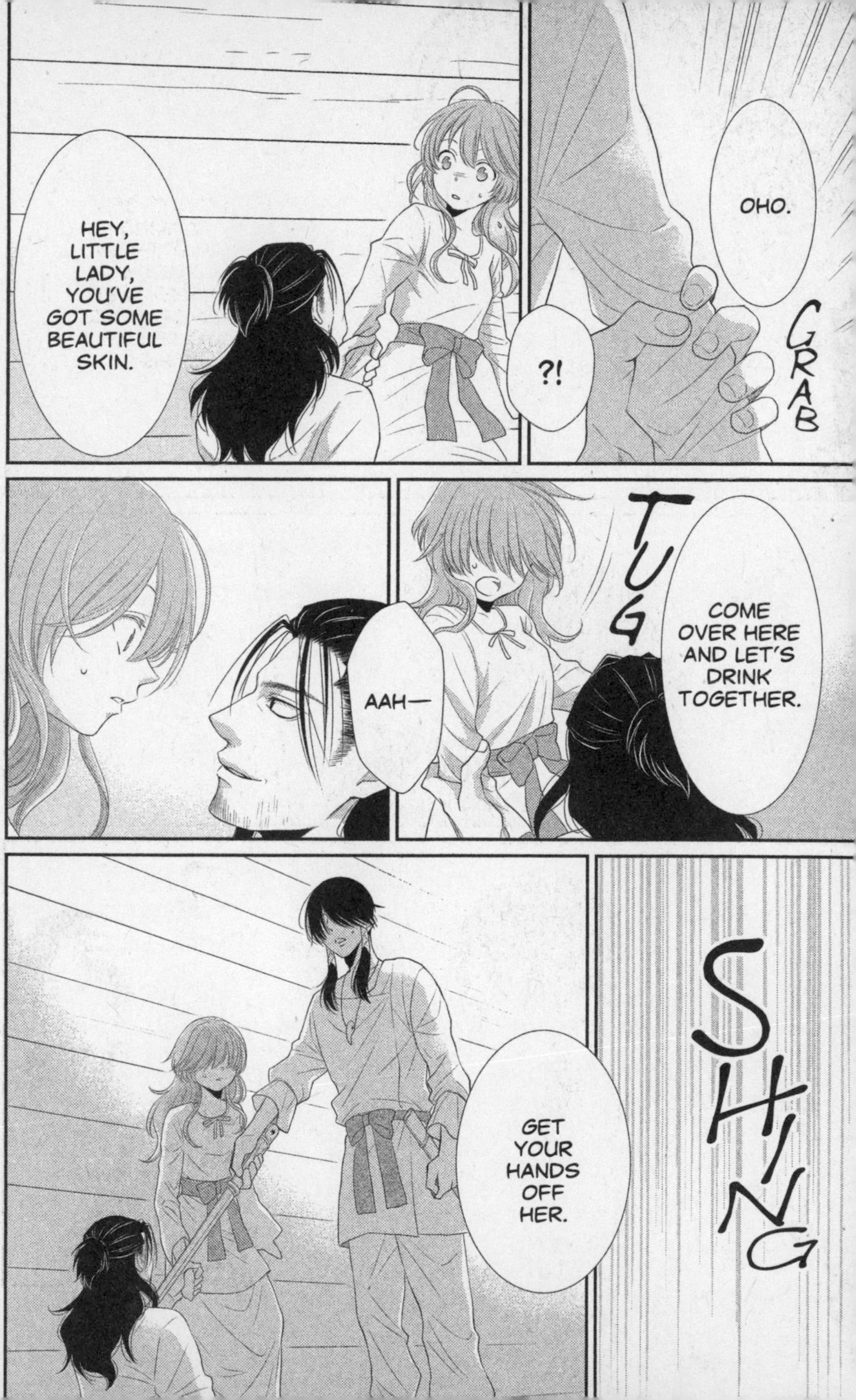
OHO.
GRAB
?!
HEY, LITTLE LADY, YOU'VE GOT SOME BEAUTIFUL SKIN.
COME OVER HERE AND LET'S DRINK TOGETHER.
TUG
AAH—
SHING
GET YOUR HANDS OFF HER.

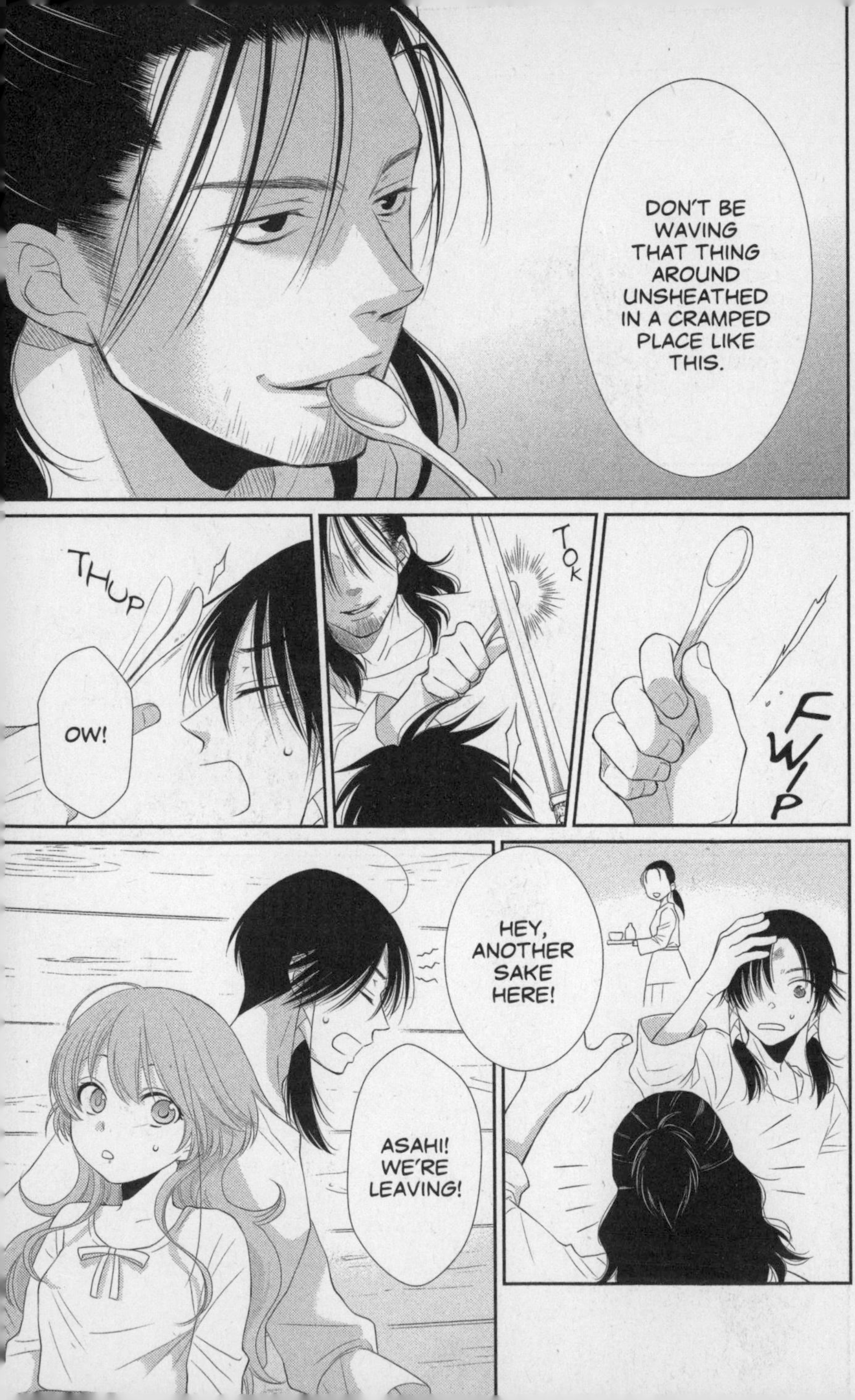
DON'T BE WAVING THAT THING AROUND UNSHEATHED IN A CRAMPED PLACE LIKE THIS.
FWIP
TOK
THUP
OW!
HEY, ANOTHER SAKE HERE!
ASAHI! WE'RE LEAVING!

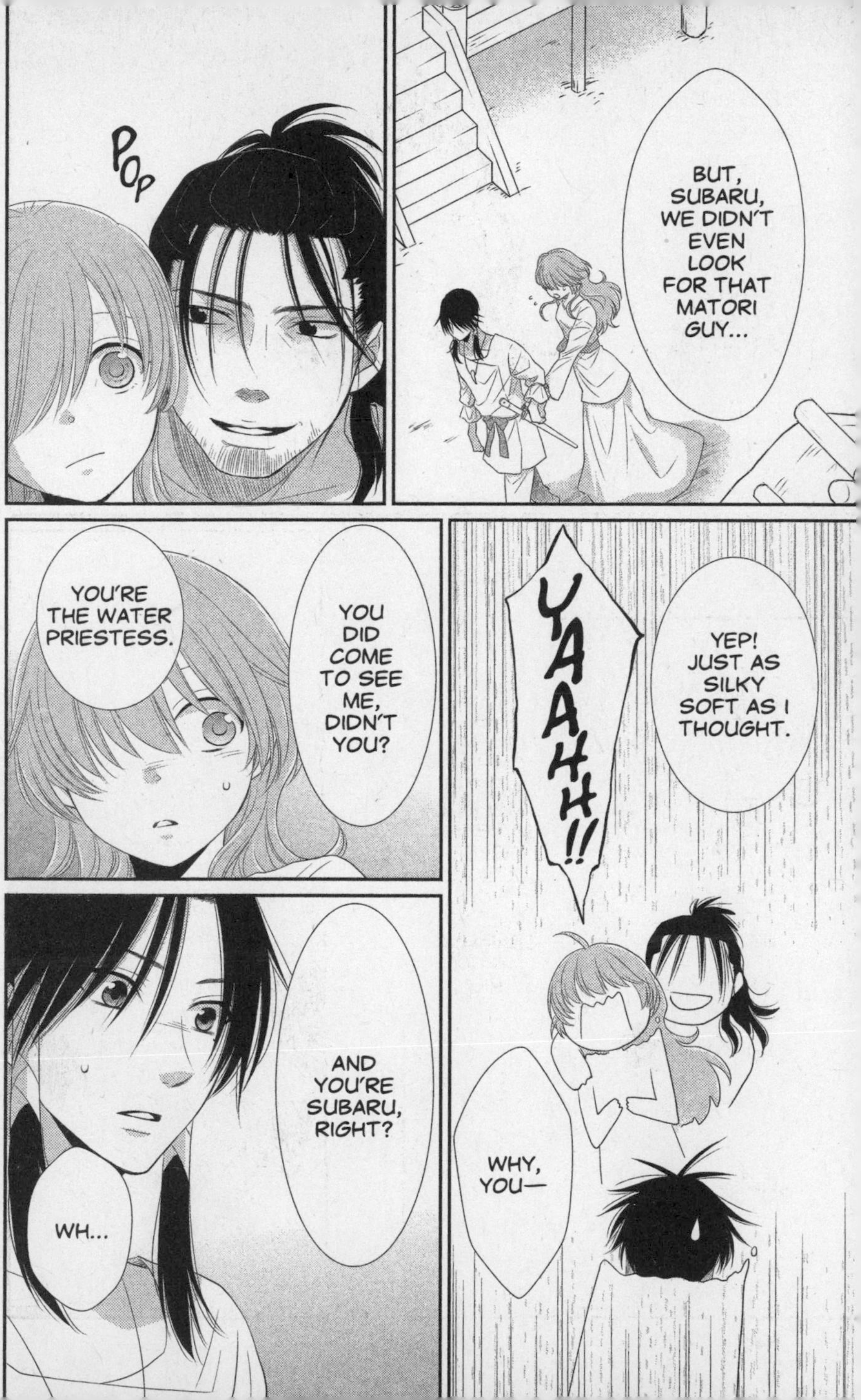
BUT, SUBARU, WE DIDN'T EVEN LOOK FOR THAT MATORI GUY...
POP
YEP! JUST AS SILKY SOFT AS I THOUGHT.
YAAHH!!
WHY, YOU—
YOU DID COME TO SEE ME, DIDN'T YOU?
YOU'RE THE WATER PRIESTESS.
AND YOU'RE SUBARU, RIGHT?
WH...

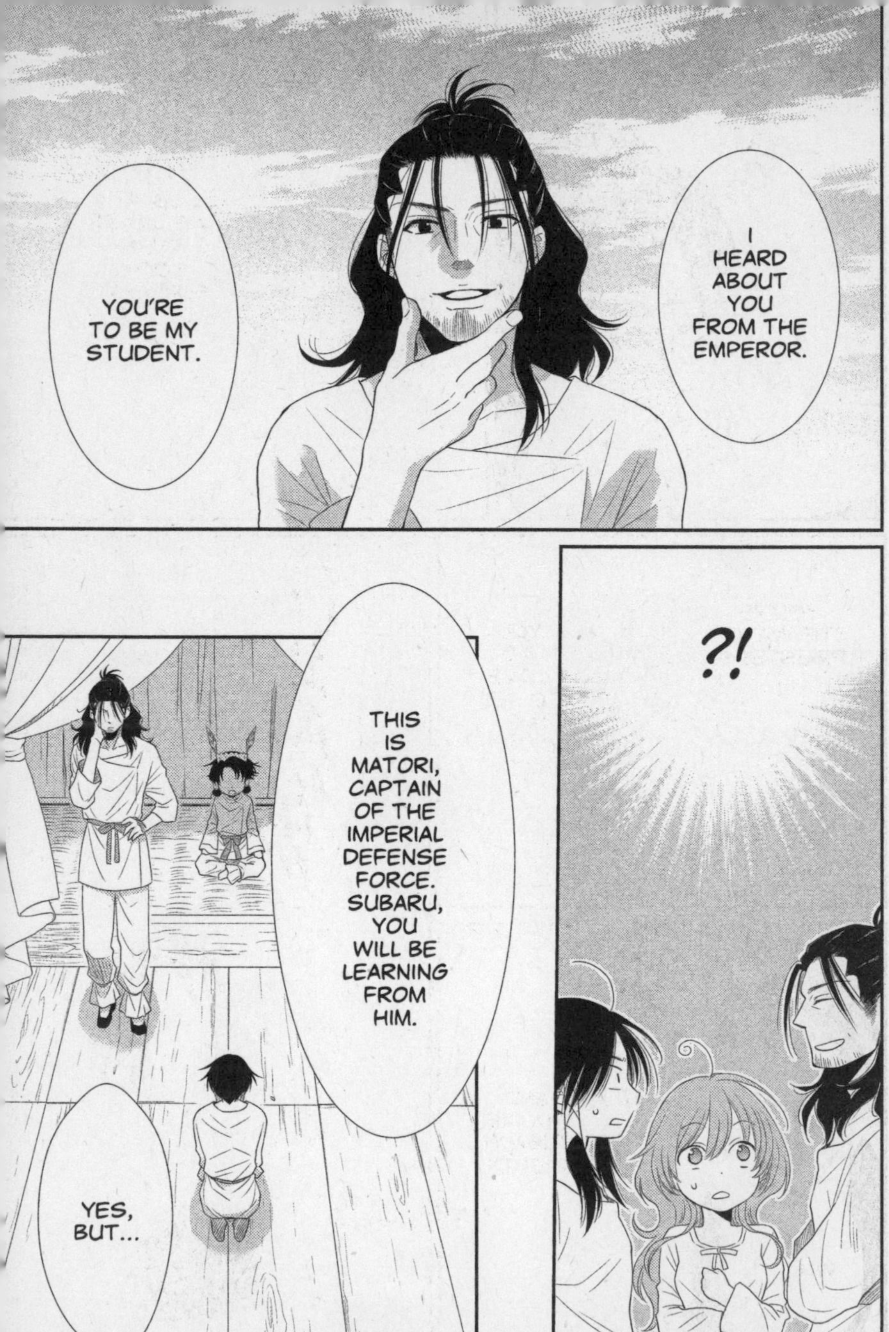
I HEARD ABOUT YOU FROM THE EMPEROR.
YOU'RE TO BE MY STUDENT.
?!
THIS IS MATORI, CAPTAIN OF THE IMPERIAL DEFENSE FORCE. SUBARU, YOU WILL BE LEARNING FROM HIM.
YES, BUT...

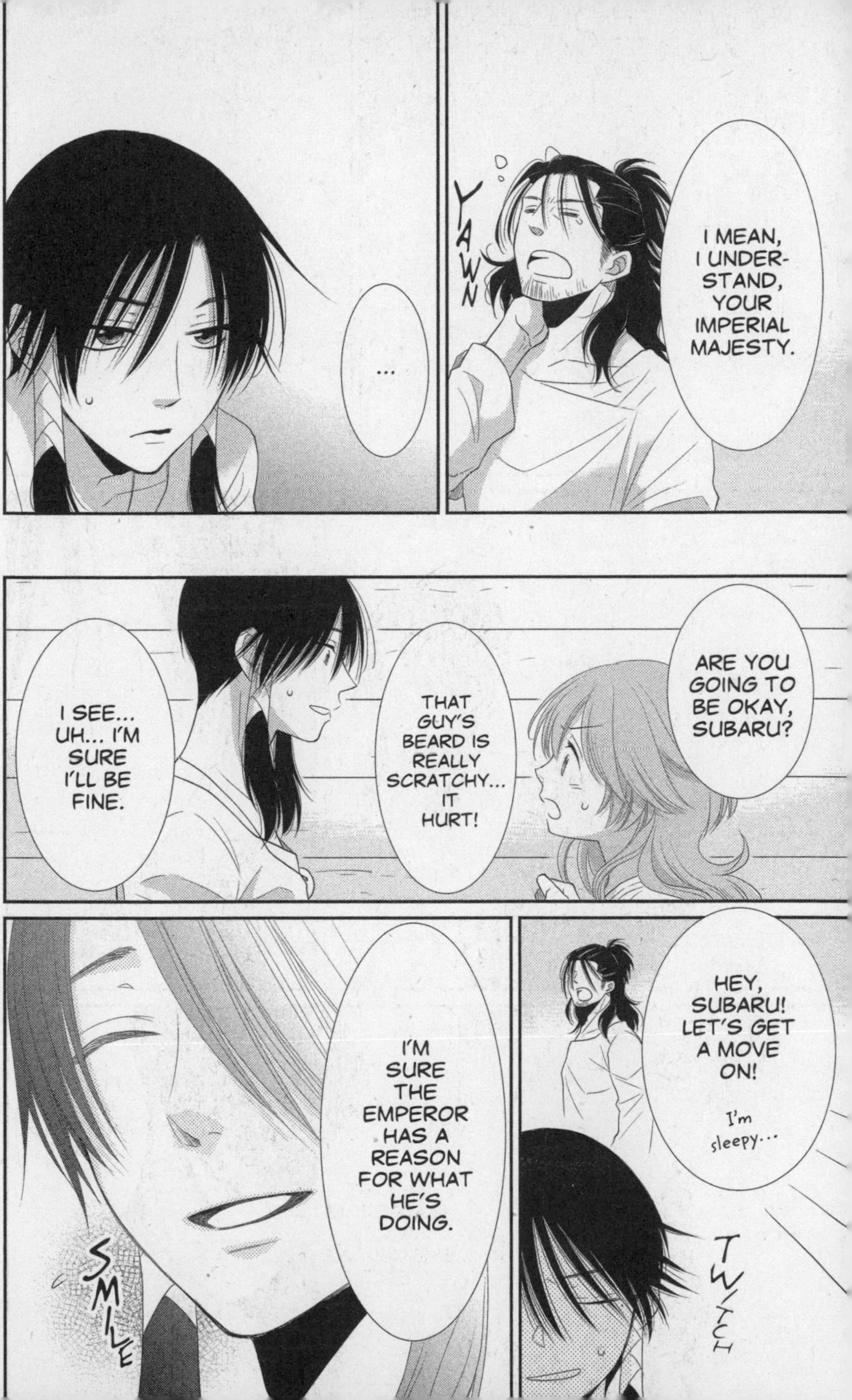
I MEAN, I UNDERSTAND, YOUR IMPERIAL MAJESTY.
YAWN
...
ARE YOU GOING TO BE OKAY, SUBARU?
THAT GUY'S BEARD IS REALLY SCRATCHY... IT HURT!
I SEE... UH... I'M SURE I'LL BE FINE.
HEY, SUBARU! LET'S GET A MOVE ON!
I'm sleepy...
TWITCH
I'M SURE THE EMPEROR HAS A REASON FOR WHAT HE'S DOING.
SMILE

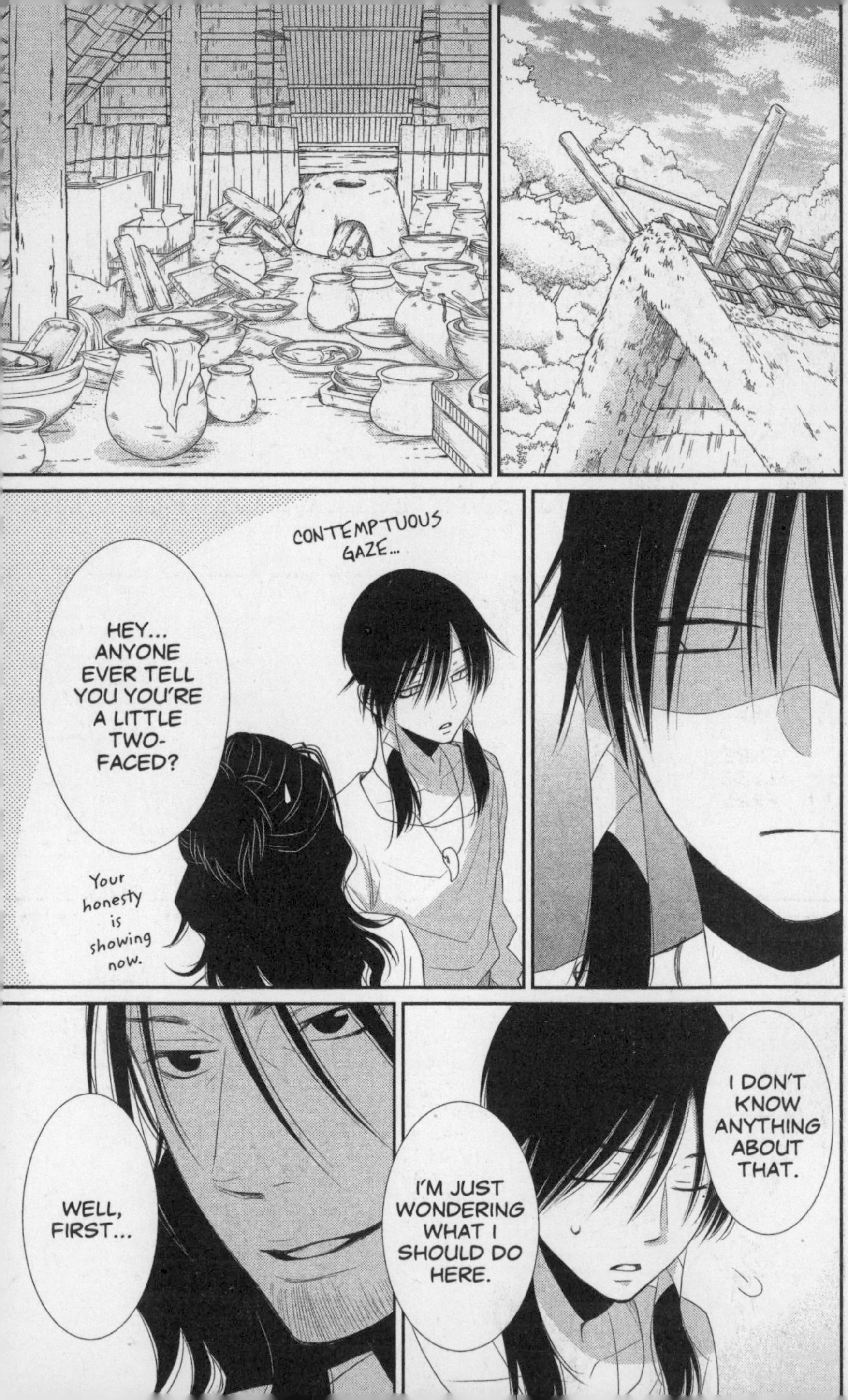
CONTEMPTUOUS GAZE...
HEY... ANYONE EVER TELL YOU YOU'RE A LITTLE TWO-FACED?
Your honesty is showing now.
I DON'T KNOW ANYTHING ABOUT THAT.
I'M JUST WONDERING WHAT I SHOULD DO HERE.
WELL, FIRST...

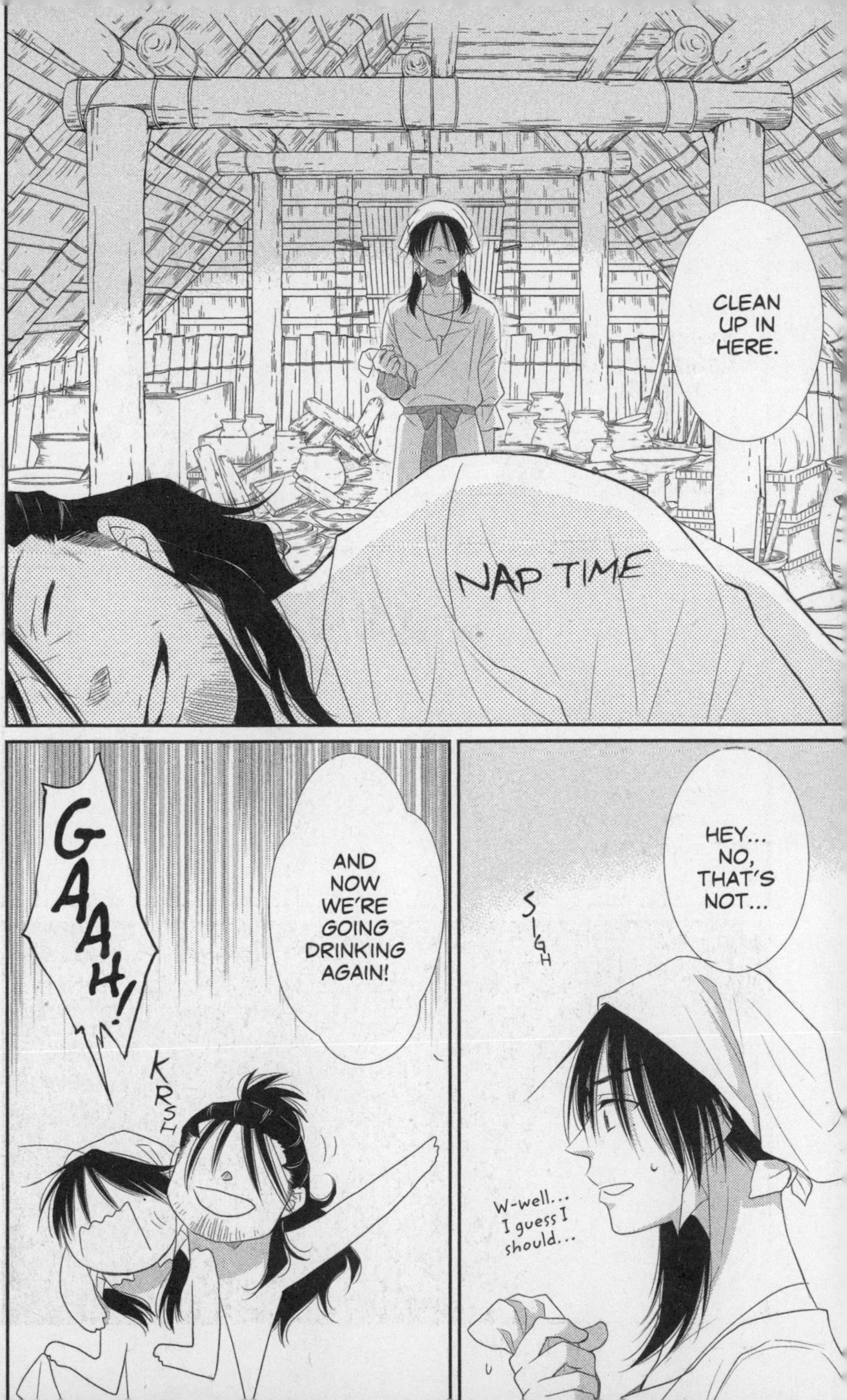
CLEAN UP IN HERE.
NAP TIME
HEY... NO, THAT'S NOT...
SIGH
W-well... I guess I should...
AND NOW WE'RE GOING DRINKING AGAIN!
GAAH!
KRSH

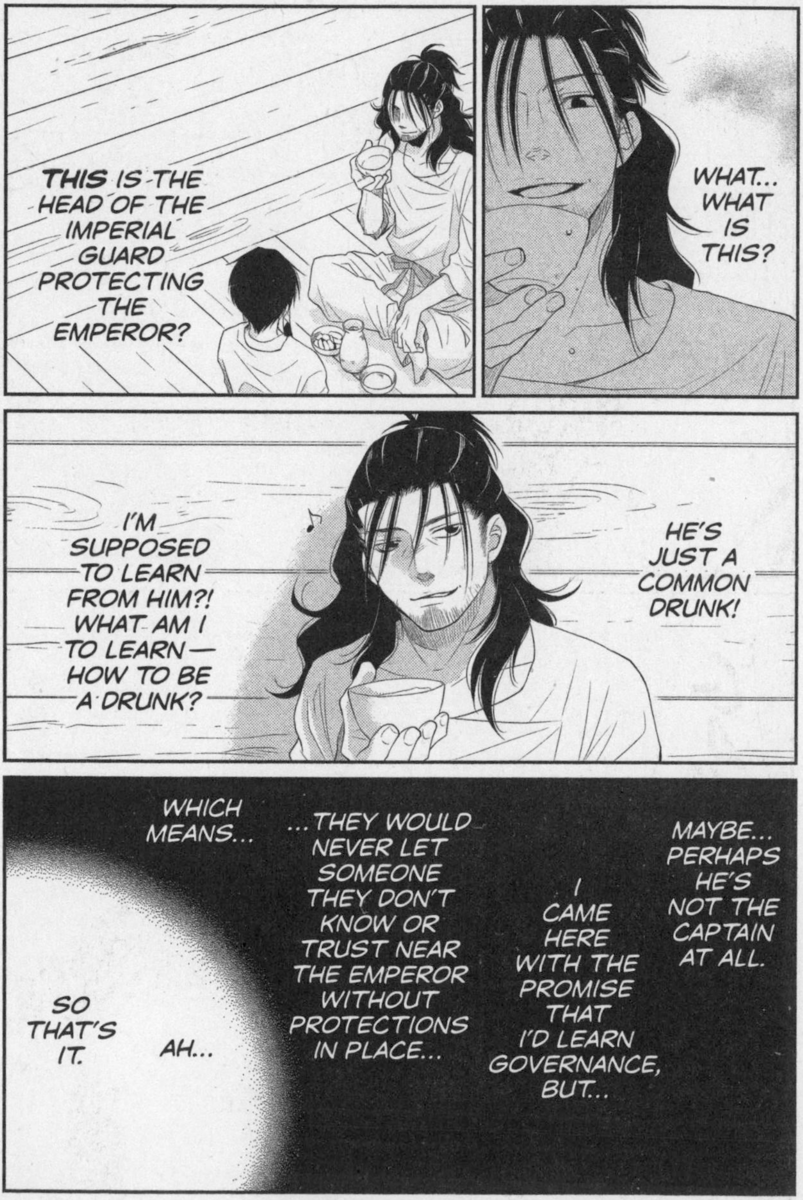
WHAT... WHAT IS THIS?
THIS IS THE HEAD OF THE IMPERIAL GUARD PROTECTING THE EMPEROR?
HE'S JUST A COMMON DRUNK!
I'M SUPPOSED TO LEARN FROM HIM?! WHAT AM I TO LEARN— HOW TO BE A DRUNK?
MAYBE... PERHAPS HE'S NOT THE CAPTAIN AT ALL.
I CAME HERE WITH THE PROMISE THAT I'D LEARN GOVERNANCE, BUT...
...THEY WOULD NEVER LET SOMEONE THEY DON'T KNOW OR TRUST NEAR THE EMPEROR WITHOUT PROTECTIONS IN PLACE...
WHICH MEANS...
AH...
SO THAT'S IT.

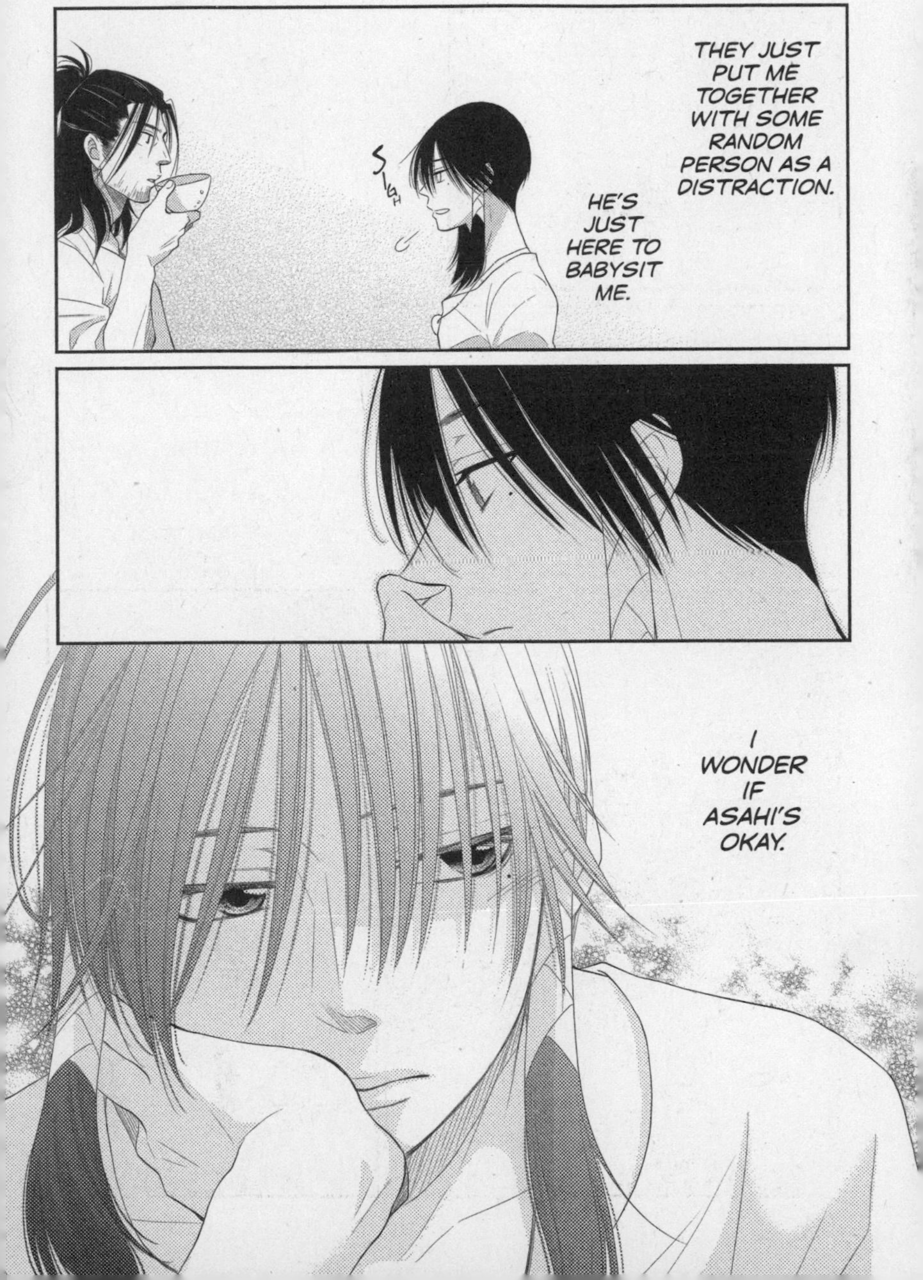
THEY JUST PUT ME TOGETHER WITH SOME RANDOM PERSON AS A DISTRACTION.
HE'S JUST HERE TO BABYSIT ME.
SIGH
I WONDER IF ASAHI'S OKAY.

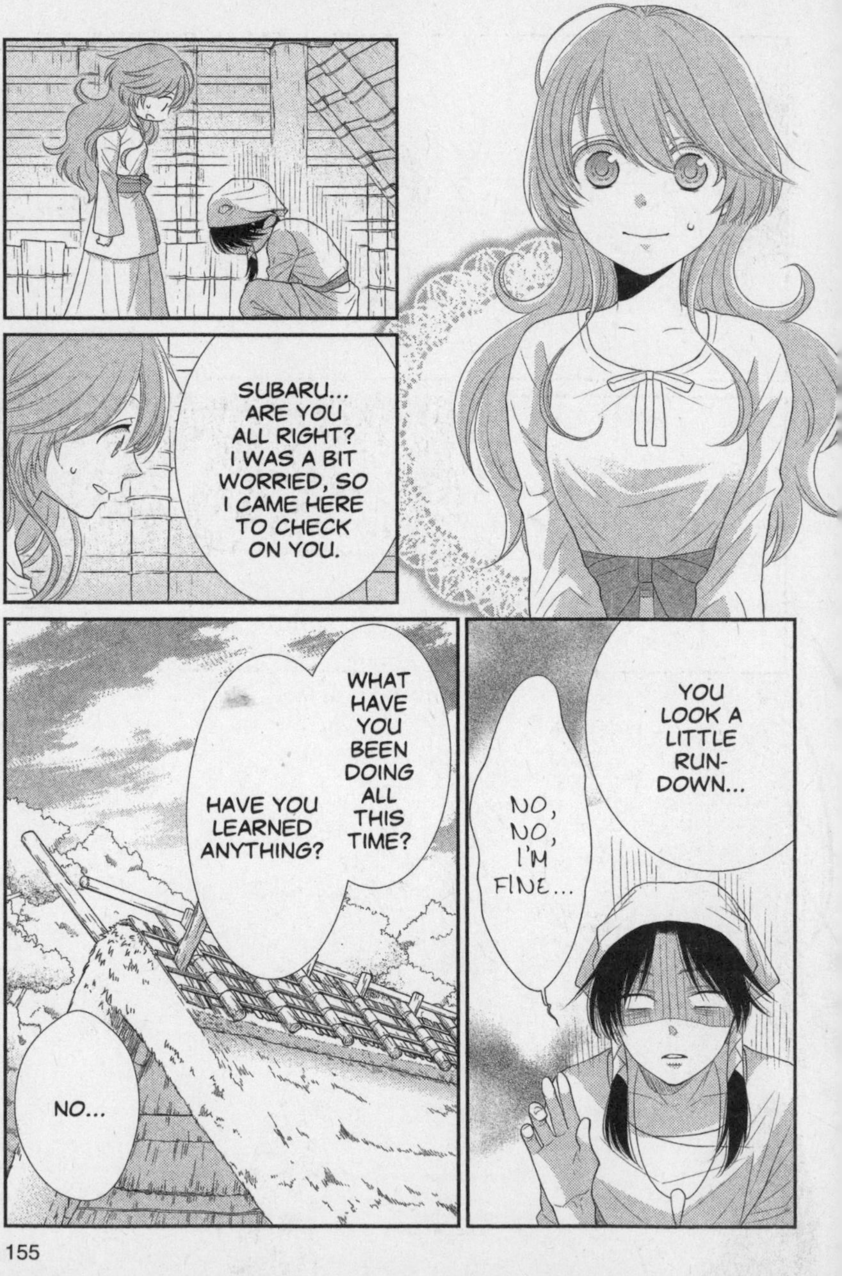
SUBARU... ARE YOU ALL RIGHT? I WAS A BIT WORRIED, SO I CAME HERE TO CHECK ON YOU.
YOU LOOK A LITTLE RUN-DOWN...
NO, NO, I'M FINE...
WHAT HAVE YOU BEEN DOING ALL THIS TIME?
HAVE YOU LEARNED ANYTHING?
NO...

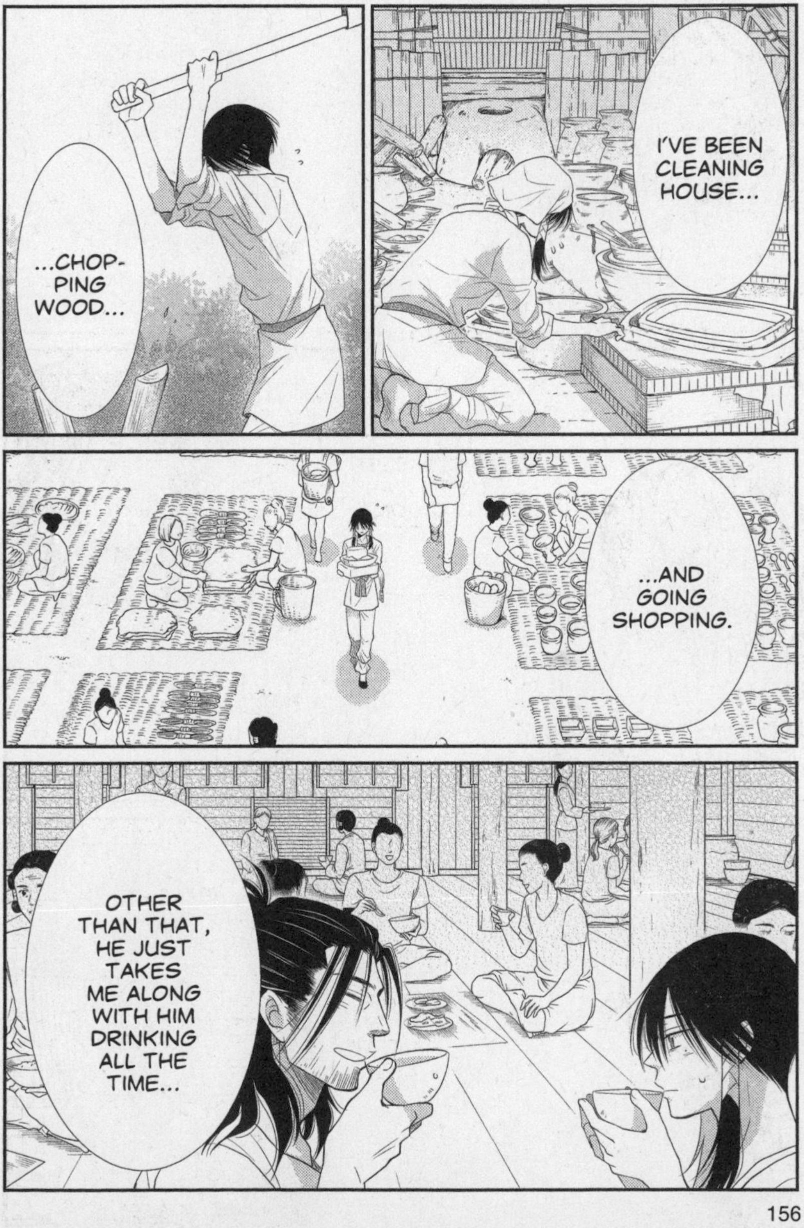
I'VE BEEN CLEANING HOUSE...
...CHOP-PING WOOD...
...AND GOING SHOPPING.
OTHER THAN THAT, HE JUST TAKES ME ALONG WITH HIM DRINKING ALL THE TIME...

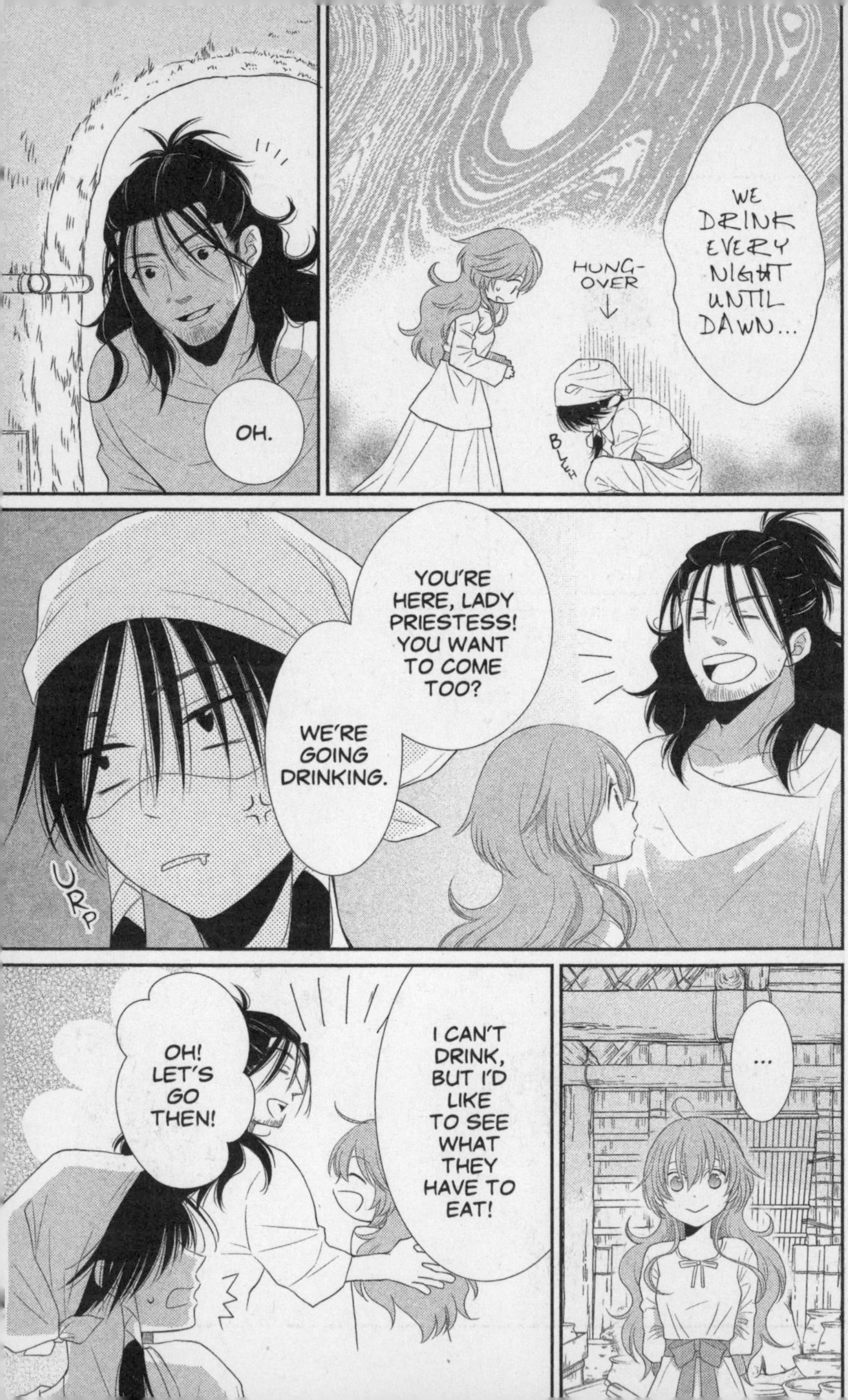
WE DRINK EVERY NIGHT UNTIL DAWN...
HUNG-OVER
OH.
YOU'RE HERE, LADY PRIESTESS! YOU WANT TO COME TOO?
WE'RE GOING DRINKING.
URP
...
I CAN'T DRINK, BUT I'D LIKE TO SEE WHAT THEY HAVE TO EAT!
OH! LET'S GO THEN!

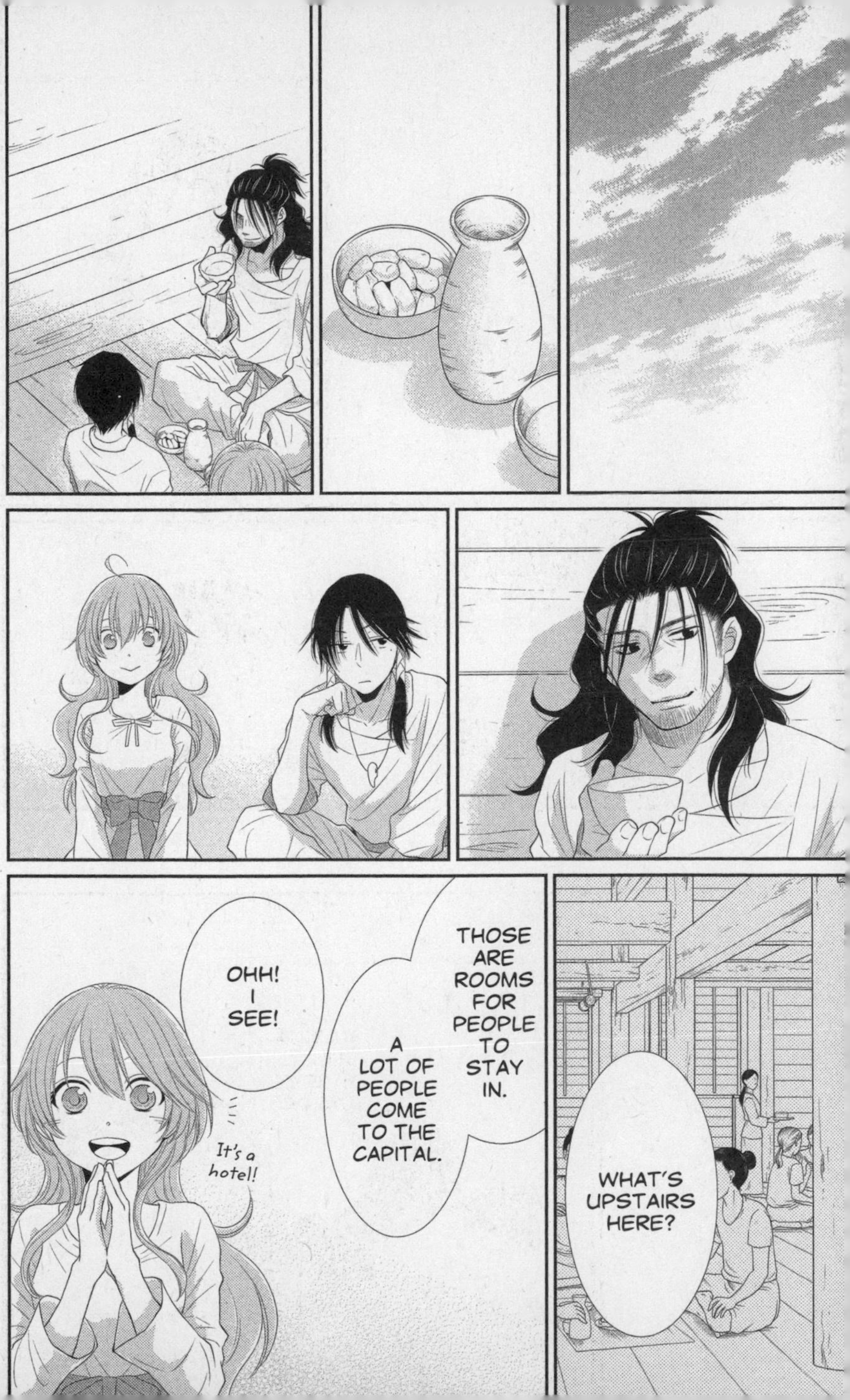
WHAT'S UPSTAIRS HERE?
THOSE ARE ROOMS FOR PEOPLE TO STAY IN.
A LOT OF PEOPLE COME TO THE CAPITAL.
OHH! I SEE!
It's a hotel!

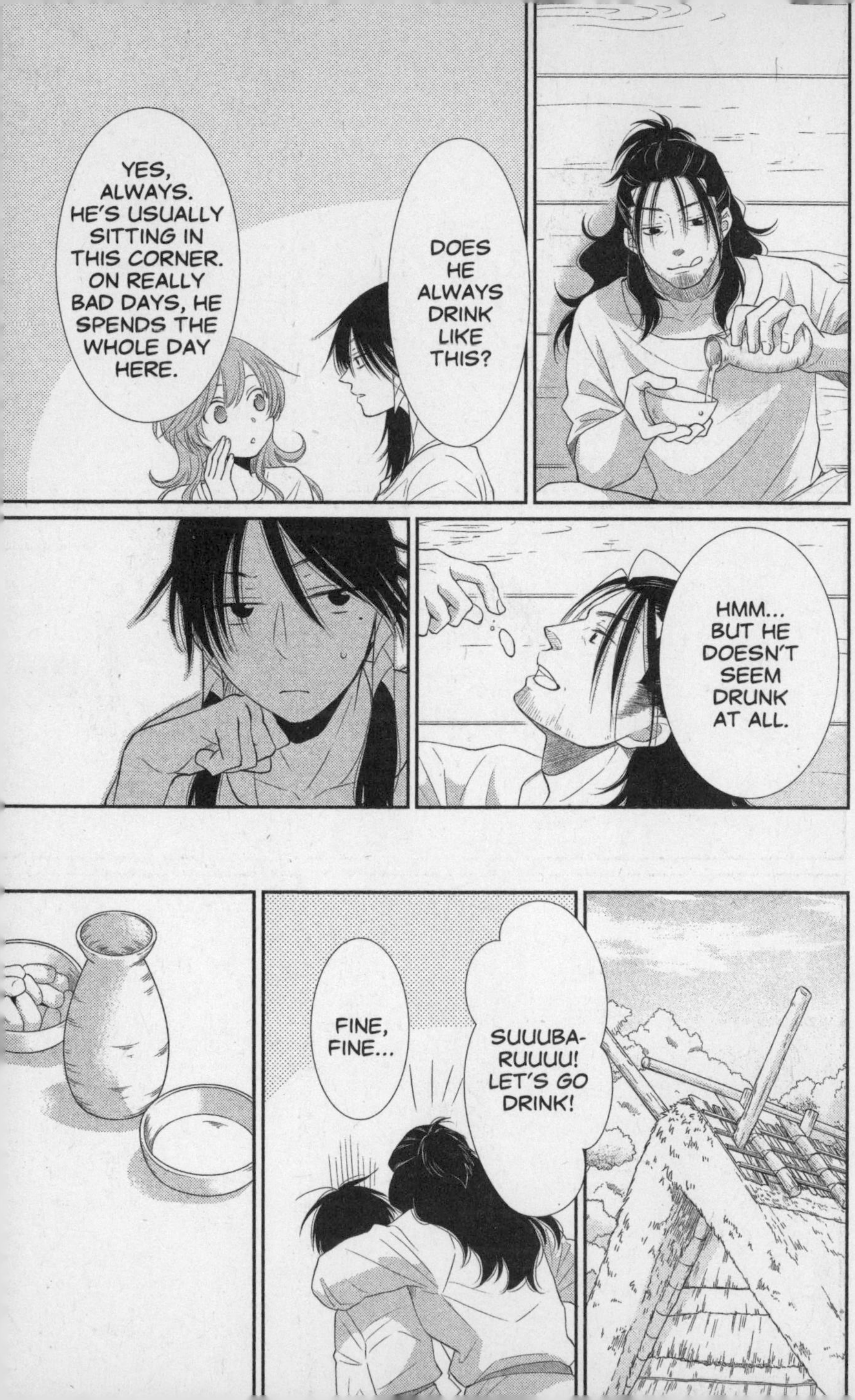
DOES HE ALWAYS DRINK LIKE THIS?
YES, ALWAYS. HE'S USUALLY SITTING IN THIS CORNER. ON REALLY BAD DAYS, HE SPENDS THE WHOLE DAY HERE.
HMM... BUT HE DOESN'T SEEM DRUNK AT ALL.
SUUUBA-RUUUU! LET'S GO DRINK!
FINE, FINE...

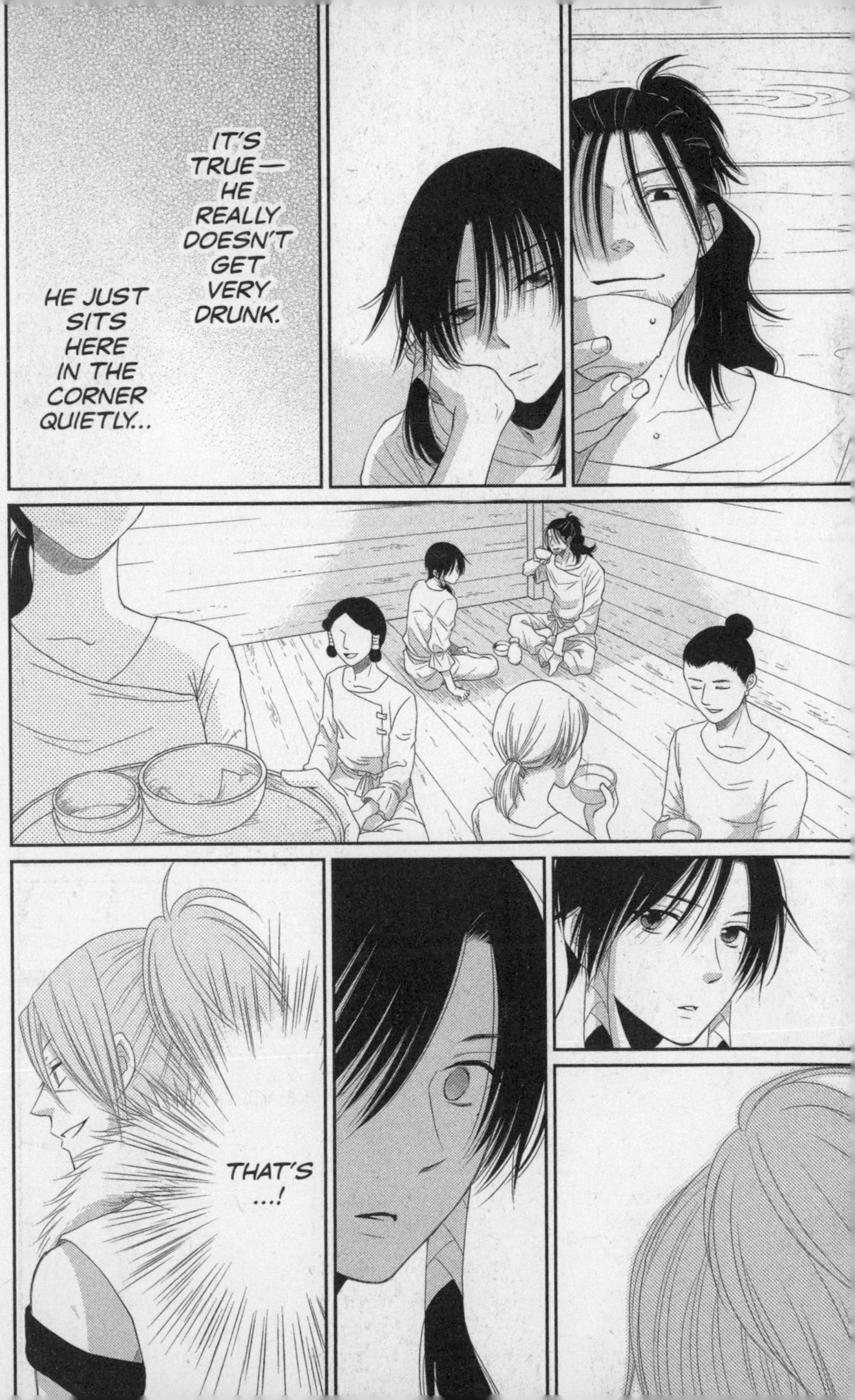
IT'S TRUE—HE REALLY DOESN'T GET VERY DRUNK.
HE JUST SITS HERE IN THE CORNER QUIETLY...
THAT'S ...!

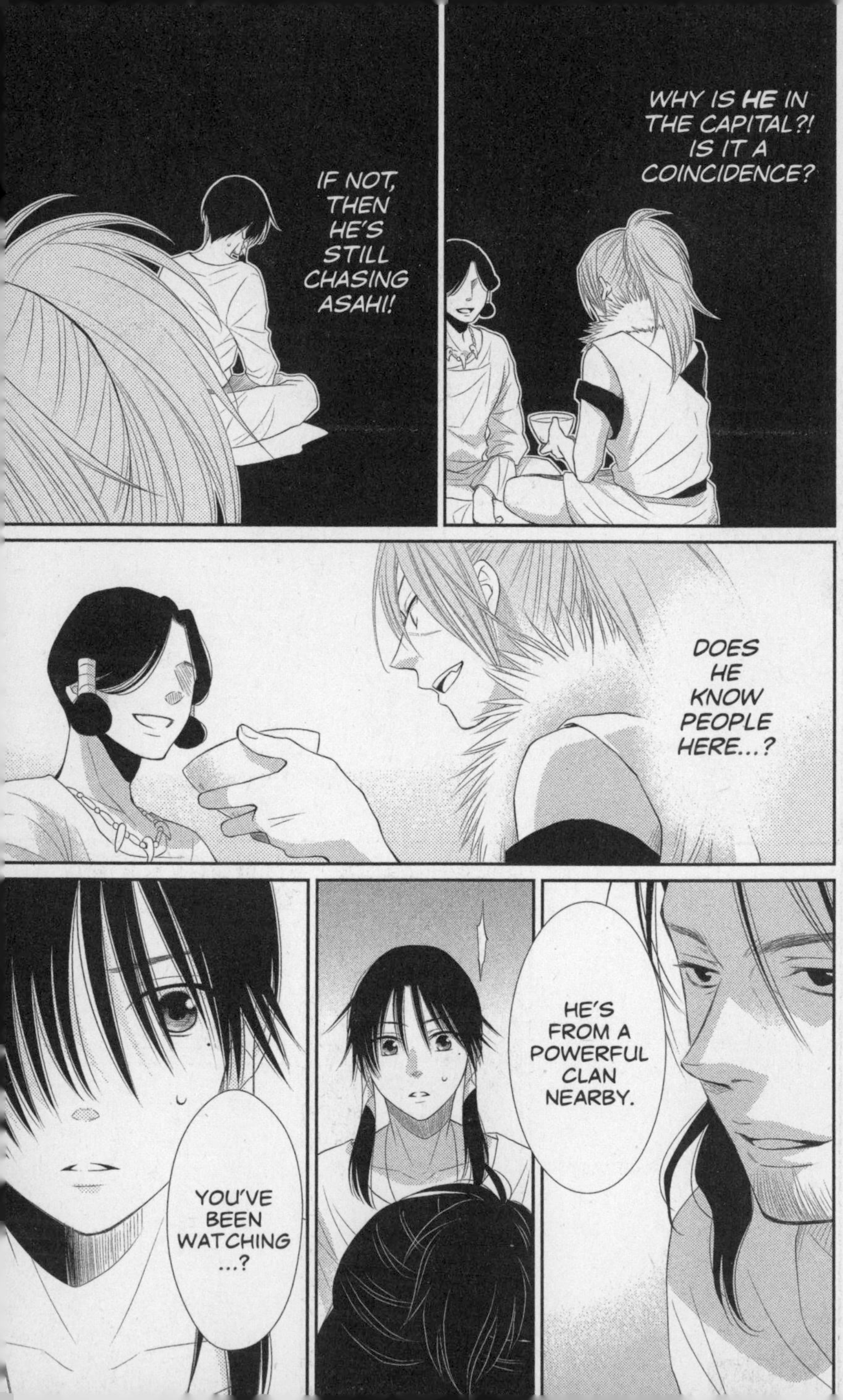
WHY IS HE IN THE CAPITAL?! IS IT A COINCIDENCE?
IF NOT, THEN HE'S STILL CHASING ASAHI!
DOES HE KNOW PEOPLE HERE...?
HE'S FROM A POWERFUL CLAN NEARBY.
YOU'VE BEEN WATCHING...?

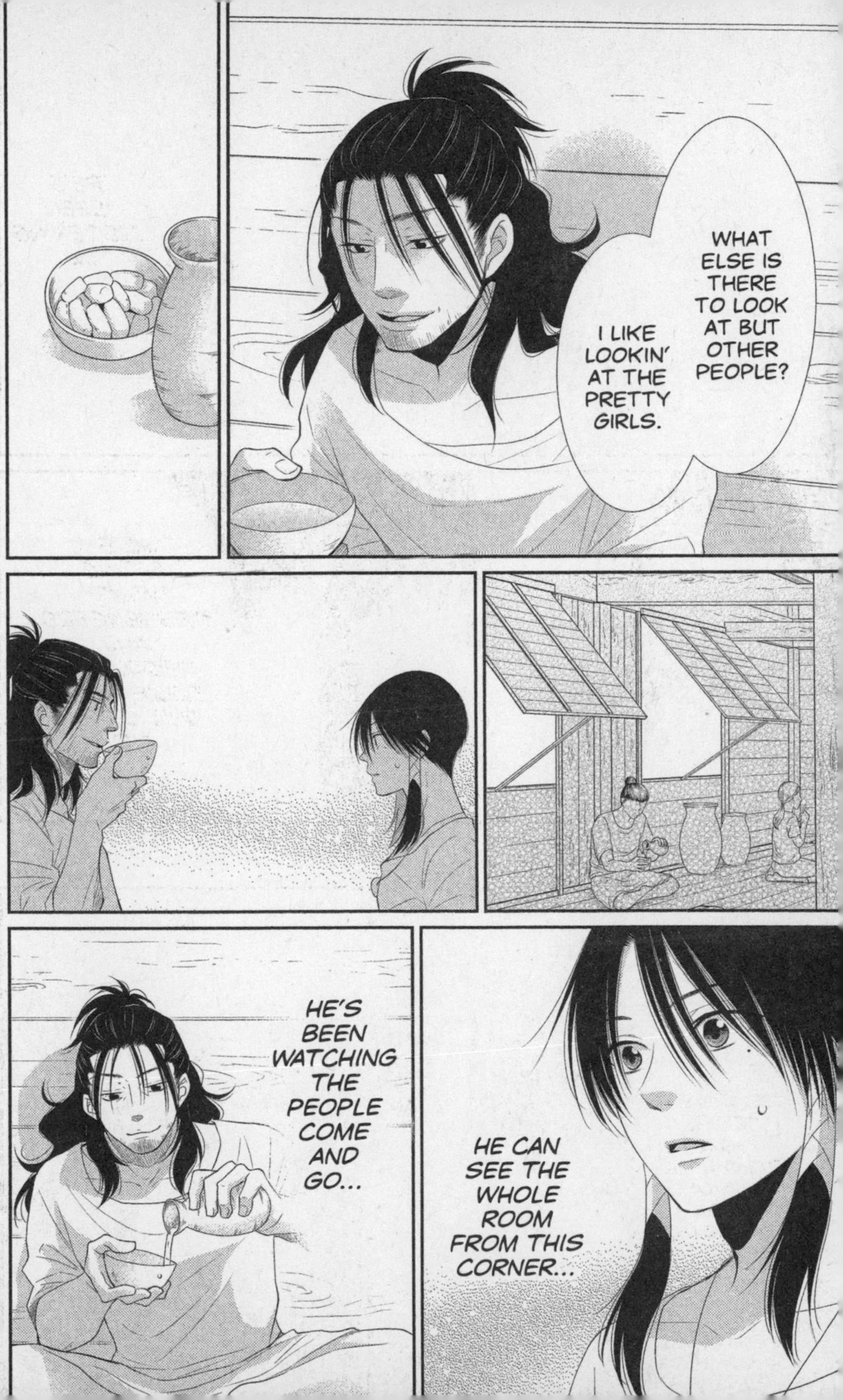
WHAT ELSE IS THERE TO LOOK AT BUT OTHER PEOPLE?
I LIKE LOOKIN' AT THE PRETTY GIRLS.
HE CAN SEE THE WHOLE ROOM FROM THIS CORNER...
HE'S BEEN WATCHING THE PEOPLE COME AND GO...

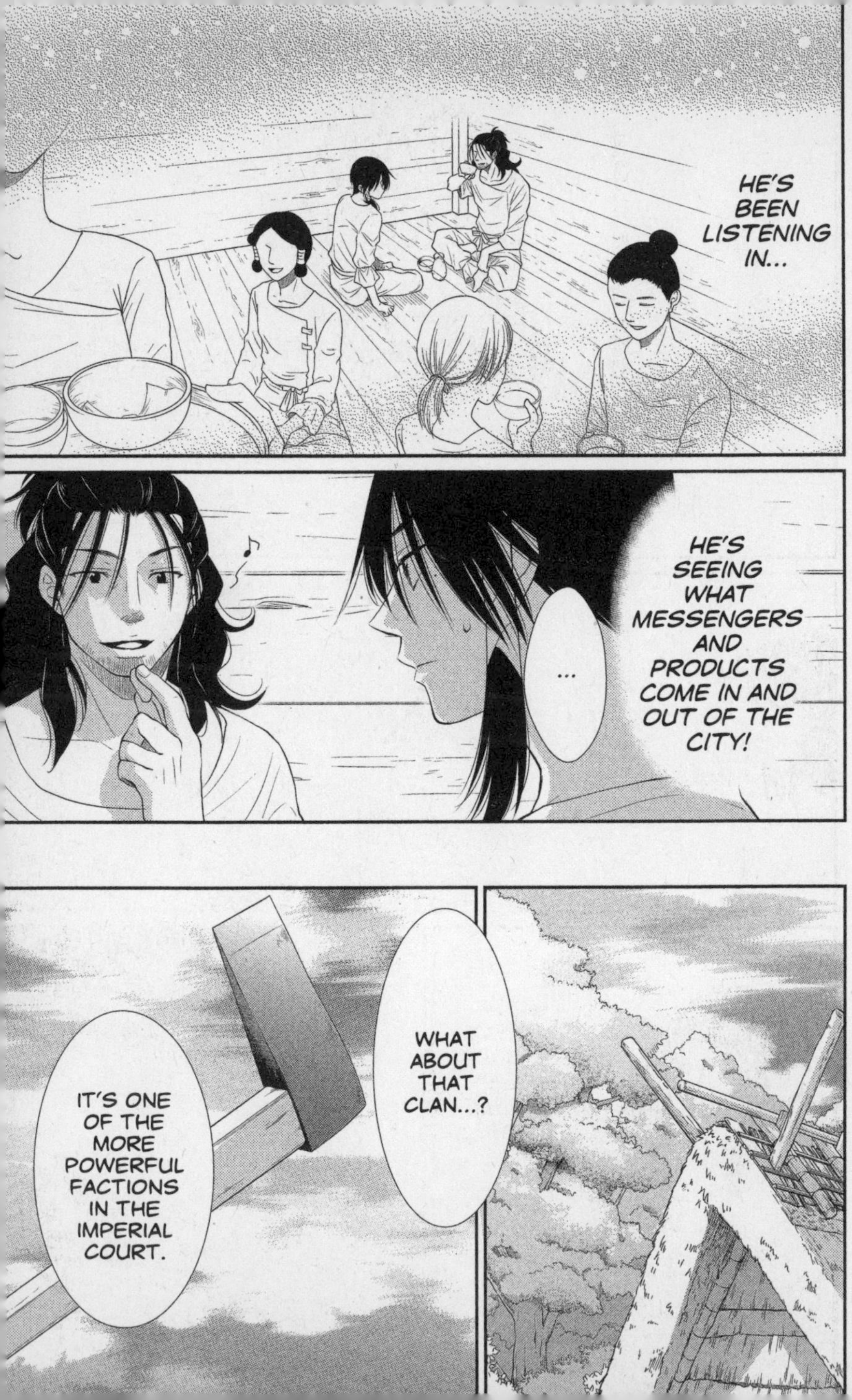
HE'S BEEN LISTENING IN...
HE'S SEEING WHAT MESSENGERS AND PRODUCTS COME IN AND OUT OF THE CITY!
...
WHAT ABOUT THAT CLAN...?
IT'S ONE OF THE MORE POWERFUL FACTIONS IN THE IMPERIAL COURT.

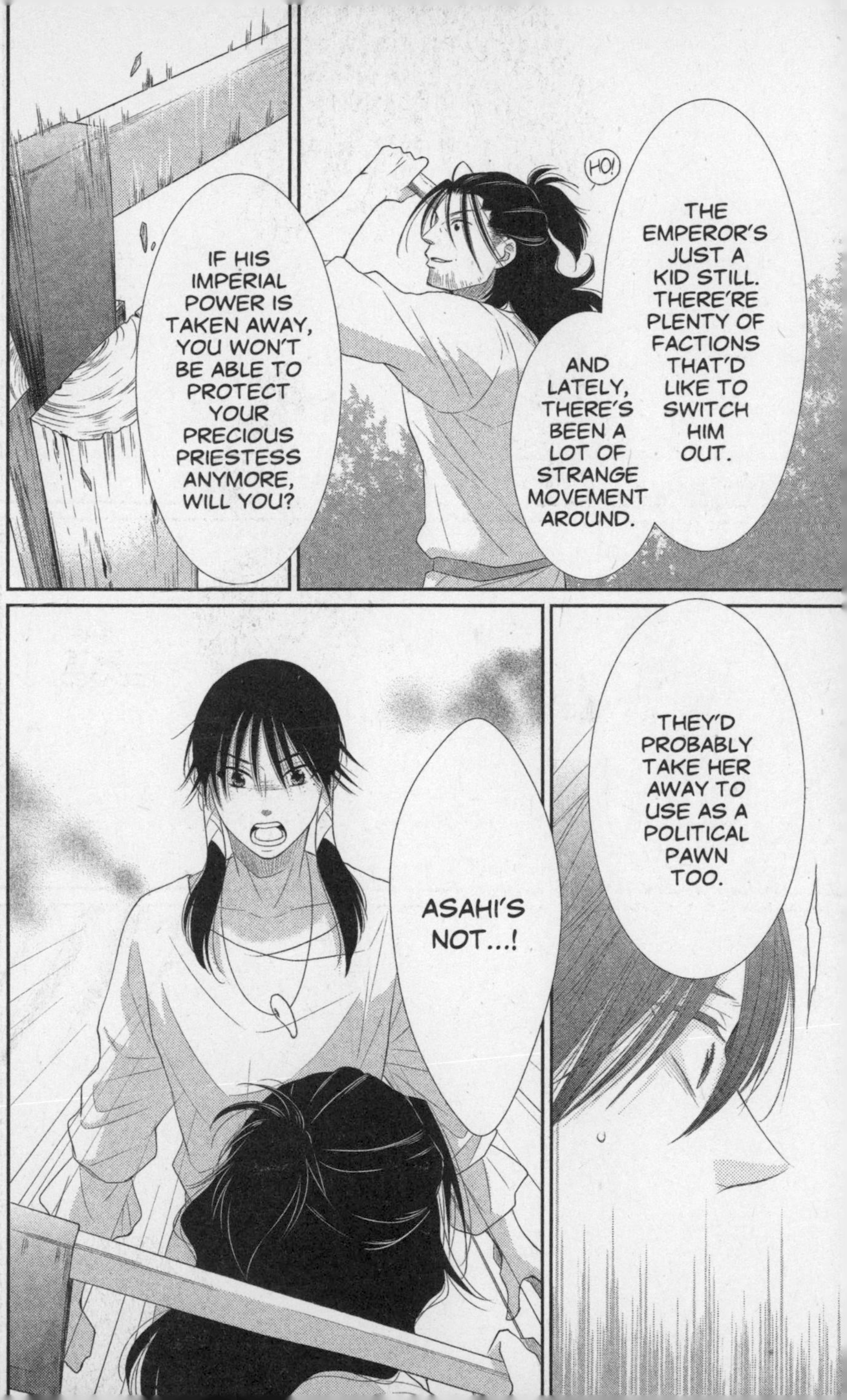
HO!
THE EMPEROR'S JUST A KID STILL. THERE'RE PLENTY OF FACTIONS THAT'D LIKE TO SWITCH HIM OUT.
AND LATELY, THERE'S BEEN A LOT OF STRANGE MOVEMENT AROUND.
IF HIS IMPERIAL POWER IS TAKEN AWAY, YOU WON'T BE ABLE TO PROTECT YOUR PRECIOUS PRIESTESS ANYMORE, WILL YOU?
THEY'D PROBABLY TAKE HER AWAY TO USE AS A POLITICAL PAWN TOO.
ASAHI'S NOT...!

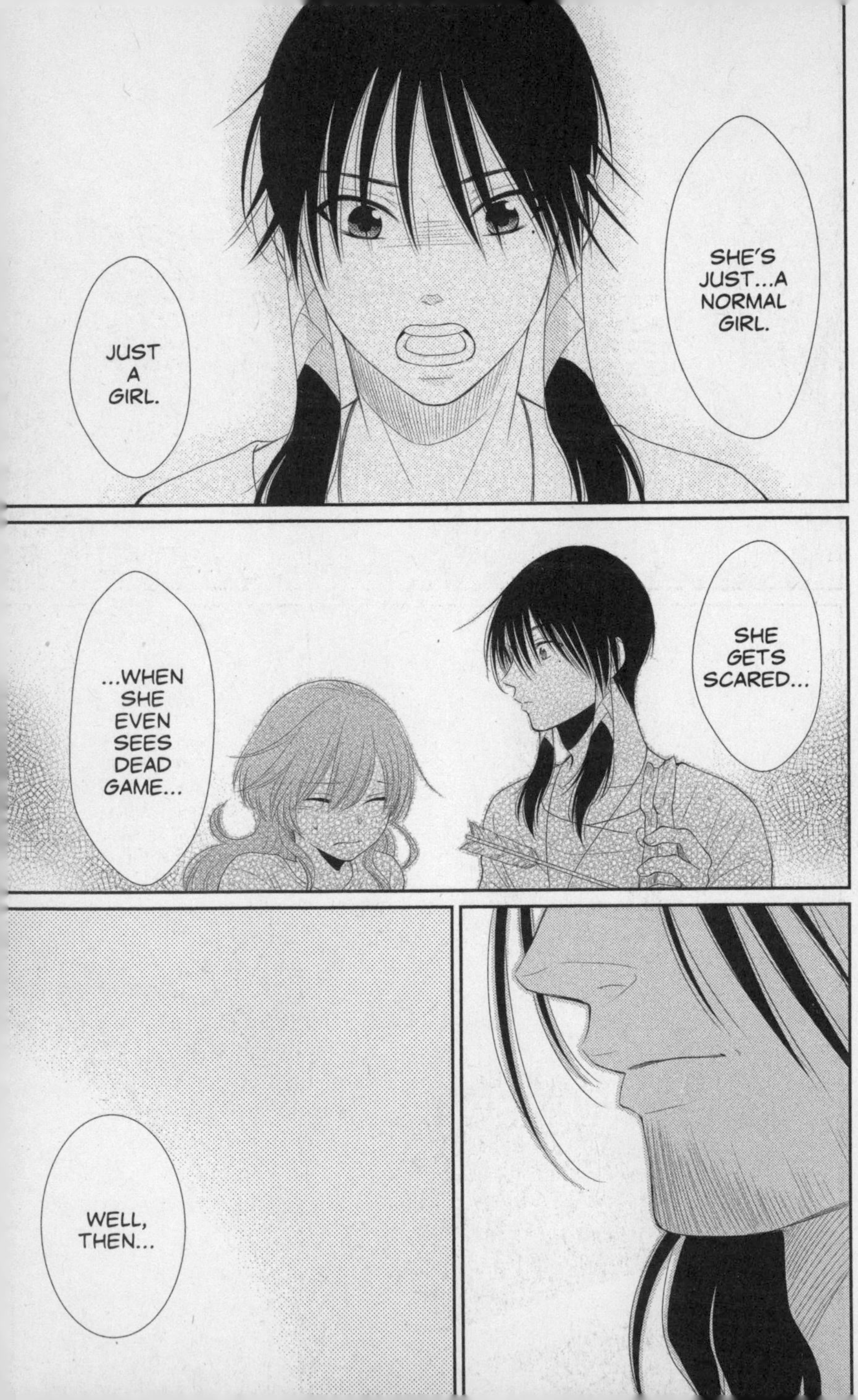
SHE'S JUST...A NORMAL GIRL.
JUST A GIRL.
SHE GETS SCARED...
...WHEN SHE EVEN SEES DEAD GAME...
WELL, THEN...

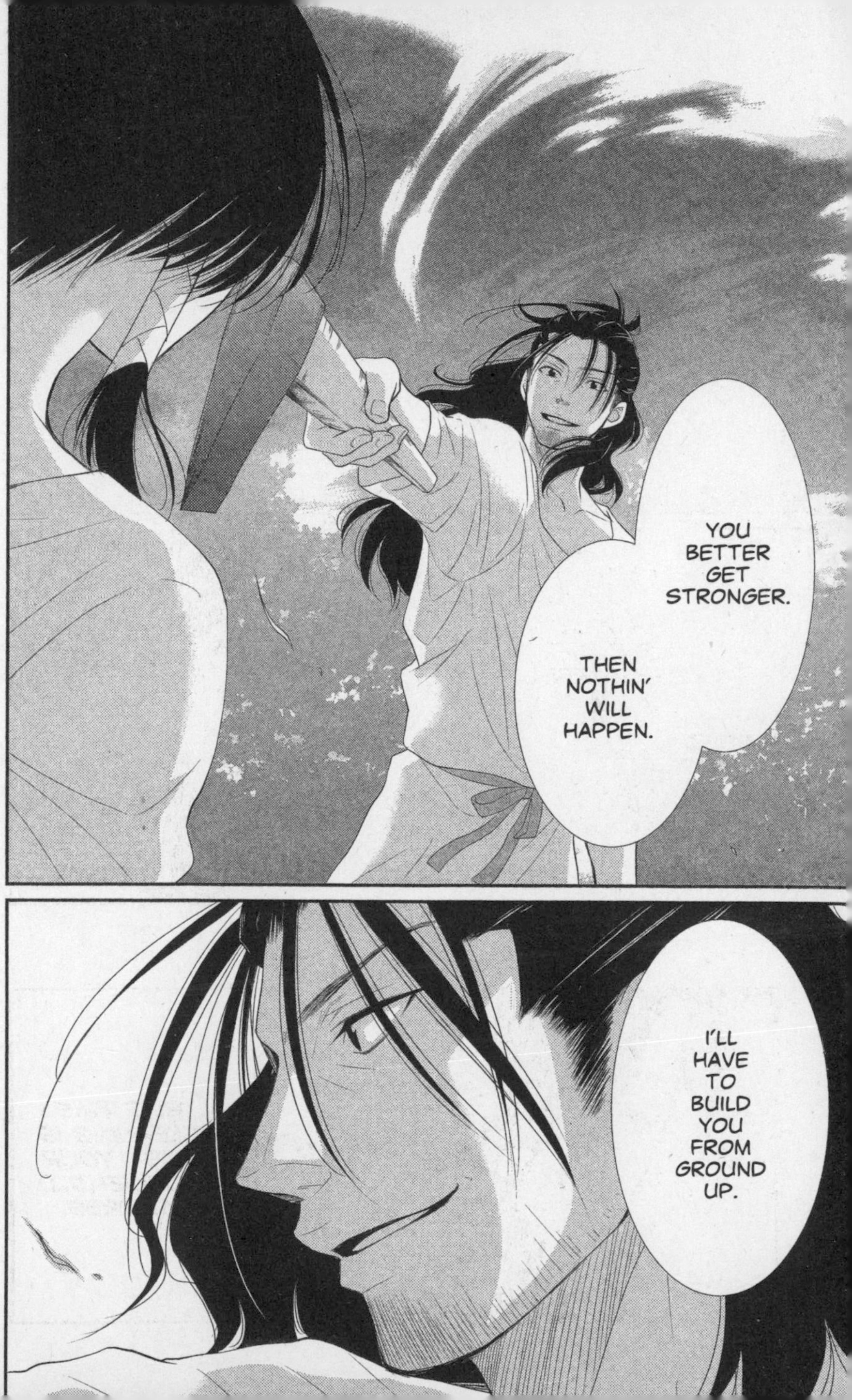
YOU BETTER GET STRONGER.
THEN NOTHIN' WILL HAPPEN.
I'LL HAVE TO BUILD YOU FROM GROUND UP.

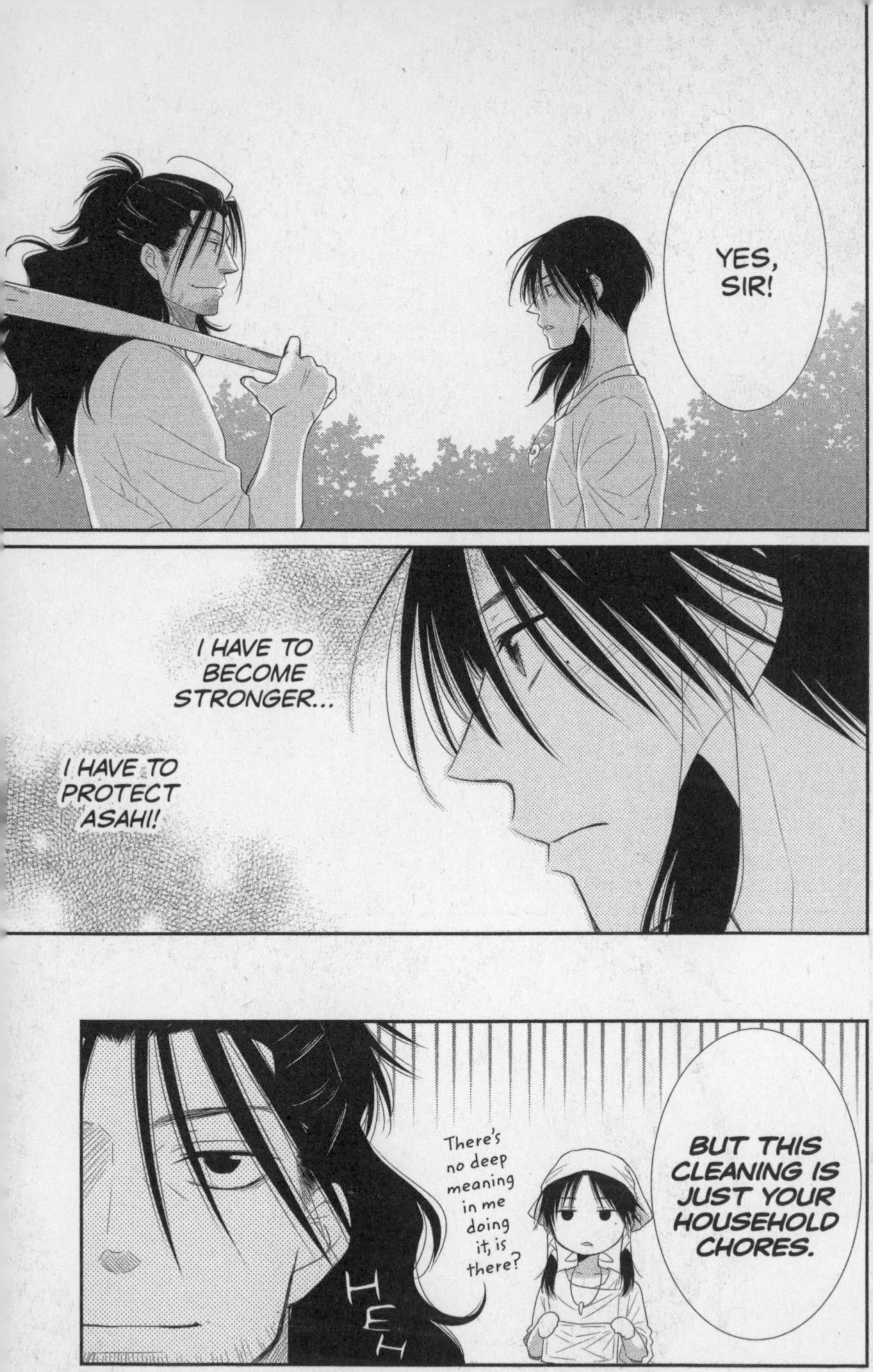
YES, SIR!
I HAVE TO BECOME STRONGER...
I HAVE TO PROTECT ASAHI!
BUT THIS CLEANING IS JUST YOUR HOUSEHOLD CHORES.
There's no deep meaning in me doing it, is there?
HEH

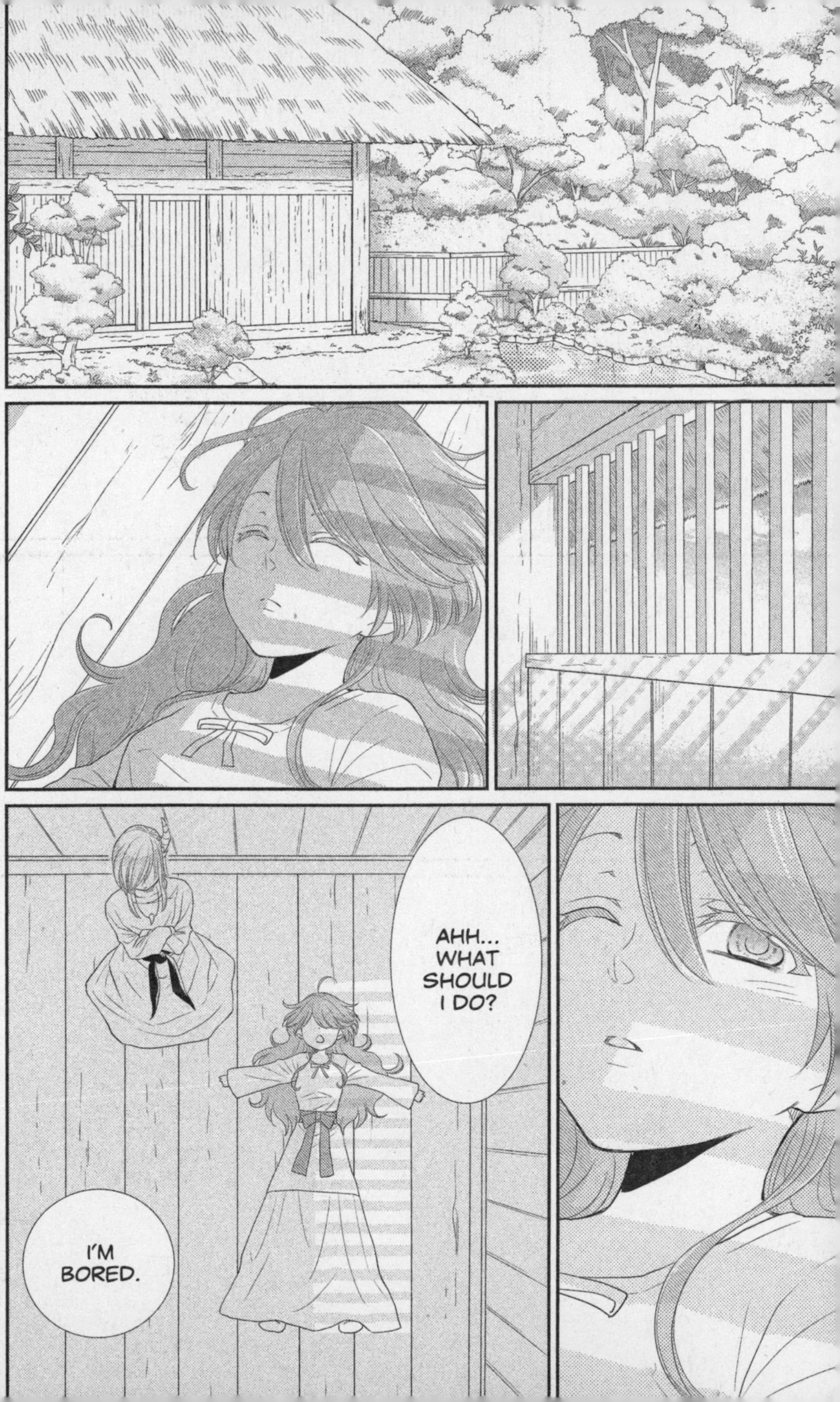
AHH... WHAT SHOULD I DO?
I'M BORED.

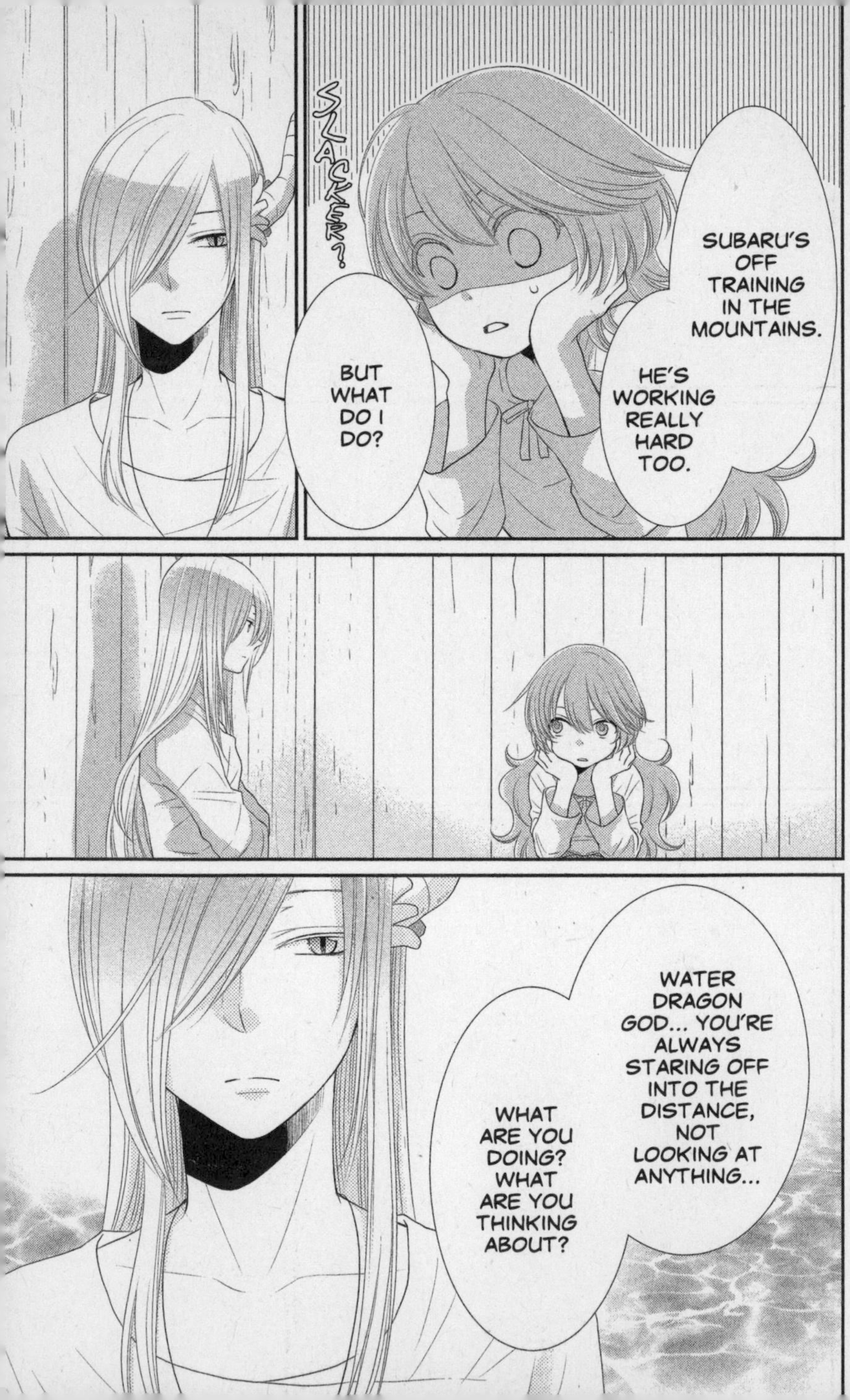
SUBARU'S OFF TRAINING IN THE MOUNTAINS.
HE'S WORKING REALLY HARD TOO.
BUT WHAT DO I DO?
SLACKER?
WATER DRAGON GOD... YOU'RE ALWAYS STARING OFF INTO THE DISTANCE, NOT LOOKING AT ANYTHING...
WHAT ARE YOU DOING? WHAT ARE YOU THINKING ABOUT?

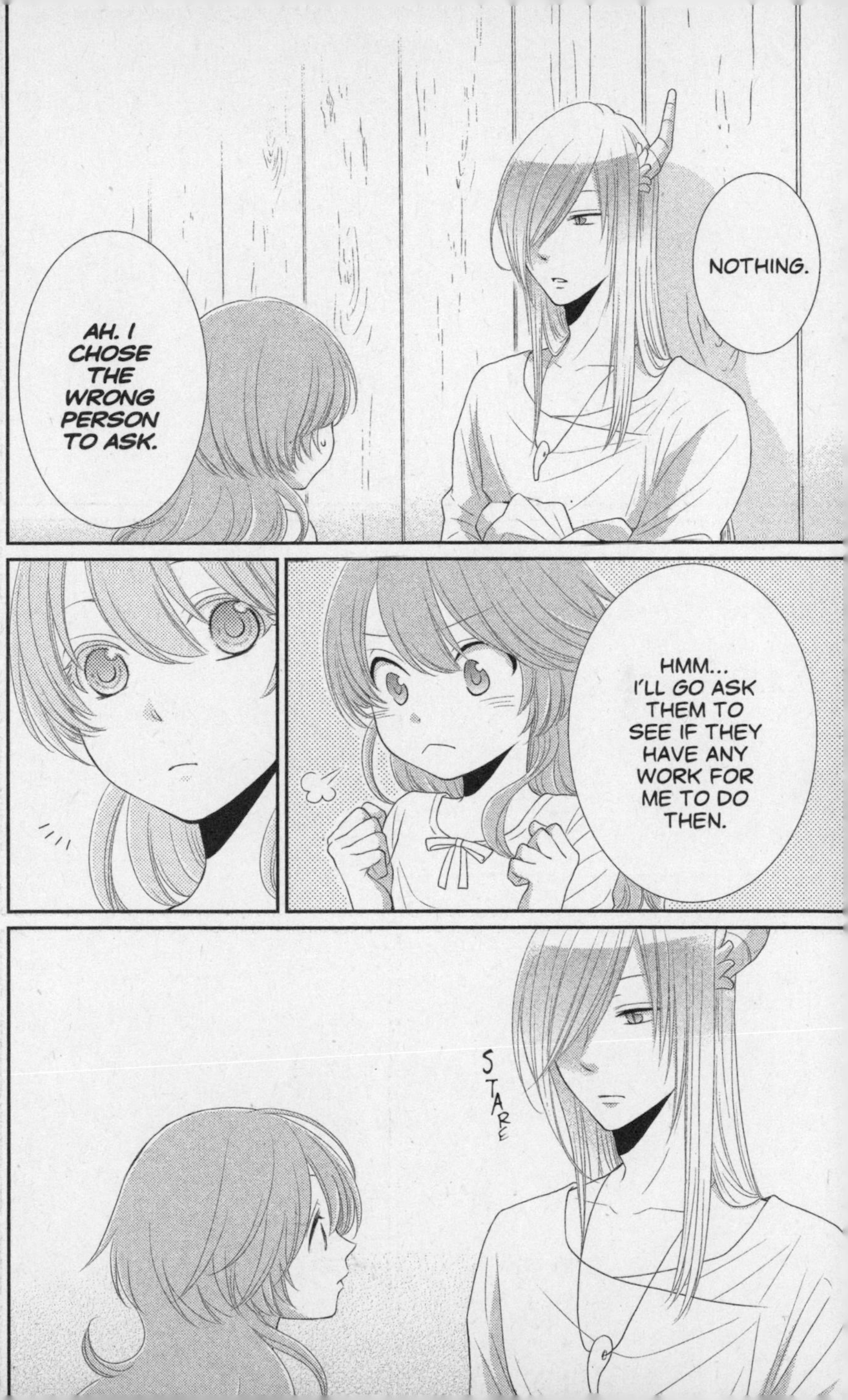
NOTHING.
AH. I CHOSE THE WRONG PERSON TO ASK.
HMM... I'LL GO ASK THEM TO SEE IF THEY HAVE ANY WORK FOR ME TO DO THEN.
STARE

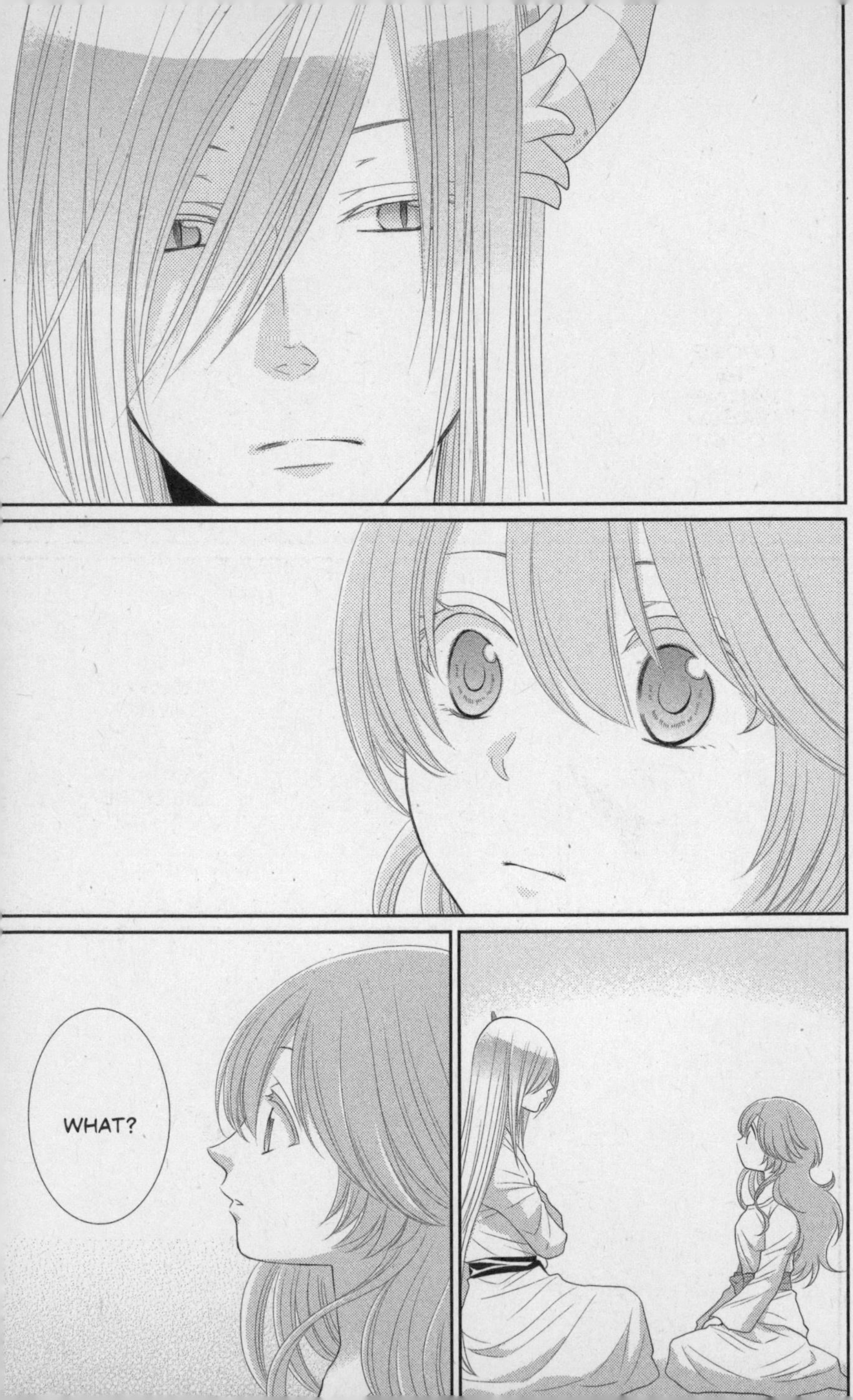
WHAT?

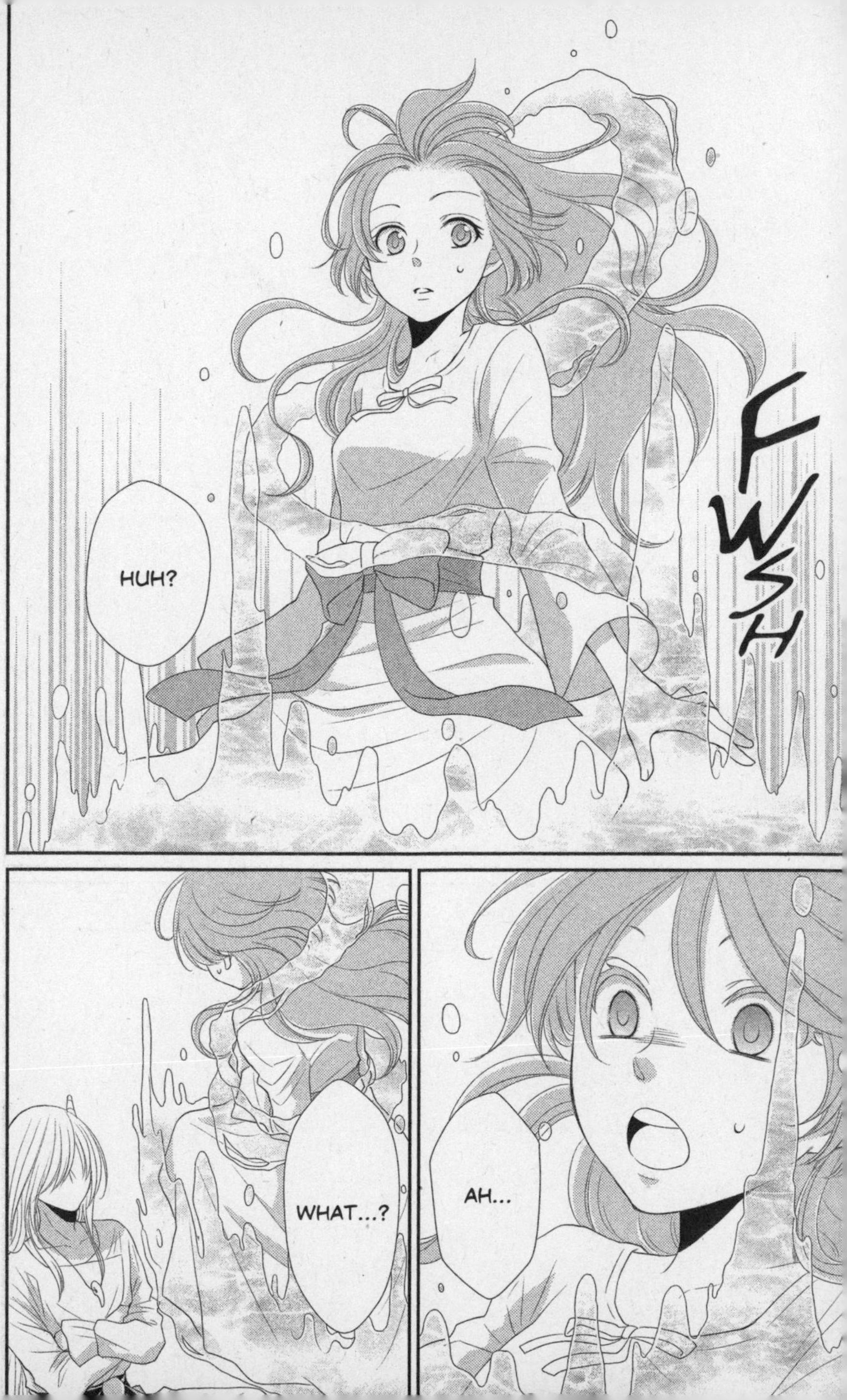
FWSH
HUH?
AH...
WHAT...?

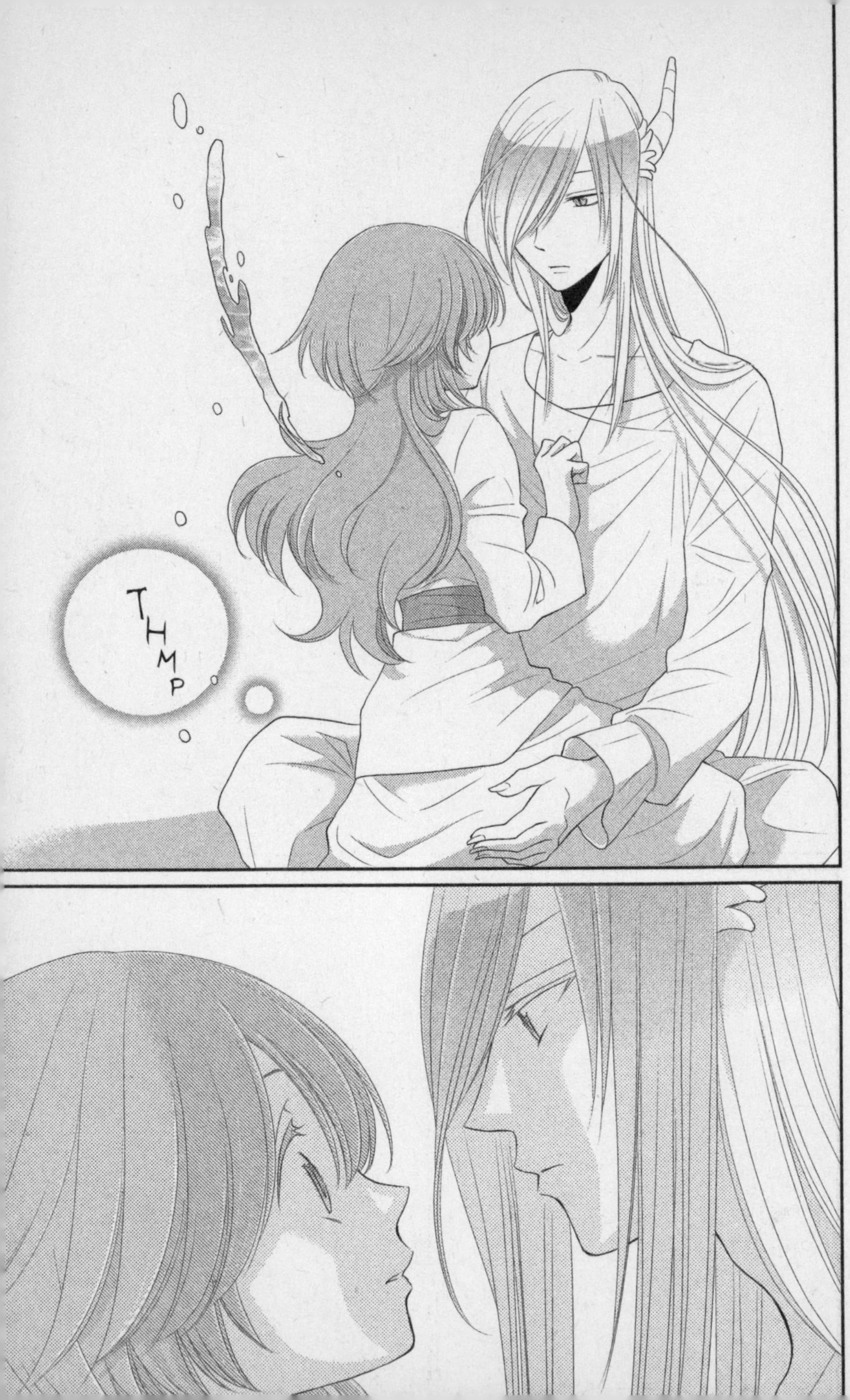
THMP

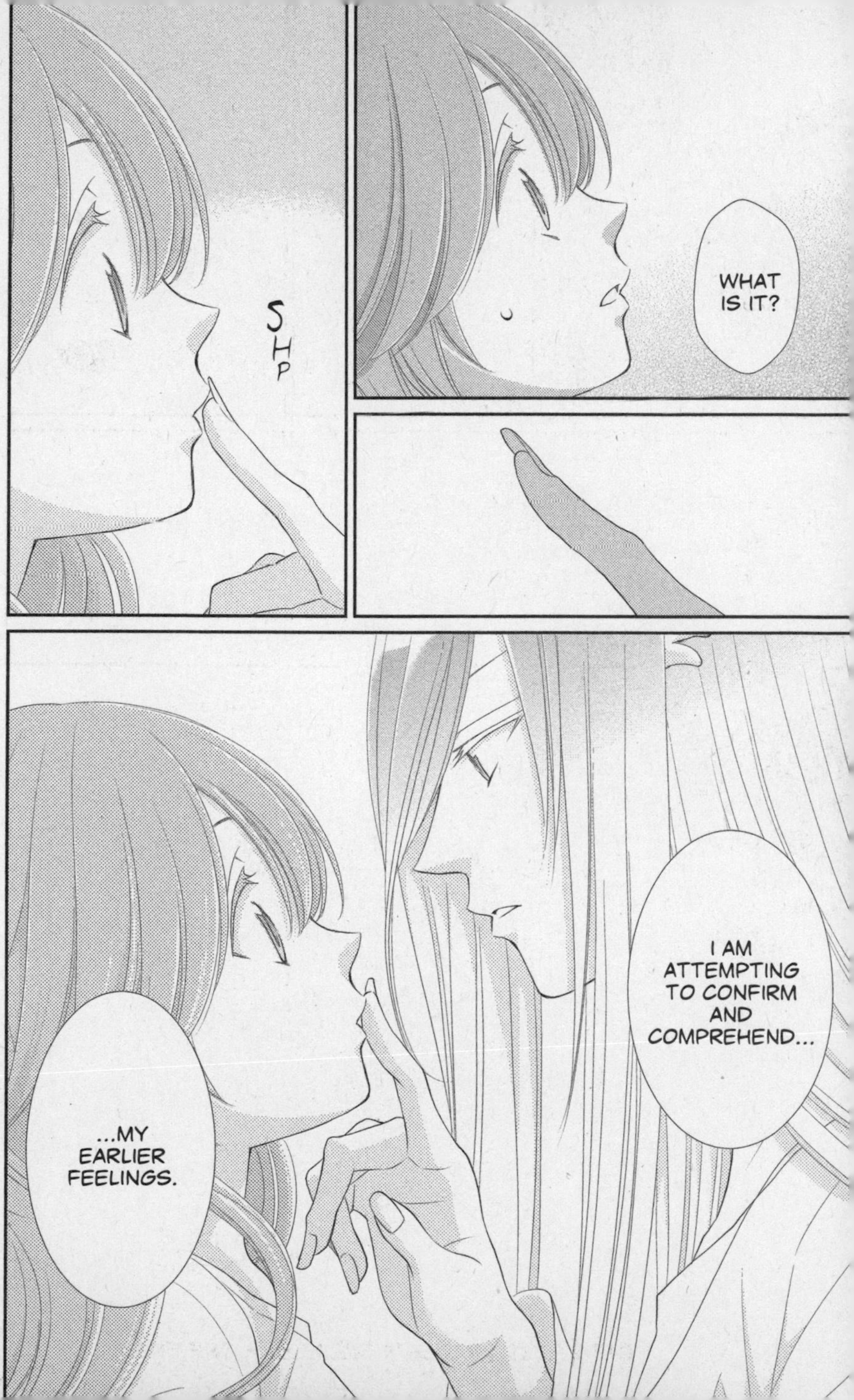
WHAT IS IT?
SHP
I AM ATTEMPTING TO CONFIRM AND COMPREHEND...
...MY EARLIER FEELINGS.

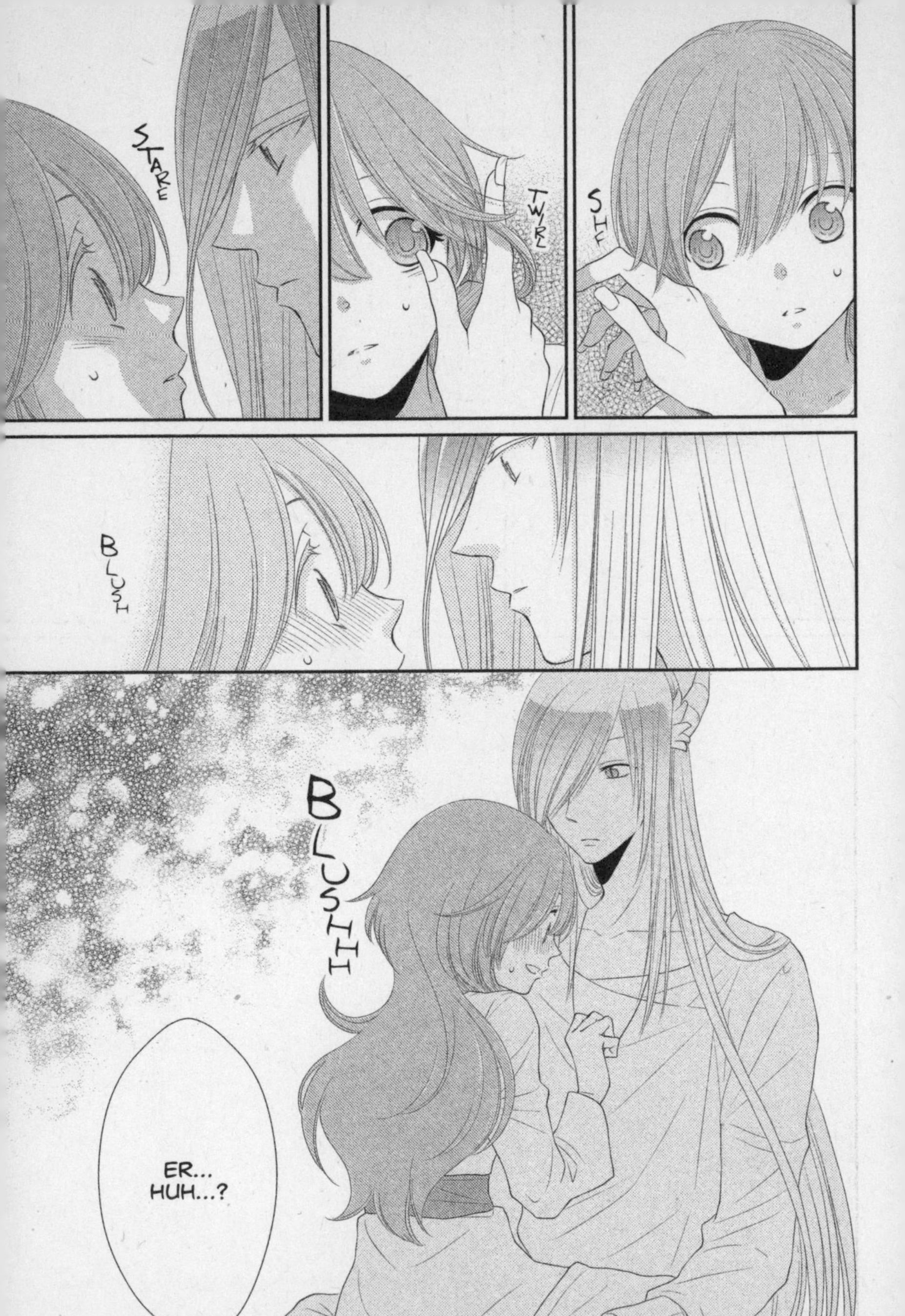
SHIF
TWIRL
STARE
BLUSH
BLUSHH
ER... HUH...?

THE WATER DRAGON'S BRIDE 5 — THE END —

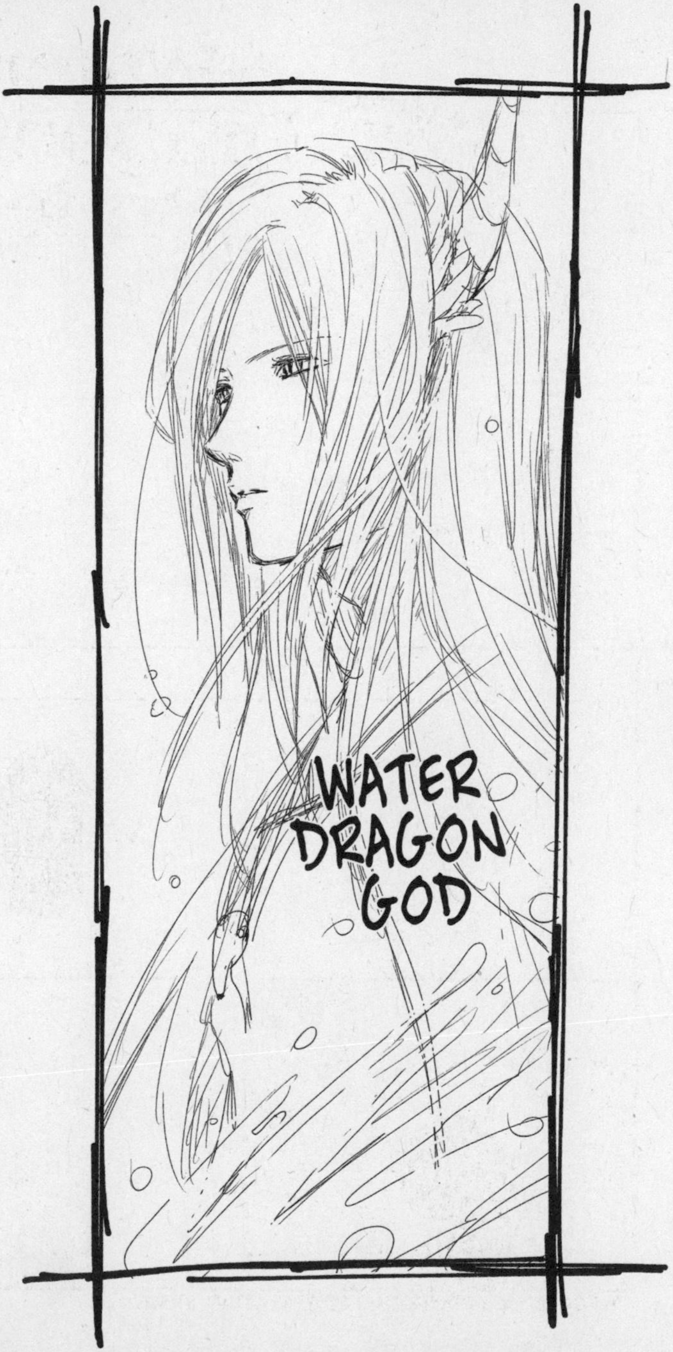
WATER DRAGON GOD

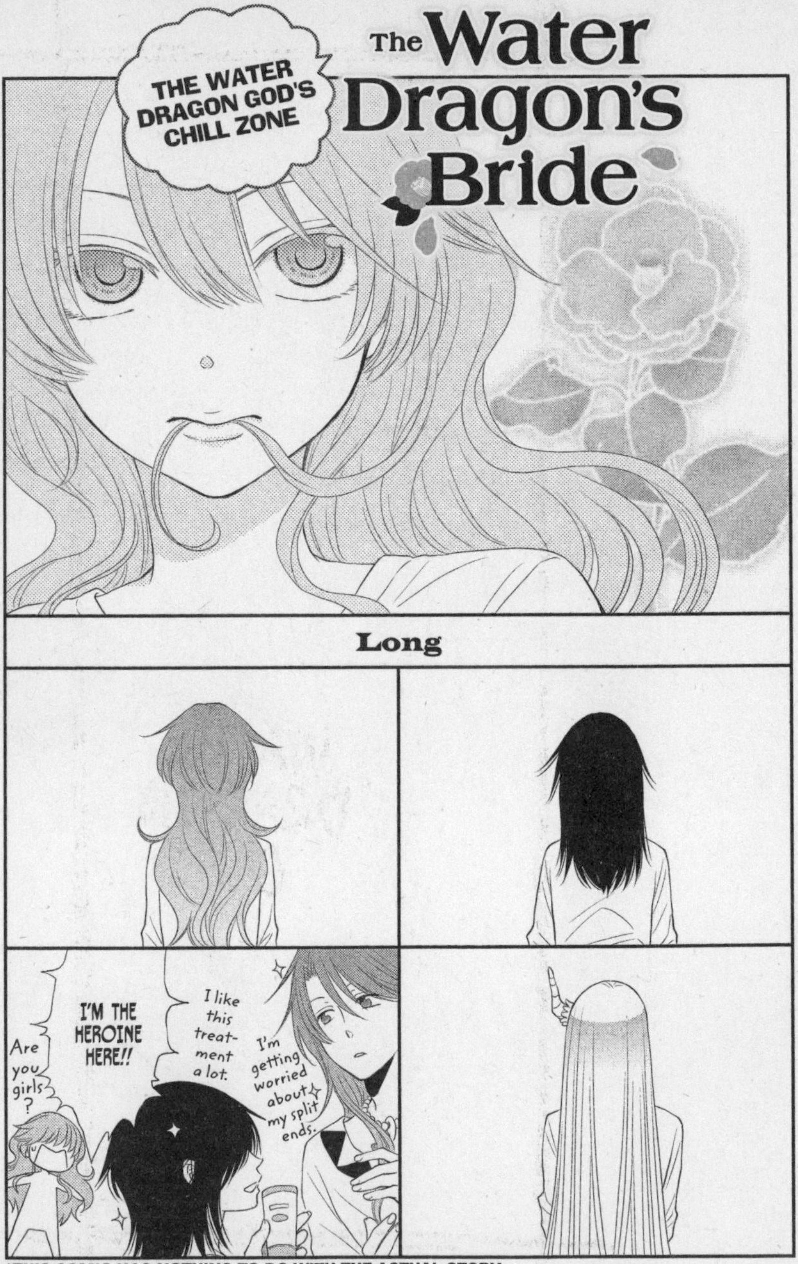
The Water Dragon's Bride
THE WATER DRAGON GOD'S CHILL ZONE
Long
I'm getting worried about my split ends.
I like this treatment a lot.
I'M THE HEROINE HERE!!
Are you girls?

*THIS COMIC HAS NOTHING TO DO WITH THE ACTUAL STORY.

Shorter

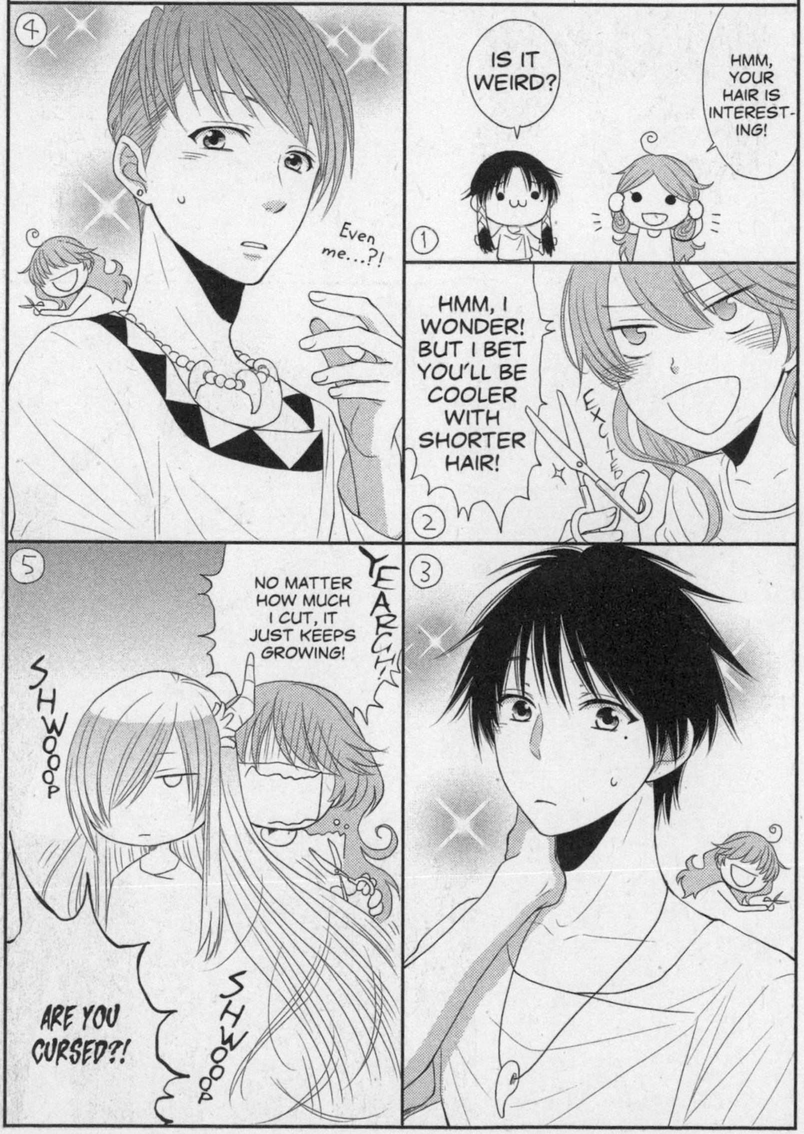

IS IT WEIRD?
HMM, YOUR HAIR IS INTEREST-ING!
HMM, I WONDER! BUT I BET YOU'LL BE COOLER WITH SHORTER HAIR!
EXCITED
Even me...?!
NO MATTER HOW MUCH I CUT, IT JUST KEEPS GROWING!
YEARGH!
SHWOOOP
SHWOOOP
ARE YOU CURSED?!

Jealousy

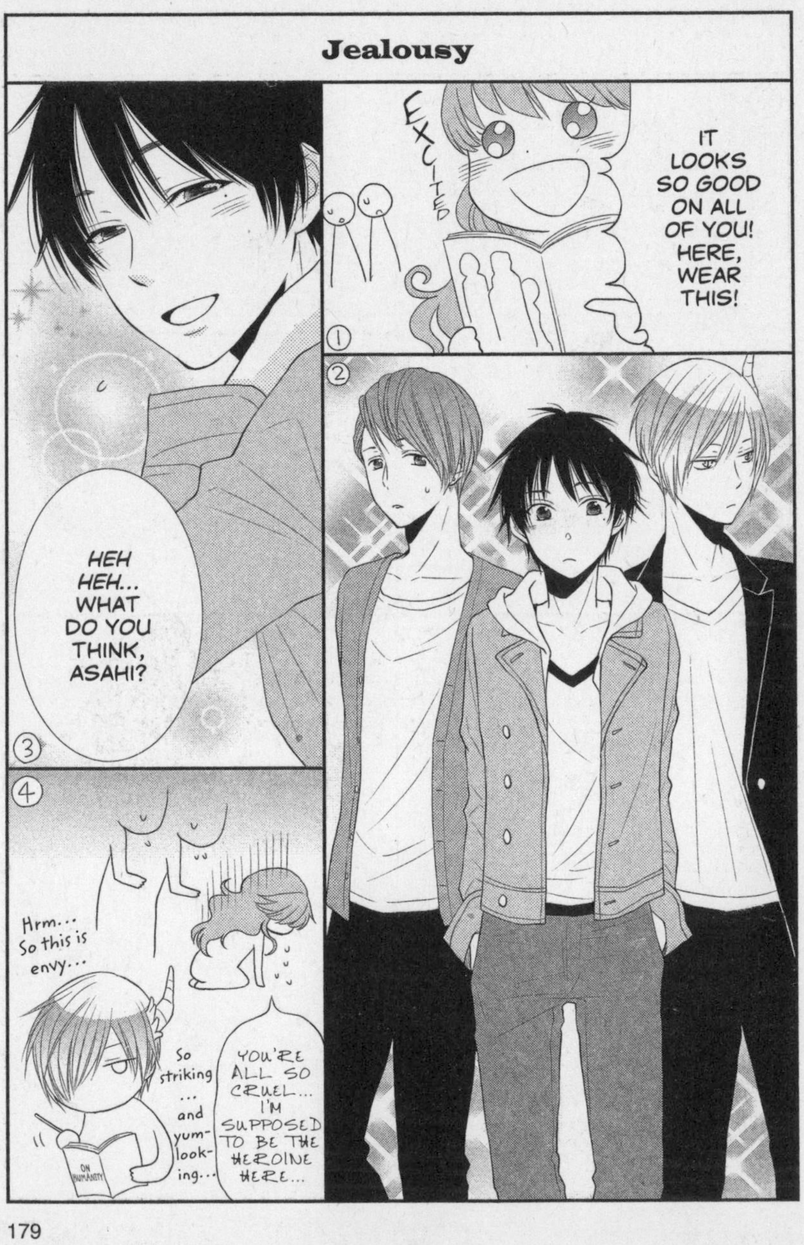
EXCITED
IT LOOKS SO GOOD ON ALL OF YOU! HERE, WEAR THIS!
HEH HEH... WHAT DO YOU THINK, ASAHI?
YOU'RE ALL SO CRUEL... I'M SUPPOSED TO BE THE HEROINE HERE...
So striking ... and yum-looking...
Hrm... So this is envy...
ON HUMANITY

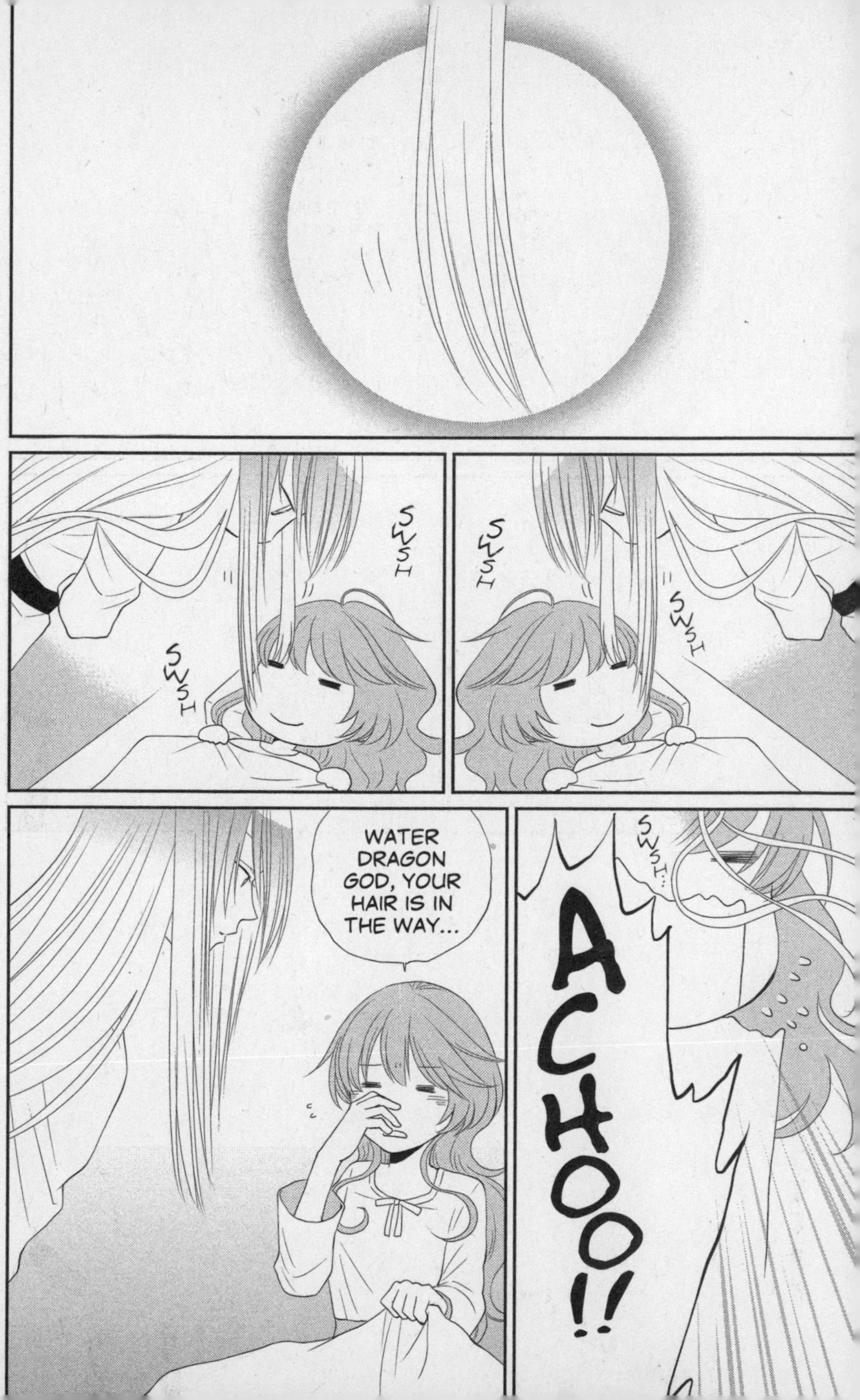
SWSH
SWSH
SWSH
SWSH
SWSH...
ACHOO!!
WATER DRAGON GOD, YOUR HAIR IS IN THE WAY...

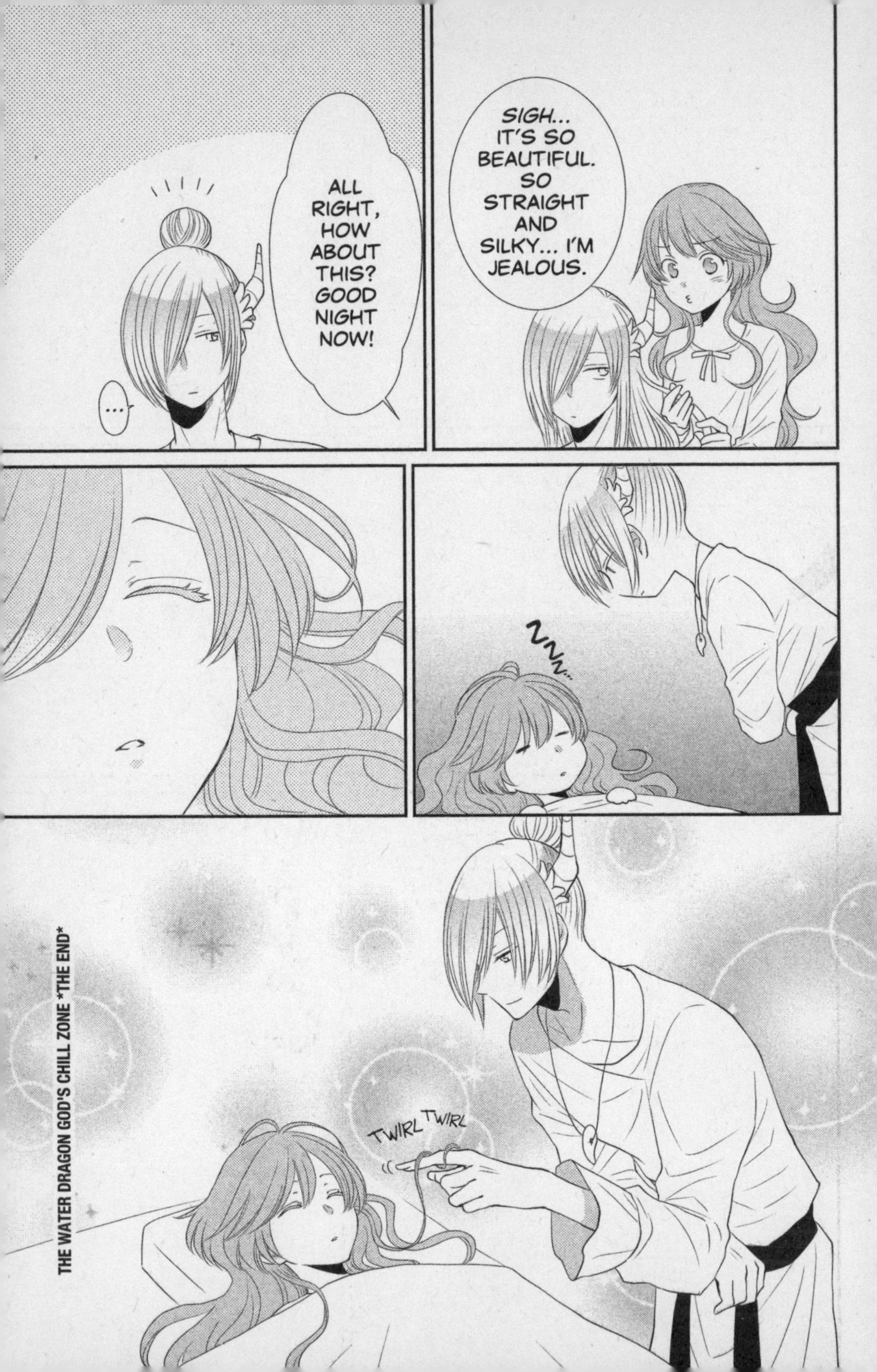
SIGH... IT'S SO BEAUTIFUL. SO STRAIGHT AND SILKY... I'M JEALOUS.
ALL RIGHT, HOW ABOUT THIS? GOOD NIGHT NOW!
...
ZZZ...
TWIRL TWIRL
THE WATER DRAGON GOD'S CHILL ZONE *THE END*

Please send your letters here! ↓ ↓
Rei Toma
c/o The Water Dragon's Bride Editor
VIZ Media
P.O. Box 77010
San Francisco, CA 94107

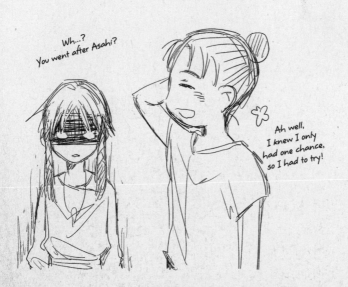

Wh...?
You went after Asahi?

Ah well,
I knew I only
had one chance,
so I had to try!

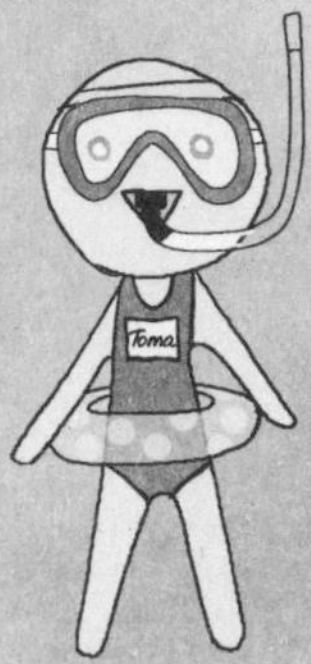
Toma

**I drew Tsukihiko in color.
I was a little conflicted about
my color choices!**

– REI TOMA

Rei Toma has been drawing since childhood, and she created her first complete manga for a graduation project in design school. When she drew the short story manga "Help Me, Dentist," it attracted a publisher's attention and she made her debut right away. After she found success as a manga artist, acclaim in other art fields started to follow as she did illustrations for novels and video game character designs. She is also the creator of *Dawn of the Arcana*, available in North America from VIZ Media.

The Water Dragon's Bride
VOL. 5
Shojo Beat Edition

Story and Art by
Rei Toma

SUIJIN NO HANAYOME Vol.5
by Rei TOMA
© 2015 Rei TOMA
All rights reserved.
Original Japanese edition published by SHOGAKUKAN.
English translation rights in the United States of America,
Canada, the United Kingdom, Ireland, Australia and New
Zealand arranged with SHOGAKUKAN.

ORIGINAL COVER DESIGN/Hibiki CHIKADA (fireworks.vc)

English Translation & Adaptation **Abby Lehrke**
Touch-Up Art & Lettering **Monalisa de Asis**
Design **Alice Lewis**
Editor **Amy Yu**

Printed in Canada

Published by VIZ Media, LLC
P.O. Box 77010
San Francisco, CA 94107

10 9 8 7 6 5 4 3 2 1
First printing, April 2018

viz.com

shojobeat.com

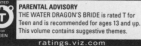